Unless Recalled Earlier

DATE DUE

MAR 1 2 2003

CHANGING DIFFERENCES

CHANGING
DIFFERENCES

Women and the Shaping of American Foreign Policy, 1917–1994

RHODRI JEFFREYS-JONES

RUTGERS UNIVERSITY PRESS
New Brunswick, New Jersey

Library of Congress Cataloging-in-Publication Data

Jeffreys-Jones, Rhodri.
    Changing differences : women and the shaping of American foreign
policy, 1917–1994 / Rhodri Jeffreys-Jones.
        p. cm.
    Includes bibliographical references and index.
    ISBN 0–8135–2166–1
    1. United States—Foreign relations—20th century. 2. Women in
politics—United States—History—20th century. 3. Women diplomats—
United States—History—20th century. I. Title.
E744.J35 1995
327.73—dc20   94-39588
                                                                    CIP

British Cataloging-in-Publication information available

For Mary

CONTENTS

Preface ix

1 Introduction 1

2 A Momentary Silence: The Survival of
Gender Distinction in World War I 11

3 From Peace to Prices in the Tariff Decade 29

4 Presidential Recognition of
the Female Vote, 1932 50

5 Dorothy Detzer and the Merchants of Death 65

6 A Tale of Two Women: Harriet Elliott,
Eleanor Roosevelt, and Changing Differences 84

7 Margaret Chase Smith and the Female
Quest for Security 105

8 Bella Abzug: Signpost to the Future 131

9   The Myth of the Iron Lady:
An International Comparison   155

10   American Women and Contemporary
Foreign Policy   174

11   Conclusion   196

Notes   201

Bibliography   245

Index   263

PREFACE

he origins of this book are in the 1960s. Then, it seemed to me
and to many of my generation of students, we were confronted
by an absurdity. On the one hand the world was becoming a more
egalitarian and democratic place. On the other war, the "sport
of kings," seemed to flourish. For this reason I became interested in the social bases of diplomacy. Encouraged by the historian Oscar
Handlin, I took up a Charles Warren postdoctoral fellowship at Harvard
University in 1971–72, to study the influence on foreign policy of six
social groups: organized labor, citizens of color, immigrants, university
students, consumer organizations—and women. This book is the belated
first fruit of that enterprise.

Over the years my research benefited from considerable generosity. I
owe major debts to the trustees of residential fellowships which created
islands of opportunity in the midst of a teaching career: those of the
Charles Warren Center for the Study of American History; of the John
F. Kennedy-Institut für Nordamerikastudien at the Free University of
Berlin; of the Ada E. Leeke Research Fellowship, Northwood Institute,
Margaret Chase Smith Library Center, Skowhegan, Maine; and of the
Canadian Commonwealth Visiting Fellowship scheme, for which I was
sponsored by the University of Toronto. I am grateful to these, as I am
for other types of financial assistance: an Overseas Fellowship from the
British Academy, several grants from the Carnegie Trust for the Univer-
sities of Scotland, and grants from the American Philosophical Society
and the Moray Fund.

The advice and criticism of a considerable number of individuals have
been invaluable. All of the following helped me in a substantial way, supplying ideas, practical assistance, interviews, and encouragement or commenting in a scholarly manner on portions of the book's early drafts:
Bella Abzug, Willi Paul Adams, Tom Barron, Crispin Bates, Christine
Bolt, Susan M. Bowden, Angus Calder, John Whiteclay Chambers, Wayne
S. Cole, Jeremy Crang, Robert A. Divine, Charlotte Erickson, Gregory

P. Gallant, Elizabeth Warnock Fernea, Lloyd Gardner, Joan Hoff, Alice Kessler-Harris, Warren F. Kimball, W. Roger Louis, Carol Miller, Ruth B. Mandel, Jim Potter, Victor H. Rothwell, Robert D. Schulzinger, Mel Small, Margaret Chase Smith, Amy Swerdlow, Emma Vincent, Margaret Walsh, Wesley Wark, and Donald Cameron Watt.

I would like to thank all the foregoing, as well as the numerous librarians and archivists who have helped me, Leslie Mitchner and the dedicated team at Rutgers University Press, my ever-supportive literary agents Frances Goldin and Sydelle Kramer, and those individuals, especially Buffy Manners in Austin, Texas, and Charles and Susan Rice in New York City, who have helped to make my research trips such a pleasure.

My daughters Gwenda and Rowena and my stepdaughter Effie refrained from playing musical instruments at crucial moments in the writing of this book, and deserve my everlasting gratitude despite their assertions that I am tone deaf.

Without the constancy and love of my wife, Mary, the completion of this book would not have been possible.

CHANGING DIFFERENCES

especially tough. Such women assume what are thought of as masculine characteristics not just for tactical reasons but because in political terms they have become men. They therefore tend to be hawks in foreign policy and are disposed to support any war that comes along.

The breakthrough hypothesis is flawed, however. Margaret Thatcher, for example—the archetypal "iron lady"—prime minister of the 1980s who led Britain to victory in the Falklands/Malvinas war—might actually claim to have been one of the most peaceful premiers in British history. The field of women and foreign policy is full of contradictions and complexities, and for that reason is particularly intriguing.

Yet despite the subject's compelling nature, there has never been a serious attempt to trace its general history—a better understanding of which is needed both in women's studies and among students of foreign policy.[3] The range of issues that needs to be addressed is considerable, and several key aspects remain unexplored. There is no straightforward answer even to the question of why women have wanted to form themselves into distinct pressure groups on foreign policy. It would be too cynical to agree with the assumption made by some male politicians that women agitate over foreign policy solely to create bargaining chips for concessions on domestic issues. For some women it is a matter of the right to have an equal say even if solutions to international problems cannot be found. For others the achievement of influence in foreign policy is, like the vote itself, a means to an end, such as a safer or more peaceful world or a better environment—while many men, of course, would support such goals, women have been particularly associated with them. Another answer might be qualitative: Whatever one thinks of men's performance as diplomats, it is surely a mistake to ignore a vast reservoir of untapped talent, the female half of the population. Still another consideration that motivates some women is the idea that they, as a group, and because of their roles as household managers, have a vested interest in certain aspects of economic foreign policy. In contrast, there is the more idealistic feminist goal to exert appropriate pressure on the U.S. government, in order to help one's sisters in foreign countries where sexual repression is worse than in the United States.

To explore these issues more fully, it is useful to look at the real influence that American women have had on American foreign policy since they won the vote in 1920. It is surprising that this has not yet been done, except that the implications of this inquiry could clearly be devastating for American feminists. Since 1960 there have been twenty-two women prime ministers and presidents worldwide, but the United States has had no woman as president, vice president, secretary of state, secretary of defense, or chair of the Senate Foreign Relations Committee. According to this measurement American women are among the missing sisters of world politics, a predicament they have shared with the female citizens of Italy, Australia, and Chile, as well as of such supposedly less democratic countries as the former Soviet Union, Iraq, and North Korea.

The measurement of women's progress, however, needs to be addressed with some care. Given the nature of the American political system, one needs to look beyond the obvious leaders in the executive and legislative branches of government, and to ask what women may have achieved through public opinion, through their representatives on Capitol Hill, and as insiders within the foreign service. The picture is less bleak when the lobbying effectiveness of women is compared with that of, say, organized labor, immigrant groups, or business. Egalitarian feminists may take comfort from the fact that the number of self-made women in Congress has risen sharply, especially in the 1990s. Moreover, some of the "stars" of twentieth-century women's history have lent their weight to foreign-policy causes. The stubborn statistician may insist that if it cannot be counted, it does not exist. But that would be to ignore the impact of such household names as Jane Addams, Amelia Earhart, Eleanor Roosevelt, Jane Fonda, Joan Baez, and even Shirley Temple. None of these famous women was part of a uniform movement, but all in their separate ways sought to influence foreign policy or to play a role in it.

The obstacles women faced in attempting to achieve self-empowerment in this area need to be scrutinized both for themselves and for their consequences. Politically active women shared in common with other insurgent groups—for example, labor unions and civil rights organizations—the fate of being labeled "Reds." They were also distinctly vulnerable to sexual smears. Sexual scandals involve men, too, of course, as can be seen in the cluster of allegations concerning Senators Brock Adams, Daniel Inouye, and Robert Packwood in the 1992 elections, and the determined attempts to besmirch the character of President Bill Clinton.[4] However, compared with men, women politicians have been at once more innocent of, and yet more vulnerable to, such charges. Eleanor Roosevelt was accused of gender impropriety simply for engaging in a public career. Senator Margaret Chase Smith was accused of having entered Congress through sexual guile. Both were the widows of sexually adventurous politicians who were never publicly accused in their lifetimes.

Even when one turns to sets of circumstances that might seem encouraging to women, sexism is sometimes a problem. One might argue that women would thrive politically in a culture of the broad left, and in a milieu such as Scandinavia—a region of "feminism without feminists"—where, theoretically, publicly active women are so common-place that gender ceases to be an issue.[5] In the United States the community of protesters against the Vietnam War might be said to have provided such an environment, especially as the nation was said to be experiencing a new wave of feminism in the 1960s. In fact, however, the number of women in the foreign service declined in that decade, as did the number of women in Congress. Many years later feminist Gloria Steinem, then an antiwar activist who worked with draft "refuseniks," still recalled with chagrin that "there was this idea, women say Yes to men who say No." Even among the "politically correct" of the day, then, women found it difficult to free themselves from the constraints of ste-reotypical roles and to make their own way.

The obstacles in the way of women are important not just because they kept women back but also because they are perceived to have shaped the character of those women who did break through. As already noted, there is a tendency to label the Margaret Thatchers of this world "iron ladies." Israel's Golda Meir and India's Indira Gandhi were alike dubbed "the only man in the cabinet." To novelist Salman Rushdie, Pakistan's Prime Minister Benazir Bhutto is "Virgin Ironpants." Margaret Chase Smith's stance on defense issues caused Soviet leader Nikita Khrushchev to dub her "the devil in the disguise of a woman."

According to some analysts, women who break through into positions of foreign policy power have "matured" and left behind women with such "traditional" attitudes as the love of peace; when all women mature, they will be just as willing as men to resort to force. According to others, loss of gender distinction is just a temporary phase: Once women are secure in their positions of high office, they will stop trying to be men. Indeed, some political candidates are already "running as women." All this lends itself to comparative analysis: How have "dy-nastic" women behaved, who have never had to fight to get to the top? Are all women who fight their way to the top belligerent in foreign policy, or is there such a thing as an "iron dove"?

Whether women are more peaceful than men is a contentious ques-tion related to a broader debate: about the existence, character, and ex-tent of an essential difference between women and men.[6] Eleanor Roosevelt insisted that "women *are* different from men." Senator Mar-garet Chase Smith said, "I definitely resent being called a feminist." British journalist Polly Toynbee asked, "Is Margaret Thatcher a woman?" The debate over such issues—and some of the ideas associ-ated with it—is relevant to an understanding of the strength and na-ture of women's impact on foreign policy.

Because little has been written about women and foreign policy the historiography of the field is immature. Nevertheless, it is possible to discern two broad schools, one succeeding the other. The first of these, which might be designated the "Peace School," took shape in the first half of the twentieth century. A prominent member was Emily Greene Balch, whose work with the Women's International League for Peace and Freedom (WILPF) made her prominent in the 1920s and 1930s. Balch subscribed to the idea of "nurturant motherhood," whereby women are different from men in being more caring and peaceful. She observed in 1915 that "the nourishing mother . . . is not only more or less incapacitated for either fight or flight during her pregnancy, but she is in a special way the companion, protector, and support of the little ones."[7]

In 1946, the year Balch won the Nobel Peace Prize, the historian Mary Beard supplied another example of antiwar feminism in her book *Women as Force in History*, in which she noted that women stood to gain from the end of physical coercion: "War, being always a foe of civilization, tends to deepen the subjection of women to men."[8] This pronouncement may have reflected a tactical aspiration: If women supported the peace movement, then the peace movement could be expected to support women's rights. But, more important, it represented the genuine belief that war, in Balch's words, "tended to lower the importance and the social power of women." War glamorized the male role, encouraged prostitution, and damaged the status of women who excelled at more peaceful, nurturant roles. Thus the dominant historiographical premise of the Peace School was based on what Balch, Beard, and others regarded as logic—violence as practiced by men subordinated women, so they were against it.[9]

In the second half of the twentieth century, there emerged what could conveniently be labeled the "Belligerent School." Its members emphasized and praised the aggressive roles played by women in history, suggesting that there was little difference between women and men in this respect. The emergence of the school may have been partly the result of frustration at the slow rate of women's progress toward further equality, a tardiness that was attributed by some to the pacifist tendencies of the women's movement in the first half of the century. Another factor that encouraged the growth of this school of thought was the nuclear shield. Once the superpowers possessed the ultimate deterrent, there ensued a period when major warfare seemed a more remote possibility. Some women seized this moment to flirt with the idea of war.

One aspect of the Belligerent School was its rejection of the idea of nurturant motherhood. The rejection stemmed in part from the perception that the duties of motherhood could be a real burden to women who wanted careers—a perception that both reflected and spawned a new trend in historiography. Several studies, to be sure, still emphasized the role of nurturant motherhood in various international activities undertaken by women, for example as missionaries, and especially in the women's peace movement.[10] Barbara Steinson argued that the outbreak of war in 1914 stimulated the credo that "women instinctively gave their unselfish devotion to the nurture and protection of life [and that the] female role was one of sacrifice and of service to others." But Steinson also brought to light an inconsistency: The nurturant motherhood instinct could be and was recruited for warlike purposes. She drew attention to the fact that women were active in nurturant and caring ways in the preparedness movement in World War I, through such organizations as the Women's Section of the Navy League.[11] Another historian has pointed out that while nurturant motherhood was and still is, in her view, an important factor, some of the peace movement's "most famous and revered women, such as Jane Addams, Emily Greene Balch, and Carrie Chapman Catt, never had children."[12]

Scholars of the Belligerent School have made a determined effort to publicize the role of heroines in the history of war. One of their purposes is to supply a corrective to the male-dominated writing of history, a prejudiced mode that has slighted the role of women. They further aim to expose the male habit of portraying women as too timid to fight or to govern. They hope to provide inspiring examples for modern women to follow. The historian Antonia Fraser is a prominent exponent of the Belligerent School. In her book *Boadicea's Chariot*, she notes the importance of "force" in history (by force she means violence, whereas Beard used it to mean power). According to Fraser, it follows that "on the one hand the traditional lack of involvement of woman in the world of 'force' will add to her air of inferiority; on the other hand her involvement in that world when it occurs, stands a good chance of raising her status." Fraser set out to prove that, from Boadicea through Margaret Thatcher, women had a set of "warrior queens" whom they could admire and emulate.[13]

This outlook is not always confined to the study of leaders. In a book that gives greater attention to the lower ranks, British journalist Kate Muir notes that women rarely served as soldiers until very recent times. But she rejoices in the changes taking place in the 1990s (more than 34,000 women served in the Gulf War in 1991) and, like Fraser, takes inspiration from history's exceptions—for example, the Amazons and the women who donned male uniforms to fight in the American Civil War.[14]

The Belligerent School is a notable and lively element in the historiography of women and foreign policy, but it does not go unchallenged. For one thing, the traditional Peace School still thrives. For example, in 1993 Harriet Hyman Alonso published a book with the self-explanatory title, *Peace as a Women's Issue: A History of the U.S. Movement for World Peace and Women's Rights.* But the discussion is no longer confined to a debate between two schools of thought. After all, the foreign policy debate is not just about a clash between pacifism and militarism. Other issues need to be discussed, and indeed new ways can be devised of approaching the old debate about war and peace. To meet some of these challenges, there has emerged a cluster of diverse scholarship with varying methodologies, which for want of a more apt term might be labeled the "Innovative Tendency."

The Innovative Tendency is a response to what is undeniably an increasing, if gradual, involvement of women in public life and in foreign policy. Emily S. Rosenberg described one of its aspects in the June 1990 issue of the *Journal of American History.* A "way of integrating women's history into the study of foreign relations," she wrote, "would be to locate those exceptional, often slighted women who influenced foreign policy."[15] A pioneering step in this direction had already been taken in 1987 with the publication of the collection of essays edited by Edward P. Crapol, *Women and American Foreign Policy: Lobbyists, Critics, and Insiders.*[16] Another approach is to study the international activities of women doing "women's work," as in the case of nursing. A third, more theoretical approach relates to "the vast world systems literature," raising the question of how people should be grouped for purposes of analysis—thus, in assessing the efficacy of an aid program, one might ask not only how it helped poor farmers but also whether it assisted or retarded the prospects of women in poor farming areas.[17]

A fourth way is to examine gender ideology and imagery. In 1978 Lloyd Etheredge published the results of his investigations in *A World of Men: The Private Sources of Foreign Policy.* Etheridge studied the makers of American foreign policy between 1898 and 1968—State Department officials, presidents, and senior advisers. He concluded that the "world of power politics" was, in being male, oriented toward ambition, competitiveness, dominance, and power, amounting to a "male narcissism syndrome" that increased the likelihood of war. He noted that wars were the work of over-self-confident men bent on irrational courses of action: "between 1914 and 1968 the initiators of violence lost 60% of their wars." Etheridge stressed the gender difference: "Males are more inclined than women to seek strength, power, activity, dominance, competitive achievement."[18]

This last approach has led to a fusion between Peace School assumptions and Innovative Tendency methodology. Exponents of antiwar feminism have published work complementing that of Etheridge, and in some cases finding inspiration in theories of literary criticism. Susan Jeffords argues that the Vietnam War changed things for women, but not for the better. Her thesis is summed up in the title of her 1989 book: *The Remasculinization of America: Gender and the Vietnam War.* She focuses on examples drawn from various types of media. For example, she cites Gustav Hasford's 1979 novel, *The Short Timers,* later made into a well-known film, in which a leading character, Joker, declares: "God has a hard-on for Marines because we kill everything we see."[19] Jeffords argues that by the use of such language a feminine space is created, into which are placed objects of low regard. (In the Rambo movies, for example, the U.S. government is feminized subject matter.) Women—who had threatened to shake up gender relationships in the 1960s—are put into the feminine space as a means of restoring their traditionally low status. For Jeffords, then, war is a cause of masculine language that serves to put women in their place.

Another scholar, Carol Cohn, has compiled a grimly amusing litany pertaining to nuclear weapons. She attacks those male defense intellectuals who humanize "smart" bombs which have their own "eyes" and "ears" and "brains," and belong to a "family" of weapons systems which represents a "new generation." These same experts dehumanize people, whose deaths are merely "collateral damage" alongside the weapons one seeks to "cripple" or "kill."[20] Taking Etheridge, Jeffords, and Cohn together, the argument would be that male dominance and war reinforce each other.

Yet another possibility for innovative investigation was suggested by a prominent contributor to the Belligerent School. For all her emphasis on bellicose feminism, Antonia Fraser points out that warrior queens are the products of hereditary monarchies—and that the United States lacks such an institution.[21] The suggestion here is that something might be gained by comparing the political culture of the United States with that of other countries. Comparisons could further understanding of how American women may be different from their foreign sisters, as well as from their menfolk at home. Potentially, comparisons can help to explain the degree and nature of American women's influence on foreign policy, and the factors that help or hinder them in their attempt to win a share of power in the diplomatic sphere.

A final issue that the historian must address is the degree and nature of women's impact on foreign policy. The matter can be partly resolved by determining the extent to which women have penetrated the foreign policy hierarchy. It is also necessary to analyze various assumptions on the character and extent of gender differences. However, a further and sadly neglected dimension of the problem is that of chronological progression—for the distinctive nature of women's impact on foreign policy has changed over time.

To outline such change one can begin with the 1920s. It is customary for historians to be preoccupied with the effects of war on society, and to view the twenties as a decade prefigured by World War I. It is true that many women reacted against the horrors of the war and supported the Republicans' peace initiatives in that decade. But they also developed a campaign that historians have never acknowledged, carrying the promise that society would influence foreign policy and not vice versa. Fearing that trade restrictions would cause high prices, prominent women led a high-profile campaign against the increased tariffs promoted by the Republicans. Goods of interest to women were particularly singled out in 1920s propaganda literature. Then, in the 1932 election, President Herbert Hoover made a strenuous appeal to women to save his high-tariff presidency, but to no avail; the Democrats won and tariff reform followed in 1934.

By the 1940s, however, housewife-led consumer awareness was on the ebb, and new concerns arose that redefined women's difference over foreign policy. Eleanor Roosevelt led the way by pioneering a caring issue in international politics. She campaigned for the United Nations Universal Declaration of Human Rights, modified it to reflect women's interests, and secured its adoption by the General Assembly in 1948. When Dwight D. Eisenhower became president in 1953, he opposed the human rights declaration and vowed to "save the U.S. from Eleanor Roosevelt." But Mrs. Roosevelt continued to fight for the rights involved in the declaration, and bequeathed to the United States and the world at large awareness of an issue that remains vitally important to the present day.[22]

But at the height of the Cold War, what worried women most was the problem of security. In 1951 Margaret Chase Smith told one of her Maine constituents that America should either use its "full atomic strength" to win the Korean War and bring home America's young men or "pull out" and "stop this endless killing." In placing her reliance on the nuclear shield and opposing "hot" wars that involved ground fighting and young Americans being killed, she helped to prepare the ground for the policies of the Eisenhower administration. But there is a question about the proposition that she was being "normative" in the sense of emulating America's male leaders. Opinion polls suggest that women as a whole in the 1950s supported nuclear deterrence to a greater degree than did men, and that women shrank disproportionately from hot wars like Korea or the Suez operation. Smith thus appears to have been representative of a new gender difference on foreign policy.

New York's Bella Abzug represented a more recent era. According to one detractor, Congresswoman Abzug's main political achievement was "a traffic light on Rivington and Columbia." But according to a respected authority on the Vietnam War, she helped to commit Congress "to a full and final pullout."[23] The latter activity would be consistent with women's opposition to hot wars in the 1950s, and the opinion polls continued to confirm that women were more averse than men to ground fighting.

However, Abzug was also associated with a sea change in women's attitudes on nuclear defense. Instead of being more supportive of it than men, women became more opposed. Abzug and a new cluster of woman politicians in the 1980s made the most of this new outlook and agitated for an end to the Cold War. Some women now believed with renewed fervor that if only they could achieve an end to military tensions, their gender would at last achieve equality. America, like Sweden, would be a land of feminism without feminists, or, as one popular postcard proclaimed in 1992: "I'll be a post feminist in post patriarchy."

In spite of all these changes since the 1920s, one aspect of gender difference over foreign policy has remained constant: Women have always been especially inclined to support peace. The format has varied: In the 1920s they linked peace to free trade; in the 1930s they linked it to arms control; in the 1950s they associated it with deterrence; in the 1960s, with anti–Vietnam War protest. In the 1980s women's interest was once again focused on limiting the spread of weapons of destruction. The principle has, however, remained the same, and the emphasis on peace is an enduring ingredient in the "gender gap" that separates women in the aggregate from men in American politics.

The phrase "changing differences" nevertheless aptly describes the relationship of women to foreign policy in the twentieth century. It suggests the need for more than one type of discussion: about differences between women and men that have helped to change U.S. foreign policy; about the ways in which those differences have changed over time; and about the women who want to take an active part in changing the differences, whether by modifying, accentuating, or eradicating them.

2 | A MOMENTARY SILENCE
The Survival of Gender Distinction in World War I

In World War I, Carrie Chapman Catt and the mainstream leadership of the American feminist movement made an implicit deal with President Wilson. The deal was full of potential repercussions for women, because Catt had considerable stature. She was known as a tough-minded feminist leader, and the reputation was deserved. Even as a girl, before she graduated from Iowa State (the only woman in her class), she had become a firm adherent of the evolutionary theories of Charles Darwin and of the individualist-competitive notions of Herbert Spencer. She believed that the path of her gender lay onward and upward through struggle. She worked tirelessly for women's right to vote, serving twice as president of NAWSA—in 1900–1904, and then in the final phase of the campaign, 1915–1920.

According to her biographer Robert Booth Fowler, peace was an important goal for Catt. She thought that voting women "would become a force for world peace." But her main aim was to establish "women's dignity," with the right to have "control over their lives," and in 1917 Catt and her NAWSA colleagues proposed to the president that if he would support votes for women, they would drop their pacifist principles and support the American war effort.[1] This deal lends itself to the proposition that American women had to become like men in order to participate in the male world of politics—because the transformation was necessary tactically and because women "grew up" politically.[2] Whether or not one agrees with this proposition, the idea that women won the vote by supporting involvement in a war was potentially influential. It carried the danger that some feminists would in future perceive women's participation in war as necessary to sexual empowerment.

Women in significant numbers fell silent on the question of peace in the important period, 1917–1920. The horrors and sacrifices of world war had a stunning effect on their peaceful aspirations. Wilson presented the conflict as a struggle for peace, a "war to end wars." But leaders who had abandoned their pacifism as a price for the vote could not convincingly turn around at the war's end to support Wilson's goal of American entry into the peacekeeping League of Nations. In contrast to other groups, such as organized labor and Irish Americans, women were relatively silent in the months when the Senate first debated and then failed to ratify U.S. membership in the League.

Yet the impression that women had "sold out" and relinquished their right to be different needs modification. When the United States entered the war, organized feminist pacifism was a very recent creation. Its initial following was too small to be decimated in any meaningful sense and in fact—compromise notwithstanding—received a fillip from the horrors of war. The history of gender-distinguished peace agitation can be seen as a continuum, with prewar origins and postwar achievements interrupted—but also inspired—by wartime persecution and experiences.

Equal rights feminism, in contrast, was a well-established movement already on the brink of success at the outbreak of war in 1914: The vote would have been achieved irrespectively. One respected historian who thinks the war did hasten the advent of the vote for women is careful not to overstate his claim: "Like prohibition, the suffrage movement had won many areas before the war, but the war accelerated the winning of the franchise by two years."[3] It is a mistake to ascribe the vote, as distinct from the timing of its achievement, to wartime compromise. It would be just as erroneous, however, to disregard the significance of the compromise, for it impaired the authority of those women who were a party to it and opened the way for unanticipated twists in foreign policy feminism in the 1920s.

The history of gender-distinguished peace agitation supplied post-1920 women with inspiring personalities, rudimentary organization, and a corpus of ideas. The personalities, organizations, and ideas cannot be said to have been particularly effective in influencing foreign policy before 1920. But they did help to shape the outlook and conduct of those women who later had an impact.

Jane Addams was the leading personality (of either sex) in the prewar peace movement. One of the first generation of college-educated women, she had rejected marriage in order to devote herself to the poor and to social reform. She pioneered the American tradition of social work through her Hull House settlement house in the immigrant slums of Chicago. She thus belonged to the social-reform wing of Progressivism, the political movement that swept the United States after 1900 and, in Theodore Roosevelt and Woodrow Wilson, produced two of the nation's most admired presidents. However, in spite of her fame, Addams cannot be assumed to have spoken consistently for the majority of Americans. The social reformers were a minority among the Progressives, and, while many Progressives were peace enthusiasts to begin with, only a minority of them held out, with Jane Addams, to oppose American entry into World War I.

The hostilities between the United States and Spain in 1898 had disgusted Addams, who began to think hard about international conflict and called for "a moral substitute for war."[4] She believed it was necessary to wean men away from thoughts of war by inventing an alternative glamour, connected with constructive, peaceful achievement. She argued that the United States had a special role to play in this regard. In its great cities and within the ambit of its democratic institutions, immigrants from all over the world had already mixed and learned to get along together. The lessons of the New World could surely be imparted to the Old.[5] Addams encouraged Americans to look outward: "Men of all nations are determining upon the abolition of degrading poverty, disease, and intellectual weakness, and are making a determined effort to conserve even the feeblest citizen to the State. To join in this determined effort is to break through national bonds and to unlock the latent fellowship between man and man."[6] Thus one of her many achievements could be said to have been that she contributed to the fund of ideas that, just over half a century later, lay behind John F. Kennedy's Peace Corps.[7]

As the most successful woman of her day, Addams supplied important leadership to those, especially women, who sought alternatives to war. For she believed that women had a duty in this regard: "Woman, the citizen . . . will bear her share of civic responsibility because she is essential to the normal development of the city of the future, and because the definition of the loyal citizen as one who is ready to shed his blood for his country, has become inadequate and obsolete."[8] Together with other women Addams helped to commit her sex to the peace cause well before the suffrage amendment took effect in 1920.

When the United States joined in the pointless carnage of European war in 1917 and Addams opposed the decision, she failed to carry the nation's women with her. By this time she had lost a great deal of her popularity and standing. When, in July 1915, she drew attention to the battlefield practice of priming men with drink before sending them into action, she attracted opprobrium for her lack of respect for dying heroes. Then, with the young Canadian Julia Grace Wales, she involved herself in a campaign to secure American mediation to end the European slaughter. But the automobile manufacturer Henry Ford seized control of the venture, and it degenerated into what critics perceived as a publicity stunt. Unrepentant, Addams continued her opposition to American entry into the war and then criticized U.S. war aims, which incorporated the "pathetic belief in the regenerative results of war." As a result Addams the American heroine became Addams the unpatriotic outcast.[9]

However, Jane Addams's infamy was to be short-lived. Her status as an inspirational figure revived after the war, and she was awarded the Nobel Peace Prize in 1931. Her message that men, and not women, should change their ways countermanded and transcended the wartime compromise whereby Catt and her followers promised loyalty to the martial ways of men in return for the vote.

A review of some of the other presuffrage leaders and of the organizations they created helps to explain the world in which 1920s women found themselves, and illustrates the links not just between women and peace but also between feminism and peace. These links went back to the earliest days of the Republic, but more recent memories for the women of the 1920s were of the war against Spain and then the brutal American suppression of insurgency in the newly acquired Philippines.[10] These events had stirred up some incipient protest during the presidency of Theodore Roosevelt (1901–1909).[11] In 1906 the social reformer Lucia Mead persuaded the American Peace Society to extend its propaganda activities to working people. In the following year Mount Holyoke College president Dr. Mary ("May") Woolley, a vice president of the American Peace Society, strenuously attacked American militarism at a Peace Congress of Women. Though impatient with the "pacifism" then in vogue, President Roosevelt recognized the force that confronted him when he met with the prominent suffragist and peace worker Anna White. A vice president of the Alliance of Women for Peace, White sought Roosevelt's support for a series of international arbitration proposals. Although White died in 1910, she belongs to that broad category of women who could be described as feminists, who helped to identify peace as an issue of special concern to women, and who contributed to the shaping of the consciousness of the women who followed her.[12]

In the years preceding American entry into the war, not just committed peace workers like Addams and Woolley but several other reform-minded women had ideas on the subject. One example is Lillian D. Wald, founder of the Henry Street Settlement in the slums of New York City. She told a New York audience in 1915 that whereas men would respond to appeals to "die for their country" and fight to "save their wives and children," women interpreted the same appeals as calls to "go out to kill" and ruin the lives of wives and children in other countries.[13] Women in the middle-class professions—few in number but significant trendsetters—also felt an obligation to speak out. For example, the pioneering female lawyer Belva Lockwood was the most vocal spokesperson of the Universal Peace Union, as well as the American secretary of the International Bureau for Peace.

Even allowing for the fact that "feminism" consists of many branches with a wide variety of beliefs, it is clear that to a remarkable degree those women committed to the furtherance of peace were in one way or another feminists, which helps to explain why they were conscious of gender difference in their approach to foreign policy issues. Hannah Hull, a leading personality in the peace cause both before and after World War I, served as vice president of the Pennsylvania Woman Suffrage Association, 1913–1914. The militant suffragist Mabel Vernon later applied her campaigning skills to the struggle for peaceful solutions to international problems, especially in Latin America. Hannah Bailey presided over the suffrage campaign in Maine and supervised the Department of Peace and Arbitration of the Women's Christian Temperance Union (WCTU). The birth control advocate Mary Dennett became the first secretary of the American Union Against Militarism. The social investigator and suffrage campaigner Crystal Eastman supported both the latter organization and the Woman's Peace Party.

In three distinct ways the pre-1920 peace women ensured that the compromise made with President Wilson would not sully in perpetuity the separate nature of the female stance on foreign policy. First, some of the campaigners, for example, Hannah Hull, supplied peace leadership in person after the attainment of the female vote. Second, others found that their direct influence was on the wane but that they had already helped to form a new generation. Notably, in the pre-1920 decade Jane Addams personally influenced and inspired Dorothy Detzer, a young woman who subsequently developed her talents to become a significant shaper of foreign policy.

The third way in which pre-1920 women had an enduring impact was in their capacity as role models or icons. Addams is clearly a case in point. Two other women who spring readily to mind are Alice Paul and Jeannette Rankin. All three were in disgrace by 1917 because of their opposition to American entry into the war, but all three came to command long-term respect.

Alice Paul's charisma was more narrowly focused than that of Addams, but was potent nevertheless as far as her followers were concerned. A Quaker descended from William Penn on her mother's side, and from the Winthrops of Massachusetts on her father's, she exuded high principle, self-confidence, and intellectual brilliance: She earned a Ph.D. in sociology from the University of Pennsylvania in her mid-twenties, by which time she had already spent three years in England, learning radical tactics from the British suffragists while she studied at a Quaker school.

Not yet thirty when war broke out in 1914, Paul brought radical tactics to bear in her native country with all the vigor of youth. She applied them to the peace crusade at a time when, in the words of one historian, there existed in the United States a new wave of women, "many of them veterans of woman suffrage, social reform, and labor organizations [who] did not share the distrust of demonstrations and a fear of indiscreet action that inhibited leaders of older peace organizations."[14] Paul was best known for her association with the National Woman's Party, dedicated exclusively to the achievement of the vote for all American women. She organized picket lines and parades and went to prison for her beliefs.

An advocate of pacifist feminism, Paul scornfully dismissed Wilson's pretensions to being a peaceful president. She retrospectively summed up her stance as follows: "The only thing that seemed to us so clear was that the women were the peace-loving half of the world and that by giving power to women we would diminish the possibilities of war."[15] As time passed and it became clear that the "war to end wars" had merely ended millions of young lives, Paul's political isolation from the majority of contemporary franchise leaders became an inspiring badge of courage. Still a young woman at the time of World War I, she remained alive for many years to remind people of her principles.[16]

The first woman to enter the British Parliament and the first woman to enter the U.S. Congress were both Americans and both advocates of peace. Lady Astor, the American who breached the barrier of gender prejudice in the House of Commons, was in the 1930s to endure considerable opprobrium because of her association with appeasement. Even more dramatically Representative Rankin forged a link between women, democracy, and peace. Alice Paul told her "it would be a tragedy for the first woman in Congress ever to vote for war."[17] Rankin did vote against American entry into World War I. A generation later, she was the only legislator of either sex to vote against the United States going to war with Japan.

A product of the pre–World War I suffrage campaigns in her native state of Montana, it was Rankin who, on January 10, 1918, introduced the suffrage amendment on the floor of the House. Like other women who achieved prominence in the period before 1920, she linked the peace and feminist causes. Aware, as she put it in the early 1920s, "that men are disposed to look down on the temperamental pacifism of women (which in spite of all the exceptions is a psychological fact)," she insisted that women would have to press for international disarmament, for "peace is a woman's job."[18] The historian Joan Hoff summed up the Jane Addams following: "There has probably never been such an influential generation of pacifists, and Jeannette Rankin remains one of its most memorable representatives."[19]

Pre-1920s women not only imprinted their personalities on subsequent history but also left a heritage of organizational structures and ideology. The main franchise organization, NAWSA, had been founded in 1890—with roots stretching back to the Seneca Falls Convention, which demanded votes for women in 1848. NAWSA was the organization that, under the leadership of Carrie Chapman Catt, compromised with Wilson and supported the American war effort in 1917–1918. In 1920, with the vote won, NAWSA became the League of Women Voters (LWV). It might be supposed that the LWV would have inherited NAWSA's mantle of compromise, even to the point of appearing tarnished. It is true that the LWV at times gave the appearance of being a rudderless crusade incapable of satisfying the expectations aroused by the suffrage triumph, and that some dynamic and committed women looked elsewhere for leadership. Yet it must be acknowledged that ever since the 1920s, the LWV and various subgroups spawned by it have addressed foreign policy issues and lobbied the White House and Congress concerning them.

Women's interest in foreign policy temporarily declined after the Spanish-American War. But such individuals as Lucia Mead, Mary Woolley, and the Shaker eldress Anna White remained active in the Roosevelt years. Of some importance, too, is the fact that middle-class women had considerable managerial experience, gained in a variety of activities that included charity organization societies, women's clubs, and such social events as assembly balls, as well as the suffrage campaign. They saw not just opportunity but also a source of frustration in the formation, between 1900 and 1914, of some forty-five male-dominated peace organizations. On the one hand these societies supplied women in every region of the United States with a "peace culture" not entirely different from that which later prevailed in India and Norway, two countries that produced peace-oriented woman prime ministers (see chapter 9)—and women did work within these societies, building specific expertise in peace agitation. But on the other hand they began to form an impression of the shortcomings of male pacifism from their point of view, and ideas about a separate, feminist initiative.[20]

Women were ready to take the lead when war broke out in Europe in 1914. On August 29 fifteen hundred women marched in silent protest down Fifth Avenue, dressed in funereal black. An organization called the Women's Peace Parade Committee was responsible for this event. Its chair was "Fanny" Garrison Villard, the only daughter of the abolitionist William Lloyd Garrison. Villard was a member of the New York Peace Society but was discontented with it, and proclaimed at a meeting of the Parade Committee, "this is a time for a new peace movement." Though the parade did not itself spawn a new organization, it brought an infusion of new blood into the peace movement—only nine of the 121-member Parade Committee belonged to the Peace Society, though they all came from New York. Then on January 10, 1915, inspired by Hungarian feminist Rosika Schwimmer and with the active participation of Alice Paul, a convention in Washington, D.C., established the Woman's Peace Party, with Jane Addams as president. In April of that year Addams and forty-six other American women traveled to an international meeting of suffragists in The Hague, in the neutral Netherlands. The 1,136 feminists in attendance made peace their central concern. They formed an International Committee of Women for Permanent Peace and elected Jane Addams its president. The Woman's Peace Party became the U.S. section of this committee.[21]

The Woman's Peace Party was a single-issue organization that failed in its immediate objective of keeping the United States out of the war, but it left a legacy. Its demand for the nationalization of the arms industry foreshadowed women's concern in the 1930s about profiteering arms manufacturers, the "merchants of death," and in the 1960s with the "military-industrial complex." Moreover, in May 1919 women who had been at The Hague convention met once again, this time in Zurich, Switzerland. They there formed WILPF. They elected Jane Addams president, and her fellow-American Emily Greene Balch secretary-treasurer. The Woman's Peace Party now became the U.S. section of WILPF, with Anna Garlin Spencer as its chair, and with every prospect of becoming a dynamic group in international relations.[22]

The enfranchised women concerned with foreign policy after 1920 drew inspiration from the personalities of their predecessors and inherited some of their institutional structures. Not unnaturally, they also fell under the influence of the attitudes and ideas of pre-1920s women. Pre-1920s ideas and the controversies that surrounded them were to condition future debates both about feminism and about women's roles in foreign policy.

If women were more peaceful than men, an assumption shared by most people regardless of gender, it was nonetheless a phenomenon in need of explanation. The most popular explanation in the Progressive Era rested on the notion of the instinct of nurturant motherhood, an instinct that made women more peaceful than men and endowed them with superior morality. As noted in the last chapter, Emily Balch advanced this view. Belief in the tenet may have been a motivating factor for some women, but references to it gradually faded away as it became plain that it could be turned into a justification for tying women to the home—which would have been self-defeating for women's aspirations in general, and in particular for their efforts to enter politics to contribute to a more peaceful world. Nevertheless, the nurturant motherhood idea could be seen as underpinning the notion, still important in the 1950s, that women were the guardians of the family, and as such on the one hand devoted to strong national defense and on the other opposed to "hot wars" that would harm their offspring.[23] Controversial though the idea was and continues to be, it is evidence of the fact that on the subjects of war and peace women had their own modes of thought in the Progressive Era, and that the habit persisted.

A remarkable feature of women's thinking about war and peace was its often distinctive character. Sometimes, of course, women supported male objectives for the same reasons as men. At other times they supported the same objectives as men, but for independent reasons. In still other cases women invented a new agenda that caught on with men and seemed to be asexual in character but still owed something to their gender. An interesting case is presented by Jane Addams's challenge to the contemporary idea of the "melting pot," meaning a homogeneous society that suppressed ethnic differences. She anticipated the "salad bowl" view of American society, embracing a peaceful pluralism from which the rest of the world could learn. On the face of it her challenge was asexual. Yet her gender may have helped her to articulate the idea of recognition of difference as a prelude to reconciliation. Similarly, her idea of a peaceful alternative to the glamour of war infused with a distinctively seductive quality the prevailing and rather stuffy philosophical thinking about a "moral substitute" for armed conflict.[24] Jane Addams inspired by her thoughts as well as by her actions, and these thoughts were not masculine in character.

One feature of pre-1920s feminism was its parodying of male manipulations of language. A satirical 1915 poster ridiculed the language of gender prejudice by inverting it. The poster was headed WHY WE OP-POSE THE VOTE FOR MEN:

> Because no really manly man wants to settle any
> question otherwise than by fighting about it.
> Because man's place is in the army.
> Because if men should adopt peaceful methods
> women will no longer look up to them.[25]

This is no isolated example of female skepticism of male propaganda. In one of Willa Cather's novels a mother mourns the death of her son in the war but consoles herself that he did not live to see the discrediting of the "ideals" for which he supposedly died.[26] To this woman the male ideology of war is just an anachronism. Such female attacks on the pomposities of male war language were not an invention of the Progressive Era. But the horrors of 1914–1918 stimulated women's disposition to criticize and link the male languages of war and sexual domination. The criticisms formed a precedent for what was to become a staple of linguistically based feminism in the wake of the Vietnam War.

Last but not least, some women in the Progressive Era linked war with the repression of their sex. It is true that Balch's idea that war had always "tended to lower the importance and the social power of women" was not universally shared.[27] Those who advocated the compromise with Wilson took the opposite view. The Civil War had been the "Negro's hour" (if briefly); the world war would empower American women, if only they supported it; after all, Catt did gain the president's ear.[28] But even this view rested on an assumption of gender difference in foreign policy—women could not have sold a principle they did not possess. More significant is the fact that, whereas the compromisers succeeded in blurring the repressive effects of war in the short term, in the longer term Balch's view was to prevail.

The history of the Progressive Era female "doves," their institutions, and their ideas is a story of shaping precedents. Ideologically as well as in terms of personalities and organizations, the development of gender-distinguished peace agitation was a continuum. World War I was at the same time a momentary interruption to feminist peace agitation and a goad that contributed to its renewal.

The great compromise with Woodrow Wilson aggravated the divisions that already existed within the feminist and peace movements but—given the impetus of personality, organization, and thought behind the feminist peace impulse—failed to destroy gender distinctiveness in the realm of foreign policy. That the compromise took place there can be little doubt. It was rooted in the peace movement's leadership crisis, a crisis brought about by presidential desertion. For, like neutrality advocates in general, peace-inclined women found themselves deprived of their standard bearer between the fall of 1916, when Wilson was reelected as the man who had kept America out of the war, and the spring of 1917, when the very same politician began to get tough with the Central Powers. This spectacular desertion stripped the peace lobbyists of an opportunity to demonstrate their strength and unity of purpose. The mainstream suffrage leaders who conceived of themselves as pragmatists now began to believe they would have to choose between the vote and peace, inclining toward the former.

The makings of the compromise were visible as early as 1915, when

Catt secured the expulsion from NAWSA of the leader of the Congressional Union for Woman Suffrage, Alice Paul. The Congressional Union had been formed in April 1913, inspired by the prosuffrage march by ten thousand women on the eve of Woodrow Wilson's inauguration. It first concentrated on militant tactics in support of a constitutional suffrage amendment, then took up the peace cause in an agitation that was to lead to the formation of the Woman's Peace Party. Catt made it clear that she was embarrassed by these peace activities. Whereas she had hitherto been associated with the peace cause and had participated in the work of the peace movement, she declared that her main loyalty now was to the campaign for the vote.[29]

In January 1917 the Congressional Union posted "silent sentinels" outside the White House. But the NAWSA president denounced such tactics. As one historian has put it, she "made it clear that she would do nothing to harm her influence as a suffrage leader," believing "that wartime service would win more support for the woman suffrage cause than pacifism." Catt argued that women could make a crucial economic contribution to the conduct of war and summoned a meeting of the NAWSA executive council with a view to formulating a "definite proposal" to the government. Reproached by a Woman's Peace Party official for condoning "czarlike" methods, Catt made a joke of the peace cause: "I was hesitating whether to assign you to the poisonous gas-bag factory or to make you driver of a military tank."[30]

The heavy flow of United States weapons to the Allies and the collapse of the domestic peace movement hastened the day when poisonous gas would cease to be an object of American mirth. Following the U.S. declaration of war in April, there were expectations that President Wilson would immediately show his appreciation of the propreparedness stance of the mainstream suffrage movement. But the president refused to endorse local suffrage bills because, according to his secretary, Joe Tumulty, he was aware of "the sensitiveness of legislative bodies to outside suggestion, particularly if made with any apparent assumption of official authority."[31]

At this point the National Woman's Party—the new name adopted by the Congressional Union at the time of the 1916 Republican Party convention—launched a campaign of peaceful picketing for the vote. Outside the White House on August 14 the pickets unfurled a banner emblazoned with the words KAISER WILSON. A mob of sailors and government employees thereupon attacked the pickets (initiating the first of several riots), only to be ignored by the police, who arrested six of the antiwar protesters. Catt castigated the demonstrators instead of the authorities, protesting that "suffrage is not won today by stunts."[32] She complained that militant tactics smelled of unpatriotic behavior and might alienate supporters of the franchise. Privately she perhaps resented the challenge to her own authority and power to dictate tactics.

NAWSA's approach contrasted with that of the Woman's Peace Party. Early in 1917 its powerful New York branch offered the support of suffragists throughout the state for the prospective war effort. Nationally Catt reiterated the offer, an act that outraged members of the Woman's Peace Party and split the suffrage movement.[33] The split meant there was a prospect of feminist opposition to the war, and this gave NAWSA a bargaining chip. In July its vice president, Helen H. Gardener, wrote to President Wilson:

> Our hope has been to secure your interest and powerful influence at that time—at the opening of the new Congress—for a real drive for the enfranchisement of twenty million of American women, as a "war measure" and to enable our women to throw, more fully and wholeheartedly, their entire energy into work for their country and for humanity, instead of for their own liberty and independence.[34]

Here there was a veiled threat—support us, or women will fight for their own liberty, not for their country, perhaps even lending their weight to the likes of Paul and Addams. The peace movement was a useful stick with which to beat the president and Congress into submission on the subject of the vote. Gardener recognized its implicit power.

The House of Representatives gave Jeannette Rankin's suffrage amendment its required two-thirds majority in January 1918. The Senate proved to be stubborn, however. Members from the southern states worried that blacks would seek the vote if women obtained it; there were also fears that women would vote for Prohibition and that they would cease to accept low wages. In an attempt to shift senatorial as well as presidential opinion, NAWSA's leaders tried to align the suffrage cause with American war aims. The collapse of the czarist regime and later the withdrawal of Bolshevik Russia from the war meant that all the Allied Powers with whom the United States fought were democracies. With the suffrage amendment pending, Gardener wrote the president on June 17, 1918: "It is unthinkable that the United States Senate can now vote to range itself on the side of Germany and Hungary, who alone of all the warring countries have denied to women the ballot this 'war for democracy and self-determination' began."[35] This argument stood on its head the notion that women, benefiting from the peaceful dimension of democracy, would favor peaceful means.

The argument does seem to have had an effect on Woodrow Wilson. Forgetting earlier inhibitions about congressional resentment of "outside suggestion," the president in June 1918 wrote to Senator John K.

Shields of Tennessee. He said he was departing from his normal custom of noninterference in senatorial affairs because of the gravity of the international situation and because "much of the morale of this country and of the world will repose in our sincere adherence to democratic principles." He was asking "very frankly" if it would be possible for Senator Shields to vote for the suffrage amendment. When Shields found it difficult to accept that a vote for the franchise was a war measure, Wilson assured him "that the passage of the amendment at this time was an essential element in the conduct of the war for democracy" and would have an "important and immediate effect." At the end of July he reinforced the message in a letter to another wavering senator: "I believe that our present position as champions of democracy throughout the world would be greatly strengthened if the Senate would follow the example of the House of Representatives in passing the pending amendment."[36]

In the fall of 1918 the president and NAWSA were especially mindful of their apparently mutual political dependency. The Germans were bogged down following the repulsion of their attack across the Marne, and peace loomed. It would be convenient for Wilson to have a Democratic majority in the Senate during any peace negotiations. The women's vote in the already-enfranchised western states might prove to be important in November's midterm elections. Thereafter the enfranchisement of twenty-six million women presumed to be peace loving might prove to be of assistance to a president who, in spite of having fought a war, still wanted to establish his credentials as a peaceful man and, in particular, to create a peace-generating League of Nations of which the United States would be a leading member.

From NAWSA's viewpoint the fall of 1918 was an important time because the president needed friends and because the suffrage amendment was coming up for another vote in the Senate. From Catt's point of view she needed results, for with the arrival of peace the president might not need women any more, given the immense popularity of the League idea in the nation at large. Worse still, the winning of the vote and the joining of the League might come in peacetime, which would mean that she had played the war card in vain.

On September 18 Catt told Wilson the amendment required just one more vote, and hinted at reward in the case of delivery: "We are not unmindful that we shall owe our victory to you and are more grateful than words can express."[37] Wilson promised immediate action, but on the eve of the September 20 Senate vote Catt had to turn to him again "in sheer desperation," this time short of two votes. Playing the patriotism card to its utmost, she asked the president to publish in the next morning's papers a statement to the effect that suffrage endorsement was "a war measure."[38]

Catt noted that the chief opposition came from the "solid South" and from the "Massachusetts senators." Her particular difficulty—and opportunity—lay with Henry Cabot Lodge. The senior senator from Massachusetts wanted to establish peace on a firm footing. But, as he explained on the eve of the suffrage vote, he wished to do so with a policy of containment toward Germany, with a system of buffer states, and by resurrecting the European balance of power. One historian suggests that, unlike Wilson, Lodge could not "gloss over" the tragedy of war "by escaping into the future and embracing the ideal of a new community of nations."[39] In these circumstances, Catt conceived it to be in her interest to play on the expectations of the president, who was already having problems with Lodge:

Many of us were shocked at the peace terms put forth by Senator Lodge. He had much of the substance, but the spirit of humanity was not there. There was none of the thrill, the exaltation which your exposition of our aims produces. We shudder to think that should the reactionary element of either or both parties become apparent at the end of the war, the world may lose the fruits for which a generation has been sacrificed.

It is therefore not alone to win two votes that we suggest this step. The country and especially the women recognize the need of constant direction of thought and feeling upward and onward.[40]

Wilson did not appeal through the press but instead took the unusual step of addressing the Senate in the course of the debate, hoping Catt would "think what I did do was better."[41] In his address he followed the line that NAWSA leaders had pressed on him:

This is a peoples' war and the peoples' thinking constitutes its atmosphere and morale. . . . Through many, many channels I have been made aware of what the plain, struggling, workaday folk are thinking upon whom the chief terror and suffering of this war falls. . . . They think in their logical simplicity, that democracy means that women shall play their part in affairs alongside men and upon an equal footing with them.[42]

Catt's desertion of the peace standard was comparable, in its effect on her supporters, to that of the president's own desertion of neutrality in 1916–1917. It could also be represented as having been a portent: On three subsequent occasions in the twentieth century—because of

the country's late entry, once again, into World War II and then because of the gradualist approaches to the Vietnam and Gulf Wars—
Americans were to be granted the time to debate entry into serious
hostilities. It could be said that Catt left to future generations involved
in those decisions the precedent of a peacetime pacifist.

Yet there is a need for caution in assessing the significance of the
Catt-Wilson deal. For one thing, the deal simply did not work. In spite
of the president's efforts, the Senate vote fell short of the requisite majority by two votes, and not until June 1919, with peace in force and
"war measures" a thing of the past, did the suffrage amendment find
the extra support it needed. Thus the accommodation could be represented as having been distinctly ineffective and hardly an inspiration
for future generations.

For women especially, the compromise could be presented in a
gloomy light. In fact, it could be regarded as having been positively
harmful to, and ominous for, the ideals of women's empowerment and
world peace at a time when the United States was about to debate the
question of entry into the League of Nations. When Wilson lost his majority in the Senate in the 1918 election and Lodge became chairman of
the Senate Foreign Relations Committee, the League of Nations proposal was assured of stiff opposition on Capitol Hill, and the president
needed all the support he could muster in the nation at large. Where
women like Catt were concerned, he needed a sudden about-face. The
former pacifists-turned-patriots would need to rekindle their crusade
for peace.

Fannie Fern Andrews was one such woman who tried her best.
Andrews had been a peace campaigner determined to instill cooperative ideals at the high school level. Her American School Peace League
had branches in thirty-five states by 1913. But then she endorsed the
war effort and became assistant U.S. commissioner for education. She
attended the Paris Peace Conference as a representative of the U.S. Bureau of Education, acting as the spokeswoman for a conference of women
delegates who had been sponsored by the International Council of
Women, a suffrage organization established in Washington, D.C., in
1888. Andrews claimed that these women were responsible for "several
of the provisions of Article 23 of the Treaty of Versailles."[43] The article
promised that the League would make efforts to combat a number of
evils: the exploitation at work of "men, women and children," prostitution, drug trafficking, the international arms trade, restrictions on international migration and trade, and the spread of diseases from one
country to another. Andrews despaired, however, of being able to arouse
the enthusiasm of the American public for such objectives.

The women who supported such objectives might in other times have been President Wilson's most formidable allies domestically, in contrast to the more fickle reformers who had blown hot and cold on peace issues. Those who had stuck to their pacifist principles might also have carried more authority in public debate when advocating an international peacekeeping organization. However, they were both embittered and marginalized by their treatment at the hands of the Wilson administration. The Woman's Peace Party gathered at Zurich instead of Versailles to form WILPF because it had been prohibited from meeting with German women at the site of the peace negotiations. The Zurich convention protested the vindictive treatment of Germany meted out at the official peace conference, insisted that Germany should be a member of the League, and urged that the peace treaty should incorporate a "Women's Charter" with an emphasis on equal rights.

But the president's policies had created a climate of opinion within which it was difficult for these women to operate. Because of her peace work, Wellesley College dismissed Emily Balch from the teaching post she had held for twenty-one years. Official government sources repeatedly smeared Jane Addams as a Red because of her peace work. (Not for the last time, a liberal American government had started a Red scare it could not stop.) By dallying with the compromisers Wilson had lost some of his best support. In the fall of 1919, after a long summer of debate, he failed to persuade the Senate to endorse the peace treaty negotiated in Paris that included, at his own insistence, the covenant of the League of Nations.[44]

The subsequent story of the League fight underlines not only the failure of the apparent Catt-Wilson strategy but also the president's uneven enthusiasm for womanly counsel. In part because of the strain imposed on him by the fight over the League issue, President Wilson fell ill in September 1919, and did not resume his official duties until early 1920. In the period of his illness, his wife, Edith, tried to ensure the government's functioning. She did not depart from the policies of the elected chief executive. But she later recalled that, at a point when the League fight was particularly acrimonious, she suggested to her husband that he compromise with the League's critics. The wisdom (or otherwise) of this suggestion is not of interest here (if Wilson had compromised with Lodge at this late hour, he would have had to return to Europe to attempt to renegotiate terms with European statesmen in humiliating and unpromising circumstances), but the fury of the president's reaction to the suggestion, which he interpreted as desertion, is. His nerves, it is true, were strained at the time. But, in the opinion of one student of presidential wives, "Edith had married a man who rarely listened to women on any substantive issue."[45] It is not whimsical to suggest that Wilson was at times distinctly unreceptive to women's views, and it is open to question whether NAWSA greatly changed his attitude.

In February 1920 Wilson congratulated NAWSA "upon the fact that its great work is so near its triumphant end that you can now merge it into a League of Women Voters to carry on the development of good citizenship and real democracy."[46] Perhaps he looked forward to the states' ratification of the nineteenth amendment, finally achieved on August 26, and was still hopeful of women's backing for his unsullied League. Responding to pressure from feminists, he had reversed his earlier ruling that women would be ineligible to hold office in the League, and no doubt expected that women would embrace the organization and its ideals.[47]

But within weeks the Senate again declined to accept an unamended treaty. In the 1920 presidential election Carrie Catt campaigned for the League and, at the last moment, endorsed the Democratic candidate, James Cox, on the ground that he was more supportive of the League than his opponent, Warren Harding.[48] But she had little impact. Far from dominating the election, the League issue simply faded away. Harding won. The League of Nations had to function without American commitment and strength, could look to an uncertain future, and could offer only a curtailed measure of hope and sustenance to internationalist American women, who had ample cause to regret their disempowering exclusion from the attempted global forum.[49]

The short-term efficacy of the Catt-NAWSA-Wilson deal is, therefore, open to doubt on the grounds that, whereas it may have sealed wartime unity, it failed to secure the vote as a "war measure" and failed to provide the means for U.S. endorsement of the League of Nations. It might be added that there are questions even about the thesis that Catt was instrumental in persuading the president to deliver his ineffectual endorsement of the constitutional amendment. One possibility is that, while political expediency played its role, the president came to support the amendment at least partly because he was intellectually committed to a progressive outlook.[50] He may have been less open to Catt's urgings than to those of two women with an exceptional personal claim on his attention: two of his daughters from his first marriage, Eleanor and Margaret, both by this time active suffragists, the former married to a powerful cabinet colleague.[51]

Another view is that the feminist who put the president under the greater pressure was not Catt but Paul. In October 1917 Paul, along with some of her colleagues, was given a seven-month prison sentence. Her offense was that she had parodied the masculine language of war conveyed in the Liberty Bond slogan THE TIME HAS COME TO CONQUER OR

SUBMIT by carrying it in a suffrage parade. In the District of Columbia jail Paul and her comrades went on a hunger strike. Paul was then force-fed, transferred to a psychiatric ward, and placed in solitary confinement. The image of the woman in her lonely cell preyed on the president's nerves and conscience. Late in November Paul was released—reportedly after striking an agreement on presidential suffrage endorsement with an unofficial White House emissary who visited her in prison. From President Wilson's point of view, Paul was a truly troublesome woman. His dealings with Catt were, at least in part, a relatively painless way of disguising his surrender to Paul.[52]

In the longer term the war-for-votes deal diminished the appeal of Catt, now tarnished with the brush of peacetime pacifism. In contrast, the Paul wing of feminism retained its relatively inspiring character even if it never attained majority status in the women's movement as a whole. In the 1920s foreign policy feminism was to diversify, concerning itself with foreign economic policy and also pursuing peace with renewed vigor in a variety of ways. These developments stemmed from the fact that the women of the 1920s inherited an unimpaired gender-distinct tradition with respect to foreign policy—with peace as that tradition's enduring ingredient.

3 | FROM PEACE TO PRICES IN THE TARIFF DECADE

he image of the frivolous flapper is beginning to fade. Gone for good is the notion that, in the wake of the Nineteenth Amendment, American women squandered their hard-won votes. Historians now recognize that early 1920s politicians on some issues feared the female vote and accordingly gave respectful support to legislation women desired.[1]

Given this renewed appreciation of the potential effectiveness of women in politics, there is every reason to scrutinize their role in foreign policy. For, as their earlier history had promised, women worked in a variety of ways for a more peaceful world. In the words of one historian, the heirs of the Woman's Peace Party "recognized a 'gender gap' in political affairs, claiming that women would vote differently from men in such areas as peace, child labor, and birth control."[2]

But women were also active in their attempts to influence economic aspects of foreign policy. One aspect of these attempts was rooted in the Woman's Peace Party's agitation in World War I, when it had demanded the nationalization of the arms industry as a means of keeping the United States out of hostilities.[3] In the 1920s and 1930s women continued to demand government regulation of the munitions industry because the arms race might lead to war. Later they were to argue ever more insistently that money spent on weapons would be better spent on improving society at home and abroad.

A second aspect of women's economic interest in foreign policy, and one of special concern in this chapter, sprang from the perception that high tariffs were inimical to the interests of women because they led to higher prices. This perception lay behind a low-tariff/free-trade campaign, which flourished as a feminist issue in the interwar years. The campaign revitalized an older idea, that the free-trade cause was an integral part of the peace crusade. The latter argument had been, and remained in the 1920s, that if countries traded together, it would be too expensive for them to start wars. During the 1920s the peace-and-low-prices outlook gradually gained ground among women and could be regarded as having had some effect on the outcome of the 1932 presidential election and on 1930s foreign trade policy.

In that the free-trade campaign harkened back to eighteenth- and nineteenth-century liberalism, it was conservative, even reactionary. For free trade was akin to laissez-faire, and the United States, like leading European industrial nations, had already traversed its "crossroads of liberalism," with most social reformers now urging a more active role for government.[4] The "conservative" advocacy of free trade was to some degree a defense against anti-Red smear campaigns directed at women in the 1920s. After all, ran the invisible text, an endorsement of laissez-faire placed one at the furthest remove from the doctrines of Karl Marx. It is true that this fear-driven retreat could not outlive the nativist mood of the early 1920s. Again, the women's trade campaign always had to coexist with more radical feminist demands for "statist" curbs on the arms industry. The antitariff agitation never quite gave way to the insistent demands of the peace movement pure and simple, and eventually sank into relative oblivion. Nevertheless, in its day the feminist linking of prices and tariffs was a significant factor, and it invites the scrutiny of the historian.

By the end of the 1920s women were well equipped, in organizational terms, to influence foreign policy. The prosperity of the decade did not affect society evenly, but it did help middle-class women raise money, not just for the major feminist peace societies but also for, in one estimate, "hundreds" of smaller women's peace groups.[5] But this was not all, for interest in foreign policy spread far beyond the confines of peace societies as such. In 1929 Florence Boeckel, education director for the National Council for Prevention of War (NCPW) noted that organization's cooperation with other groups not primarily devoted to the peace cause, for example the American Farm Bureau Association (AFBA) and the American Association of University Women (AAUW). The far-reaching NCPW has been described as "the most effective pressure group of the peace movement."[6] Boeckel observed that all the leading women's organizations elected, in the course of the 1920s, to make international affairs their prime concern. She listed twenty-six such organizations (including five that had been formed "wholly in the interest of world peace"). Claiming that the total membership of the twenty-six associations reached "well up into the millions," she argued that "women through their organizations are the greatest present factor in educating public opinion for a world order."[7]

Women did help to exert a check on the lobbying effectiveness of what President Dwight D. Eisenhower later dubbed the "military-industrial complex," notably playing a role in frustrating the navy's plans for shipbuilding. The navy's goal was the completion of the ambitious naval building program set forth in the Naval Bill of 1916, which reflected, in one historian's words, "the Imperial Roman maxim: to ensure peace, prepare for war."[8] In 1918 and again in 1920, Secretary of the Navy Josephus Daniels announced a three-year plan that would build for the United States the world's biggest navy.[9] Yet after the war, in 1921, nine powers met in Washington, D.C., for a disarmament conference.

American public opinion was a major factor behind the conference. The historian Robert Ferrell has observed that in the decade following the Armistice of 1918 there was, at a time when "many diplomats held office by will of the people," a "citizen campaign for peace."[10] In the United States in particular there was, in another historian's words, a "popular revolt against navalism."[11] Rooted in the protest engendered by naval expansion at the time of the American quest for empire at the turn of the century, this revolt gathered considerable momentum in the 1920s. When Republican Senator William H. Borah of Idaho in 1920 introduced a motion calling for a conference on naval disarmament, and subsequently called for a 50 percent reduction in naval construction, he had widespread support.[12] The American taxpayer recoiled at the prospect of renewed arms competition. Business organs like the *New York Journal of Commerce* took up the taxpayers' cause and counseled restraint in defense spending. There emerged on college campuses a National Student Committee for the Limitation of Armaments. The churches formed their own organizations to the same purpose, and delivered an impressive number of petitions to Congress. Organized labor, too, had its General Committee on the Limitation of Armament.[13]

Women played the leading role in the naval disarmament campaign, and throughout its course constituted its most salient feature. Borah's efforts had been flagging in early 1921, the point at which women intervened, deluging Washington with telegrams and letters and stirring up other groups. The Women's Committee for World Disarmament (WCWD) "stimulated," according to one specialist study, "all other existing groups."[14] This small but energetic committee was an offshoot of the National Woman's Party (NWP). Under Emma Wold's leadership and with Senator Borah's encouragement, it marshaled other women's associations such as the National League of Women Voters (LWV), the Women's Non-Partisan League (WNPL), the National Congress of Parents and Teachers (NCPT), the AAUW, the WCTU, the Women's Missionary Council (WMC) of the Board of Missions of the Methodist Episcopal Church, and the Federation of Business and Professional

Women's Clubs (FBPWC). These groups in turn proselytized in society at large. Borah declared himself "delighted with their work."[15]

On April 18 the Women's Committee sent a delegation to the White House, demanding an early disarmament conference and a moratorium on naval spending. President Harding stalled but reportedly informed the women that they "would not be disappointed."[16] On the local level the committee was active in thirty states. For example, every town of substance in Michigan received a visit from a local "Woman's Flying Squadron for Disarmament." The aim was to bring pressure to bear on individual legislators who might talk to the president, and who would then vote to ratify any arms-reduction treaty negotiated—a point to be stressed in light of the Senate's recent failure to ratify the Versailles peace treaty incorporating American membership in the League of Nations.

Harding appears to have been conscious of a need to propitiate the woman voter on the peace issue. He agreed to see women's delegations and to the calling of the disarmament conference. He then appointed four women to a subcommittee of the American delegation. Later in the year, when the Washington proposals were under consideration and some women were disappointed that only partial disarmament was being achieved, the president revealed his reasoning in an orchestrated and widely publicized correspondence with one particular woman who had written to him. Mrs. Ella Fried of the Brooklyn Citizen's Committee for Universal Disarmament was a person of no special political significance. (If she had been, as the White House doubtless calculated, she might have given the president more trouble.) Her importance lay in the fact that she was a woman with pacifist hopes. "I think I ought to correct your impression about the expectation for universal disarmament," wrote the president. "It is very erroneous even to contemplate going as far as that. If we can get a reasonable limitation we shall think that great things have been accomplished."[17] By showing his readiness to write to an "ordinary" woman like Fried, Harding aimed to keep the majority of her gender on his side.

It is appropriate to note here that the administration was struggling to manage public opinion. Secretary of State Charles Evans Hughes had convened the Washington conference and was mainly responsible for the American approach to it. In some ways public opinion was a nuisance to his plans. He desired the substitution of American power based on economic strength for British and Japanese power based on military force. He showed himself to be shrewd in negotiations and was assisted by a factor having nothing to do with public opinion—the United States had broken Japan's secret codes, was reading Tokyo-Washington messages, and was able to bargain in the knowledge of Japanese fall-back positions. However, the force of public opinion was such that he felt under pressure to come to terms, and he found it difficult not to make unilateral concessions. Only by playing for time did he manage to secure a moderate, multilateral arms reduction agreement instead of an ill-considered unilateral reduction on America's part.[18]

Whatever one's assessment of Hughes's tactics, women do appear to have taken a leading role in organizing public support for the Washington conference and for the treaties that arose from it. Fresh to electoral politics, they were not, in terms of foreign policy lobbying, as well organized as they were to be later in the decade, and they tended to take their cue from Borah and other male leaders.[19] But they were helped by the current vogue for public opinion—Walter Lippmann published his notable book on the subject in 1922—and by the fact that, with the science of opinion sampling some years in the future, politicians skeptical of the press had little option but to consider well-led groups to be representative of opinion at large.[20]

Following the Washington conference, Italy, France, Britain, Japan, and the United States agreed to limit the total tonnage of the major or "capital" ships in their respective navies, and with other nations signed a series of treaties increasing security in the Pacific and Far East. In 1922 the navy obtained not the $680 million appropriation it had requested from Congress but $395 million, with the allotment for naval construction halved. According to one subsequent critic, Hughes sank "more of our fleet than the Japanese did at Pearl Harbor." All too soon it became evident that reductions in capital ship tonnage would not curtail the race for supremacy in other, lighter types of ship. Furthermore, Japan was angry when it later found out about Hughes's techniques of deception. But most arms agreements are imperfect and in need of periodic review, the Washington accords helped bolster international confidence at least in the short term, and women remained proud of the part they had played in "a noble experiment."[21]

B ecause their antimilitary stance could be misrepresented as unpatriotic—and because America was going through one of its nativist, anti-Red phases—female peace campaigners were now subjected to vilification and smears. Spokesmen for the army and navy led the assault. Deputy Chief of Staff General James G. Harbord inveighed against "all that fascinating inconsistency of mingled charms and hysterics which so often characterizes lovely women—without whose approval no war has ever been waged." Secretary of War John D. Weeks, who felt he had a grievance against feminists, was particularly vehement. He had been one of the Massachusetts senators opposed to the franchise amendment in 1918; then, in that year's elections, feminists campaigned successfully against him and he lost his seat in spite of Republican gains elsewhere. Further goaded by the military reductions of the early 1920s, Weeks took his revenge. He said he had to defend the United States from the threat within. In line with the nativist impulse of the times, he accused WILPF of being a Red conspiracy.[22]

The Navy's Rear Admiral Fiske expressed similar apprehension in 1925:

No man respects and admires women more than I do, but some women have faults, and the fault most commonly found is a seemingly insatiable desire to interfere in matters they do not understand. War they understand least, and from it they instinctively recoil. There is a danger in this situation. Women now have the vote and they outnumber the men. There must be some action by the men which will bring women to realize that it is for their comfort and protection that all wars are fought. It is to the interest of women that they permit men to obtain the necessary armament. Only in this way can they be assured of the comfort and protection they need. In spite of themselves, we must protect the ladies![23]

These militaristic sentiments may well have encouraged some women to take a more cautious line. On the other hand, they did not undermine the antimilitarist campaign or reverse the downward spiral in military expenditure. Furthermore, Red-baiting and nativism had passed their peak by the mid-1920s in the nation at large, and there was less reason for women to feel inhibited about expressing their views on foreign policy in the later 1920s.

Women's strong interest in peace issues continued throughout the 1920s. Opposition to naval expansion was important to American women because they inhabited an oceanbound nation that placed greater reliance on warships than it did on tanks. However, they never restricted themselves to criticisms of the navy. For example, WILPF had campaigned for reductions in the general level of military expenditure—and in response to such pressures between 1920 and 1922 Congress halved the number of soldiers in the army.[24]

Former suffrage leader Carrie Chapman Catt directed her bureaucratic instincts into a new channel, which culminated in the formation in 1925 of an institution designed to coordinate the peace efforts of the main women's associations—the Committee on the Cause and Cure of War, of which she remained in charge until 1932. Meanwhile numerous specific groups remained firmly committed to the idealistic peace cause. The AAUW steadfastly identified international issues as matters requiring "emergency" attention. Among these issues were the arbitration of international disputes and proposed U.S. membership in the World Court.[25] In all, seventeen women's groups joined to form a World Court Committee. They formed an impressive lobby, even if they failed to persuade the United States to join this League of Nations institution.

The U.S. failure to join the League of Nations itself remained a weakness in the international efforts of the women's movement. In fact, it could be argued that American women had a counterproductive effect on the first stirrings of a serious movement for world government. The Catt-Wilson war deal had already eviscerated the 1919–1920 campaign for the League. Catt, moreover, had opposed the formation within the League of a women's bureau. Thereafter a serious split occurred in the American feminist movement, between those who favored an Equal Rights Amendment (ERA) to the U.S. Constitution and those who wanted special protective legislation for women, that imposed itself, through the vigor and financial resources of American women active in Geneva, on the international feminist community. In the long run the split produced a constructive debate on how women's rights and conditions could be improved, and on how women could contribute to world peace. But in the short run the internationalization of the U.S. feminist split prevented women from speaking with a united voice through the League. Thus, having failed to join their international sisters in 1919–1920, American women who turned up as unofficial guests in Geneva in the 1920s and 1930s proved to be a divisive force.[26]

Just as American women failed to be an asset to the League of Nations, so the League fell short of being a unifying force in the U.S. feminist peace movement. Ferrell argued that although American peace groups in the 1920s were larger and more influential than their European counterparts, they suffered from naïveté concerning international politics, and from a diversity of goals that tended to dilute the effectiveness of their work in any one direction. Whereas European internationalists campaigned mainly in support of League of Nations peacekeeping endeavors, Americans spent their efforts not just on the League, but on the campaigns for U.S. membership of the World Court, for disarmament, and against militarism (for example, the marines' interventions in Nicaragua). Yet Ferrell observed that some of the "radical" organizations, such as WILPF, "battled hard and effectively" for the peace cause. WILPF mounted a determined effort in support of bilateral treaties to outlaw war. The main "outlawry" advocate, French Prime Minister Aristide Briand, was so convinced of his following among the American people that he appealed directly to them for support, instead of going solely through diplomatic channels. In December 1927 President Calvin Coolidge received Jane Addams and a WILPF delegation at the

White House. They presented him with a thirty-thousand-signature petition supporting the idea of a treaty outlawing war. The president promised the WILPF delegation he would respond to Briand's proposal. However, because he and his secretary of state, Frank Kellogg, perceived in Briand's overtures an attempt to commit the United States to the defense of France should Germany attack again, Kellogg developed a counterproposal. The result was the Multilateral Treaty for the Renunciation of War, also known as the Kellogg-Briand Pact, which was ultimately signed by most of the world's nations.[27]

In spite of the Washington treaties and the Kellogg-Briand Pact, some women began to worry that they were not making enough impact. Florence Boeckel suggested a model by which women's influence could be judged, observing that women could influence international affairs in three ways: as actors in the executive or legislative branches of government; within political parties, where they might influence foreign policy platforms; and through public opinion. But in 1929, the year of her survey, she concluded that only in the last respect had they made a significant impact.[28]

Boeckel's observations invite a reexamination of the 1920s. Such a review suggests that both her pessimism and her qualified optimism are defensible. No American woman had an executive say in the making of foreign policy. As for the legislature, the historian William Chafe has suggested that most 1920s congresswomen were products of the "widows' game," easily manipulated by male politicians and generally occupying for just one term the seats they inherited from their departed husbands. (Actually, of the nineteen congresswomen who served in the 1920s, only five succeeded deceased spouses—and one had taken over from her dead father. One might anyway question the logic of the assumption that political widows are less effective than, say, privileged sons—of whom there have been a great number in the history of every country.)[29] Within the political parties there were, in fact, some feminist stirrings. Belle Moskowitz served Al Smith as campaign manager for his four terms as governor of New York, sat on the Democratic National Committee, and directed their publicity during Smith's presidential candidacy in 1928. While Smith lost, Moskowitz's activities did foreshadow the emergence in the 1930s of a major female political party boss, in the person of Mary W. ("Molly") Dewson. Nevertheless, Boeckel's reservations about women's standing in the executive, legislative, and political party spheres are understandable.[30]

Boeckel was more optimistic about women's impact on public opinion. But even here some qualifications appear to be in order. If one measures women's influence on public opinion in the concrete form of voting behavior, the results from the feminist standpoint are not immediately reassuring: In the 1920s observers worried about low female turnout at the polls and about a tendency among women to vote the same way as their men.[31]

Though these concerns illustrate the uncertainties that beset pioneering American political women in the 1920s, they were not entirely well founded: The indications are that women in the mass *did* have some potency. Low turnout at the polls was a feature of the decade, regardless of gender, and therefore not an indication of feminist weakness. Historians have justified their view that wives voted with their husbands in the 1920s by citing Paul Lazarsfeld's study of voting intentions in 1944 and retrospectively applying his conclusion that only one in twenty-two wives intended to differ from their husbands.[32] But people change over time: The women of the 1920s may have had a less "normative" outlook than did their war-blitzed successors in the 1940s. And Lazarsfeld and his colleagues appear to have missed something crucial about the women they studied: American women were distinctly more critical of World War II than were their menfolk, according to a 1942 survey conducted on behalf of the Office of War Information.[33] Finally, the statistical deduction that wives follow their husbands's voting intentions does not hold up logically—after all, husbands could be voting with their wives. Lazarsfeld and others have offered impressionistic evidence indicating that wives defer to their husbands, quoting, for example, claims to that effect by apparently compliant women. However, to accept that evidence at face value would be to ignore the phenomenon of wives and daughters who subtly influenced husbands and fathers while leaving intact the cherished illusion of patriarchal control. It would also contradict the findings of leading post–World War II female politicians that "women write [political] letters . . . for the family" and that "men listened to their wives, daughters, and sisters."[34]

Women may well have suffered from a sense of letdown in the 1920s. Their expectations had been high, and some politicians may have had an inflated opinion of the power women would wield, leading to depressed esteem in the later 1920s. But Boeckel was justified in being relatively sanguine about the force of female public opinion, especially as the nativist, Red-baiting tide receded. Certainly American women started from a low political base in 1920, and had a long and arduous journey in front of them. Again, it does seem possible that Red-baiting caused them to change their emphasis. But the argument that women were weakened or politically impotent in the 1920s simply does not hold water.

It therefore makes no sense for historians to ignore the impact of women on the 1920s tariff debate, as they have done hitherto. It is true that the full force of women's impact was not felt until the tariff changes of the 1930s; indeed, female tariff campaigners and their allies suffered serious reverses in the 1920s. However, the feminist tariff agitation can only be understood if one examines its roots in the 1920s, and it is to the same decade that one must turn to appreciate the underpinnings of the changes in the following one.

Until the 1920s American farmers had been in the van of the campaign for lower tariffs. They had attacked Hamilton's protectionism, the "Tariff of Abominations" (1828), and the McKinley tariff (1890) largely because they believed that industry was being protected at a cost to the consumer. The actual word "consumer" was on the tariff-debate agenda well before the 1920s. For example, in 1867, the protectionist wool manufacturer John L. Hayes tried to counter "the popular argument of the opponents of our policy" in a pamphlet entitled *Protection a Boon to Consumers*.[35]

By the 1920s the farming free-traders were on the defensive, for the United States was on the brink of becoming an urban society. The farmers' lobby, while still strong, seemed on the point of eclipse. Profiting from this and from the reaction against internationalism that set in following the war and the League of Nations debate, urban manufacturers and wage earners seemed well placed to carry the day. In the period of their ascendency, the Republicans fostered the notion that higher tariffs would bring larger profits, full employment, higher wages, and continuing prosperity. It was into this context that newly enfranchised women stepped—in their capacity as the new champions of a particular type of consumerism.

Here it is necessary to distinguish between four types of "consumerism," for women, unlike the farmers, were widely enmeshed in all four—a fact that has hitherto helped to obscure their contribution to the tariff debate. The first type of consumerism had to do with moral pressure. Josephine Shaw Lowell had established a National Consumers' League in the nineteenth century. Under the subsequent leadership of Florence Kelley and with the active support of prominent women like Eleanor Roosevelt and New Deal cabinet member Frances Perkins, the league used the power of women as consumers in support of social reform goals—women were urged to boycott goods and services supplied by businesses that exploited women and children.

The National Consumers' League at the same time alerted women to their wider economic role as consumers. This second type of consumerism manifested itself in the 1920s, and particularly during the depression, in the rise of consumption-oriented economics. The supposition that high-spending consumers could redeem U.S. economic fortunes elevated consumerism to a new plane. At the same time it served as the prelude to the oft-derided "consumer society" and "culture of consumption," and came to be associated with "sexy" advertising and the exploitation of female stereotypes to sell goods and services at home and abroad.[36]

A third variety of consumerism spanned the years from the publication of Upton Sinclair's *The Jungle* in 1906 to the launch of Ralph Nader's *Unsafe at Any Speed* in 1965. Although it was a fight to protect consumers from the unscrupulous production of dangerous items, ranging from contaminated canned meat to unsafe automobiles, there was also an element of self-interest here. Those who persuaded Congress and the president to accept laws purifying food and drugs (under Theodore Roosevelt) or regulating working conditions on American ships (under Woodrow Wilson) were, to be sure, protecting the health of the American family and the welfare of the American sailor—but they were also protecting their own stomachs and their own lives at sea.

A potent blend of idealism and self-interest likewise affected the fourth type of consumerism, consumer agitation over prices and, what is of concern here, consumer militancy over the tariff—an important element in foreign economic policy. According to one influential line of reasoning—though there were economists and politicians who dissented from it—higher tariffs caused higher prices. As they affected the quality of family life, higher tariffs were therefore morally regrettable. Idealists also maintained that tariff fluctuations could damage the economies of some of America's weaker trading partners, causing social suffering. Furthermore, high tariffs were supposed to create international tensions that might lead to war, whereas free trade (according to its idealistic advocates) made war uneconomical and less likely.

While these idealistic arguments appealed to women, their support for low tariffs can also be seen in another, more materialistic light. Lower prices—thus lower tariffs—appealed to the consumer interest of what the culture of the time would call the shopping female. It could, of course, be argued that this appeal was too abstract to affect women's political behavior. But low-price economics did fit in with women's general outlook in the 1920s, a decade when rising living standards meant more leisure and more time to spend money. It was a decade when not a few women, according to historian Alice Kessler-Harris, shunned longer working hours, simply wanting "more time to live."[37] While one cannot generalize for all classes, there was a tendency for women to want to escape the wage slavery of the nineteenth century; widespread acceptance of the idea of work as career, with its more positive connotations, lay some distance in the future.[38] Ending as they did in the catastrophic

1929 crash, the 1920s could be portrayed as the decade of the irresponsible, high-spending flapper. Yet one can also describe those years as a decade when women had some money to spend and time to spend it, and as an era when they looked for value for money through reasonable prices.

Observers of women's economic behavior had for some time assumed that they were the nation's spenders. The economist Thorstein Veblen, in his classic study *The Theory of the Leisure Class* (1899), interpreted their devotion to such fashions as the high, deeply curved French heel as an ostentatious rejection of work: "It has come about that obviously productive labour is in a peculiar degree derogatory to respectable women, and therefore special pains should be taken in the construction of women's dress, to impress upon the beholder the fact (often indeed a fiction) that the wearer does not and can not habitually engage in useful work."[39] In a similar vein Bertha June Richardson declared in her 1904 book, *The Woman Who Spends,* that women had "thrown off the yoke of economic production" and were now interested in spending their husbands' wages. Then, in 1912, the sociologist Wesley C. Mitchell complained about "the dominance of women in spending." He criticized the amateurism of that spending (he thought there should be an educative campaign to make consumers' choices more expert). In coining his famous phrase the "backward art of spending money," Mitchell reflexively and by no means atypically imputed weakness to a pecuniary sphere associated with the feminine.[40]

After World War I political commentary confirmed these perceptions. Mabel C. Costigan spoke on the issue in the fall of 1919, when the national women's vote was about to be courted for the first time. Costigan was president of the Consumers' League of the District of Columbia, chair of the Food Supply and Demand Standing Committee of the newly formed LWV, and the wife of Edward P. Costigan, a U.S. tariff commissioner who later served in the Senate. In a letter to state LWV chairs she noted that there had been a 65.9 percent increase in the price of household items since the war. This was a women's issue because "about 90 percent of the money, representing wages brought to the home, is spent annually by women." Acting on Costigan's premise that the majority of women had "practically no training in business principles," the LWV pressed for legislation to facilitate the teaching of home economics.[41]

The feminization of consumption was not just an advertizing gimmick that exploited women. It had a serious economic dimension and remained constant in economic discourse throughout the 1920s. A leading Republican woman, Mrs. George Orvis, in 1929 urged her party to focus on the housewife's interest in the tariff because "according to the most conservative estimates, women form 85 percent of the ultimate consumers of the country."[42] These figures may have been exaggerated. They would have been more credible as references to *net* disposable income—after mortgage, automobile, and other major payments in which men probably had a considerable if not dominant say. On the other hand, men did spend less on drink (and women possibly more) in the Prohibition decade. Whatever the truth of the matter, women were popularly conceived to be the nation's consumers.

Women scholars, too, turned their attention to the economics of consumption, perhaps contributing to the neoclassical impulse that led to the emergence of the "Chicago school" after 1930.[43] In her influential book *A Theory of Consumption* (1923), Hazel Kyrk argued that the home had become a unit of consumption, as opposed to production. Women were "the heads of modern households." Theirs was the task of "making market choices," and they were "deputed to speak for the whole body of consumers."[44] Other female economists now turned their attention to different facets of consumption. Books by Theresa S. McMahon (1925) and Jessica B. Peixotto (1927, 1929) reexamined existing theories on underconsumption and emulative spending. Elizabeth E. Hoyt's *Consumption of Wealth* (1928) was a study of family budgets.[45] In the 1920s women showed a keen interest in consumption and in the related issue of prices.

Newly enfranchised women did not immediately organize against the tariff. Yet their potential was recognized. In 1921, when Republican plans were afoot for an upward tariff revision, Herbert E. Miles formed the Fair Tariff League (FTL). Miles was a retired farm machinery manufacturer, a former vice president of both the U.S. Chamber of Commerce and the National Association of Manufacturers, and a veteran low-tariff agitator. Consumer welfare was at the top of his list of announced priorities, and his new organization soon turned its attention to women, as consumers, in an attempt to recruit popular support for its opposition to the Fordney-McCumber Bill.

In April 1922 the FTL circulated a leaflet titled "Women and the Tariff: No. 1." The leaflet aimed to impugn the rich protectionists but perhaps appealed to the condescending middle classes when it attacked proposed duties on woolen stockings and cheap lace, "the kind of lace which poor women wear." It exhorted women to petition their legislators, claiming that hitherto "Congress [had] ignored the consumer."[46] Another FTL pamphlet, *Corsets and the Tariff*, suggested a relationship between women's physical and political freedoms:

> Women dress humanely now. Corsets are fitted to the person. She is no longer encased in a form-made steel compress. Distance, alone,

is sufficient protection, as says an American corset manufacturer, unless his European competitors send fitters here. . . .

This corset tax is because women haven't known, and haven't voted.[47]

A third FTL leaflet concentrated on food prices. Once again, the exhortation was the same: "The consumer, the women, who are to pay these tariff-swollen prices, should be heard from NOW."[48]

Agitation over the anticipated impact of higher tariffs on prices failed to influence the outcome of the debate. The 1922 Fordney-McCumber Act terminated the policy of trade liberalization that had been evident in the Democrats' 1913 Underwood tariff. The act imposed an average *ad valorem* rate of 33.22 percent on free and dutiable goods. Clearly this was a slap in the face for those who had hoped that women would come to the rescue of international free trade.

There remains the question of whether women, if offended in sufficient numbers by the passage of the new tariff, effectively punished its perpetrators at the polls. There was, however, no organized feminist campaign to rid Congress of high-tariff legislators. What can be more readily shown is that none of the leading 1920s high-tariff sponsors—Fordney, McCumber, Hawley, and Smoot—survived politically to inspire their successors in the 1930s with an image of high-tariff political triumphalism. High-tariff legislators had their way in Congress, but their policy won little support at the polls—least of all, it can be surmised, among women.

Joseph W. Fordney of Michigan sponsored the 1922 tariff bill in the House. He was motivated to defend his state's sugar-beet interests against the threat of importation of cheap Cuban sugar.[49] Yet he tried to argue that the tariff did not damage consumer interests. He claimed that importers were already charging high prices by adding profit margins of up to several thousand percent. Thus there was "not the slightest necessity" that his bill would "increase the cost to the American consumer." Fordney also made a slight verbal gesture toward the recently enfranchised gender: "The proponents of this act believe in American institutions, in American industry, in American labor, in American men *and women,* and by this law present to the country a purely American act."[50] Politically sensitive, Fordney anticipated and tried to preempt women's argument that they spoke for the whole nation rather than for vested interests. It is possible that his verbal gesturing toward consumers and women—in itself recognition of new forces in politics—might have saved him from electoral defeat. But he decided not to face the people and announced his retirement.

The tariff bill's other sponsor, Senator Porter James McCumber of North Dakota, likewise failed to supply proof that a leading high-tariff advocate could survive at the polls. Although his defeat in the 1922 Republican primary does not lend itself to simple analysis, it is in some ways suggestive. He lost to Lynn J. Frazier, a former governor with credentials of a type that commended him to politically conscious 1920s women. It is true that Frazier advocated agricultural support prices, but he had favored women's suffrage and opposed militarism and corporate privileges.

In contrast, McCumber had alienated female voters by attacking the franchise campaign in 1918. At the time he had observed that women needed to care for children free of life's worries, such as participation in the political process. For this reason alone, and perhaps independently of his high-profile liability for the 1922 tariff, McCumber was vulnerable to a gendered vote. In the event Frazier not only unseated McCumber in the primary but succeeded in holding the seat for the Republicans in the November election at a time when there was an exceptionally large swing against the GOP nationwide, generally attributed to their recent tariff. Peace feminists thereby gained an unswerving ally: Every year from 1926 to 1937, the new senator was to introduce the Women's Peace Union's amendment (usually known as the "Frazier amendment") to the Constitution, which, if adopted, would have outlawed war. While detailed opinion analysis was still a thing of the future in 1922, it is possible to detect in the preferences of the North Dakota voters a tendency to favor candidates free of the blemishes of sexual chauvinism, militarism, and industrial protectionism. It is not inconceivable that women were partly responsible for that tendency.[51]

After the passage of the Fordney-McCumber Act, women took a more active stance on the tariff. The LWV decided to conduct its own educational campaign. In April 1922 the FTL's acting secretary, Alfred B. Mason, asked the LWV to endorse and circulate his organization's literature on the tariff. The LWV's congressional secretary replied diplomatically that the question would have to be put to her organization at its next annual meeting, which would not be until 1923, well after the midterm elections. Thereafter, the league resisted FTL appeals for direct endorsement. This was not, however, for any lack of political sympathy; rather, the league's leaders wished to make their own policy. They were encouraged in this direction by the 1923 housewives' boycott of sugar to protest its high price. At its 1924 convention in Buffalo, the league decided to add the tariff to its study program. At this point some FTL leaflets did find their way into early LWV study materials. But they soon gave way to the league's own, more substantial literature on the tariff and consumers. By 1925, according to one LWV officer, the tariff was in "several" states "the really popular study subject."[52]

The LWV adopted a low-tariff position and engaged in active propaganda in pursuit of its goal. It took advantage, for example, of the possibilities for persuasion inherent in radio, a medium whose novelty gave its messages charisma and which could be expected to target the millions of American housewives who were still mostly confined to the home. In March 1929, the league and the National Broadcasting Company (NBC) jointly sponsored a talk—by Raymond T. Bye of the University of Pennsylvania—on "The Tariff and the Consumer." Twenty-four radio stations broadcast the talk, in which Bye claimed that "our cost of living is considerably higher than it would be if we did not have so many import duties." The tariff did not protect jobs. As demonstrated in the case of sugar, Bye claimed, it reduced the purchasing power of foreigners dependent on exports to the United States, so curtailing U.S. exports to them and causing unemployment in America. The LWV not only sponsored this talk but arranged for its text to be published in the press. Its commitment to tariff reductions was clear and determined.[53]

Later in 1929 tariff-reduction campaigners rallied to oppose proposals for a new round of customs-duty increases. The bill sponsored by Senator Reed Smoot of Utah and Representative William C. Hawley of Oregon mooted a general rise in tariff levels. A group of politically experienced women now launched a campaign against the envisaged increases. Former Republican National Committee member Mrs. George Orvis on September 2 accepted the chair of a bipartisan Consumers' Committee to Investigate Living Costs. Members of her eleven-woman-strong committee made up an impressive if not particularly egalitarian array, composed of such persons as a former president of Republican Business Women, Inc. The willingness of senior Republican women to cross party lines on the tariff issue is perhaps an indication that they had not yet "arrived" as machine politicians—but it also spelled trouble for the GOP in the not-too-distant future.

Orvis believed that there was an obvious connection between the tariff and the family budget, and that women, "being the ultimate consumers of the country," should be heard. Her committee addressed the moral as well as the economic issues that concerned so many women. Caroline O'Day, a Democratic member of the committee, pithily if patronizingly expressed the perceived connection between women, prices, tariffs, and war: "Excessive protective tariffs mean international antagonisms, and international antagonisms mean wars. We must make the women understand that the increase in the price of sugar and shoes means sending their sons and grandsons into war."[54]

Orvis complained that Congress had overlooked the consumer during the Smoot-Hawley hearings.[55] This sense of grievance, which was
politically significant in the 1920s and 1930s, invites historical scrutiny.
How credible was the complaint that Congress ignored women on the
tariff, and how could Capitol Hill ignore half the electorate? One factor
already noted is that the congressional response may not have been entirely rational—some male politicians would ignore women even at the
risk of placing their political future in jeopardy. Another is that some
women may have been relatively apathetic toward the tariff. The LWV
was not apathetic, and it was a major organization with a far-reaching
network of links with other pressure groups, but then, it did consist
mainly of middle- and upper-class women. Perhaps less socially exalted
women mutely coveted not lower prices but tariffs that protected their
husbands' jobs.[56]

Less conjectural is the fact that women did not present a united front
on the tariff. In 1925 Edith Nourse Rogers (Rep., Mass.) inherited the
seat left vacant by her deceased husband, John Jacob Rogers (sponsor
of a law that had placed the Foreign Service on a more professional footing). She was to serve longer in Congress than any other woman (1925–
1960), and took an active interest in foreign affairs. Yet she was out of
tune with the more salient strains in 1920s feminism. She was a firm
supporter of army and navy appropriations and an advocate of the protective tariff. Her father had been a mill owner in Lowell, and she wanted
a tariff system that would protect the economic interests of her constituents. Moreover, she was far from being a mere cipher in the House.
On one occasion she dramatized her case by wearing on the floor a
Lowell-made cotton smock adorned with a white gardenia. On another
she mounted a display of foreign-made goods outside the Capitol; inside the building she vehemently attacked the trade and price tactics of
Germany and Japan.[57]

There was, of course, opposition on Capitol Hill to the prevailing
tariff policies. But the case of the George amendment suggests that low-
tariff women were ignored even by their allies. Introduced by Senator
Walter F. George on October 15, 1929, the amendment called for the
presidential appointment of a Consumers' Counsel of the United States
Tariff Commission. Senator George's state, Georgia, was not untouched
by the stirrings of feminism, incidentally. When Tom Watson died in
1922 and his widow declined to serve in his place, Rebecca Felton had
taken his seat in the U.S. Senate. Known as a biographer and a campaigner on political issues, the octogenarian Felton was, in the estimate
of the *Atlanta Constitution*, Georgia's leading woman citizen. She
served for only a day before resigning to make way for George. Yet she
was the first woman to serve in the Senate, and, though her placement

smacked of southern chivalry at its stifling worst, and her public endorsement of mass lynchings of black men as a warning to potential rapists made her a reverse inspiration for the years to come, she could still be regarded as a feminist of sorts. Felton had supported the franchise and in 1917 opposed, as a result of what she "saw during the Civil War . . . conscription for Georgia boys."[58] Moreover, Jeannette Rankin had taken up residency in Georgia. She had lost her congressional seat but none of her political zest. Rankin worked for the National Consumers' League and, in 1928 founded the Georgia Peace Society.[59] Given the high profiles of Felton and Rankin, there would appear to have been an opportunity, in Georgia, to form a propeace, low-tariff, farmer-women coalition.

But George took no heed of the potentialities of the female lobby. Like so many politicians over the past century and a half, he saw the farmer as the real consumer. The *Minneapolis Tribune* summed up his case: There was in politics a potentially powerful but presently disorganized animal, the "general consumer," and "the interest of the general consumer is coincidental with the interest of the farmer."[60] Neither George nor the *Tribune* saw fit to discuss the gender of the consumer. When the Senate passed his trailblazing consumer representation measure with a large majority, the senator must have felt confident that his political tactics were in no need of critical attention. But his triumph was unreal. President Hoover saw no need to implement the proposal, and consumer representation in matters affecting foreign trade did not occur until the mid-1930s.[61] Arguably George should have paid more heed to women as a potential source of support. But he did not, and the complaint by low-tariff women that they were being ignored in Congress was, on the whole, well-founded.

The journalist Anne Hard epitomized women's resentment at the demeaning oversights of leading politicians. An expert on industrial efficiency who had serious reservations about free-trade feminism, Hard nevertheless revealed, in an article in the December 1929 issue of *Ladies Home Journal*, her anger at male political attitudes over the tariff. Her article was entitled "Am I Blue? The Housewife's Interest in National Legislation That Enters the Kitchen." She took her theme not from the recent Wall Street crash but from a "jazz-sorry voice" on the radio that reminded her of the carping criticisms emanating from the consumer. After making inquiries on Capitol Hill to see how the proposed tariff legislation would affect her own household menus, Hard concluded that prices would return to normal soon after Smoot-Hawley was enacted. She explained by means of an agricultural example: Domestic farmers would respond to short-term price increases with increased planting, bringing prices down as supply once again matched demand. The Federal Farm Board, established and equipped with a half-billion-dollar budget by the Agricultural Marketing Act of June 1929, would if necessary contribute to price stability. After all, Hard reminded her readers, prices had returned to equilibrium after the 1922 Fordney-McCumber tariff.[62]

Yet Hard fumed at male attitudes on the Hill: "Every time I get one of these gentlemen in Washington started on my very simple proposition of 'what shall I pay for food?' he immediately leaves what seems to me, as a woman, just a plain question and goes leaping off into broad generalities and says that 'tomatoes are a Mexican problem.'" She suspected that congressmen used arguments about foreign policy to camouflage the fact that they were serving sectional interests at home. Like many women, she regarded her gender as being above self-interested politics and as constituting a national lobby for the public interest. Indeed, her lobbying stance was in danger of becoming nationalistic and even xenophobic. This outlook set her apart from the generality of women's groups lobbying on foreign policy, which succumbed only with relative rarity to the tide of economic nationalism that swept the United States with the onset of the Great Depression. But she did typify women's belief that they were now being politically neglected, and their desire to rectify matters—in Hard's case she forced a number of U.S. senators, even if just for a few uncomfortable minutes in the course of her research interviews, to think about foreign economic policy from the female consumer's viewpoint.[63]

To outward appearances, at least, women agitating over the tariff failed in their purpose. The Fordney-McCumber Act was an initial setback; then the Smoot-Hawley Act entered the statute books in 1930. The 1922 measure had imposed a 33.22 percent *ad valorem* rate; in 1930 the rate reached an unprecedented 40.08 percent, with the average impost on dutiable goods being 52.8 percent.[64] The appearance of failure was undoubtedly based in good measure upon reality, and it is possible to discern a number of weaknesses in the women's lobby on the tariff. The first weakness is generic: Women were one of many lobbies on foreign policy, and not all politically active women gave the issue a high priority. The second is politicians' growing belief—perhaps erroneous but nevertheless important for policy formation—in the 1920s that women could with impunity (and even should) be ignored. The third weakness has to do with class. While leaders of either sex tend to be drawn from a social and educational elite, the generally genteel ladies of the LWV could be regarded as representing women with no jobs and with husbands' money in their pocketbooks, as distinct from the overwhelming majority of women who thought of themselves less as consumers than as producers—either wage earners themselves or wives, daughters, and mothers of wage earners. According to the popular conception, tariffs protected jobs for the wage earners of America, and one might argue that the millions of poorer women for this reason had little sympathy for bourgeois trade liberalism. Finally, as Boeckel's analysis signified, women could claim to influence policy only through public opinion and its concrete expression at the polls, and not in their capacity as executive officials, diplomats, senators, or policymakers within the Republican and Democratic parties.

In the early 1930s hidebound politicians still persisted in ignoring women, even to their peril. Representative William Chatman Hawley of Oregon belonged to that band of male politicians who sometimes seemed blind to women's existence, let alone their aspirations. On May 4, 1932, he stepped into the road outside the House office building on his way to the Capitol. An automobile knocked him down. Picking himself up, Hawley observed that the driver was a woman. She asked the congressman if he was hurt, but Hawley gallantly waved her on without taking her name.[65]

But an even more severe shock awaited the physically shaken coauthor of the recent tariff. On May 23 a recount in the southern Oregon Republican primary gave State Corporation Commissioner James W. Mott a narrow victory that ended Hawley's long spell in Congress. Immediate reactions suggested that Oregon had rejected Hawley because he was a "dry"—Mott was an advocate of liquor-law modification. By the fall, however, the reasons for the voters' preferences had fallen into a different perspective. Journalist Arthur Krock observed that Hawley was a victim of antitariff sentiment in Oregon, a state that had suffered "direly" under Republican duties. It was on this point that the primary voters had delivered their verdict.[66]

When the 1932 election results began to come in, some of those with a complacent belief in the political formulas of the past decade received a rude shock. Reed Smoot is said to have "suspected that someone was playing a ghastly joke on him." There were several reasons for Smoot's defeat at the hands of a hitherto obscure Democratic opponent. Unemployment was a major factor, with 35.8 percent of Utah's wage earners out of work.[67] Low prices tormented the state's farmers: As a *New York Times* analyst put it, "the Senator could not talk against 30-cent wheat, $3 steers and 8-cent wool."[68] Ironically, the argument that high tariffs make for higher prices should have worked in Smoot's favor. But—along with Fordney, McCumber, and Hawley—he failed to convince men and made no effective appeal to women, and he did not survive. In all this there is more than a hint of a double negative—blind though they may have been to the fact, politicians who did not appeal to women did not have a high chance of survival at the polls.

W omen's influence on foreign policy in the 1920s was limited, but it was not insignificant. As an approximation one might argue that women had less influence than business but more influence than Irish Americans.[69] There were sound business reasons for the Republicans' peace strategies in the 1920s, but they also developed within the framework of the expectant female half of the electorate, and it is not only conceivable but probable that women would have punished at the polls any gratuitous manifestation of militarism.

The women who favored liberal trade policy may have been upper-crust and economically unsophisticated, but upper-crust minorities with crude ideas are notoriously capable of shaping history. These women helped to educate the generation that, in the mid-1930s, made America a more open trading country. They left to their daughters the legacy of an economic approach to foreign policy, even if the nature of that economic approach was to change in the years ahead. In the shorter term they contributed to the ending of the Republican ascendancy that had begun with the election of Lincoln in 1860. But first the women of America were to be subjected to the pleas of an increasingly desperate president—on the ground that his foreign policy was made for them.

4 | PRESIDENTIAL RECOGNITION OF THE FEMALE VOTE, 1932

By the end of their sometimes successful campaigns in the 1920s, leading women had come to regard themselves as a national lobby. That is to say, they saw themselves as being above the petty struggles of pluralistic politics, and removed from male Americans' eternal squabbles over local issues and vested interests. This national outlook gave women a sense of potential affinity with the government official who represented the democratic will of the people as a whole—the president of the United States.

The incumbent, Herbert Hoover, tried to take advantage of this potential affinity with women when he made a special appeal to them in the presidential election of 1932. In doing so he showed his appreciation of the fact that leading women saw themselves as having a further national affinity—with foreign affairs, an aspect of public policy mainly associated with the national executive. Hoover further realized that, in the early 1930s, this meant that women were interested in peace and in the tariff.

President Hoover did not change his policies to suit women. However, he did vigorously explain those policies to the female half of the electorate. Whereas some congressmen had ignored women at the risk of political self-destruction, Hoover made an effort to recruit their support. In this sense it could be said that women "arrived" in politics in 1932.

But Hoover lost the election, and Governor Franklin Delano Roosevelt of New York became president. The message of the election was tortuously ambivalent for those who hoped for signs of women's political power. On the one hand the election results suggested that women had enough political independence to resist even a direct and flattering appeal for their support. On the other hand it seemed to show that elections could not be won by appealing to women.

Clearly Hoover would have won reelection had he retained the support of a certain percentage of the female vote. The reasons for his failure to win that support, as well as the manner of his appeal to women, therefore invite attention. To anyone who believes that elections are mainly won on domestic economic issues, the reason for Hoover's failure is obvious: With thirteen million people unemployed by the end of 1932, he stood no chance. Yet Hoover tried to recoup his fortunes by appealing to women on two foreign policy issues: the Republicans' peace record and the prosperity-enhancing properties of the tariff. Unluckily for him the continuing crisis in China following Japan's invasion of Manchuria in September 1931 reminded all women and men of the fragility of the Republicans' peace accomplishments. And the state of the economy fatally weakened any defense of his administration's foreign economic policy. In any case the president was attempting to persuade certain influential and strong-minded women to believe in foreign policy principles they had already rejected and against which they were actively campaigning. The quality of his arguments availed him little in a hostile climate.

Ironically Hoover was, to a greater degree than any of his predecessors, a president who was genuinely sympathetic to women and to their concerns. An orphan by the age of ten, he had been brought up by Quaker aunts whose influence he fondly remembered and who left him with ideals that—if they fell short of pacifism strictly defined—still imbued him with a yearning for peace. His wife, Lou, was mildly but pointedly feminist—she urged Girl Scouts to look for careers and invited black women to the White House. Hoover supported her in the controversy over the latter initiative and was no doubt influenced in turn.[1]

From an early point in his public career Hoover had tried to accommodate women in his scheme of things. He was aware of the peculiarities of gendered politics. In World War I, for example, he played on the special role of women as consumers. As President Woodrow Wilson's U.S. food administrator, he urged women to practice thrift in order to conserve food supplies, thus making more nutrition available to American families and to America's allies in Europe. Perhaps with half an eye on morale and psychological warfare, he asked the American woman to forgo "four-o'clock teas and late suppers," to let ducklings grow up before eating them, and to "re-establish the old habits of personal marketing, so that by actual knowledge of prices and of abundance or scarcity of foods she may purchase more easily for herself and in the interests of the whole food supply question."[2]

By August 1920 Hoover was immersed in his successful efforts for the relief of famine in war-torn Europe, and again he appealed to women's thrift, this time in moral terms. He vehemently denounced extravagant expenditure on luxuries; one pair of silk stockings was a "venial lapse," but collectively the wastrels of America were doing enough "to stagger the world." They should remember "the millions of people in Europe who have no stockings at all." Though "it is true that not every woman in this country signs her husband's checks," women were "very largely the guardians of the American pocketbook." They should restrain their expenditure to avoid "the creation and maintenance of class feeling." He issued a prophetic warning to those who "spend $200,000 every night in New York City alone on restaurant suppers": They should remember the "hard times" that followed on the extravagances of the Civil War and Reconstruction.[3]

Hoover's outlook seemed to transcend party politics, a point that in itself was a potential commendation to women with an antidivisive, national outlook. Though he eventually became a Republican politician, both major parties had initially courted his allegiance; in 1920, in the words of his biographer Joan Hoff, the Democrats had looked to him "as the only national figure who might ensure them the progressive, pro-League, and woman vote."[4] The perception that he would appeal for women's support was well founded. In 1923 Secretary of Commerce Hoover told the LWV journal, the *Woman Citizen,* "there is no cause more worthy of earnest and devoted effort of American women than those efforts which lead constructively to the elimination of the causes of war." The *Citizen* appreciated Hoover's attention to women. It commented that Hoover's visit to the LWV's Des Moines convention, "to start the Administration campaign for American entrance into the World Court, says something about the way the League of Women Voters' influence is regarded."[5] Nor was this appreciation confined to the relatively staid LWV. Both Hoover and his Democratic opponent, Al Smith, appealed for the women's vote in the presidential election of 1928, but it was Hoover who won the endorsement of the radically feminist Woman's party—and won the election.[6]

Yet Hoover's natural and cultivated political rapport with women did not save him from retribution in the two years preceding his electoral defeat. He failed to win over the feminist doves. This was not because of lack of effort or because of ineptitude on his part, and not because the Democrats offered a convincing alternative. Rather, the widening breach between Hoover and his peace critics reflected the latter's high expectations in a period when, for reasons beyond the president's control, nations were once again preparing for war.

Hoover was sincere in his desire for disarmament, and his policies were informed and logical, even if they—indeed, like any constructive policies—were impossible to implement in the distrustful international climate developing in the wake of the 1929 stock market crash. In January 1930 Hoover and the British prime minister, Ramsay MacDonald, convened another naval conference in London. Their plan was to obtain further reductions, in order to reap what in more recent times has been labeled the "peace dividend"—money saved on warship construction was to be used to combat the effects of the economic slump. Agreement was reached, in principle, to limit tonnages of lighter vessels omitted from the Washington treaties. But implementation was slow, and Japan, regarded by Hoover as "our first line of defense in the Far East," was allowed certain increases.[7] Disappointed with the stalemate at the conference, the American branch of WILPF criticized the U.S. government for its perceived intransigence, showering the State Department with protests. The league's secretary, Dorothy Detzer, emerged from a strained two-hour meeting with President Hoover on April 25, 1930, convinced of his obstructive intentions.[8]

The League of Nations now planned a further disarmament conference, this one to meet in Geneva in February 1932. For the first time the League's council allowed women to take an active part in the work of such a conference. Detzer threatened Hoover with punishment at the presidential election unless he included a woman in the American delegation. When Hoover rejected WILPF's first nominee on the ground that she was a Democrat, Detzer pressed the case of its alternate choice, Mary Woolley, a Republican. The daughter of a Civil War chaplain who had instilled her with pacifist principles, Dr. Woolley was, as well as president of Mount Holyoke College, a vice-chairman of the American Civil Liberties Union (ACLU), which had supported the Sacco-Vanzetti defense; had once been blacklisted by the Daughters of the American Revolution (DAR) (of which she was a member); and was a supporter of the aims of WILPF.[9]

Hoover did appoint Woolley. She herself, according to one biographer, was never to exaggerate her role in the Geneva conference, "calling it only an entering wedge for women in diplomacy." Yet, as the same biographer notes, Woolley "was hailed as the first woman to represent the country at an important diplomatic conference."[10] Perhaps recognizing the significance of the appointment, Secretary of State Henry Stimson was not overjoyed. After Hoover telephoned him with the news, Stimson is reported on good authority to have told a colleague: "She is a woman of 69 years of age, and knows nothing about the subject. I assume, however, she knows how to read."[11] Stimson personified the continuities of the male foreign policy establishment—his first cabinet appointment had been as secretary of war in 1911, and his last was to be to the same position in 1945 (when he was seventy-eight). The poor grace with which he conceded boded ill for women's immediate ascent into executive foreign policy positions.

When the disarmament conference convened, millions of peace petition signatures were delivered to Geneva in its support. Expectations were high among America's feminist peace campaigners. In Hollywood, California, a group of WILPF activists met to plan a "Transcontinental Peace Caravan." Led by Mabel Vernon, the caravan visited 150 cities in a two-month tour, whipping up support for disarmament and collecting several hundred thousand signatures as the U.S. contribution to the "Golden Book" petition presented at Geneva. Public meetings were held, the last at New York's Belasco Theater. Vernon recalled that she "was using [her] Woman's Party experience, modeling it on the same lines."[12] Like those in the later campaign against the Vietnam War, the tactics were inspirational, and attempts were made to draw in female "stars." For example, the idolized aviator and feminist Amelia Earhart pledged her support on the eve of her solo flight across the Atlantic, the first by a woman. WILPF's spiritual leader Jane Addams finally carried the American petitions to the White House, at the head of a spectacular, mile-long procession of automobiles. In the meantime, Mary Woolley was given a rousing send-off at a mass meeting and banquet in New York.[13]

But the Geneva conference met under a shadow, for on January 28, 1932, the Japanese attacked the major Chinese city of Shanghai. Nevertheless, the conference dragged on, and Woolley plied Hoover, in the month of May, with petitions asking him to take a lead with disarmament initiatives. In June the president did transmit the "Hoover plan," urging the abolition of offensive weapons and a one-third reduction of armies. Yet the conference ended in failure, serving only to awaken people to the shortcomings of the world's peace machinery. A bitterly disillusioned Detzer blamed Woolley for "timidity," but the influential lobbyist was also disappointed with the Hoover administration as a whole. Thus Hoover was a politician with a record of appealing to women for their support on peace issues, but not with universal success.[14]

Whereas the radicals of WILPF found Hoover wanting on the peace front, the more moderate LWV turned its attention, in the period 1930–32, to the shortcomings of his foreign economic policy. Here, the passage of the Smoot-Hawley Act had left the Hoover administration open to criticism. The law was a convenient, readily identifiable target for those who wanted to cut through the complexities of economics and make a case against Republican policy.

All kinds of objections were voiced against Smoot-Hawley—giving women a menu of criticisms from which to choose. Latin American "economic resentment" of the United States was traced to the act, which was held responsible for the slashing of U.S. imports from Latin America from more than a billion dollars' value in 1929 to a quarter of that sum four years later.[15] Again, by 1932, twenty-four countries had retaliated against the United States with tariffs or embargoes of their own. To circumvent these imposts, American industrialists built, within two years, 250 factories on foreign soil—to the detriment of employment back home. By 1932 American exports had fallen by half.[16] According to one school of thought, Smoot-Hawley contributed to this loss not only by inviting retaliation but also by inhibiting price falls domestically, thus further undermining the competitiveness of U.S. exports.[17]

The economic nationalists and protectionists who supported Smoot-Hawley believed that higher prices were necessary in order to give manufacturers the confidence to invest. But real weekly earnings in manufacturing industry fell from $24.76 in 1929 to $21.32 in 1932.[18] The American consumer would be less able to pay for goods at higher prices, and there was the political consideration that he—or, in the discourse of the 1920s, she—would be reluctant to do so. The effects of individual imposts were keenly felt in straitened times. The leading American economist and tariff reformer F. W. Taussig noted that "an amusing list can be made of a series of duties that pursued the family from top to bottom":

> For the men, straw hats were subjected to much higher duties. . . . The duty of 1922 had been equivalent to 60% . . . ; the new one was about 150%. Women came in for attention of a similar sort; their leather gloves "embroidered or embellished" went from 70% to a compound rate equivalent to 140%. The children were not forgotten. The toy duties of 1922, one of the absurdities of that measure, were in general retained—toys at 70%, dolls at 90%; but some very cheap celluloid dollies were now subjected to still higher duties, again compound, equivalent to 160%. The boys naturally could not be let off more easily than the girls; and fire-crackers of the cheapest grades, which had been 8 cents a pound in 1922, now were put at 26 cents (about 135% on the value).[19]

Though Taussig joined in public debate on the tariff, the rigorous techniques and abstractions he and other economists like Hazel Kyrk often used needed to be reduced to simple terms disseminated to a wide audience. The LWV took on itself the task of enlightening American women about the implications of the tariff. In principle the LWV's publications were still apolitical, and nonpartisan on the tariff question. In practice, however, they favored the trade liberalization advocated by the Taussig school, and this had the effect of helping the Democrats.

L WV concerns are exemplified in Idella G. Swisher's *An Introduction to the Study of the Tariff*, a book published in handsome format in 1931 by the league's Committee on Living Costs. Swisher drew from protariff arguments, as well as from those of Taussig. She noted, for example, that some women worried that their husbands' wages might be undermined if protectionism were removed. But she claimed that women as a whole were very concerned about the anticipated effects of the tariff. She stated that tariffs had added 12 percent to the cost of living in 1903, then 15 percent, for "the average family," in 1910, and there was a danger that history would repeat itself yet again.[20] She suggested that tariffs hit hardest at the necessities of the poor. High tariffs were the work of a few determined lobbyists who stood to make great gains, at the expense of the relatively apathetic majority who suffered smaller but keenly felt losses. Thus Swisher appealed to the social conscience of the women's movement, but on the minimal-government lines of classical liberalism. She favored safeguarding the dollar in the pockets of the needy, rather than instituting invasive governmental reforms on their behalf.

For use in conjunction with Swisher's book, Louise G. Baldwin, chair of the LWV's Committee on Living Costs, prepared an instruction manual, *Study Questions on the Tariff*. She urged her students to ponder the following questions: "What are the arguments used in political discussion to gain the support of labor in maintaining a protective policy? How have economists answered these questions? . . . Explain in your own words what is meant by "Real" wage. . . . What do we mean by the purchasing power of wages? How is it affected by the tariff?" Other questions referred to the Republicans' packing of the Tariff Commission, to Taussig's proposals for reforming it, and to the voter's role in helping to bring about reform. The student was further asked: "What role does the lobby play in tariff-making? Is there an organized presentation of the consumers' interests?" In this way, Baldwin turned the didactic query into a leading question for propaganda purposes.[21]

Baldwin worried about the elitist composition of the LWV and tried to do something about it. She insisted that it should be brought home to women that high tariffs did not affect just "Paris gowns and imported luxuries." It should be stressed that they had "a very direct relation to our market baskets." She suggested that tariff luncheons be held with a plain menu of her own devising:

Grapefruit

* *

Creamed Chicken with Mushrooms—Peas

Rolls   Cherry Preserves

Tomato Salad

*   *

Chocolate Ice Cream

*   *

Wafers   Coffee

The procedure would be that "each participant takes a course of the luncheon served and discusses the relation of the tariff to the foods in that course."[22]

Luncheon, it may be surmised, would have lacked appeal to working women; Baldwin's culinary tactics could be regarded as having been more an admission of weakness than a restorer of strength. But the over-all picture is of a significant women's campaign against the tariff. Organized in every state, the LWV laid detailed plans to educate every type of woman on the subject of the tariff, putting into plain language, in pamphlets and radio broadcasts, the arguments honed by Taussig and his followers. In spite of his lifelong receptivity to and respect for women, Hoover was in trouble, in the years 1930–1932, with both the peace and the tariff feminists.

This added to the misfortunes of a president who, in 1932, had his back to the wall on account of the international economic depression. In trying to limit the political damage inflicted by the slump, Hoover might well have had more to fear from the enmity of his previous supporters, than from the electoral opposition. Norman Thomas, the third-party Socialist candidate, had no great charisma and was as likely to take away Democratic votes as Republican, thus giving Hoover an advantage. The Democrats' Franklin D. Roosevelt proved to be a leader of formidable political skills, once in presidential office. But in 1932 he was still an obscure politician. On the tariff, which the *New York Times* proclaimed had become "a dominant issue" for the first time in twenty years, Roosevelt was a hopeless vacillator.[23] In any other election year, the presidential challenger might have been put on the defensive, forced to explain why he was making deceitful and contradictory promises in an apparent effort to please different audiences. But this was 1932. The nation was in economic crisis, and any alternative to the incumbent looked attractive. Roosevelt did not even try to appeal to women. He did not have to. The onus was on President Hoover to hold on to groups that had once supported the Republicans, to defend his policies and to show that those policies were not responsible for the calamity that had befallen his country.

Late in September, with the election little more than a month away, Hoover began his tactic of explaining his policies to women. He tried to reach them in the place where most Americans still expected them to be—their own homes. Though far from being a great communicator like Roosevelt, the president had an unshakable faith in radio. In his evening broadcast from the White House, Hoover responded to an invitation from the Women's Conference on Current Problems, then in convention in New York, to comment on women and "local advancement." Rather reluctantly he did address this theme, but only after a prefatory observation that he "could have taken part of [his] time to speak . . . about such problems as world disarmament, American policies in advancement of world peace, the importance of the forthcoming Economic Conference in Europe [the ill-fated London conference, which, in 1933, with Roosevelt in the White House, failed to stabilize international currency markets]." Hoover was clear in his own mind about the agenda he thought would really interest women.[24]

Republican women did give the president some effective support. The Women's Division of the Republican National Committee published a pamphlet called *The What Why and How of Tariff.* This pamphlet stated that the Republican party had implemented protectionism throughout its seventy-five-year history, with good results not just for the farmer, wage earner, and businessman but also for the consumer. Yet the Democrats always complained about high tariffs: "When the Hawley-Smoot bill was making in 1930, Democrats undertook to frighten the American people, and especially the American housewife, with their usual solemn warning that if it became law a billion dollars would be added to the cost of living. Instead, the cost of living has decreased three billion dollars."[25]

As the day of the election approached, women featured in Hoover's campaign in three respects. They organized a "Hoover Day" on October 7, they spoke on the radio on behalf of his candidacy, and the president made a special appeal to them in the final stage of his whistle-stop electioneering tour of the nation.

Mrs. Arthur L. Livermore, chairman of Women's Campaign Activities for the Republican National Committee, played a leading part in organizing Hoover Day activities in the eastern states. She told the president's secretary Lawrence Ritchie that her group was keen to have Hoover speak on the radio to women gathered in groups, believing that more than a million would listen in this way. She afforded a glimpse of the diversity among Republican women. Her own group had suggested that the forgathered women should "occupy themselves at that time in making clothing or knitting sweaters for the children of the unemployed." But "in some of the larger places women have been invited to play bridge or other games." Rural groups like her own realized that they could not prevent city women from playing bridge, but they would make every effort to suppress stories about bridge playing and publicize instead the knitting for the unemployed, "feeling that this is a better feature than playing cards."[26]

The president took advice on the contents of his October 7 address to women. White House secretary French Strother noted that a prefinal draft of the address embodied "nearly all outside suggestions."[27] But the president's speech, though drafted by Strother, was his own.[28] Felix Hebert, eastern manager for the Republican National Committee, told Hoover that the Women's Division wanted the text of the address to be on child welfare. Hoover did mention child welfare toward the end of his talk but did not give it the pride of place Hebert suggested. He may have been influenced by the need, suggested in notes for the speech, to avoid being "too patronizing." Thus, he may have decided to avoid the appearance of confining women to a narrow, maternalistic sphere—though he could not resist the semipatronizing observation, an elaboration on women's claim to be above party politics, that "women take a longer view of national life than a great many men."[29] His final draft conformed more closely to the urgings of Grace Morrison Poole of the General Federation of Women's Clubs, who urged him to talk politics and to emphasize his desire for "a real reduction in armaments."[30] There can be little doubt, though, that Hoover took advice for purposes of fine tuning only. He was convinced that he knew how to put over his firmly held views in a manner that would appeal to women's aspirations, aspirations he had studied for more than a decade. In giving prominence to foreign policy issues, he followed his own instincts.

Hoover's defense of higher tariffs rested on the assumption that the Democrats were unpragmatically, even ideologically committed to "free trade," a phrase that low-tariff advocates were now rather loath to use. At the Democratic National Convention in Chicago, Senator Cordell Hull of Tennessee heightened the sense of interparty difference when he insisted on the adoption of a low-tariff policy based on the principle of reciprocity.[31] But the Democratic presidential candidate, though prone to temporize and to make low-tariff speeches to selected audiences, listened to the advice of his "brain trust" chief, Raymond Moley, who cautioned against naive free-tradism. On September 20, in a speech written by Moley and delivered in Seattle, Governor Roosevelt announced: "I have advocated and continue to advocate high-tariff policy, based on reason, on good old-fashioned horse sense."[32] His statement meant that the Republicans could not go on the counteroffensive or profit from the argument that Democrats would sacrifice jobs on the altar of free trade. Instead they were kept on the defensive, required to prove, as best they could, that their particular brand of protectionism was in the national interest.

In his Hoover Day broadcast, the president appealed to women on several fronts, promising, for example, greater sexual equality and better homes.[33] He made a special plea to what he portrayed as women's special sense of morality, stating his hope that it would help to keep the United States out of war. The Republicans, he reminded his listeners, had negotiated the Kellogg-Briand pact. With the Manchurian debacle in mind, he claimed that his administration was effectively mobilizing world public opinion against international aggression. The Republicans would achieve disarmament in the future. If Hoover's own "vital plan for the reduction of armaments throughout the world" was accepted, "the world will be relieved of an enormous burden of taxes" to the benefit of "men and women whether in the home, at the shop, or at the desk."

Most important in terms of keeping alive the distinction between Democratic irresponsibility and Republican economic realism, Hoover tried to counter the view that the depression stemmed from the Republican tariff: "No one will deny the fact that such a depression would never have taken place had it not been for the destructive forces loosened by the Great War." The protective tariff had prevented "enormous increased unemployment." Women should take heed, for "some 10 millions of you are engaged in gainful employment." The tariff, moreover, was helping to protect farmers from price falls even more catastrophic than the ones they had already endured.

Hoover's recognition of the female vote was a salient feature of his campaign. The *New York Times* reproduced the text of his October 7 broadcast, giving it front-page publicity under the headline PRESIDENT APPEALS FOR WOMEN'S VOTE TO REBUILD NATION. But this radio address was only one of three dimensions of his major effort to court female support. From September 29 to November 6, women broadcast over NBC and CBS on behalf of the president every Wednesday, Thursday, and Friday, with the exception of two cancellations to accommodate the World Series. The last talk, by tennis champion Helen Hull Jacobs, went out at 9 P.M. But all the preceding transmissions were in midafternoon, evidently aiming at the nonworking housewife. The female broadcasters included several women who owed their prominence to their husbands, a disproportionate number of DAR members, the president of Radcliffe College, and no representative of organized labor. But they did include one Native American, and one black. The Women's Division of the Republican National Committee had shown an awareness of the need to pick a representative cross-section of American women, even if its effort met with mixed success.[34]

Edith Nourse Rogers, an ardent defender of the protective tariff, was one of three women who were particularly prominent amongst those who backed the president in radio broadcasts related to foreign policy. Her CBS broadcast on October 27 addressed the question, "How will the election of the president of the United States affect me and my family?" It consisted mainly of a convoluted, extended metaphor that likened Hoover to one of the stock heroes of the interwar years, the airplane pilot. After delivering her thoughts about running out of gasoline and flying through fog, Rogers claimed that Hoover was the candidate "who can guide the plane through the adverse trade winds of foreign competition; who can battle the storm of foreign supremacy in armaments because he knows something about foreign countries."[35]

The second example of a prominent woman who broadcast in support of President Hoover's foreign policy is Carrie Chapman Catt. The architect, a decade and a half earlier, of the deal with President Wilson that supposedly gave women the vote in return for prowar loyalty, Catt again displayed, in her November 2 broadcast, a taste for the politics of respectability.[36] In her opening few remarks, she told Americans not to vote for the socialist candidate. She pleaded for a conservative response to the depression crisis: "This is no time to make over human society, as Norman Thomas would have us do; no time to protest against President Hoover because some favorite plan is not included in his platform. It is no time to stop the machinery in order to revise the tariff. A tariff law rarely consumes less than a year of time."

Responding to Al Smith's barb that Hoover had converted prosperity into depression, Catt said that Smith was incorrect in pointing to bad management under the Republicans: "The Great War, and nothing else, caused the world-around depression." In attempting to answer the question, "If the war caused the depression, why did it not affect us before 1928?" Catt hinted that the U.S. government had compounded the nation's economic problems by lending too much money to foreigners, creating a speculative spiral. Yet "there was no power that could have saved us from our share in the world's penalty for the Great War and its wastefully spent 187 BILLIONS OF DOLLARS."[37] As one who had supported the American war effort, Catt appeared to be playing a contortionist game with her conscience. However, her argument that Republican economic difficulties stemmed from Democratic warmongering was welcome to Hoover partisans and must have seemed well attuned to the presumed peace-and-prosperity goals of the woman voter.

The day after Catt's broadcast, Mary Woolley went on the air in a further CBS transmission on behalf of the Republicans. In a short and pointed talk, she addressed herself entirely to the "international" reasons for President Hoover's reelection. Despite the rejection of the

Hoover plan, she described its recent presentation at Geneva, "with its concrete proposal of abolition of bombing from the air, tanks, heavy mobile artillery and chemical and bacteriological warfare, and approximately one-third reduction of other implements of warfare and of effectives." She claimed that the plan had "galvanized the Conference into new life" and that it was "the most constructive proposal made to the Conference during its six months." She went on to assert that Hoover had restored the United States to "a position of moral leadership such as it has not held since the days immediately following the war." She warned of the danger of foreign disillusionment with the United States if Hoover were not reelected to continue with his peace program. According to Woolley, Europeans would say: "You are good at initiating plans in the United States, but you do not 'stand by': You began the League of Nations but you did not join; the World Court is your conception, but you have not become a member; you gave the Conference the Hoover plan for disarmament, but you have not supported it in your election."[38] It must have seemed that Woolley's reasoning, like Catt's, would serve the Republicans politically by striking the right chord with women. It was a fitting prelude to the third dimension in Hoover's appeal to women—his own eleventh-hour efforts to persuade them to vote Republican.

Speaking from Saint Paul, Minnesota, two days after Mary Woolley's broadcast, the president gave a hint of the emphasis that would appear in the final stage of his campaign. He remarked in his radio broadcast that he had "long experienced [women's] courageous and tenacious abilities in organization for public purposes." He said that he had worked with them in the war, in postwar relief—"It was with the women that I organized the measures that saved the lives of 10 million European children"—and subsequently in the areas of child protection and home improvement.[39]

On November 7 the presidential campaign wound its way through the Rocky Mountain states on its way to Palo Alto, California, where Hoover would join his wife to vote on the following afternoon. At noon the train stopped in Salt Lake City. Hoover addressed a gathering of twelve thousand people in the Mormon Tabernacle. In Utah, where memories of polygamy survived, the president avoided the subject of women's rights and role. However, he did address another of his major campaign themes that mattered to women. For Utah was the home of Reed Smoot, the thirty-year veteran of the U.S. Senate and cosponsor of the Smoot-Hawley tariff law who was up for reelection along with his fellow Republican president. Hoover therefore spoke squarely to the tariff issue, praising Smoot's reform of the Tariff Commission.[40] His speech ensured that no voter who read a newspaper before going to the polls the next day would be spared exposure to Hoover's view on the tariff.

After its ninety-minute stop at Salt Lake City, the train rolled westward toward the Nevada Desert. As the evening encroached, it pulled into a siding at Elko, then a one-street town described by a New York correspondent as an outpost of the Old West, "with gambling houses open and the wild, free life of decades ago still in evidence." With the distant mountains darkening beyond the alkali-white vastness of flat earth, the exhausted candidate emerged on the back platform to deliver a few words to the miners, cattlemen, and "other frontier types, deeply interested in the proceedings," who had gathered to hear him.[41]

But the main business of the evening was to take place at 7:40 P.M. in the club car adjoining Hoover's private accommodation, which had been equipped as a studio. In this studio, Hoover made his last-minute electoral address to the nation. His special plea was to women. On election day, he said, they should exercise their function of "the guardianship of the fundamental ideals." He appealed to women's desires for order, peace, and security both at home and abroad. Describing the United States as a "nation of progressives," he used the typically Progressive tactic of smearing the left with the charge of disorder: "I am a believer in party government. It is only through party organization that our people can give coherent expression to their views upon public issues. There is no other way except by revolution, but we in America have ordained that the ballot shall be used for peaceful determination and not violence."

Hoover promised that the Republicans would look after the long-term welfare of American families and would "secure . . . obedience to law." His main theme was a gender-tailored externalization of the same message: "It is [the women of America] who are mobilizing new public regard to our obligations to home and children of the future; it is they who are mobilizing the maintenance of peace in the world." The president added: "The men of our country carry the frontline of battle through their initiative, their enterprise, their hopes, their courage." But, although the latter observation undermined the effect of the former, Hoover does appear to have appealed, in his last throw of the electoral dice, to the peaceful instincts of women.[42]

In the election Roosevelt defeated Hoover by a decisive margin. The depression largely accounted for the result. Yet, while the economic factor is important in determining voting behavior, it is not necessarily all consuming. Following FDR's reelection in 1936, the country plunged into the "Roosevelt depression," with almost one-fifth of the work force out of a job. Though the economy began to pick up as World War II increased the demand for American goods, there were still nine million unemployed when Roosevelt ran for a third term in 1940. In spite of his failure to put the economy right after two full terms, he was still reelected. Clearly, the economic factor is not always supreme in American politics.

Hoover was an able president with arguments and policies just as good as those of his opponent, and his special appeal for the women's vote was both credible and good politics. It is just conceivable that he could have offset the effects of the depression. But certain factors ensured that this would not happen. Compared with Roosevelt, Hoover lacked humor and charm. His recruitment of humorist Will Rogers did not save his image, nor did the manipulation of his name, as in Hoover Day and Hoover Plan. The streets filled instead with those notorious jibes about "Hoover blankets" (newspaper wrapped around homeless sleepers) and "Hoover flags" (pockets turned inside out, indicating the absence of assets). Whereas Hoover may have earned the respect of women in happier times, they never grew to love him; conversely upper-class women in particular took to the socialite Roosevelt and his inspirational wife, Eleanor. As Mabel Vernon put it, "the Roosevelts were really awfully nice people."[43] All this was ominous for a candidate who was already bound to disappoint both the peace feminists and the more "respectable" women of the LWV who wanted a lower tariff.

The election of 1932 virtually ended the alliance between militant foreign policy feminists and the Republican party that had helped to underpin the peace initiatives of the 1920s. Politically active women began to look with greater sympathy at the Democrats. But there seemed no special need for the Democrats to take them seriously. It is true that women had won a great deal of political recognition in the Republican campaign. But the outcome of the 1932 election was disempowering. Theoretically Hoover's appeal to women may have saved him from an even heavier defeat. However, the more obvious message was that it did him no good at all. Having shown the lead in the nineteenth century and in the feminist peace movement up to the 1930s, American women were entering an era, stretching from the 1930s to the 1960s and beyond, when they could be described as the "missing sisters" of international politics. Yet they were on the eve of sharing in two great triumphs, triumphs that reflected the pressures they had exerted in the 1920s and were still capable of applying until the mid-1930s: These were tariff reform and American withdrawal from the arms trade.

5 | DOROTHY DETZER AND THE MERCHANTS OF DEATH

Dorothy Detzer has faded into undeserved obscurity. Historians writing about the 1930s have paid far more attention to the president's wife, Eleanor Roosevelt, than to Detzer, a woman who made it on her own.[1] Yet in spite of her subsequent neglect, Detzer was one of America's most effective political women. Those few historians who have examined her activities have noted her wide-ranging lobbying activities in the Republican years and her "pivotal role" in the unsuccessful opposition to the Lend-Lease law of 1941.[2] They have concurred in the *New York Times* contemporary verdict that she was "the most famous woman lobbyist" of the 1920s and 1930s.[3]

Above all, the minority of historians conversant with her career have credited Dorothy Detzer with "a crucial role" in instigating the Senate munitions investigation of 1934.[4] Chaired by North Dakota's Gerald P. Nye, a Democrat, this inquiry examined the role of bankers and arms manufacturers, the so-called "merchants of death," in fomenting World War I for the sake of profit. The Nye committee's findings underpinned American neutrality as the international community slid toward another world war in the 1930s.

In that Detzer helped to bring about the Nye investigation, she had a significant impact on American foreign policy. Detzer's opportunity to exert influence first came in 1924, when the U.S.–section president of WILPF, Hannah Clothier Hull, invited her to become WILPF secretary in the United States. In the years leading up to the Nye inquiry, WILPF was by no means the only women's organization interested in promoting disarmament as a means to peace—the Women's Peace Union, for example, was strenuously active in 1932 at the World Disarmament Conference. But Detzer managed to combine in her outlook a series of beliefs that proved suited to the politics of the 1930s. She stressed the role of gender difference in international affairs; she expected women to be able to act as a differentiated bloc of voters; she thought that women could sway public opinion, and that public opinion was the key to a more peaceful foreign policy. Though she verbally genuflected in the direction of free trade, she opposed the international commerce in weaponry and demanded government intervention to stop it. With all these beliefs, she combined the asset of prodigious talent as a Capitol Hill lobbyist.[5]

To evaluate more fully the degree of Detzer's influence, one must take into account contextual factors: not only the strength of feminist public opinion that eased her task but also nongendered opinion and preexisting congressional receptivity to her views. After all, there are few single-handed victories in a democracy. Any estimate of Detzer's effectiveness must be qualified in another way, too. For it is prudent to distinguish between Detzer's short-term success in furthering neutrality, her medium-term failure in preventing United States entry into World War II, and her long-term success in helping to establish the agenda for the modern gender gap on American foreign policy.

Yet there can be little doubt about Detzer's overall effectiveness, and for an explanation of that it is sensible to start any inquiry with the woman herself. Her very early years do not provide obvious reasons for her later achievements. She had a conventional upbringing. Born in 1893, she grew up in Indiana and worshiped in an Episcopalian church. Though in the 1930s she was known for her "charming and disarming personality" and took pride in her femininity and sartorial elegance, in her own memoir she unassumingly chose to recall that she had been "no beauty" as a girl.[6] She understood that it is sometimes wise to appear to be a part of the conventional crowd one is trying to mold. In this connection her family's concept of patriotic duty gave her insight into the conservative mind. Her parents supported the U.S. war effort in 1917–1918. Her older brother, Karl, served with the army in France and became a captain in the Division of Criminal Investigation, the military's secret police (he later became a minor Hollywood scriptwriter). Her twin brother, Don, to whom she was emotionally close, also fought in France, while her younger brother, Juny, embarked on a naval career.

Before her political awakening Detzer supportively volunteered for service with the Red Cross. When the Red Cross turned her down because she was too young, she volunteered for social work at Hull House. There for the first time she encountered pacifists. For four years she worked with Jane Addams. No easy infatuation ensued, for by now Addams was a reviled figure on account of her opposition to the war. But in 1920, on Jane Addams's urging, Detzer joined a Quaker relief mission based in Vienna. She worked for a time at the "Volga famine front," fifteen hundred miles east of Moscow. Her experiences in Russia and with ill-nourished children in Vienna radicalized her and turned her against war. Her twin brother's fate intensified her commitment to the antimilitarist cause. Don had suffered mustard gas poisoning at the front, and Dorothy had to witness the creeping agony of his death.[7]

In her work as a lobbyist Detzer demonstrated her belief in the efficacy of public opinion and was determined to exploit to the full the opportunity that the Nineteenth Amendment had laid at the feet of women. She saw herself as an individual lobbyist backed by mass support. Affected as she was by her moral fervor, she believed that she and her supporters would prevail because their cause was just. According to her outlook, there were good lobbyists and bad, and the two were mutually exclusive. Among the worst of the bad were the corrupt and corrupting Washington representatives of the munitions lobbyists. She regularly and contemptuously refused their attempts to persuade her, with lucrative salary offers bordering on bribery, to change sides.[8] Like other women newly emergent in politics, Detzer was a stranger to the male culture of wheeling and dealing, and could view and depict herself to others as a reformer above faction. A worldly observer might think that this rendered her naive and impractical. But it seemed plain to her that those who worked for a good cause could succeed within the American political system:

> I discovered that public opinion when informed, effectively organized, and buttressed with moral principle, could be the single most powerful factor in American political life.
>
> To be sure, public opinion is not always enlightened. And even when it is, it can be thwarted by the pooled resources of powerful interests. Yet my own experience demonstrated that these powerful interests can be checked and controlled by the will of an active and alert citizenship.[9]

Detzer's passionate commitment, her integrity, and her faith in public opinion were qualities that commended her to potential and actual supporters. She furthermore proved capable of organizing her own following, which was to stand her in good stead as a peace campaigner. The growth of WILPF testifies to Detzer's success at organizing grassroots support for her cause. Of course, she had the help of other able and charismatic women such as Jane Addams and Emily Balch. But the figures do suggest that Detzer was competent in significant ways. In 1921 the U.S. section of WILPF had two thousand members in 9 branches. By 1937 it had thirteen thousand members in 120 branches.[10]

The increase is significant because the women concerned were dynamic, and had an influence out of proportion to their numbers. They could be relied upon to organize the sending of thousands of letters on key issues to legislators, the president, and the secretary of state. WILPF galvanized other women into action, too—and Detzer was especially adept at coalition politics within the broad left. She cooperated with the National Association for the Advancement of Colored People (NAACP) and was arrested for demanding the desegregation of Capitol Hill restaurants. Other allies included the American Civil Liberties Union, the Southern Tenant Farmers Union, and her friend Norman Thomas, presidential candidate of the Socialist Party of America.[11]

In her international activities the furtherance of peace was her consistent theme. To that end Detzer worked with the League of Nations and urged support for the World Court. According to Senator William E. Borah, her campaign for the ratification of the Kellogg-Briand pact saved it from defeat; she also supported Senator Frazier's perennial attempts to promote a constitutional amendment outlawing war. Her special interest in disarmament had led her to exert pressure on President Hoover over the 1930 London Naval Conference and the 1932 Geneva Disarmament Conference. The consistent focus of her activities allowed Detzer to acquire, in the words of one historian, wisdom "in the ways of committees and pressure groups" in pursuit of her particular goals.[12]

Detzer responded to two crises in the Republican years with results that illustrate some of her strengths and weaknesses as a peace campaigner. One of these was the civil war in the Central American nation of Nicaragua, where strife was virtually endemic. Since the fall of the José Zelaya dictatorship in 1909, the United States had regularly intervened on the pretext of restoring order. Repeated invasions by the U.S. Marines had prompted Amy Woods, Detzer's predecessor as WILPF secretary, to draft a Senate resolution banning the use of the army and navy to protect private U.S. interests abroad. But the Senate did not adopt the Woods resolution, and a majority in the chamber undoubtedly disagreed with the economic radicalism underlying it.

Nevertheless Detzer took up the issue a few years later. In 1927 the marines clashed with rebel forces led by the ruthless but charismatic Augusto Sandino. The U.S. deployment of a squadron of dive-bombers against the diminutive nationalist force was a military innovation whose bloody effectiveness was demonstrated only at the price of loss of U.S. public support for the intervention. The Senate Foreign Relations Committee held a hearing in February 1928. Criticism of U.S. policy was mounting, and the marine actions became a popular topic in school debates. At a time when Americans condemned Japanese intervention in China, the Hoover administration was embarrassed by its own involvement in Central America, and finally pulled out of Nicaragua. The withdrawal heralded President Roosevelt's much-admired undertaking, at the 1933 Montevideo Pan-American Conference, that the United States would not intervene in the internal affairs of other American nations. Detzer recalled that Amy Woods's resolution for the Senate thus turned out to be "the daring forerunner of the policy which the world was later to know as that of the Good Neighbor."[13]

The *Nation* credited Detzer with having helped to achieve the historic U.S. withdrawal from Nicaragua, and the WILPF secretary does appear to have made a contribution to a successful campaign. But the special attribute of the affair was that, as the hemispheric superpower, the United States could unilaterally decide on intervention or withdrawal. This meant that public opinion, with which Detzer and other women lobbyists claimed a special affinity, was a relatively important factor. The Senate could afford to listen to the voice of the people, at the same time being aware of other considerations involved in the marine occupations. These considerations included the folly of alienating Latin American trading partners who sympathized with the Nicaraguans' protestations of sovereignty, and the issue of congressional control over foreign policy—especially in the case of undeclared "banana wars" or counter-insurgency campaigns.[14] Detzer's achievement was real enough, yet, like many other human achievements, reflected favorable circumstances.

The September 1931 Japanese invasion of Manchuria presented Detzer with a new and contrasting challenge. For Japan, unlike the United States' Latin American neighbors, was a major power. This placed a constraint on U.S. options, and limited the significance of American public opinion. Yet it appeared that the need for some kind of action was more urgent than had been the case in Nicaragua. In common with other informed observers, Detzer could see that the attack on Manchuria was ominous. As she later remarked, Japan's aggression threatened the viability of the Versailles peace, of the League of Nations, of the 1922 naval agreement, and of the Kellogg-Briand nonaggression pacts. It "precipitated the first major test of the world's peace machinery."[15]

Detzer was, in fact, exceptionally alert to the critical threat to those values that feminists linked together: democracy and peace. She had started to speak out against Hitler in 1926, well in advance of some of those who later took her to task for her opposition to rearmament.[16] Now, she called (in vain) for the withdrawal of all Western ambassadors from Japan and supported the League of Nations call for a boycott of Japanese goods.[17]

In December 1931 Detzer signaled the policy she and her allies were to achieve in the mid-1930s to the consternation of so many interventionists and subsequent historians. She persuaded Congressman Hamilton Fish Jr., of New York, a Republican member of the House Foreign Affairs Committee, to introduce a motion providing for an embargo on the export of arms to warring nations. WILPF would support the move by organizing a Foreign Affairs Committee hearing. Her intention was to build on public indignation over the Manchurian war with a view to achieving a general arms embargo.

On this occasion she did not succeed. On February 9, 1932, the press and speakers assembled in readiness to appear before the Senators. But the committee suddenly retreated behind closed doors, and voted to suppress the hearing. Members stated privately that the reason was the desire not to offend, variously, Japan, China, and the Department of State. Detzer now visited Assistant Secretary of State James Grafton Rogers, who confessed that his department had, in response to a telephone call from the committee's executive session, requested a cancellation of the hearing. Detzer told him that the government was supporting the arms industry. He said that she failed to appreciate the delicacy of the Far Eastern situation and that the arms embargo question was academic anyway, because the United States was exporting only a negligible quantity of weapons.[18]

There now occurred an incident that furnished Detzer with the opportunity to demonstrate her effectiveness in shaping WILPF policy. On February 11 the *Washington Daily News* reported the loading of "large quantities of nitrates believed to be for the Sino-Japanese War" at the wharf of the Atmospheric Nitrogen Company in Hopewell, Virginia. Detzer ascertained that the company was tied to the Mellon-owned Gulf Oil Company, a circumstance she described as "illuminating" because Andrew Mellon was secretary of the treasury at the time. In a Philadelphia meeting two days later, Detzer stressed this point to a group of enthusiastic reporters, but later complained that all the local papers except the *Philadelphia Record* suppressed the story. Such suppression, real or imaginary, merely fanned her indignation and encouraged her to press for a radicalization of WILPF policy. The following year, WILPF adopted a resolution accusing the arms firms of fomenting war scares, stimulating excessive arms expenditure, spreading false reports, and bribing officials. Corruption and the concomitant denial of fair play were issues likely to increase the reform fervor of feminists who saw in their everyday lives instances of the unfair treatment of their sex. The arms manufacturers were now up against a reinvigorated demand for an investigation of their lobbying methods, as well as an embargo campaign.[19]

Although this campaign eventually succeeded, Detzer's attempt to induce the United States to adopt a policy that would stop Japanese aggression in China failed. This was not because of a lack of sympathy for China among the American public. On the contrary, there was widespread indignation against Japan. There is every reason to suppose that Detzer's natural constituency, the women of America, formed part of the Sinophile consensus. *The Good Earth*, Pearl Buck's compassionate novel about life in China, won the Pulitzer Prize for fiction in 1931, and was destined to surpass all other works as a source of images of China in the minds of Americans in prominent professional and public positions. Several other American women were to "go native" in China and record their sometimes influential views.[20]

It is not improbable that Americans of both sexes shared Detzer's views on Manchuria. But this was to be an instance of democratic impotence. Detzer and her colleagues could bring pressure to bear on the U.S. government, but not on the government of Japan. Japan was too powerful to be constrained other than by force, and Detzer's circle would and did not lobby for military action. On the diplomatic front, WILPF and its allies might have achieved more had the United States been a member of the League of Nations, but it was not. Thus by 1932 Detzer had demonstrated her potency as a foreign policy lobbyist in the United States, but the limitations to her influence in the international sphere were already evident.

However, the main thrust of Dorothy Detzer's lobbying activities remained in the direction of arms control. Following Franklin D. Roosevelt's inauguration, Detzer, WILPF, and their allies were poised to launch the decisive phase in their antimunitions campaign. The protagonists of armed deterrence and of international disarmament were drawn up in stark opposition to one another. In the eyes of some legislators, the postwar demobilization had gone too far. They believed that, in a worsening international climate, U.S. defenses were becoming dangerously exposed. On withdrawing from the League of Nations in March 1933, Japan publicly indicated its intention of renouncing the naval limitation agreements with the United States and other Pacific powers. Against this background the House had before it a naval appropriation bill to provide funds for the building of new warships up to the limits permitted by the 1922 and 1930 naval treaties at a possible cost of just over $500 million—in a later flight of hyperbole, Detzer called it the "Billion Dollar Navy Bill."[21]

Detzer and her supporters turned to the new president for support. The outlook seemed promising. Roosevelt had subscribed to the 1920s disarmament consensus and favored nonintervention in Latin American affairs.[22] On May 2, 1933, Emma Guffey Miller, a Democratic National Committee member from Pennsylvania, wrote to the president's secretary, Louis Howe, reminding him of the president's disarmament commitment and requesting an audience for Detzer and her colleagues.

But although Roosevelt was a man of liberal sympathies, he was also a skillful politician who did not want to be enmeshed in the concerns of the women's peace movement. Howe informed Miller that his boss would see no delegation that month. The Bonus Expeditionary Force was supposedly responsible for the decision. Impoverished by the depression, this "army" of World War I veterans had first marched on Washington in the final year of the Hoover administration, demanding immediate payment of their service bonuses due in 1945. They were now encamped once again on the outskirts of the city, ready to resume their marches along the Mall, and the president did not want to set a precedent, in seeing Detzer, that would oblige him to meet the veterans. But Roosevelt did, in fact, see two other delegations, one of them from a fraternal organization called the Tall Cedars. Acidly (if in private), Detzer referred to the latter as "a lot of men dressed up in yellow coats, green trousers and yellow caps." She was furious at Roosevelt's reluctance to receive her, noting the contrast with Coolidge and Hoover, who had both agreed to meetings. She vented her spleen on Howe, who was widely believed to have influence over the president. But in reality Howe's influence on the president was waning, and the evasion may well have come from the president himself. Under pressure two years later to receive a further WILPF delegation, Roosevelt perhaps betrayed his underlying attitude in a remark to his assistant secretary: "I suppose I have to see them."[23]

If, on her part, Detzer had reservations about the president, she was too astute to express them. Instead she redoubled her efforts in Congress. There she focused her attention on the efforts of the navy bill's supporters, led by its sponsor, Representative Carl Vinson of Georgia. As usual Detzer criticized her antagonists' tactics. In a statement prepared for antimunitions campaigner and war correspondent George H. Seldes (the older brother of the critic Gilbert V. Seldes) she complained: "When Jeannette Rankin, Legislative Secretary of the National Council for the Prevention of War, and I both begged Mr. Vinson to let us appear against the bill, and to have time to call in those representatives of groups who wished to oppose it, he refused. . . . His manner was that of a dictator and not that of a representative of a democratic people."[24]

When the bill passed the House and came before the Senate Naval Affairs Committee, on January 30, 1934, the opposition was given twenty minutes' notice of its chance to appear. Detzer and Rankin raced over, but the hearing was cut off after half an hour.[25] The bill's sponsors were insensitive in other ways, too. Roosevelt denied that the bill initiated a big-navy policy, but Vinson crowed, "It means real fighting ships."

Detzer told the president that she was "puzzled" by the "conflicting reports."[26]

The insensitivity of the bill's sponsors provoked indignation that, in turn, fueled the campaign for an investigation of the arms industry and its lobbying methods. The campaign drew further strength from Detzer's assiduous tact. Her correspondence with Seldes provides one illustration of her sensitivity. After Seldes asked her permission to quote certain passages from the statement she had sent him in an article he was writing for *McCall's Magazine*, she replied asking for modifications as "a matter for my own protection in the Senate."[27] Among the sentences she changed was the following: "When we could not be heard in the House Committee, we began to bombard the Senate Naval Affairs Committee whose chairman is Mr. Trammell." She deleted "bombard" and substituted the words "demand this from."[28] More than one factor was at work here: There was the inappropriateness of the use of the word "bombard" by a peace advocate and, at the same time, Detzer's awareness that such language would not do on male-dominated Capitol Hill. Ladies did not "bombard" gentlemen if they expected to get their way. The incident illustrates Detzer's tactical qualities, which could be very effective given the right support and the appropriate circumstances.

Detzer now began to agitate for an inquiry into the munitions industry's influence on foreign policy. Her role in the achievement of that inquiry illustrates in cameo one of this book's main themes—that women have had a significant influence on foreign policy. But to understand properly Detzer's achievement—to appreciate both how she succeeded and why she could not have succeeded without the help of allies and favorable circumstances—it must be placed in context.

Detzer's campaign took place in a favorable climate. There was widespread hostility to the business of arms manufacturing. War veterans, whose patriotism it was impossible to impugn, complained about the profiteering of the arms manufacturers at the expense of ordinary soldiers who had risked their lives. The popular patriotic organization the American Legion encouraged the idea of a check on wartime profiteering. Supportive though the legion was of universal conscription and war mobilization plans, it nonetheless backed the idea of taking the profit out of war.[29]

In the country at large an isolationist spirit was evident that, in a perverse way, helped the cause of those internationalist women who wanted peace and a curb on the arms trade. In the Senate, with its special privileges in the making of foreign policy, an isolationist bloc posed a formidable obstacle to those who favored rearmament and interventionism. As some of these senators were key supporters of the New Deal,

President Roosevelt had to respect their foreign policy preferences. Among the more prominent isolationists in the Senate were Borah of Idaho, Hiram Johnson of California (Republican), Burton K. Wheeler of Montana (Democrat), Henrik Shipstead of Minnesota (Farmer-Laborite), and Robert M. La Follette Jr. of Wisconsin (Progressive Republican), as well as Nye of North Dakota, who was to head the arms inquiry.

The climate of opinion stemmed to some degree from the scholarship of the revisionist historians, who were making known their doubts about official propaganda on the causes of American entry into the Great War. Their ranks—which included such talented writers as H. E. Barnes, Charles Beard, C. Hartley Grattan, Walter Millis, and Charles Tansill—had captured, for the time being, the commanding heights of historical opinion. They disagreed over some issues, for example President Wilson's personal responsibility for U.S. entry into the war, and they tended to embrace a broad economic determinism rather than one that focused on the arms industry, yet these revisionists collectively raised serious doubts about the official reasons for American entry into the 1914–1918 war. (Even FDR expressed retrospective regret at the departure, in 1915, of Secretary of State William Jennings Bryan, who resigned in protest against Wilson's drift toward intervention.)[30]

Then, as the historian Warren Cohen put it, in the spring of 1934 "the manufacturers of war materials were subjected to an intensive muckraking."[31] The March issue of *Fortune* carried an exposé of the arms industry that captured the imagination of the public—and of Borah, who was clutching a copy of the magazine when he appealed for an investigation in a forceful Senate speech.[32] At the same time there appeared the book, by Helmuth C. Engelbrecht and Frank C. Hanighen, whose title became the catchphrase of the arms debate: *Merchants of Death*. This publication became a Book-of-the-Month Club selection and appeared in condensed form in the mass-circulation *Reader's Digest*. Antiwar groups and individuals in the meantime flooded Capitol Hill with petitions and letters.

Detzer felt that "Washington had never been more alive to, or more conscious of, the people's will" than in the initial phase of Roosevelt's presidency.[33] It is open to question whether "the people's will" was reliably expressed by WILPF, an organization accused of having a "Mayflower complex." Yet, in practical terms, women's elitist leadership was formidable. For Detzer was helped by the development of what historian Susan Ware has called a women's political network in the 1930s.[34] Using Boeckel's breakdown (discussed in chapter 3) of how women could or could not influence foreign policy, the potential impact of the network on foreign policy might be laid out as follows.

In 1929 Boeckel had looked in vain for evidence of women as actors in the executive branch of government. Roosevelt, however, at last provided some encouragement to American women by appointing Frances Perkins secretary of labor (she served throughout his long presidency). Although her foreign policy concerns were to be concentrated in the economic sphere, her elevated position nevertheless gave heart to those women who wished to influence policy in other respects. Similarly Roosevelt seemed to have satisfied another of Boeckel's unfulfilled aspirations—a greater role for women in the councils of political parties. He entrusted his wife and senior adviser James Farley with the task of setting up a Women's Division of the Democratic National Committee. Molly Dewson became its director and, in that position as in subsequent posts, succeeded in coordinating the lobbying efforts of women's groups and bringing their concerns to the attention of the president and his wife, with both of whom she enjoyed a close relationship.[35]

Boeckel longed for the day when women would achieve a more peaceful foreign policy through the legislature. The biographer Ingrid Scobie has suggested that women did not exercise such a reforming influence in Congress until 1945, partly because the typical female legislator of the 1920s and 1930s was a political widow.[36] Although there were in reality fewer players in the "widow's game" than some people imagined, it is true that Boeckel's day had not yet arrived when Detzer mounted her campaign for a munitions inquiry in 1934. The 73rd Congress, which convened that year, contained eight women, compared with nine in the 71st Congress (1929–1931), which Boeckel had found wanting. Moreover, from the WILPF viewpoint, the foreign policy attitude of the women in Congress was distinctly unpromising. The one ardent campaigner for international peace, Ruth Bryan Owen, had resigned her seat on being dispatched as U.S. ambassador to Denmark. Although hers was a symbolically important appointment (she was the first woman sent abroad to represent the United States), her removal weakened WILPF on Capitol Hill. Only two of the 73rd Congress women took a prominent interest in foreign policy: Edith Nourse Rogers opposed neutrality legislation, and Florence Prag Kahn continued the propreparedness policies of her late husband, Julius Kahn, on the Military Affairs Committee, which he had chaired and whose seat on the committee she inherited. The women of the 73rd Congress may have served as a useful reminder that male hegemony could now be challenged, but they were not of direct assistance to Dorothy Detzer.[37]

This leaves the phenomenon from which both Boeckel and Detzer took the greatest encouragement, public opinion. In this department the peace women were blessed with inspiring leadership. Preeminent in this regard was the president's wife. Eleanor Roosevelt subscribed to her own version of the "moral equivalence" argument: "War . . . appeals to the idealism of youth. . . . We must find a substitute." Her "New Patriotism" dictated that toymakers should change the discourse of their artifacts, making "armies of foresters" instead of "tin soldiers." She was one of the most influential women to live in the White House. In the period of the munitions debate, she gave female peace organizations her open and conspicuous support. She endorsed the Nye investigation and its postulated connection between munitions profiteering and war. She campaigned for the World Court in 1934–1935 and, as late as 1936, for the Quakers' Emergency Peace Campaign, which, in calling for disarmament and neutrality, challenged some of the president's views. In these senses and in this period, Mrs. Roosevelt was an independent leader of public opinion, even if she was simultaneously a voice in the executive mansion and one of its apologists.[38]

Another woman who helped to raise women's consciousness on the peace issue as the war clouds gathered, and as Nye and his supporters fought for neutrality legislation, was Mabel Vernon, the organizer of the 1932 Transcontinental Peace Caravan. On September 6, 1935, Vernon launched a "People's Mandate" campaign, which led to radio hookups with Europe to discuss peace issues, a campaign to support the 1936 Inter-American Conference for the Maintenance of Peace, and meetings with President Roosevelt.[39]

Instrumental in arranging the White House meetings was a woman described by Vernon as being "a great friend of Eleanor Roosevelt's."[40] Caroline Love Goodwin O'Day had received a genteel upbringing in Georgia. She acquired an international perspective by working in Europe as an artist and fashion designer and on her return to the United States devoted herself to WILPF and the peace cause. Elected to Congress from New York's Rye district in 1934, she became, as it were, an agent of influence for the pacifists because of her stalwart support for the New Deal, an exhibition of loyalty that meant that the White House door remained open to her. Less pleasing to President Roosevelt than her support for domestic reform was her stance on foreign policy. She not only upheld WILPF's aims in the mid-1930s but opposed modification of the neutrality laws even after Hitler's attack on Poland in 1939.[41]

Detzer was not the only female lobbyist seeking to take advantage of the popular mood and the pacifist upsurge among women. The activities of others both indicate that hers was not a solo performance and help to explain her effectiveness. Jeannette Rankin was one lobbyist who supported her on Capitol Hill. Though Rankin had lost her congressional seat in 1919, she was able to draw on her experience and indeed was sufficiently in touch politically to be reelected in 1941. Another of

Detzer's allies on the Hill was Estelle Sternberger, a former executive secretary of the National Council of Jewish Women who now headed the peace publicity organization World Peaceways.[42]

Outside politics the network from which Detzer drew support included Amelia Earhart, the aviator, who, in the words of a biographer, "flew for women" and was "a close friend of Eleanor Roosevelt." As a popular heroine with a media image boosted by the activities of her publisher husband, G. P. Putnam, Earhart formed a link between women inside and outside the elitist network. On September 11, 1934, Earhart endorsed the Nye investigation, declaring "I am emphatically opposed to all that has to do with war and activities of munitions makers."[43]

The degree to which women were to the fore in 1930s peace agitation is reflected in Engelbrecht's later propaganda—in his 1938 book, *Revolt against War*, he emphasized the effects of war on women, for example as victims of pattern bombing and as prostituted camp followers.[44] His political judgment is understandable, as is the enthusiasm with which Detzer proclaimed that public opinion was behind her.

Detzer portrayed Congress as the chief obstacle to arms-trade reform. WILPF had already subjected both Hoover and Roosevelt to intensive pressure to institute a specific arms embargo against Bolivia and Paraguay, which were at war over claim to the Chaco Boreal, a plain at the foot of the Andes. An estimated one hundred thousand soldiers were to die "in a wholly fruitless contest over erroneously charted oilfields."[45] When League of Nations arbitration failed, WILPF supported the League's position that as neither Bolivia nor Paraguay had its own arms industry, the war could be snuffed out through a munitions embargo. First Hoover and then Roosevelt agreed to put the embargo before Congress. But Detzer failed to obtain the desired result. In June 1934 she remarked that "the embargo resolution was the only piece of legislation which the President asked to have enacted into law during the short session of the spring of 1933 which was not passed by Congress."[46]

Detzer did not publicly attack the president. In this way she kept open her lines of communication to FDR and Eleanor Roosevelt. Just as, centuries earlier, one attacked the king's advisers and not the king himself, Detzer directed her fire away from the White House. For example, she attacked the National Recovery Administration (NRA), the newly established New Deal agency charged with working out codes of fair practice for each industry, because the NRA did nothing to control the international munitions trade. She remarked: "The State Department approved the idea of having two persons, one an expert from the munitions department of the State Department, watch the code. We have reason to believe that the State Department sent the proposal to the President, and that the President approved it, and forwarded it, but nothing has come of it."[47]

Detzer noted that General Hugh Johnson, the NRA administrator, was responsible for blocking the idea of monitoring weapons via the codes. Frances Perkins had already foisted on Johnson a Consumers' Advisory Council, and he was digging in his heels in an effort to allow large corporations the latitude to fix prices, make profits, and operate free of the disadvantages then associated with competition, low prices, low tariffs, and over-regulation.[48] Because Johnson's toleration of monopolistic practices was odious to some of Detzer's allies in the Senate—notably Borah and Nye—he was a convenient target for attack.[49] But he was no more than the faithful executor of Roosevelt's 1933–1934 policy of boosting business confidence against a background of severe deflation and low demand—even to the point of rescuing the nation's economic fortunes via international arms sales.

Detzer chose to ignore the president's involvement in his own policies, in effect backing an unwilling horse. As Secretary of State Cordell Hull put it (later, with the wisdom of hindsight), FDR was "marking time" on the arms question, going along with the antimilitarists only in anticipation that their public support might wane.[50] Roosevelt had been undersecretary of navy in the Wilson administration, and his private correspondence in fact reveals that he already entertained a contempt for "professional pacifists."[51] Detzer may have seen through this facade, but the intricate etiquette of mutual political dependency dictated a tactful silence on the issue. Concerned as she was with winning immediate struggles, Detzer may have realized that she could exploit public postures, even if they were insincere and might well prove transitory.

Detzer was more aggressive in her treatment of Congress. Yet here, too, she used techniques that had served her well in the White House, such as flattery. By protecting Roosevelt she had put him under pressure to remember his promises and to do her bidding. With similar effectiveness, she cajoled her senatorial allies Nye; La Follette; George W. Norris of Nebraska; and, above all, Borah. According to Detzer's memoir, Borah, known as the "Lion of Idaho," was guarded by his secretary, Cora Rubin, a "tiger" whom she had to "tame." Detzer won over Rubin and gained the senator's confidence by fiercely defending Borah's reputation. For example, she asserted that he was a "scholar" and not, as his detractors claimed, "inexperienced in foreign affairs." In a shameless flight of hyperbole, she later recalled: "One sensed at once the incorruptible quality of this strong, western, untamed personality."[52]

Detzer shrewdly chose, as her congressional allies, senators of agrarian provenance. Nye's North Dakota and Norris's Nebraska were rural, while neither the brewing industry in La Follette's Wisconsin nor the metalliferous mining interests in Borah's Idaho constituted, in foreign policy terms, an influence likely to modify agrarian "isolationism." None of their mainly landlocked states had an interest in naval manufacturing; none was noted for the production of munitions.

This qualification by default affected the case of Gerald P. Nye. After taking advice from the experienced Senator Norris, Detzer concluded that Nye should lead the munitions inquiry. A vigorous and reasonably able Progressive Republican, Nye had already chaired one inquiry, a Senate investigation into the notorious Teapot Dome oil-lease scandal. But, had he been vulnerable to the powerful arms lobby, Nye might not have accepted his munitions assignment. When determined to unseat its opponents, this lobby could in several states deliver both cash and votes. The lobby's power unnerved politicians who might otherwise have been sympathetic to munitions restraint. For example, in an era of high unemployment, it had been difficult for the representatives of states with shipbuilding interests to withhold support from the Vinson-Trammell Bill. But Nye was not up for reelection for another four years, and North Dakota was probably the least military state in the union—in 1960, at any rate, it had fewer defense interests than any other state. Thus Nye was in an unusually good position to lead a fearless inquiry.[53]

Once Nye had agreed to take the responsibility, Detzer increased her efforts. As usual she organized a flood of letters and petitions—still a very important expression of opinion in the prepollster age. WILPF and its allies held mass meetings, with Nye the star speaker at several of them. However, when Jean Frost of WILPF conducted a Senate poll, it indicated that there would still be stiff opposition. This resistance gave added significance to Detzer's role. She redoubled her ambushes of slow-moving senators in the Capitol's corridors. But her blandishments were insufficient, and several reform-minded New Dealers who allied with Nye and Borah on other issues remained uncommitted. Detzer saw that she needed a signal of approval from the Roosevelt administration. She therefore targeted and managed to pin down Secretary of State Hull.

Hull's experience of rural Tennessean politics and international outlook predisposed him to listen. On March 19, 1934, he endorsed her call for an inquiry. According to Detzer the position was still parlous, and "the measure was finally put through by an extremely clever parliamentary move on the part of Senator Nye."[54] In effect Nye resorted to blackmail. In a routine piece of congressional thuggery, he lined up nine senators who were willing to filibuster the current tax bill, then agreed to call them off in exchange for unanimous support for his own resolution.

On April 12 the Senate agreed to the munitions investigation. Roosevelt bowed to the inevitable and even, in a message to the Senate on May 18, expressed gratification over the inquiry. However, he used the occasion to indicate, indirectly, his reservations on the issue, when he asked the Senate to understand that it would be unwise to act unilaterally to control the "evil" of the arms trade. He favored a closer international monitoring of the arms trade, and a policy of mutual reductions arranged through international conferences.[55]

Detzer's main achievement was her effort in the campaign to set up the Nye inquiry. An assessment of Detzer's significance for American foreign policy must begin, then, with an evaluation of her role in that campaign. The prominent newspaper columnist Drew Pearson was in no doubt about her importance: "Chief credit goes to a young lady who initiated the idea long before anyone else but quietly remained in the background. She is Miss Dorothy Detzer of the Women's International League." In October 1934, with the papers and radio covering the Nye inquiry, the Pennsylvania WILPF branch *Newsletter* noted the "conspicuous credit" being given Detzer. According to one writer in the *Christian Century*, the inquiry "would not have happened without the persistence of one individual," Detzer. Asked about the role of the American Legion in the campaign for the inquiry, Senator Nye said it had not been obstructive, but "all credit" was due to WILPF and other peace organizations; "the help these gave and especially that of Miss Dorothy Detzer are not to be in any way discounted."[56]

The evidence for the foregoing paragraph comes entirely from items in Detzer's own papers in the Swarthmore Peace Collection. Though she cultivated an image of deference and self-effacement as a lobbyist, her collection and retention of such items, though by no means unusual, is suggestive. It is probable that she had an eye on her place in history: For the benefit of contemporaries she lionized her friends, but for the benefit of historians, herself.[57] Because of World War II, she felt compelled to write an account of her antiweapons efforts in the 1930s, and in 1948, she published her political autobiography. *Appointment on the Hill* is a riveting and highly plausible tale. Those historians who credit Detzer's influence have tended to use the book as their sole source on the point, using it as a fleeting reference to a fleeting mention.[58]

Writing to his biographer in 1962, Nye complained that in her book Detzer "was taking much more credit unto herself and others for the conception of the investigation and the legislative steps to bring it about."[59] Nye's judgment was subjective because he wanted more credit for himself, yet it is true that several factors were at work that helped Detzer win her cause. Moreover, Detzer was in some ways a liability to her fellow campaigners. Considering that she was not a socialist, she used the word "left" with an abandon that could have occasioned gratuitous harm to her main cause in a country that was merely resting between major bouts of anti-Red hysteria.[60] Her advocacy of public ownership of the arms industry was based on an assumption that seems questionable in light of the strength the military lobby was to achieve in some Cold War Communist countries; the proposal was never widely popular in the United States.

However, on balance, Detzer's claim to special influence in the munitions campaign does ring true. Detzer's idealism and her independence from any special interests made her attractive, compared with other lobbyists who were geared toward the profit motive. Despite certain liabilities, she did have helpful attributes: organizational skill, charm, tact, restraint, and a willingness to benefit from other people's judgment and experience. She was not an original thinker, but she did present the antimilitarist point of view coherently and helped to win publicity for an argument the media might otherwise have ignored. She did make a difference in the campaign for a munitions inquiry.

The main schools of thought on the Nye investigation differ in their assessment of its wisdom and benignity. Led by William Langer and Everett Gleason, the war apologists saw the inquiry and its exposure of World War I munitions-lobbying tactics as dangerous nonsense. According to the apologists Nye and his colleagues oversimplified the causes of American entry into the Great War. They were responsible for U.S. embargo policies in the 1930s—a reluctant Roosevelt signed the first of these, an embargo on arms exports to belligerents in future wars, on August 31, 1935. The follies of these policies were exposed in the ease of Italy's invasion of weapons-starved Ethiopia, the fall of Spain's underequipped democracy, and the ineffectually resisted expansion of Nazi Germany. Even the preparations for the defense of the mainland United States suffered delays. So the munitions inquiry was malignant and all too effective, though mercifully short-lived in its consequences.[61]

Turning to the other major school of thought, the more sophisticated among the revisionists would have said that the Nye committee's perspective was oversimplified in its concentration not on the economic system as a whole but on specific villains: arms manufacturers, shipbuilders, bankers, Woodrow Wilson.[62] But there was agreement that its findings, if narrow, were nonetheless accurate. The seven reports of the Munitions Investigating Committee based on hearings in the years 1934 to 1937 established beyond doubt that the arms manufacturers had made huge profits out of World War I, and that they used unsavory tactics on Capitol Hill to frustrate international disarmament.[63] So the investigation had an educational impact, even if it was overtaken by the events leading to World War II.

One interpretation of the whole affair would be that Detzer was involved in no more than a transient drama. She is open to the charge that she moved in a purblind circle, tragically unaware of 1930s realities that would soon shatter hopes for a more peaceful world. For example, her friend and fellow WILPF officer Anna Graves lived in Geneva, yet failed to perceive the nature of the situation unfolding in Germany. In 1931 she and Detzer had conferred in the Maison Internationale, WILPF's international headquarters in Geneva, on the problems affecting Liberia, where the rubber-planting plans of the Firestone company had aroused fears of neoslavery.[64] Graves and Detzer had insisted on the desirability of a benevolent American intervention.[65] In July 1933 they were still corresponding on the issue, and, in one letter, Graves incorporated into her harangue against Firestone a lengthy aside on the British and American exploitation. She "really was ashamed to see" prominent members of the NAACP condemning the treatment of Jews in Germany, yet doing so little in the case of Liberia. "Nazi fury," she added, "is a drop in the bucket to the ruthlessness" of economic imperialism.[66]

While Detzer herself had been an opponent of Hitler since 1926, she could be faulted for not galvanizing her friends to resist the military menace personified in the German dictator. On the other hand, her restraint meant she could continue to advance a collective philosophy for American foreign policy. She explained her circle's vision at a Nye hearing on April 10, 1935. Using the collective "we" to suggest she was speaking for WILPF, she advocated the extension of the "Caribbean" nonintervention policy to the rest of the world, and a cautiously modified version of pacifism, a "policy which contemplated as a first step only the actual defense of continental United States." If war threatened, the law should provide for a popular referendum on the issue, and a "government-controlled radio" should afford equal opportunity to the advocates of each side of the case. To eliminate the profits from war, she reiterated, "the munitions industry should be nationalized.[67]

Detzer was unremittingly internationalist in outlook. She fell out with Borah because, in writing the foreign policy planks for the 1936 Republican party platform, he showed himself to be against the League of Nations and the World Court, and devoid of ideas or commitment on disarmament. She fell out with some conservatives in WILPF because of her support for the American League against War and Fascism, which contained some Communists; then, she fell out with the Communists because they put Communism first and peace second. She yearned to help the antifascist cause in Spain, and later regretted the application of the American arms embargo to the civil war in that country. Her internationalism dictated her unwavering personal opposition to Hitler, confirmed in her remark in 1938: "Anyone who knows the nature of fascism, knows that fascism must expand and Hitler has obligingly laid out his plans for all to read in *Mein Kampf.*"[68]

At the same time Detzer never came around to supporting the idea that the United States should encourage armed resistance to the Nazis. After Hitler's invasion of Poland, she attacked President Roosevelt's "sinister" preparations for war.[69] Talk of running her as a peace candidate for the presidency came to nothing in 1940, but then she threw herself into the unsuccessful campaign against the Lend-Lease Act of 1941, the law designed to help the British continue to fight against the apparently invincible Germans.[70] Nor did U.S. entry into the war blunt her critical instinct. In 1944 she wrote a furious letter to Eleanor Roosevelt, accusing her of being an apologist for the U.S. military leadership, who wanted to deny Red Cross relief money to small occupied countries like Holland: "Surely it is not maudlin emotionalism to insist that there are values which transcent [sic] even the wisdom of general staffs. . . . Even the political state at war cannot escape the Christian imperative which has rung down the ages."[71]

By this time Detzer's influence on American foreign policy had declined to the point of negligibility. Her failure to endorse a military stand against Hitler in the late 1930s consigned her to virtual oblivion. Yet she had shown that American women could influence the general agenda of U.S. foreign policy, if not the conduct of powerful foreign countries. She had forced President Roosevelt to concede the "evil" nature of the arms trade and helped to set a new economic agenda for the discussion of national security policy.

Equipped with their new agenda, women were to achieve influence once again in the 1960s. For the realization gradually dawned that foreign policy cannot be conducted on the premise that any powerful foreign leader might turn out to be another Hitler. It turned out that Detzer's faith in arms limitation had not, after all, been an aberration in U.S. foreign policy. Others, for their own reasons, were to reach similar conclusions. President Eisenhower having denounced the influence of the "military-industrial complex" on American national security policy, Bella Abzug capitalized on the feminist impulse of the 1960s by leading a congressional assault on American militarism, and the world achieved a measure of disarmament by the 1990s. Thus, in the short term, Detzer and her legion of supporters succeeded by launching the Nye inquiry; in the medium term, they failed to prevent World War II and their country's entry into it; but in the long term, they blazed a trail for critics of the nuclear arms race.

6 | A TALE OF TWO WOMEN
Harriet Elliott, Eleanor Roosevelt, and Changing Differences

In the realm of foreign policy, the decade from the late 1930s to the late 1940s was one of changing gender differences. Because of a transformation in attitudes toward the consumption function of the "housewife," women came to be less closely associated with low prices and low tariffs, and their particular association with free trade virtually disappeared. Another change occurred because of developments overseas. The full horrors of the Hitler and Stalin regimes became evident in the mid-1940s, powerfully stimulating American women's interest in human rights, which they proceeded to export to the rest of the world. Yet not everything changed in the decade under consideration. While America's entry into World War II was a major setback to the peace movement, it was during the war that the first statistical confirmation emerged of a "gender gap" on foreign policy. Its chief ingredient was women's pronounced taste for a defensive war strategy, a preference consistent with their foreign policy outlook both before and after the great global conflict.

The activities and fates of two women encapsulate these changing differences and telling continuities. Harriet Elliott was a government adviser who continued the interwar campaign to preserve the rights and interests of the American consumer in matters of international trade. However, tariff reform did not survive as a gender issue, and in that respect Elliott was ineffective. Like Elliott, Eleanor Roosevelt had been involved in the peace movement, but she was a much more prominent and successful activist. After the war Eleanor Roosevelt led the agitation for a Universal Declaration of Human Rights, to be promulgated and monitored by the new United Nations (UN).

Harriet Elliott became a senior adviser on trade and consumer matters in May 1940, when President Roosevelt appointed her to the National Defense Advisory Commission. A suffragist and antiwar Quaker before American entry into World War I, Elliott showed her willingness to compromise when in 1918 she agreed to chair the education department of the North Carolina Division of the Women's Committee of the Council of National Defense. In the 1920s she moved once again with the mainstream when she joined Carrie Catt's Conference on the Cause and Cure of War. In 1935 she became dean of the Women's College at the University of North Carolina. In February–August 1935, at the behest of Democratic National Committee Chairman Jim Farley and of Molly Dewson, she worked for the Democratic Party's Women's Division, running an educational program on the aims of the New Deal. Farley rewarded her by placing her nephew Allan Pearce in a Honolulu job in 1936. By the advent of war in Europe, Elliott was a friend of Eleanor Roosevelt as well as of Molly Dewson. She was evidently a trustworthy choice for high position, a woman whose loyalty had been cemented in time-honored fashion. Roosevelt must have anticipated that she would be a malleable bureaucrat.[1]

Elliott's failure to achieve her desired objectives does not mean that she was incompetent. On the contrary, she was an intelligent and determined bureaucrat. Her problem was that the free-trade feminists were already in a defensive and largely untenable position. These women failed partly because they had succeeded in the short run: when they won some of their objectives in the mid-1930s, they turned their attention elsewhere. The free-trade feminists also failed because they were disarmed by FDR's political skills—indeed to such an extent that they were later unable to revive their campaign, even when World War II began to destroy the structures of international trade.

In his effort to propitiate free-trade women, Roosevelt started at a disadvantage, for he had courted the opposite side in the debate and indeed pursued protectionist policies at the outset of his presidency. Both of the major pieces of early New Deal legislation—the National Industrial Recovery Act and Agricultural Adjustment Act (AAA)—aimed at price maintenance. Furthermore, according to the respected financier Bernard Baruch, the National Industrial Recovery Act would, by raising wage levels, make tariff increases inevitable.

But the President rejected Baruch's point of view when it was put to him in a press conference on May 26, 1933. His policies kept free-trade women on his side and helped to defuse a campaign that might have damaged him politically. A short account of his tactics will help to explain why Harriet Elliott had such limited impact. One point is that Roosevelt was rarely short of a plausible answer to criticism. For example, in his rebuttal of Baruch he claimed that tariff increases would not be necessary if other countries agreed to prop up their own prices, so removing the threat of cheap imports to the United States.[2]

The pragmatic president always seemed able to offer at least some reward to lower-tariff lobbyists. Shortly before the Baruch challenge, Ann Caner had written to the president:

> I am ten years old and I'm in Fifth Grade. At the school I go to we have Weekly Readers. In one of them I read about tariffs. The Government as I understand has to have them. I read also that high tariffs was one cause of the depression and that you were in favor of low tariffs. I haven't slept very well because they're all I can think of. . . . I think medium sort of in between tariffs ought to be had. What do you think? (You may think this letter the funniest thing in the world but I mean business).[3]

Because the president was "terribly busy," Tariff Commission secretary Sidney Morgan responded with the assurance that tariff problems kept older people awake, too. Morgan told Miss Caner that "the 'medium-sort-of-in-between tariffs' that you speak of, the kind that will encourage trade with our foreign neighbors and also improve business at home, I think, are just what we are all looking for."[4] Women concerned with consumer issues could not reasonably complain that Roosevelt ignored their concerns. The president courted a wide range of groups in search of a supportive coalition, and made encouraging gestures in the direction of the nation's consumers. For the continuing low-tariff agitation was part of a wider concern with consumer affairs in domestic American politics. The famous trial lawyer Clarence Darrow was just one of several prominent public figures who allied themselves with the cause. Popular books had been published on the subject, and by the mid-1930s there had developed, according to the historian Arthur M. Schlesinger Jr., a "consumer mystique."[5] Thus, even on the occasion of the establishment of the price-boosting National Recovery Administration (NRA), Roosevelt had deemed it prudent to announce: "The aim of this whole effort is to restore our rich domestic market by raising its vast consuming capacity. If we now inflate prices as fast and as far as we increase wages, the whole project will be set at naught."[6]

In the early phase of the New Deal, FDR went beyond verbal gestures. He accepted consumer representation on the NRA and on the AAA, as well as through a joint Consumers' Council.[7] When he explained his plans for setting up a National Emergency Council (NEC) in December 1933, he promised that "a representative of the Consumers' Council" would be included. He duly appointed Mary Harriman Rumsey to head the NEC's Consumers' Division. Rumsey was the daughter of railroad magnate E. H. Harriman, shared a house in Washington with Secretary of Labor Frances Perkins, and was a powerful member of Washington's women's network. One of Rumsey's experts wrote to Molly Dewson explaining NEC plans and expectations: "The Administration has always insisted that the interests of consumers, as well as those of owners and workers, shall be represented," and it would deal with any price complaints.[8]

In June 1934, Congress passed the Reciprocal Trade Agreements Act. This appeared to be a definitive response to the agitation of those who championed free trade, world peace, and the rights of the consumer. For one thing, the law effectively removed tariff-making powers from congressmen who might favor local constituents, giving it to the executive instead.[9] Potentially this favored women's lobbies, as they claimed to be more effective nationally than locally. The terms of the legislation were also promising, allowing for handsome tariff reductions affecting the trade between the United States and specific foreign countries. Under the reciprocal agreements that followed bilateral negotiations, reductions as high as 50 percent were achieved. Secretary of State Cordell Hull was an apostle of liberal trade and proved to be a determined battler against economic nationalists, achieving fifty bilateral agreements by the outbreak of World War II. Though his outlook was essentially agrarian—he described his trade agreements as "treaties of peace . . . indispensable to the prosperity of our farms"—his actions and language were congenial to peace-through-trade women.[10]

But, while the reciprocity legislation was to a significant degree a triumph in which peace-through-trade feminists could share, it tended to have the long-term effect of making their campaign redundant—and in the short term it did little to enhance their power. Here, one can take note of FDR's skillful political tactics. The president would encourage a whole range of potential supporters, from blacks to women through farmers and organized labor, and he would make concessions to them verbally or in policy. But he was careful to keep the control of events in his own hands. There was no advantage in surrendering power to people on whose loyalty he could count anyway. If gestures were not enough to satisfy bonus marchers and sharecroppers, auto workers and radical writers, he sometimes tried to give the impression that what he conceded he had intended to allow anyway. Thus he conveyed a sense that his government was already aware of problems and taking care of things, and there was no real need for him to heed people's demands for real representation and power in high government. Through his manipulation of political signals, Roosevelt outwitted those among his supporters who might have caused him political difficulties.

The consumer lobbyists soon began to experience the limitations to their power. Secretary Morgan of the U.S. Tariff Commission refused to cooperate with the NRA's consumer advisers.[11] The NRA team could not even expect any backing from the head of their own agency, General Hugh Johnson, who was skeptical of the idea of consumers as a political force. When Frances Perkins broached the matter of stronger consumer representation on the NRA, Johnson bellowed at her, "Who is a consumer? Show me a consumer."[12]

The NEC was hardly more effective as a channel for consumers' pressure. To be sure, Rumsey's subordinate Paul Douglas set out to establish consumers' councils all over the United States. But by this very process he bypassed the consumers' and housewives' own organizations, effectively sapping their spontaneity and activism. NEC member Walton H. Hamilton later observed to Molly Dewson that the consumer interest had been represented on the council "under rather inhospitable auspices."[13]

The female consumer lobby suffered a reverse in November 1934, when it lost Mary Rumsey, who died from the effects of a riding accident while fox-hunting on her farm in Virginia. Her money, her judicious political entertaining, and her zeal in promoting an alternative viewpoint to those of big business and big labor had all been useful to the consumer cause. But an even greater setback was to occur on May 27, 1935. On that day, "Black Monday," the Supreme Court in its *Schechter* v. *United States* decision rejected the constitutionality of the NRA, thereby dealing a further blow to the already flimsy structure of consumer representation. FDR at first reacted by trying to restructure consumer representation within the doomed NRA—he put Walton Hamilton in charge. Then, he transferred the Consumers' Division of the NRA to the Department of Labor. Even with Frances Perkins at the helm, this was sending a snowball to hell—her department was by definition biased toward producers, not consumers. At the same time the president dealt with a militant display by the AAA's consumer advisers by dismissing them. The chief executive was determined to remain in control.[14]

The overall picture is of declining consumer militancy in the face of a politically adroit president. Yet the continuation of that decline stemmed, at least in part, from the administration's promotion of additional consumer-friendly measures. Signing the Sugar Control Bill into law in 1937, Roosevelt played on the themes of consumer welfare and open competition when he attacked "the little group of seaboard refiners who, unfortunately, for many years were able to join forces with domestic producers in the maintenance of a continuing and powerful lobby in the national capitol and elsewhere." He declared that "the end of the monopoly is definitely in sight" and added: "The monopoly costs the

American housewife millions of dollars every year and I am just as concerned for her as I am for the farmers themselves."[15]

President Roosevelt displayed his political skills in dealing with a wide range of issues, and trade policy was no exception. By the time war broke out in Europe in 1939, he had ensured that feminist consumer militancy was little more than a memory. Nevertheless he continued to deal with trade policy in a political manner, and he intended Harriet Elliott to be part of his solution when he appointed her to the National Defense Advisory Commission.

O stensibly Elliott's appointment placed a woman in the higher reaches of the national security bureaucracy and gave her the opportunity to shape policy in ways that would satisfy women's needs and aspirations. But in practice Elliott was to be a token representative of women, a token representative of consumers, and an example of yet another friend to whom the president turned a deaf ear.

In May 1940 the president set up the National Defense Advisory Commission (NDAC), the predecessor of the wartime Office of Price Administration (OPA). The NDAC's composition offered an opportunity for the exercise of presidential patronage. Roosevelt nominated Elliott to be the consumer protection representative on the eight-member commission. This stung Frances Perkins, who wanted two labor men on the NDAC—a representative of the AFL, in addition to the already appointed Sidney Hillman of the CIO. She asked Roosevelt why he did not drop Elliott to make way for a second labor man. In her paraphrase, the president replied he "wasn't going to have two labor men; too much trouble to have two."[16]

So Roosevelt's appointment of Elliott to a high-profile body may have been a maneuver to limit the power of big labor. Another perspective on the composition of the NDAC came from the playwright and government official Robert Sherwood, who suggested that the president wanted people who demanded policies "he did not want to advocate publicly for political reasons at the time." According to Sherwood, Roosevelt occasionally "wanted to be 'attacked' for inactivity and thus 'goaded' into action by public demand."[17] Elliott, like the others, may have been appointed for this purpose.

Roosevelt himself is the source for a final perspective on the Elliott appointment. He told Perkins: "We have to have a woman. Got to pacify the women. If there is a woman, you won't have women's protests against actions that are too military, against giving too much help to the allies. The presence of a woman on the commission will stop all that." Perkins further recalled that the president had been "adamant. I never knew him to be so stubborn."[18]

It seems to have been Roosevelt's intention to make a political gesture toward women by making a token appointment to his war advisory commission. Further, he intended to channel women's attention into consumer matters in order to divert attention from the much more contentious war-and-peace issue. Not content with this, he tried to ensure that Elliott had little say, even on policies affecting the consumer. When he announced the composition of the NDAC, journalists latched on to the question of the enforcement powers to be vested in Elliott. The president replied evasively. At first, he said, she would not have much to do, because of current surpluses. But she might later have to take matters up with the Agriculture and State Departments, and with the antitrust division of the Department of Justice.[19]

Elliott had a proven capacity for compromise, as well as personal ties to the president and his administration. It would not be demonstrably unfair to label her a "peacetime pacifist" who responded with alacrity to the call of war. Yet she proved to be rather more than a token woman and gave the president some trouble. On July 12, 1940, she rebelled over two issues—both stemming from the question of U.S.–Latin American relations and the price of coffee—that would have been custom made for the 1920s feminists. The problem arose from the effect of the European war on Latin American coffee production. The State Department proposed a system of country-by-country import quotas. This flew in the face of free-trade principles but had the advantages of stabilizing production and supply and of giving the United States a lever for political influence in a region where the European fascists hoped to make their mark. But at the same time the proposal raised the specter of maximum quotas that would injure the consumer. The fear was that restrictive quotas would limit supplies in a way that would have an inflationary effect on the price of every cup of coffee in America.

Elliott's first rebellion was over representation. She was convinced that the State Department was hostile to the consumer interest, and that her office should "be placed in a position to follow, and, where appropriate, to participate in the negotiations upon which these decisions affecting American consumers are based."[20] Elliott wanted the NDAC's foreign trade adviser, Henry J. Tasca, to take an active part in policy formation instead of W. Averell Harriman, another offspring of the railroad tycoon and a close adviser of FDR's, whom Tasca portrayed as unsympathetic to consumers.[21]

On August 2, 1940, Roosevelt made mollifying noises about Elliott in an address delivered, at her request, to representatives of civic organizations meeting in Washington to discuss consumer problems. He told the delegates it was "just grand of you to come down here" and praised the "vitally important job" Elliott was doing, but without specifying exactly what it was or how he was going to support her.[22] Consumer economist Caroline Ware now warned Elliott of State's view that Tasca was too junior and peripheral to be admitted to membership of the influential Executive Committee on Commercial Policy (ECCP). She also warned her against "pushing the issue at the present time." By the end of August 1940 Elliott had had to agree to a compromise whereby Tasca sat in as an observer on ECCP meetings deemed by its chairman to be relevant, with Harriman agreeing to supply on request such trade information as Elliott might desire. Elliott's consumer bureaucrats had been put in their place.[23]

Elliott's second rebellion was over policy. At her instigation her economic adviser, Ben Lewis, challenged the State Department's position with a counterproposal. He recommended that the preamble of the contemplated coffee agreement should indicate it was an emergency, temporary measure and not a departure from the trade agreements principle of 1934. He further suggested that a minimum aggregate quota be stipulated, on the model of the consumer protection clause of the 1937 Sugar Act. Elliott and Lewis wanted to protect American families, especially poor families, from excessive scarcity-induced price increases.[24]

Elliott explained her fears in a letter to Averell Harriman in November. If the quota system were adopted in the case of one commodity, she argued, it might be extended to others and jeopardize the trade agreements program. She asserted that "the vital interests of the consumers in any permanent foreign policy lie with the sound and tried principles of the trade agreements program." Accepting the need for temporary quotas, she nevertheless demanded consumer guarantees. But when he received her letter, Harriman (or one of his State Department aides) penciled scornful comments in its margins. For example, Elliott's suggestion of a ban on coffee reexports to protect U.S. consumers elicited the remark: "This seems hardly necessary."[25]

On January 2, 1941, Elliott revealed her growing impatience with the White House when she wrote to Molly Dewson protesting Eleanor Roosevelt's proposal that a society lady, possibly Nancy Astor, should organize American women in a campaign against inflation.[26] Lady Astor was the Virginian who had married a viscount, settled in England, and won election as Britain's first woman member of parliament—she served as a Conservative from 1919 to 1945. At Cliveden, the Astors' country seat, Astor enacted the role of a formidable political hostess. At the start of the war the press on both sides of the Atlantic denounced the so-called Cliveden set for allegedly promoting appeasement, and even for conspiring with Hitler. Seemingly impervious to these attacks, Astor set out to help the war effort, and, at the suggestion of her close friend

Lord Lothian, the British ambassador to Washington, turned her attention on her native country. She wrote to Eleanor Roosevelt, offering to "talk to the women" on behalf of the embattled British, and the first lady apparently thought that, as the United States was still neutral, Astor might campaign against price hikes instead.[27]

Elliott thought Astor could not possibly appeal to "rank and file" women, and the hostess's reputation for appeasement in any case made her politically unacceptable to the Roosevelt administration. The president wrote to Lady Astor saying he did "not feel that Eleanor or I should ask you to make the sacrifice it would surely be to leave England in these critical days."[28]

This did little to assuage Elliott's discontent. Her public pronouncements began to take the hue of incipient criticism of government policy. When coffee prices rose in the spring of 1941, she issued a press release in which she claimed the increases were unjustified in the light of existing stocks and production surpluses. She threatened to force an increase in the aggregate coffee import quota. Justifying her threat, she argued that coffee was of "vital importance" to the administration's "Good Neighbor" policy with the Americas, and "essential" to the maintenance of civilian morale. But she failed to elicit a satisfactory response. On November 21, 1941, she wrote to Eleanor Roosevelt complaining that consumer interests were not being taken seriously by the government. The next day she resigned from the NDAC. Her resignation letter to the president contained no mollifying statements, and she refused to respond to high-level pleas to change her mind.[29]

Shortly after the Japanese attack on Pearl Harbor on December 7, Roosevelt accepted Elliott's resignation.[30] In a way the rift between them seems to have been trivial and fleeting. Just two months after Elliott's resignation, Congress passed a law giving effect to one of her main proposals—the Emergency Price Control Act. The law provided for the establishment of the NDAC's successor, the OPA, later credited by its admirers with holding down prices in the inflationary war years.[31] But although Elliott accepted a new job promoting the sale of war bonds, she was given no role in the OPA. She was not on the same wavelength as the president. Elliott regarded the world crisis as permitting the continuation of the New Deal by other means, but Roosevelt saw national security as his transcending goal—and feared that persistence with New Deal policies might alienate the business community at a crucial time.[32]

Pearl Harbor's domination of the headlines ensured that there would be no great fuss in the media or in government circles over the resignation of Harriet Elliott. She had in any case already been relegated to the margins of Washington's policy-making world. She had failed to achieve the principle of effective consumer representation in matters of foreign trade, and had failed to become more than a token and relatively unknown woman in the circles devoted to the economic planning of the war effort. It is evident, however, these failures did not stem from her own inadequacies but rather from the political skills FDR had deployed from the very beginning of his presidency.

B y the 1940s the feminist low-price campaign that had underpinned earlier free-trade demands had lost its sting. Women were not, in World War II, the devotees of lower prices that they had once been assumed to be. The government secretly polled women in the seven months following Pearl Harbor and found that they were undistinguished by any special enthusiasm, compared with men, for price controls.[33] For the first time evidence was available—at least, to the select government officials privy to it—to show that women en masse may have been fairly similar to men in their outlook on prices. When the government findings are considered in conjunction with the evidence of Gallup polls, it can be inferred that men as well as women favored price controls. In March 1941, 68 percent of the people polled wanted a price freeze for the duration of the war. In August 1945, 74 percent of the Gallup sample opposed decontrol.[34] It seems reasonable to suppose that these were male as well as female proportions.

The laissez-faire thrust of pre-1940s middle-class foreign policy feminism had given women's attitudes a deceptively monolithic and distinctive appearance. Nevertheless, although contemporary assumptions that women were the dominant consumers and thus given to a free-trade bias had been influential politically, they cannot be sustained statistically. It is still a matter of speculation how many important expenditure decisions men may have made within the pre–World War II family. However, the available figures on family expenditure between 1935 and 1950 are rather more substantial. From these it would appear that while consumer spending expanded rapidly, it did so unevenly on certain commodities. Thus spending on clothing increased by 53 percent, but spending on recreation and automobiles went up 185 and 205 percent, respectively.[35] It seems likely that in the immediate postwar years men had a greater relative say on recreation, and they were probably dominant in the purchase of automobiles. In other words, as prosperity increased, so did the role of men as consumers. What further cemented this process was the spread of credit finance and of checkbook banking. As time passed, the rise of the credit card and the emergence of the fashion-conscious, status-seeking male hastened the equalization of expenditure between men and women.

One reason for men's more vigorous activities in the marketplace was their incipient displacement at the point of production—as men devoted more time to spending, they made way for women on the job front. In the immediate aftermath of World War II, American culture plucked women from the factories and placed them in the home—to the fury of 1960s feminists. But increasingly women came to value job opportunities because of the scarcity vested in them by the depression, because of the encouragement offered by the World War II production boom, and because, in a galloping process of cultural change, middle-class women demanded careers instead of rejecting paid work as socially demeaning. Not only did more women seek work, but they included in their ranks a greater number who were married. As the economic historian Claudia Goldin put it in 1990, "the increase in married women's work over the last half-century is . . . the rising portion of a U-shaped process that extends across the last two centuries."[36] Within the family, then, women earned money, accentuating their association with the production process even if many of them did not work in factories. It is revealing that, whereas the 1920s had produced a special breed of female consumption economists like Hazel Kyrk, no such cadre existed in the 1950s.[37]

This does not mean it is impossible to find individual women who still advocated free trade. In 1967 trade adviser Persia Campbell reflected traditional concerns in reminding Senate Finance Committee chairman Russell Long of Senator George's argument in 1929 "that the interest of the consumer requires the liberalization of trade," and in pressing upon him her conviction that protectionist trade blocs menaced "not only economic progress but also world peace." At the time of Senator Long's hearings, the occasional witness still reflexively referred to the consumer as "she." One might also cite the more recent case of President Bush's trade negotiator Carla Hills, who saw the collapse of communism as an opportunity to "rip down confining economic barriers" and "build a new world order."[38]

But these women could no longer claim to represent a feminist or distinctively female viewpoint. Price stability was not a distinctively female concern in the second half of the twentieth century. For example, according to 1971 Harris polls, an equal proportion of men and women (78 percent) blamed inflation on the Vietnam War. In identifying the most serious problems confronting the nation, men proved to be more worried about prices than women, while women were relatively more concerned about the war.[39] In more recent years there have been no prominent feminist overtones to the debate over the North American Free Trade Agreement (NAFTA). Either women's attitudes changed in the 1940s, or the middle-class leaders' presumption of "virtual representation" of female opinion on prices and the tariff in the prepollster era of the 1920s and 1930s had been questionable all along.

By the 1940s the crusade for low prices and world peace via lower tariffs had ceased to be a feminist concern. It crumbled for several reasons. It was to a degree stifled by its own success, the achievement of free trade reform in the 1930s. It was discredited by failure—free-trade reform did not prevent World War II. It fell victim to the skillful political maneuvers of President Roosevelt, as evidenced in the marginalization of Harriet Elliott. Finally, the impact of the feminist consumer on foreign economic policy was killed by the perception that female spending was no longer different from male spending.

Nevertheless it would be a travesty of the facts to suggest that money matters dominated women's outlook in 1940s, to the exclusion of concern over the deadlier aspects of World War II. Women were deeply concerned about the conflict, and a number of deductions can be made about their attitude. Most women supported the war. However, women did not lose their distinctively strong yearning for the ways of peace. Moreover, it is clear that this yearning was not confined to the middle-class elite of the women's movement.

Mainstream female leadership support for the war is evident from the reactions of women in Congress. There were nine female members of Congress when war broke out in 1941, compared with just one in 1917. The nine included one senator, Hattie W. Caraway of Arkansas, and a member of the House Foreign Affairs Committee, Representative Frances P. Bolton of Ohio. Eight of the nine women in the Seventy-seventh Congress joined the entire male contingent in supporting the decision to go to war.

Interventionism was, in fact, rife among the women of Capitol Hill. In a special election in May 1941 caused by the death of her husband, Maryland's Katharine E. Byron stood and won specifically as a preparedness advocate. Byron duly supported Lend-Lease. Senator Caraway seldom spoke in debates, but she had supported appropriations for a larger army and navy in the 1930s, when she won substantial military contracts for Arkansas. "Silent Hattie" had two sons in the army, and voted for Lend-Lease. Mary T. Norton and Edith Nourse Rogers were two experienced legislators who also supported interventionist legislation. Rogers had been the first, in Congress, to attack Hitler's treatment of minorities. Finally, Margaret Chase Smith supported intervention. Like Bolton, Caraway, and Rogers, she was a widow who had inherited her seat from her husband. In voting for Lend-Lease and to arm U.S. merchant ships, Smith brought her own fervor to the military cause, defying the rest of the Maine delegation and received "black looks" in the process.[40] In terms of weight, experience, and determination, the interventionist women carried the day in Congress, even before Pearl Harbor.

The support women gave the war effort was undoubtedly important economically, as large numbers of women entered the work force. It was also significant in terms of morale—good morale on the home front encouraged the soldiers fighting overseas and contributed to industrial productivity. Furthermore the political support of America's women meant that Roosevelt could exercise unencumbered war leadership.

Women's patriotism flourished partly for a negative reason: Female opponents of the war lacked effective leadership. It is true that Congress did contain some potential dissenters: Foreign Affairs Committee member Bolton had taken an isolationist stance and voted against the Lend-Lease Bill; Caroline O'Day had worked with WILPF and similarly voted against interventionist and war measures; Jessie Sumner was strenuously isolationist. Yet none of these women made a major impression in the country at large, and none voted against the declaration of war. (Sumner later opposed the plan to invade Europe, but this was a rare instance of dissent.) Women offered no concerted opposition to the military campaigns in Europe or the Pacific, and made no significant attempt to pressure the government into making peace overtures. The women who had occupied the space associated with resistance to war had effectively vacated it, leaving a leadership void.

A similar argument could be made about the executive. The president and his wife had, if not quite to the same degree as President Wilson, occupied a propeace leadership role only to desert it, leaving antiwar Americans without an inspiring leader at the helm. In FDR's case the change was merely from reluctant support of neutrality to circumspect opposition to it. But Mrs. Roosevelt had been much more important to the peace cause, especially in the inspirational sense. Jason Berger, author of a study of Eleanor Roosevelt and foreign policy, claimed that his subject "succeeded Jane Addams as the most visible leader of the women's peace movement."[41] As late as April 1940 the first lady appealed to the readers of *Good Housekeeping* to make common cause, as women, in the general pursuit of peace. But by this time she had endorsed particular conflicts. She supported the armed struggle of the Loyalists against the Franco forces in the Spanish Civil War, and, from 1939 she supported the Allied war effort and America's preparations to join the battle.[42] Few of her impressive band of supporters could find it in their hearts to condemn her, and no American woman could hope to step into the particular inspirational niche she had abandoned.

The collapse of the trade-and-peace ideology and of the Washington lobby associated with it was another blow to the prospects of an antiwar coalition. As yet there was no replacement ideology to guide the thoughts of peace feminists. Dorothy Detzer and her colleagues had developed a critique of what in future would be called the "military-industrial complex," but it would have seemed inappropriate to apply it to the United States exclusively at a time when other nations were rearming at an alarming pace.

The prospects for a feminist antiwar coalition were further undermined by yet another factor. This was the split within the feminist movement between social reformers, who believed in special legislation to protect the welfare of women, and the proponents of an Equal Rights Amendment to the U.S. Constitution. The split had a deadening effect on feminist political action. In the words of one historian, the woman's movement was, by 1940, "paralyzed by its own involvement in the politics of mutual recrimination."[43]

The foregoing weaknesses of leadership, ideology, and organization help to explain the absence of a strong feminist opposition to American participation in World War II. So does the fact that many women as well as men were caught off guard by the Japanese surprise attack at Pearl Harbor, which inevitably precipitated the country into war without a thorough debate, in spite of the protracted isolationist-versus-interventionist controversy that had preceded it.

Yet the war had few attractions for women. Given the moral and caring dimension claimed by women for their foreign policy campaigns, it could be argued that the Holocaust must have generated women's hostility to Germany, and enthusiasm for the war effort. But the Holocaust does not explain women's support for the war, for the timing is wrong: Hitler's "Final Solution" took shape only in the latter part of 1941—the first gas chamber became operational in March 1942—and the whole operation was shrouded in secrecy.[44] World War II was not morally attractive to women. Most of them supported it, but only out of loyalty to their country and their men, and because of the weakness of the opposition.

Women's reluctance to endorse war was sufficiently evident to worry the politicians. In the years preceding Pearl Harbor, interventionists had worried about women's peaceful tendency. President Roosevelt saw them as diplomatically unreliable. In 1937, under pressure to appoint a woman emissary, he told Molly Dewson that a woman ambassador could only be sent to a country "not likely to be drawn into a European conflict."[45] Roosevelt did not have the advantage of his predecessor President Wilson, of being able of buy women's support with the promise of the vote. He took other precautions. In May 1940, as previously noted, he appointed Elliott to "pacify the women" who might otherwise protest "against actions that are too military, against giving too much help to the allies." Roosevelt appears to have shared Lord Lothian's view, expressed three months earlier, that America's "emotional pacifism" could be attributed to "mothers and wives."[46] Clearly, 1920s expectations that women would be a force for peace had not entirely receded.

The conscious articulation of the view that women had a distinctive peace mission survived even as the United States slid into war. Following Hitler's invasion of Czechoslovakia and Poland, the embattled WILPF considered combining forces with male peace organizations in the interest of strength through unity. WILPF polled its membership— should it drop "women" from its title? The result, reported in January 1941, was an endorsement, in the ratio 10:4, of the existing gender orientation.[47]

But women's opposition to the war was much more widespread than this, and it was diverse in character. By no means all the objectors were feminists, liberals, and internationalists. A substantial proportion of them consisted of isolationist, conservative women who resented in equal measure the New Deal and attacks on "family values." Thus women's opposition to war can be shown to have been broad-based, a common denominator of some resilience in a pluralistic society.

The America First movement of 1939–1941 (not to be confused with the America First Committee), a mostly female effort to keep the United States out of the war, was a network of right-wing mothers' groups. For example, in 1939 Josephine Mahler started the Mothers of Sons Forum in Cincinnati. By June 1940 the forum had gathered 65,000 names on a petition against the enactment of the Selective Service Bill. In Chicago, We, the Mothers Organize for America had more than twenty thousand members. The enthusiasts in these organizations believed that Soviet Russia was a greater menace than Nazi Germany—some of them were later active in supporting the 1950s anti-Communist activities of Senator Joseph P. McCarthy. They saw in the New Deal the menace of creeping socialism. To the fury of their critics, the isolationist women exploited the "nurturant motherhood" notion for propaganda purposes. So did the war's supporters, for example Cincinnati's First Armored Division Mothers' Club, and the nationwide 75,000-member Blue Star Mother organization. But the war's right-wing opponents were unrepentant. In 1944 they still commanded tens of thousands of supporters and were still demanding an end to rationing, price controls, and the draft— and calling for the impeachment of President Roosevelt.[48]

Although the antiwar women were poorly represented in Congress, there was one inspirational exception. This was the redoubtable Jeannette Rankin. Throughout the 1930s Rankin had campaigned for peace and neutrality, endorsing the revisionist view that World War I had been an economic conspiracy and supporting the Nye investigation. In 1940 she won election once again from her native Montana. Although she ran on a "pacifist" ticket, she was not a strict pacifist. Her slogan was: "Prepare to the limit for defense; keep our men out of Europe." She believed in the idea of an American defensive perimeter running from the Aleutian Islands to Labrador by way of the Hawaiian Islands, the Panama Canal, and Maine—in this sense she showed a preference for peace with security that was to be felt by many women in the post-war nuclear age. True to her word, once elected, Rankin fought against Lend-Lease and other interventionist provisions. Then, on December 8, 1941, came her famous—some called it infamous—vote against the war. She was the only legislator to vote thus. She had voted against U.S. entry into the First World War because she felt that doing so was incumbent on her as a woman. She saw her 1940s stance in feminist terms, too: "The *women* elected me because they remembered that I'd been against our entering World War I."[49]

In the seven months following Pearl Harbor, pollsters gathered evidence that confirmed the existence of a gender gap on the war, even after the Japanese attack. Between December 1941 and July 1942, the National Opinion Research Center at the University of Denver conducted eight nationwide polls in which it compared male and female attitudes on war-related matters. In August 1942, the Bureau of Intelligence of the newly established Office of War Information prepared a confidential summary of the findings, called "Women and the War." The findings are of interest because they reflect not elitist and leadership attitudes but general opinion. For the report's compilers, the polls brought to light what they hitherto had not suspected: "On a surprisingly large number of war issues today, women exhibit consistent patterns of opinion which differ from the male half of the population."[50]

Though the government survey suggested no differences between men and women on some issues, it did bring to light dissimilarities in other areas. The women in the polled samples were more inclined than men to detest Japan as compared with Germany. They were also relatively distrustful of Russia.[51]

On the subject of war and peace the women expressed themselves in ways that confirmed some of the suspicions voiced earlier by President Roosevelt and Lord Lothian. Compared with men, they were more realistic about the likely duration of the war, doubting that it would be over in two years. Though only 8 percent of them would have favored peace negotiations with Hitler, that was double the number of men thus inclined. Women were significantly more displeased than men by U.S. nonmembership in the League of Nations—though, perhaps because of disillusionment, they were no more enthusiastic than men about the proposed "Organization of Nations." Notably they were, as the report put it, "less bloodthirsty" than men about the war. Twenty-six percent of women, compared with 20 percent of men, were prepared to accept a merely defensive war against Japan, and women were relatively loath to bomb Japanese cities.[52]

Unaware of the outcome of the government's secret opinion polls, some women pursued their own peace agenda. Although rank-and-file support for the proposed United Nations was less than wholehearted, the idea found strong backing among the female political leadership. High-profile women who had supported the war were particularly likely to support a new international organization. Notably Carrie Catt, though later criticized by the historian Mary Beard for having "intermingled" war talk with her peace ideology, campaigned for the proposed United Nations. Catt's flexibility is indicated in the changing nomenclature of the organization she headed. In 1943 the National Committee on the Cause and Cure of War became the Women's Action Committee for Victory and Lasting Peace. At the war's end Catt dropped the words "Victory and." Her conduct in two world wars marks Catt as a peacetime pacifist who was unwilling to incur the unpopularity that inhered in wartime protest. But if her character was weak, her personality was strong, and her endorsement of the United Nations significant.[53]

Eight women had served in the Seventy-seventh Congress alongside Jeannette Rankin, and none of them supported her solitary protest against the declaration of war—yet, with one exception, all of them joined Rankin in her call for a postwar organization to replace the League of Nations.[54] After the war leading women were to continue their support for the UN. Representative Helen G. Douglas, for example, criticized the Truman administration for acting unilaterally in Greece and Turkey in 1946 instead of proceeding through the UN.[55] The idea of a prestigious international institution appealed to prominent American women with ample personal resources and domestic organizational experience. In 1919–1920 they had been distracted by the franchise campaign and deflected by the Catt-Wilson deal, and had missed an opportunity to press for American membership in the League. In 1945–1946 they suffered from no such impediments and gave their unstinting support to a new instrument for world peace.

Eleanor Roosevelt's support for the United Nations infused vitality into certain key aspects of that organization's work. Her activities also helped to prepare Americans to accept a new internationalism and gave women a visible profile in the shaping of international affairs. As the historian Susan Ware has noted, the role played by personalities in maintaining the standing of women in American public life had become important: The film actress Katharine Hepburn, the aviator Amelia Earhart, and the journalist Dorothy Thompson, for example, helped to inspire a new generation.[56] One need not subscribe to a "great woman theory of history" to accept that Eleanor Roosevelt invested the campaign for the UN with "star" quality. Although her access to power may seem unfair, her influence was real enough and she contributed to public life in ways that Harriet Elliott could only dream of.

Such is the adulation still received by Eleanor Roosevelt that it should be remembered that she had numerous detractors. Within the women's movement of the 1930s, she had been a social reformer and not a supporter of the ERA. Her insistence that "women *are* different from men" alienated some feminists.[57] It could be argued that she was a poor role model for women, in that she acquired her influence through marriage, remained at her husband's side despite his persistent philandering, and passively accepted his adoption of a warlike foreign policy.[58] She was also attacked for the opposite reasons—for being too independent of her husband, for dominating him, for being too left wing, and for being interventionist.[59]

Yet every strong personality attracts criticism, and because her charisma also stemmed from her personality, Eleanor Roosevelt's inspirational qualities remained undiminished. As a young woman she had not at first had much self-belief. But her uncle as well as her husband had served as president of the United States, and that background helped to build her confidence.[60] Her considerable personal attributes included a burning sense of public duty, exceptional vitality, organizational ability, and a human warmth that was visible not only to her wide circle of friends but also to the millions of American men and women who followed her career and read her books and newspaper columns.

In the first part of her husband's presidency, Eleanor Roosevelt was a committed peace worker. She was upset when, at the time of the 1932 election, her husband turned his back on Wilsonian idealism and rejected the idea of American membership of the League of Nations. It will be remembered that she agreed with Senator Nye's indictment of the "merchants of death," and called for government regulation of the armaments industry. This was no superficial commitment: In the spring of 1935 she hosted a reception in the White House to mark the twentieth anniversary of WILPF, and in the fall she chaired a radio discussion on the theme "Women Want Peace." There can be no question that her later support for the war damaged the peace cause, but because so many other women followed her lead, because of her emphatic endorsement of peace before the war, and because Hitler's misdeeds made the war justifiable retroactively, Mrs. Roosevelt was forgiven and was once again able to supply a lead.

The distinctly humanitarian tinge of the first lady's foreign policy motives reflected her domestic concerns. At home she had campaigned successfully for the abolition of child labor. Turning to foreign problems, she lobbied in 1939 for the Jewish Children's Refugee Bill introduced by New York's Democratic senator Robert Wagner and Representative Edith Nourse Rogers—the law would have admitted to the United States twenty thousand children to be cared for by Quaker families. FDR withdrew his support for it under pressure from anti-Semitic critics—but Mrs. Roosevelt had not campaigned in vain, for in drawing attention to the plight of Europe's Jews she had helped to prepare the ground for postwar opinion.[61]

Even if the United States had not entered World War II for humanitarian reasons, these concerns came to fore as the war continued. Gradually the idea gained ground that World War II was a "just war," and when the full horror and scale of the Nazis' genocidal atrocities became known, the idea became firmly entrenched.[62] Just as Eleanor Roosevelt had had a hand in shaping attitudes on human rights before the war began, afterward she was among the first civilians to talk to Holocaust survivors and to tour the concentration camps. In the words of her biographer Blanche Wiesen Cook, her knowledge of the Holocaust created for Mrs. Roosevelt "a sense of urgency for a Declaration of Human Rights."[63]

After President Roosevelt's death in 1945, his successor, Harry Truman, appointed the former first lady to the U.S. delegation to the UN. The other delegates were all men, and men of distinction, but it was the president's widow who commanded the attention of the media. "The first lady of the world" was widely reported in her advocacy of the UN and its aims, and in addition had her own daily newspaper column ("My Day") and radio programs. The male hierarchy tried to restore order by assigning her to chair Committee Three, which had to do with social, humanitarian, and cultural affairs—a "domestic" and unimportant realm considered suitable for a woman. However, Mrs. Roosevelt proved to be disconcertingly effective in charge of Committee Three and as chair, also, of the Human Rights Commission on Refugees, from 1946 to 1952. She often captured the limelight for her own committees' work, and she brokered unlikely agreements between dissenting factions. Notably, when the Russians wanted recognition of citizens' economic and social rights, she essentially agreed with the Russians from her perspective as a social reformer that these were important both in themselves and in the prevention of future wars. However, she was distrustful of Communism, and in a well-publicized confrontation obstructed Soviet attempts to force refugees to return to Eastern European countries where they might be killed and/or mistreated.

Her great achievement was the leadership she provided in the drafting of, and campaign for, the Universal Declaration of Human Rights, adopted by the UN General Assembly on December 10, 1948. She was not entirely in control, however, of the American input into the declaration. For example, the National Woman's Party, the pressure group for an ERA, lobbied the UN to secure a change in the wording of the first article of the declaration: the phrase "all men are created equal" gave way to "all people are created equal."[64] But Mrs. Roosevelt's concerns nevertheless show up in several places in the declaration. Various clauses condemned sexual or other discrimination, asserted the rights of workers to join labor unions, insisted on equal pay for equal work, claimed "the right to leave any country, and to return," and—in a passage that Eleanor Roosevelt must have held dear—stated, "Motherhood and childhood are entitled to special care and assistance. All children, whether born in or out of wedlock, shall enjoy the same social protection."[65]

Eleanor Roosevelt's achievement at the United Nations must be kept in perspective. She was not the first American to be concerned about human rights—for example, there had been a campaign on behalf of czarist prisoners in the Siberian labor camps in the nineteenth century. Nor was she the only American to have a major humanitarian impact on the work of the UN. Policy on the repatriation of refugees, for example, was largely overseen by a charismatic male politician—Fiorello LaGuardia, the former mayor of New York City, had been put in charge of the United Nations Relief and Rehabilitation Administration.[66]

Furthermore, her campaign for human rights suffered setbacks and difficulties. On the election to the presidency of a Republican, General Dwight D. Eisenhower, she had to resign from the UN. The Eisenhower administration distanced itself from human rights issues, which were now denounced as Communistic. In 1954 President Eisenhower played to the McCarthyist gallery by mocking her and observing that the opponents of the UN human rights policy were "trying to save the U.S. from Eleanor Roosevelt."[67]

Undiscouraged, she went to work for the American Association for the United Nations. When John F. Kennedy was elected president in 1960, he realized the advantage of having a Democratic icon at his disposal. He reappointed her to the American delegation to the UN, and persuaded her to preside over his Commission on the Status of Women— on the eve of her death in 1962 Eleanor at last gave up her forty-year opposition to the ERA. But the human rights issue continued to enjoy a checkered history. In the 1960s and 1970s, the United States itself came to be associated with human rights abuses in countries like Vietnam and Chile. President Jimmy Carter pushed for human rights improvements worldwide, in right- as well as left-wing dictatorships. But critics like Henry Kissinger and Jeane Kirkpatrick called for greater realism in foreign policy. Americans continued to debate such questions as whether trade embargoes should be employed to force foreign nations to treat their citizens fairly; in May 1994 President Clinton decided to trade with China in spite of that country's continuing violations of human rights.[68]

Yet Eleanor Roosevelt's achievement is unquestionable. She widened the human rights campaign to include matters of concern to women; she attached it to the first serious attempt at world government, the UN; and she made human rights a major issue in the foreign policy of her own country. Try as he or she may, no future U.S. president is likely to be able to ignore it.

The foregoing tale of two women encapsulates some of the changes in the nature of gender differences over foreign policy in the period from the late 1930s to the late 1940s. A new outlook, which included concern for human rights and distrust of the Soviet Union, replaced the peace-through-free-trade emphasis of the 1920s and 1930s.

The tale makes it clear that, while the rise of women, especially the achievement of the vote, can be broadly equated with the spread of democracy, unelected women would still be able to play a role in the shaping of American foreign policy. At the same time the advent of opinion polling makes it possible to look beyond elite women like Harriet Elliott and Eleanor Roosevelt. A popular gender gap on foreign policy had probably existed all along, but one can point to it with certainty in the years during and after World War II.

The political significance of the gender gap during the war itself was minimal, because the government did not make known the results of its polls. But its historical significance is all the greater: The polls furnish proof that women were not the inveterately price-conscious creatures they were once assumed to be. They indicate that women supported the war, yet in a distinctive manner tended to favor a restrained kind of national defense. In peacetime this was to translate into popular support for a policy of national security with minimal risk.

The Spendthrift Woman. This "decoration" accompanied a 1920 article by Herbert Hoover, in which the future president attacked the irresponsible rich and appealed to the economic and moral instincts of internationally minded women: "If those who wear silk stockings could see the millions of people in Europe who have no stockings at all and indeed no shoes, they would take less satisfaction in the sheen and pattern of their costly hose." (*Ladies Home Journal*, August 1920)

Guardian of the American Pocketbook. This further "decoration" accompanying Hoover's article illustrates two themes: the lingering military image of women after suffrage leader Carrie Catt promised support for the war in exchange for the vote, and the notion that women were in charge of the family budget—with distinctive viewpoints concerning prices and tariffs on imported goods. (*Ladies Home Journal*, August 1920)

Jeannette Rankin: Congresswoman Against War. A Republican from Montana, she was the first woman to serve in the U.S. House of Representatives. In her first term (March 4, 1917–March 3, 1919), she joined a minority in the House and Senate in voting against American entry into World War I. In her second (January 3, 1941–January 3, 1943), she cast the sole vote against entry into World War II. (*Library of Congress and Office of the Historian, U.S. House of Representatives*)

Rebecca Felton: Senator for a Day. While the Democratic party's Georgia politicos fought over who should succeed the deceased Tom Watson in the U.S. Senate, the eighty-seven-year-old Felton was appointed to occupy the seat for one day. An editorial in the *New York Times* (October 5, 1992) rejoiced that "Southern chivalry" had upstaged the National Woman's party, and the press agencies distributed the richly stereotypical image, shown here, of the old lady strumming "old-time melodies" on her guitar instead of "worrying over her duties as U.S. Senator." But the spell had been broken: Men no longer monopolized the senate, and the way was open for women to "advise and consent" on foreign policy. (*Library of Congress*)

Dorothy Detzer, Lobbyist. Dorothy Detzer served as national executive secretary of the Women's International League for Peace and Freedom, 1924–
1946. She was the foremost woman lobbyist on Capitol Hill in the interwar
years, and was instrumental in setting up the mid-1930s Senate investigation of the arms industry chaired by Gerald P. Nye of North Dakota. The
investigation helped to keep the United States neutral in the 1930s, and
was a controversial episode in the history of American anti-militarism.
(*Photo by Peggy Duffy, courtesy of Swarthmore College Peace Collection,
Swarthmore, Pa.*)

DOUGLAS-MARCANTONIO VOTING RECORD

Many persons have requested a comparison of the voting records of Congresswoman Helen Douglas and the notorious Communist party-liner, Congressman Vito Marcantonio of New York.

Mrs. Douglas and Marcantonio have been members of Congress together since January 1, 1945. During that period, Mrs. Douglas voted the same as Marcantonio 354 times. While it should not be expected that a member of the House of Representatives should always vote in opposition to Marcantonio, it is significant to note, not only the great number of times which Mrs. Douglas voted in agreement with him, but also the issues on which almost without exception they always saw eye to eye, to-wit: Un-American Activities and Internal Security.

Here is the Record!

VOTES AGAINST COMMITTEE ON UN-AMERICAN ACTIVITIES

Both Douglas and Marcantonio voted against establishing the Committee on Un-American Activities. 1/3/45. Bill passed.

Both voted on three separate occasions against contempt proceedings against persons and organizations which refused to reveal records or answer whether they were Communists. 4/16/46, 6/26/46, 11/24/47. Bills passed.

Both voted on four separate occasions against allowing funds for investigation by the Un-American Activities Committee. 5/17/46, 3/9/48, 2/9/49, 3/23/50. (The last vote was 348 to 12.) All bills passed.

COMMUNIST-LINE FOREIGN POLICY VOTES

Both voted against Greek-Turkish Aid Bill. 5/9/47. (It has been established that without this aid Greece and Turkey would long since have gone behind the Iron Curtain.) Bill passed.

Both voted on two occasions against free press amendment to UNRRA appropriation bill, providing that no funds should be furnished any country which refused to allow free access to the news of activities of the UNRRA by press and radio representatives of the United States. 11/1/45, 6/28/46. Bills passed. (This would in effect have denied American relief funds to Communist dominated countries.)

Both voted against refusing Foreign Relief to Soviet-dominated countries UNLESS supervised by Americans. 4/30/47. Bill passed 324 to 75.

VOTE AGAINST NATIONAL DEFENSE

Both voted against the Selective Service Act of 1948. 6/18/48. Bill passed.

VOTES AGAINST LOYALTY AND SECURITY LEGISLATION

Both voted on two separate occasions against bills requiring loyalty checks for Federal employees. 7/15/47, 6/29/49. Bills passed.

Both voted against the Subversive Activities Control Act of 1948, requiring registration with the Attorney General of Communist party members and communist controlled organizations. Bill passed, 319 to 58. 5/19/48. AND AFTER KOREA both again voted against it. Bill passed 8/29/50, 354 to 20.

AFTER KOREA, on July 12, 1950, Marcantonio and Douglas and 12 others voted against the Security Bill, to permit the heads of key National Defense departments, such as the Atomic Energy Commission, to discharge government workers found to be poor security risks! Bill passed, 327 to 14.

VOTE AGAINST CALIFORNIA

Both recorded against confirming title to Tidelands in California and the other states affected. 4/30/48. Bill passed 257-29.

VOTES AGAINST CONGRESSIONAL INVESTIGATION OF COMMUNIST AND OTHER ILLEGAL ACTIVITIES

Both voted against investigating the "whitewash" of the AMERASIA case. 4/18/46. Bill passed.

Both voted against investigating why the Soviet Union was buying as many as 60,000 United States patents at one time. 3/4/47. Bill passed.

Both voted against continuing investigation of numerous instances of illegal actions by OPA and the War Labor Board. 1/18/45. Bill passed.

Both voted on two occasions against allowing Congress to have access to government records necessary to the conduct of investigations by Senate and House Committees. 4/22/48, 5/13/48. Bills passed.

NIXON FOR U. S. SENATOR CAMPAIGN COMMITTEE

The Douglas-Nixon Pink Sheet (excerpt). An infamous ingredient in Congressman Richard M. Nixon's 1950 Senate campaign against Helen Gahagan Douglas, this smear was suggestively printed on pink paper and was a factor in ending the career of an able Capitol Hill woman: Helen Douglas's areas of special interest included foreign policy. (*Regional Oral History Office, Bancroft Library, University of California, Berkeley*)

Margaret Chase Smith Commands Respect. In January 1962, Senator Smith shook hands with John McCone, director of the CIA, across Senator Leverett Saltonshall, chairman of the Armed Services Committee. These men had to take her seriously, but was this because she had conformed to male norms and become indistinguishable from the men in the U.S. Senate? (*Northwood University Margaret Chase Smith Archives, Skowhegan, Maine*)

Smith in Splendid Isolation. The senator was surrounded by men during the Test Ban hearing on August 12, 1963—she insisted on the establishment of a subcommittee on safeguards to monitor Soviet compliance, and became the senior Republican on the Senate Armed Services Committee. (Note Secretary of State Dean Rusk to the right.) (*Northwood University Margaret Chase Smith Archives, Skowhegan, Maine*)

The Iron Lady: Margaret Thatcher. The Soviet news agency TASS dubbed her the "Iron Lady." The phrase caught on and was applied in several nations to women who fought their way to the top in the male world. But Thatcher's warmongering reputation arose from gender prejudice. She was among the more peaceful prime ministers in British history. (*Courtesy of Margaret Thatcher*)

Bella Abzug: Foreign Policy Feminist. A Democrat from New York City, Abzug served in the House of Representatives from January 3, 1971 to January 3, 1977. She took a lead in legitimizing opposition to the Vietnam War, and in the 1980s played a major role in shaping the politics of the gender gap, demanding an end to the arms race and better relations with Moscow. (*Courtesy of Bella S. Abzug*)

7 | MARGARET CHASE SMITH AND THE FEMALE QUEST FOR SECURITY

Margaret Chase Smith was the first woman to gain a powerful position in America's foreign policy hierarchy. She was Maine's first congresswoman and then served four terms in the Senate, where she was minority leader on the Armed Services Committee. Her support for a strong defensive shield based on atomic weaponry gave her a hawkish reputation. When the Soviet leader Nikita Khrushchev attacked her in September 1961 as "the devil in the disguise of a woman," he seemed to imply that in being so tough, she was not a real woman at all. Smith's own position on feminism was ambivalent. She campaigned for women's rights in the armed forces and took pride in her acknowledged status as one of the best-dressed women in the public eye; however, she rejected the significance of gender in politics.[1]

Smith could therefore plausibly be portrayed as a woman typifying "breakthrough syndrome." Though she was a person of strong character, she was generally, like "Silent Hattie" Caraway before her, one of the quieter members of the Senate. She could be seen as "dancing backward" to please men and to gain acceptance among them. Undoubtedly she was under pressure to conform to the masculine Cold War stereotype. One student of the Cold War has observed that World War II had been a "boon to American masculinity." Soon Hollywood was to draw "an explicit connection between sexually liberated women and the Communist menace," and the Red-baiting FBI director J. Edgar Hoover stored information on Eleanor Roosevelt in his "Sex Deviate File."[2] When Smith ran for her Senate seat in 1948, her opponents had smeared her with Red-baiting tactics and tried to taint her character with sexual innuendo. To a certain extent Smith could be said to have beaten her conservative critics by joining them.

Yet the story is by no means as simple as that. At one point Senator

Smith made a famous stand against the activities of Senator Joseph R. McCarthy. Additionally Smith has to be regarded in the context of what women in general thought about foreign policy in the 1950s. In fact her thinking appears to have been in tune with theirs. She did not have to distance herself from those of her gender in order to advance her political career. She seems to have been representative of female opinion both in her emphasis on national security and her opposition to "hot" wars involving ground fighting. In her way she was a peace-seeking stateswoman, her chosen means being nuclear deterrence combined with military restraint. When she departed from her peaceful ways to support the Vietnam War (out of loyalty to U.S. soldiers on the battlefield, and against her better judgment), she ran afoul of her own gender and lost the Senate seat she had held for so long with distinction. Margaret Chase Smith needs to be considered not just as a lone, powerful woman but as an indicator of other women's views and influence on foreign policy—in both the hour of her success and the moment of her defeat.

Like approximately one-fourth of the women to enter the House of Representatives by 1991, Margaret Chase Smith originally filled a congressional seat left vacant by the death of her husband.[3] Her political career stemmed from her association with and marriage to Clyde Smith—and so did her political problems. In the 1948 senatorial contest her opponents used an obscure woman, Cora E. Edgerly, to smear Margaret Chase Smith sexually. Edgerly complained in a privately circulated leaflet that Smith had "slipped into Congress [in 1940] on the coat-tails of her dead husband" and more pointedly declared that she did not "like the way she got her husband" in the first place.[4] The reference here was to the rumor, still circulating in her native Skowhegan in the 1990s, that Margaret Chase discovered that Clyde Smith was having an affair and threatened to expose him and ruin him politically unless he divorced his wife and married her instead. Later rumormongers put out the story that Senator Smith was herself having an affair with her personal assistant, Bill Lewis. But the politically hurtful allegation was that she had entered Congress only through sexual guile.[5]

The smearing of Margaret Chase Smith took place at a sensitive time. Until the 1948 campaign, no woman had been elected to the Senate in her own right.[6] That year's election thus promised a major political breakthrough for American women. As Smith attempted to reassure the voters that it would be safe to elect a woman who had stepped outside the male shadow, it was tempting for her to cling to safe political norms. Accusations of moral deviation only increased the temptation to be straitlaced—politically as well as personally. The accusations against her thus may help to explain Smith's Cold War orthodoxy as well as her rejection of overt feminism.

Margaret Smith was potentially vulnerable to sexual innuendo, but only in consequence of her husband's activities many years ago. Though Clyde Smith had been an effective legislator with a strong social conscience, he had as a young politican been attracted to high school girls who two-timed him and generally gave him difficulties.[7] Margaret Chase perhaps fanned speculation in being twenty-one years his junior; he revealed his own consciousness of the age difference when he referred to her in private correspondence as his "dearest little girl."[8] However, the idea that she exploited him sexually is unsound. As the Smith camp pointed out in a chronology prepared in 1948, Clyde Smith's first wife started divorce proceedings in 1913, but the Chase-Smith marriage did not take place until 1930—an improbably long time for blackmail to take effect.[9] The sexual smears aimed at Margaret Chase Smith were politically motivated and had as their purpose the aggravation of an anticipated "sexist" prejudice among voters—that women could only succeed in public life by exploiting their sexuality. The smears reflected not her own activities but those of her late husband, who, profiting from ethical double standards, had combined a not-unblemished personal life with a rewarding political career—a luxury well beyond the grasp of America's emergent political women.

Though innocent of the charges leveled against her, Margaret Chase Smith's reaction to them was a partial retreat into an asexual fortress. She avoided remarriage as well as any appearence of romantic involvement, let alone sexual impropriety. The retreat from sexuality could be construed as a personal response to bigoted criticism, but it could also be regarded as a conscious political tactic. She was later to recall: "I would not have been elected as 'a woman candidate' in 1940. And I knew that. As a woman candidate I would not have won in the Second District, a labor district."[10] Smith remained firm to the end of her life in her denials of gender politics—"I definitely resent being called a feminist."[11]

However, despite her later denials of feminism, Smith's early interests in Congress reflected her viewpoint as a woman. It was this differentiated viewpoint that led her indirectly into her main area of long-term concern, defense policy. Smith was assigned to the Invalid Pensions and War Claims Committee in 1940, and to the Naval Affairs Committee in 1943, a year in which Americans also saw Clare Boothe Luce named to Military Affairs. Smith's interest in defense policy sprang in part from nongendered circumstances, reflecting the presence in Maine of the Kittery-Portsmouth naval shipyard, one of the state's most important sources of wealth and employment. Her defense may also have sprung from the fact that Maine, in the words of one historian, "juts hundreds of miles toward Europe as if to meet an incoming armada."[12] According to Smith, "America must keep up its defenses, and especially in a state like Maine."[13] There can be little doubt, however, that Smith's original involvement sprang to a marked degree from her concern for women:

> At the beginning of the war we were unprepared. I visited Norfolk, Virginia, at a time the fleet came in. The situation there was deplorable. Wives and girlfriends would flock to the town to be with their men. There were no places for them to go, nowhere to stay. Girls couldn't find their own men because no information was supplied; it was just confusion. So they started to go off with other men. The authorities there responded badly—they even sent some girls to jail. I demanded better treatment and shocked them on the Navy committee, of which I was member, as a woman who made these points.

To deal with the problems, Naval Affairs Committee chairman Carl Vinson appointed a Congested Areas Subcommittee and persuaded Secretary of the Navy James V. Forrestal to arrange for hearings and a report. President Roosevelt commended the report and initiated an effective program to deal with prostitution, schooling, housing, and cleaning, "even sidewalks." Half a century later, ex-Senator Smith still spoke with animated pride about her successful efforts to clean up America's naval bases.[14]

The newspapers poked fun at Smith, calling her the "Vice Admiral."[15] But she continued to press the case for women during and after the war, when she became a member of the House Armed Services Committee. With Representative Frances Bolton, she now pressed for regular status for women in the military. By August 1947, according to a Gallup poll, a majority of both sexes favored women's participation in the peacetime armed services. Nevertheless there was fierce resistance to the proposed change, as there would be in the following year to President Truman's executive order prohibiting discrimination against blacks in the armed forces. Confronted with predictions that high numbers of women would have to be released because of "menopausal symptoms," the navy's surgeon general attacked the idea as a "popular fallacy" and said it was "well known that men pass through the same physiological change with symptomatology closely resembling that of women." With the assistance of such testimony, the Smith-Bolton campaign produced the Women's Armed Services Act, signed by President Truman in July 1948; according to a student of Smith's efforts, it was she who "tipped the balance" in Congress in its favor.[16]

Between 1940 and 1948, then, Smith became a noted advocate of women's rights in the defense field. By her own account she was a "moderate" politically, but had "always been considered a great liberal,"[17] particularly by her critics: "When people thought of me as a foreign policy liberal, they were thinking of my wartime record, of my support for the destroyer-bases deal and Lend-Lease, and of my vote for the Marshall Plan—though I would have preferred a plan for European recovery that was less of a giveaway."[18]

The "liberal" label did have some credibility. To be sure, she could not match the record of her late husband, who according to the *Lewiston Journal* sponsored "practically all the labor measures" considered by the Maine legislature in the 1920s.[19] A convention of Maine's CIO and Railroad Brotherhoods refused to endorse her in the elections of 1944.[20] But Smith did believe that FDR's New Deal policies had been responsible for rescuing the United States from the effects of the 1930s depression.[21] In a consistent vein, she accepted the invitation of Secretary of Labor Frances Perkins to represent Congress at the International Labor Organization (ILO) debate in connection with the establishment of the UN. Furthermore, she voted against freezing social security taxes, and against legislation that would have punished absenteeism from war work.[22]

She also voted against the Smith-Connally Bill, enacted over President Roosevelt's veto on June 25, 1943. The law, which banned strikes in government-operated plants, imposed a thirty-day-cooling-off spell before any strike could be called and forbade political donations by labor unions in the course of national elections. Smith's vote against this first antilabor measure in a generation induced one of her rare disagreements with William C. Lewis Jr. Lewis was already an important figure in Smith's life, whom she had met when he was assigned, as a young naval officer, to the committee investigating wartime naval bases. He had written the committee's report in a way that impressed Smith. From 1948 until his heart attack in 1971, he was Smith's political adviser. In contrast to Smith, who came from a humble family and had not completed college, Lewis was independently wealthy and had gained a master's degree in public relations from Harvard University. He was, in addition, politically shrewd. Smith and the conservative Lewis were rarely to diverge on policy matters, but the occasion of Smith-Connally was an exception, and she declared that Lewis was "quite shocked when I voted the way I did."[23]

It is understandable that right-wingers later looked at Smith's pre-1948 record and used it to calumniate her as a "liberal." Smith was correct in distinguishing between her reputation for liberalism and her real political beliefs, but that liberal reputation was sufficiently discernible to be a potential embarrassment in the 1948 election year. The race turned into what the *Portland Press Herald* termed "the most bitterly contested senatorial election in years," and for that reason it produced a change in Smith's political stance.[24]

Because of Maine's traditionally safe Republican majorities, the only real hurdle for Smith was the primary. She was up against two serious opponents, the incumbent Governor, Horace Hildreth, and a former governor, Sumner Sewell. Their campaigns were well financed, whereas, largely because of her own scruples, her funds were modest.[25] It was in the primary campaign that her unofficial opponents circulated leaflets containing sexual smears. But she also had to contend with a different kind of smear: On two occasions opponents used the direct-mail technique to charge that she was a Red sympathizer. The *Bangor Daily News* publicised the first list of charges, circulated anonymously. It ran to three pages and complained, for example, that Smith "opposed machinery for Congressional investigation of un-Americanism."[26]

The initiator of the second mailing was Dorothy Sabin Winslow, a Portland businesswoman who had responded to Hildreth's request for help. She addressed the "great many women, especially club groups," who were supporting Smith "primarily because she is a woman." She claimed that an analysis of 242 House votes by Smith showed that she had voted the same way as New York's congressman Vito Marcantonio on 107 occasions. Marcantonio had in the 1930s sponsored the long-running antiwar amendment proposed by the Women's Peace Union and supported in the Senate by Lynn Frazier; Marcantonio was perhaps the major left-wing figure on Capitol Hill. Dorothy Winslow tried to contaminate Smith by associating her with Marcantonio and further said that, unlike other Representatives from Maine, Smith voted consistently for "CIO measures." Thus she voted "contrary to a majority of the Republicans 30% of the time."[27]

Within a short space Smith had been depicted as a scarlet woman and as a Red politician. But she won the primary decisively and in the ensuing contest gained a record majority over her Democratic opponent. She succeeded for several reasons. One factor that assisted her was the political skill of Bill Lewis, who chose his moment well in issuing an authoritative disclaimer on Smith's voting record—when a complete instead of selective analysis was made of her more than fifteen hundred votes, she turned out to have been a Republican loyalist, voting with her party more than 95 percent of the time.[28] In issuing this disclaimer Smith's supporters repeated a time-honored appeal to the sentiment that the American left was illegitimate—Carrie Catt had similarly disowned socialist support in 1917, in spite of the left's pioneering work on behalf of votes for women, and the "Pink Sisters" smears of the 1920s had occasioned a further ideological retreat.[29] The disclaimer tactic had the effect of broadening the immediate opportunities available to women but threatened to limit their capacity for challenging political morés.

Smith further benefited from the fact that Maine had a feminist tradition. Maud May Wood Park, the first president of the LWV, lived in the state. By the 1930s there were seven women in the Maine legislature. In this context it may be noted that Smith enjoyed the support of Guy P. Gannett, who in 1919 had introduced the suffrage proposal to the Maine state senate—and who controlled four radio stations as well as the state's newspapers, with the single important exception of the *Bangor Daily News.*[30]

Smith played on this background in the political debate. Her appeal to women was one of two notable features in her rhetoric. In spite of her later denials, she referred to certain feminist issues. Perhaps she believed that the state of Maine as a whole, given its feminist tradition, was less male dominated than the lumber-oriented Second District; perhaps she played on the sympathies of those women who were already inclined to rally to her side because of the inherently unfair nature of the sexual smear campaign against her. Tactically it made sense to appeal to women and then to deny that this was her tactic in order to maximize her vote amongst men and nonfeminist women.

Smith had an instinct for those foreign policy issues that would appeal to women. Responding to a questionnaire from the Gannett papers just before the June primary, she said she supported the United Nations, opposed isolationism, and favored "the progressive reduction of trade barriers." She supported the Marshall Plan for the economic reconstruction of Europe as a means toward securing "a peaceful world."[31] The Smith campaign targeted several categories of women— for example, businesswomen and farmers' wives—and played on gender pride. For example, one campaign postcard contained the following exhortation: "The Opposition Says That Margaret Chase Smith Must Be Defeated Because She Is A Woman. ANSWER THIS CHALLENGE."[32] Commenting on her "stunning victory," the *Washington Post* downplayed the importance of gender, noting that Smith was "no ordinary feminist." But Smith had touched on some internationalist issues dear to the hearts of prewar feminists, and in her moment of elation she chose to portray the victory as "having significance to thousands of women" in the United States.[33]

Because Maine's Senate race took place early, in September, the newly elected Smith invited comment and was in demand as a speaker on behalf of the Dewey-Warren Republican presidential ticket. She appealed to women in a national radio broadcast, declaring "there are really two basic issues in the campaign—high prices and foreign policy."[34] Smith still—and understandably in light of the Truman administration's problems with inflation and the Soviet Union—cleaved to prewar feminist priorities. At the same time she revealed, in an interview with the *Christian Science Monitor*'s Helen Henley, a viewpoint to which she was in future to adhere with ever-increasing tenacity. "Women are people," she declared. There had been no such thing as a "women's bloc" in either the June or the September elections. She had not, she claimed, appealed to the "woman's vote."[35]

But a second notable feature of Smith's line of argument was her hardening Cold War stance. In her primary literature she gave pride of place to her role as "an active leader not only in the support of National Defense measures but also in the actual formulation of national defense policy."[36] She stressed the need to rearm, to assist non-Communist countries in Europe, and to beware of "Russian trickery."[37] In the November campaign she declared herself "confident that the American people want no more repetition of the past two years during which Russia has fully capitalized on our division at home—and on the 'politics playing' blunders in our foreign policy."[38]

Margaret Chase Smith had joined the Cold Warriors early and was never to deviate from her stance. Undoubtedly this—like her disavowal of Marcantonio—owed more than a little to the political pressures of the 1948 campaign, and to the ensuing Red-baiting orgy known as McCarthyism. Yet one feature of her 1948 rhetoric invites particular attention, and lends credence to her own claim that she was a "moderate." She said she believed in "a firm foreign policy that neither offends nor appeases, but a foreign policy backed up by necessary military strength."[39] The phrase "neither offends nor pleases" indicates her desire for a balance: She wanted to combine strength and security with restraint.

If the election of 1948 helped to shape Smith's outlook, the growth of anti-Red hysteria in 1950 confirmed her in her stance. That January former State Department official Alger Hiss was convicted on charges relating to his alleged spying activities on behalf of the Soviet Union. In the late 1940s careers could be built on the wings of anti-Communism. The ambitious young Representative Richard M. Nixon had insisted that charges be pressed; Hiss was subjected to an unfair trial in a courtroom supercharged with hate; and the whole episode increased nationwide hysteria over the "Communist menace" within the United States. Then, on February 9, 1950, Senator Joseph R. McCarthy stated in an ill-researched but sensationally reported speech in Wheeling, West Virginia, that the State Department was infested with Communists who were guiding U.S. foreign policy. The "great fear," or McCarthyism, had begun.

On June 1, 1950, Margaret Chase Smith rose to her feet in the Senate and spoke for fifteen minutes. She delivered a plain-speaking attack on the Red-baiting hysteria that seemed to be carrying all before it. Though still a freshman senator, she became the first Republican of any standing to have the courage and the conviction to confront the senator from Wisconsin. She persuaded six of her fellow Republican senators to join her in signing a "Declaration of Conscience." It concluded with the words:

> It is high time that we stopped thinking politically as Republicans and Democrats about elections and started thinking patriotically as Americans about national security based on individual freedom. It is high time that we all stopped being tools and victims of totalitarian techniques—techniques that, if continued here unchecked, will surely end what we have come to cherish as the American way of life.[40]

Smith's speech won great respect both for its content and for the courage she demonstrated in making it. For in her insistence on high principle she had risked her political career; when she survived the counterattacks of her enemies, her place in American political iconography was assured.[41]

But her speech nonetheless failed to stanch the welling fear of Communism, a fear swollen by events in Asia. On June 25, 1950, Communist North Korea attacked neighboring South Korea. Fighting under the UN flag, American soldiers helped to fight off the totalitarian aggressors. But at home there were populist suspicions that Communist sympathies in the Truman administration were weakening the U.S. foreign policy stance, tempting the Soviet Union to expand, and leading to the needless deaths of thousands of America's finest young men. That these suspicions were all too easily transferable into electoral politics became evident in the course of the Nixon-Douglas Senate race in California.

The notorious Nixon-Douglas contest confirmed the dangerous impact of smear campaigns on women attempting to break through in politics. It also halted the career of a woman with a strong interest in foreign policy, who might arguably have had a considerable impact but for the use of McCarthyist tactics against her.[42] Helen Gahagan Douglas brought useful personal attributes into the political arena when she was elected to Congress from California's Fourteenth District, bordering on Hollywood, in 1944. Her career as a Broadway actress, international opera singer, and film star had not been startlingly successful and was on the wane, but it gave her confidence, glamour, and contacts that led to her friendship with Eleanor Roosevelt and admission to the charmed inner circle of the New Deal. A champion of the dispossessed, she had a strong appeal in the underpriveleged Fourteenth District. In the 1930s she had been an early critic of Austro-German anti-Semitism, and canceled an operatic tour in protest of the treatment of Jews.[43]

Once elected to Congress, Douglas took issue with Truman's aid to Greece and Turkey in 1946. She believed that it was wrong to bypass the UN in order to assist regimes that were not democratic in the first place: "Terrorism from the extreme right is as oppressive as terrorism from the extreme left. In our opposition to communism, we must not make the mistake of backing remnants of corrupt and decaying systems."[44] The following year Douglas was critical of the Truman Doctrine for the same reason. Later still, though she claimed to be one of the authors of the Marshall Plan, she thought it should have been presented as a purely economic program, and not "as an anti-Communist measure."[45] Although her criticisms prefigured later correctives to U.S. foreign policy—Presidents Carter and Bush tried to encourage democracy evenhandedly—her stance made her vulnerable to two charges in the McCarthyist era. She could be portrayed as a Democrat who was disloyal to her own party's foreign policy, and she could be smeared as a Red. The ever-ambitious Nixon used both tactics against her in the 1950 California senatorial campaign. Nixon's Republicans issued a "pink sheet," reminiscent of the anti-Smith leaflets two years earlier, that once again compared a candidate's voting record with that of Vito Marcantonio. Nixon volunteers meanwhile inundated the state with penny postcards reading, "Vote for our Helen for Senator," and signed, "Communist League of Negro Women." This time the atmosphere was more poisoned, and the smear tactic appeared to work. Nixon was elected to the Senate with a resounding majority.[46]

The contest left its mark on foreign policy in various ways. In the long term it made Nixon the bête noire of the American liberal left, which eventually took its revenge on him in the early 1970s, punishing him for his Watergate transgressions and curtailing his foreign policy powers. In the shorter term it seemed to confirm the message of the 1948 campaign—women stepped out of line at their own peril. As if the message were not plain enough for Smith in the nation at large, Maine's Guy Gannett press turned against her in the wake of her "Conscience" speech. In February 1950 the *Portland Press Herald* had lavished praise on her as one of the few Republicans likely to save America from "creeping Socialism" and the Fair Dealers. But the paper could not forgive Smith for tampering with McCarthyism, the Republicans' special weapon in the forthcoming presidential campaign. In 1951 the *Herald* protested that Mainers were not "moderate" like Smith, and the state's Republicans were "in no mood for temporizing with the foe."[47]

In response Smith went to some lengths to show that she really did detest the Communists. In October 1951 she told a constituent that the United States should either use its "full atomic strength" to win the Korean War and get the boys home, or simply "pull out" to "stop this endless killing."[48] Her appetite for nuclear warfare seemed to increase as the war continued. In August 1953 she speculated, "Maybe the atomic bomb will bring the Red barbarians to their senses as it did the Japanese."[49] On the domestic front, too, Smith took care to exhibit her anti-Communist credentials. With the blessing of President Eisenhower, she cosponsored a bill to deprive Communist "conspirators" of citizenship. The journalist I. F. Stone noted that the bill "represents the betrayal of American democracy by the respectables." Smith and her allies, he believed, "seek to ensure their own political future by outdoing McCarthy."[50]

It was at this point, in the early weeks of 1954, that there occurred the infamous Senate vote on a $214,000 appropriation for McCarthy's permanent investigative subcommittee. Only J. William Fulbright voted against the measure. Smith was, in the words of one historian, who singled her out as one of the "resolute" and "popular" members of the Senate, "among those who did not find it possible to join" the senator from Arkansas.[51] Her response invites comment, especially when one considers that later in the same year she was to break a world tour with the single object of voting for the Senate motion of censure against McCarthy. It is possible that by early 1954 Smith wanted to distance herself from anti-McCarthyism in order that she might diversify, and that she had too much ambition to rest on her laurels solely as the woman who had stood up to McCarthy.[52] Again, she herself later made a distinction: "If McCarthy had done his job properly and focused on Communist sympathizers like Hiss, he would have rendered a real service to his country. . . . I voted for the appropriation because I believed in the principle of investigation. I did not consider the vote to be a vote for McCarthy, the man."[53] Smith did later condone what she considered to be proper investigations, for example of the affiliations of WILPF and of Dorothy Detzer.[54] Whether or not this was consistent with her earlier "moderate" positions, her mid-1950s image was certainly that of an ardent Cold Warrior.

Smith's support for well-armed opposition to international Communism was in part a political shield. In qualification of this interpretation of her political outlook, it must be conceded that she was fairly conservative to begin with, especially compared with, for example, her husband Clyde, or Helen Douglas. Again, her rejection of feminism was to be more marked in her later career, when she fell out with the peace feminists and especially those women who protested against the Vietnam War. In her own way, moreover, Smith continued to advocate the rights of women regardless of the events of 1948 and 1950. Furthermore, in the years of her political maturity Smith would not be nearly so bloodthirsty a Cold Warrior as her words on Korea imply. Yet, in spite of these qualifications, it seems reasonable to suppose that the sexual and anti-Communist smears directed against her at a formative time took their toll. Smith was a major American example of a successful female politician who suffered from what one might call acute breakthrough syndrome.

S mith's advance within the Senate hierarchy was explicitly linked to her distance from gender identity, and to her willingness to adhere to prevailing political norms. Carl Vinson, chairman of the House Committee on Naval Affairs, had always been appreciative of her help in his efforts to build "the greatest navy in history."[55] After her election in 1948 he wrote to Chan Gurney, chairman of the Senate Armed Services Committee, urging Smith's appointment as a member. He recalled that when "she was being considered for appointment to the House Naval Affairs Committee in 1943 there were some who felt that a woman should not be on the committee," but that her effective work since then had vindicated his choice. "While Mrs. Smith retains her charming femininity in a manner that commands the highest respect, she never insists upon feminine prerogatives and privileges. She is an exceptional woman—but she is an extremely effective champion of National Security before she is a woman."[56]

National security stalwarts in the Senate soon took to Smith. As early as September 1949, Arthur H. Vandenberg, the architect of a firm bipartisan defense posture, referred to her as one of the "old dependables" in the matter of arms appropriations.[57] The rules of seniority dictated that Smith received no major committee appointments until 1953, when in one fell swoop she found herself on the committees on Appropriations, Government Operations—and Armed Services.[58] But by this time she was known to be a reliable supporter of the arms lobby.

In her years of political maturity as a U.S. senator, Smith supported the development of the nuclear deterrent—a policy that did not immediately endanger the lives of American young men and that appealed to a wide female constituency. For polling evidence indicates that although modern American women have been significantly less likely than men to approve of "hot wars," or actual fighting, they have been keen to support military spending for deterrent purposes.[59]

If Smith was a hawk, she was a quiet one. She was proud of her attendance record in the Senate, where for several years she never missed a roll call. But she rarely spoke. She even took a special interest in America's "silent service," the CIA, becoming in due course a quietly supportive member of the subcommittee that oversaw, or, more accurately, rubber-stamped, the activities of the American intelligence community.[60] Saying that she was quiet is by no means the same as saying that she was inactive in important policy discussions. Indeed she was a conscientious committee member who was unafraid of new challenges, for example those presented by her membership of the Aeronautical and Space Sciences Committee from 1959 to 1972 (while she also continued to be active on the Appropriations and Armed Services Committees). Yet the impression is conveyed of a politician whose earlier, bruising encounters had led her to speak both infrequently and with circumspection.

This impression is strengthened by a consideration of what must have been her sense of isolation in a male world. As the only woman in the Senate, Smith suffered the expectations, the prejudices, and—in what was a strain as well as a matter of pride—the constant scrutiny of large numbers of people. Smith had to be the personification of rectitude. That she never remarried in spite of her pleasing appearance and personality may have reflected her fear of such gossip as would have attended a public woman's courtship—she could not feel the same immunity from press scrutiny that had protected her husband's career and would attend the philanderings of President John F. Kennedy. The photographs showing Smith at work among Senate colleagues and staff depict an island of female impeccability in a sea of males.

Informal accounts of Smith's political life convey the quality of her isolation. Lady Bird Johnson recalled the evening of January 16, 1964, when she and Lyndon Johnson entertained sixty-four guests at an early dinner, so that the president could inform congressional leaders of the administration's budget plans:

> As soon as we had all filed into the Blue Room and shaken hands, Lyndon announced that he would like the gentlemen to accompany him to the little theater where there would be a briefing. I asked the others to go upstairs—perhaps some of them might like to see the second floor, the family living quarters. So we all trooped up, except for Senator Margaret Chase Smith, who went with the gentlemen.[61]

Clearly the tensions implicit in this kind of episode must have recurred time and time again. It was a strain being the only woman senator, as Smith was for most of the time between 1949 and 1973.[62] To be sure, it gave one "star" quality, which Smith enjoyed up to a point, but not to the extent that Britain's Margaret Thatcher did in later years. The presence of more women in the Senate would have been a source of comfort and support, and Smith apparently felt the need for reassurance. Perhaps still resentful from the days when the ambitious young Margaret Chase ran away from household chores, her mother had been economical with praise for her political achievements. Smith remembered that at a White House dinner on the occasion of her swearing in as a senator, her mother irritably told a guest who had been singing her praises: "You know I have other children."[63] Her feeling of isolation must have been deep seated.

Given these pressures, Smith retreated into her self-imposed prison of military orthodoxy. Yet, in the late 1950s and early 1960s, events occurred that gave her an opportunity to modify her stance. One of these was the first stirring of what later came to be known as the "new feminism," a force that might conceivably have supplied the lone senator with moral backing. A second event was the revival of the women's peace movement. WILPF was no longer the force it had been before the war, but it could derive encouragement and support from the activities of other people, of both sexes, in the numerous branches of a burgeoning peace movement, as well as from the evident if frustrated desire of President Dwight D. Eisenhower to effect some kind of demilitarization.

The women who supported WILPF had similar objectives to those who supported the nuclear deterrent—they wanted security for themselves and their families—but they advocated new arrangements for the achievement of that security. In 1956 WILPF urged the cancellation of the forthcoming series of American nuclear tests in the Pacific.[64] By the early 1960s many women were concerned about the contaminating effects of nuclear tests. Under the leadership of Dagmar Wilson, a book illustrator whose political inexperience only added zest to her charisma, a new group, the Women's Strike for Peace (WSP), put pressure on the White House to conclude a nuclear test ban treaty with the Soviet Union. By this time John F. Kennedy was president. Whatever historians have written since, Kennedy at the time had a liberal reputation and seemed prepared to listen. The bad old days of McCarthyism seemed well and truly in the past, and the way was open for Smith to adapt her posture.

But Smith did not move with the times, and resisted the proposed nuclear test ban treaty. This was in part because she distrusted Kennedy. Soon after the Bay of Pigs episode, she told a gathering of students in Missouri:

Our international position reached an all-time low with the Cuban débacle.

Today just ninety miles from the shores of our country—a small country that we gave freedom to is now a Communist nation that may soon be an arsenal of missiles and weapons for Khrushchev to aim at us or to use for international blackmail against us.[65]

In the same speech she complained that Kennedy was giving up in Laos. Such was the force of her continuing exhortations to Kennedy to stand firm against Soviet imperialism that Khrushchev denounced her and his wife complained in a letter to a member of the WSP that she was a "warmonger."[66] Smith basked in this vilification. The following year she rebuked 175 university professors who had appealed to Kennedy not to escalate the arms race:

In substance, these critics contend that the Soviets are bad because *we* make them bad. Hence, if we reduce *our* military strength, their attitude will improve, and they will become more tractable.
—Do these good and sincere people who are so critical really believe that we would be better off *without* a margin of military advantage across the board?[67]

According to Smith's assistant Bill Lewis, the senator felt fully vindicated when the Cuban missile crisis developed: Kennedy's firmness on this occasion was admirable, but, had it been in evidence in the first place, the Russians would have been deterred and the crisis need never have taken place.[68]

Smith was one of a smallish group of nineteen senators who voted against the nuclear test ban treaty on September 24, 1963. She described her ballot as "one of the most difficult votes [she] had ever cast as a United States Senator."[69] Yet she had consistently fought against the treaty, filing numerous queries. She skeptically asked, for example, to what precise degree atmospheric testing caused "genetic damage and leukemia to the living and as yet unborn."[70] She was also determined to retain the sting in America's deterrent. Secretary of Defense Robert S. McNamara assured Smith that the United States would still be able to "destroy the Soviet Union" after the treaty's implementation, but she regarded McNamara as slippery and unreliable, and paid no heed.[71]

Smith's dogged opposition to the test ban treaty might seem to indicate that her political attitude, originally shaped by the pragmatism of a breakthrough female politician, had now stiffened into a hidebound conviction that closed her mind to new ideas on the enhancement of national security. Certainly she was out of touch with America's burgeoning and sometimes influential antinuclear culture.[72] However, she was still in touch with important segments of opinion in Maine. Her staunch advocacy of atomic deterrence (to which the test ban treaty was just a minor setback) would help to ensure that jobs in Maine, where nuclear submarines were serviced, would be a little more secure and her political future commensurately brighter. Whereas public opinion nationally had favored ratification, mail from her own constituents ran eight to one against.[73] The Gannett press rallied to her defense: Her vote would "signify to her admirers the same courage with which she has reacted on other public issues."[74] Clearly Smith had not misjudged the politics of her home state.

Again, one should not conclude an assessment of Smith's 1963 defense posture without taking into account a particular facet of the test ban issue as she remembered it. In October 1964 she addressed the Air War College at Montgomery, Alabama, on the subject of the "Role of Congress in National Security Policy." She focused on the work of the Senate Preparedness Investigating Subcommittee, of which she was a member, and which had conducted hearings on the test ban treaty. "At first glance," Smith said, "it would appear that this committee exercised no influence on the final outcome." But in fact the committee had obliged the president to accept certain safeguards and became "the monitor maintaining continuous surveillance over these safeguards."[75] These safeguards included the development of facilities for the measurement of Soviet compliance (or noncompliance) with treaty provisions. The Soviet Union did in effect accept the principle of missile-site verification—a principle perhaps more important in its long-term effects than the ban on atmospheric testing. It was a step on the confidence-building road to later détente. Smith's pride in her contribution to the treaty modification suggests an incipient interest in mutual arms limitation.

In 1964 Smith made a bid for the office in which she would have been America's single most important foreign policy influence: the presidency. In 1952 she had decided against running for the vice presidency in spite of her fame as the woman who had faced up to McCarthy, and a booster campaign on her behalf in *Newsweek* and elsewhere.[76] Twelve years later she was still a readily identifiable figure who would have captured media attention and made an impression on the electorate. Her financial affairs and campaign funding were beyond reproach. She was not a machine politician and might well have been more suited to executive office than to legislative duties.

Smith took the fight all the way to the convention floor, where she arrived with sixteen committed delegates—having also been courted along the way as a vice presidential candidate. Though she may not have been a likely victor, she did win respect. Just as she had been the first woman to be elected to the Senate on her own merit, she was the first serious woman candidate for the presidency. (The precedents were by no means contemptible, however. The feminist Victoria Claflin Woodhull had run in 1872. In 1884 Belva Lockwood, the first woman admitted to practice before the U.S. Supreme Court, had won the electoral vote of Indiana.[77]) The first professional politician to make the attempt, she was conscious of her role in attempting to "break the barrier and pioneer the way for women."[78] Her effort occurred in the wake of the election in Ceylon of Sirimavo Bandaranaike, the world's first democratically chosen woman prime minister, and of the election of America's first Catholic president. Barriers did seem to be falling, even if it remained apparent that black Americans and women still had much to overcome.

Margaret Chase Smith was beset by the multifarious problems of a woman trying to break through at the top levels of political life, and shielded herself with conservative beliefs and a commitment to high arms expenditure and anti-Communism. Yet she never quite abandoned her earlier "moderation." In her responses to Barry Goldwater's 1964 presidential campaign there is a glimpse of what she might have been or, given morale-boosting political success, become. She spoke on behalf of the Republican candidate in Maine, but in her speeches made clear her reservations about his policies:

> I don't agree with Senator Goldwater's position that military field commanders [in Vietnam] should be given discretion to use nuclear weapons. I don't agree with Senator Goldwater's opposition to any form of medicare as I do believe there is a compromise form of medicare that permits options and private insurance participation.[79]

Smith was not in fact a hidebound conservative hawk. There is further evidence of this in her insistence on the rights of minorities within the defense forces. In 1965 she clashed with McNamara over the issue of the integration of the National Guard. As the disastrously provocative all-white policing of race riots would soon show, Smith was raising an important issue. On March 1, 1965, McNamara claimed that "great strides" had been made toward integration, so that there were "no segregated State Guards today." Smith pressed him for details and finally, in August 1967, condemned him: "Is one per cent honest integration and non-segregation? . . . The truth is that the Secretary of Defense was not honest in his statement of March 1, 1965, to the Senate Preparedness Investigating Subcommittee."[80] By this time, however, black Americans were beginning to complain about being *too heavily* represented in the Vietnam fighting forces.[81] Smith was about to lose touch on the issue that would contribute to the loss of her Senate seat. Nevertheless, her intention was clearly to advance the cause of tolerance in the armed forces.

For this reason, among others, Smith displayed some animus toward the Defense Department. Her inherent distrust of Secretary McNamara was escalated into fury by her belief that he and his department were helping the Democratic administration politically by making information known on a selective and politically partisan basis. Her good relationship with President Johnson did not prevent her from firing the following salvo at the defense secretary:

> On December 15, 1963, President Johnson . . . warned me that the Kittery-Portsmouth Naval Shipyard was on its way to being closed and to be braced for such closing. . . .
>
> When, on December 16, I made a Senate speech warning about the closing of the Kittery-Portsmouth Naval Shipyard, the Department of Defense vigorously denied to the press that any closing of that shipyard was contemplated. . . .
>
> But then, as I had warned, two weeks after the November 1964 election, you publicly announced the decision to close the Kittery-Portsmouth Naval Shipyard.[82]

Gannett's *Portland Sunday Telegram,* which backed Smith on the subject of political leaks and the credibility gap, had earlier reported her charges that the White House and Defense Department issued news in advance to a "favored few."[83] Smith favored a strong national defense, but it could not be said that she had a sweetheart relationship with the bureaucracy in charge of it.

Smith was so disenchanted with the defense establishment that her hostility carried over to the Republican Nixon administration. She did express some reluctance, however: "Because I was the top Republican on the Armed Services Committee, I had no desire to take the lead in opposing the Republican President."[84] But there was a vastly expensive plan afoot to build a network of ground-to-air missiles that would intercept incoming Soviet intercontinental ballistic missiles (ICBMs) in the event of a nuclear attack. Smith made a determined fight against the deployment of the proposed anti-ballistic-missile (ABM) system.

According to one historian, the coalition she led consisted of the "liberal, more dovish Republicans and Democrats."[85] But Smith's personal reasoning was not based on "dovish" considerations. After one of her votes against ABM, she explained to her constituents that it was because the system "would be obsolete before it could be installed."[86] Attacking ABM in the Senate on August 6, she declared that "offensive strength" was the "better deterrent." She had not developed a sudden aversion for advanced weapons systems. On the contrary, she placed her faith in the technology of the future, "laser defense."[87]

Smith appears to have been out of touch with the complex bargaining processes being developed by Henry Kissinger, whereby a phantom ABM system would be a bargaining chip on the table in the great poker game with the Russians, a game that would lead to the Strategic Arms Limitation Treaties (SALT), U.S. withdrawal from Vietnam, and the opening of diplomatic relations with Communist China.[88] Perhaps she was considered too honest a person to be a likely recruit to the duplicitous world of international diplomacy. Again, though the ABM vote was a close-run thing—in the final, August vote there was a fifty-fifty tie, with Vice President Agnew casting the decisive proadministration vote—Nixon and Kissinger got what they wanted, so there was no need to take her on board. Smith, with her straightforward faith in national security and her sincere if defeminized espousal of moderate causes, had been a woman suited to the season of the Cold War. But rapid changes in international affairs and in the domestic forces that shaped American foreign policy meant that, notwithstanding her qualities, she was destined for obsolescence.

By the time of the ABM debate, Senator Smith's political judgment and appeal were beginning to fade. Her reactions to the "hot" Vietnam War with its extensive ground fighting bear this out. In general, like a substantial number of women of her generation, Smith supported deterrence, but opposed "hot" wars. Her flirtation with the use of nuclear weapons in the Korean War had signified a distaste for ground-level shooting with American casualties. Similarly she told her constituents in 1967: "I have repeatedly stated both publicly and privately that I did not feel that we should have become militarily involved in Vietnam."[89] However, once American troops had been committed in Southeast Asia, she gave the U.S. war effort her stubbornly loyal support. In doing so she contributed to her eventual political demise.

A personal factor encouraged Smith's support for America's presence in Vietnam. She was a person of strong preferences and loyalties, and President Johnson was one of her favorite people. They had been elected to the Senate together and had enjoyed parallel careers on the Armed Services, Appropriations, and Space Committees. Lady Bird Johnson confirmed the special relationship: "There is a bond between them, a great respect and liking untrammeled by the difference in parties."[90] Smith recalled at a 1977 symposium that "the one principal issue that Lyndon Johnson and I always agreed on was the defense program."[91]

Smith's reaction to governmental secrecy and deception further explains her support for the war. In May 1964 she complained that both the Kennedy and Johnson administrations kept people in the dark. If she, as a member of committees taking secret testimony, did not know what was going on, ordinary citizens must be even more ignorant; as a presidential candidate she had a right to know.[92] In policy terms her reaction to this clouded vision was not to counsel restraint but to demand better military equipment in Vietnam. Already distrustful of McNamara's bureaucrats, she charged that the administration had suppressed information about the antiquated state of the airplanes being used by "our side." She accused the administration of failing to go for a clear-cut victory against the Communists.[93]

Despite her membership of informationally privileged congressional committees, Smith was taken in, like so many of her senatorial colleagues, by the administration's version of the Tonkin Gulf incident of August 1964. The false story about an unprovoked North Vietnamese attack on U.S. Navy ships produced the resolution that gave President Johnson his carte blanche for the conduct of the war.[94] Smith's speeches on the Tonkin episode display an uncritical approach to the developing war, wrapped up in the language of Cold War sophistication. She told the Pierian Club in Presque Isle, Maine, that although the Vietnamese were not the same as the Chinese, they were of the same racial origin and did the bidding of Peking. But neither the Vietnamese nor the Chinese were the same as the Russians. Apparently unaware that informed observers had known about the rift in the Communist world since the 1940s, she said she had predicted the Sino-Soviet split as early as 1957. The Russians, she surmised, welcomed the "retaliatory" American bombing response to the Tonkin "attack," because they wanted a chance to usurp the now-discredited Chinese as the champions of Vietnam. She could therefore present American aggression as a measured response that would not alienate the Russians.[95]

Fortified by such beliefs, Smith supported the American war effort in Vietnam. She regarded her role as that of the "loyal opposition" and argued that every American should support the fighting men in Vietnam, "whether one does, or does not, approve of our conduct of the war there." She herself was unhappy about the conduct of the war, pointing in one speech to various "tragedies," notably the "pilot shortage" and "bomb shortages." She criticized McNamara for overoptimism, and for issuing a constant stream of misleading information leading to "unresolved credibility conflict."[96] To her mind McNamara fomented confusion and doubt by issuing complex data on the efficacy of the bombing of North Vietnam. When in such doubt, Smith's reaction was to attack the secretary of defense and then to opt for continuing hostilities. In March 1967, for example, she was against the proposal that there should be another bombing pause to allow for further efforts at peace negotiation.[97] At this point she claimed that the Russians were building ABM sites as decoys in order to evoke an economically ruinous response from the United States, and gave notice that her support for the American ABM system was waning. Instead she supported escalating budget allocations both for American forces in Vietnam, and for military assistance to indigenous "free-world forces" in Southeast Asia.[98]

Smith's viewpoint was not very far removed from what later came to be known as the neoconservative approach—that the war was morally defensible, and that it could have been won but for halfhearted support in Washington and near-treasonable opposition among certain segments of the American public. Consistent with this outlook was the view that the press had been responsible for American misfortunes in Vietnam.[99] Smith pointed to reporters' misinterpretation of the Vietcong's February 1968 Tet offensive, which in her view had shocked the American public and caused Johnson not to seek reelection: "If this story is properly written in history, . . . it will show clearly how we smashed the Tet Offensive and how LBJ would not only have been a candidate again but he would have won overwhelmingly and gone down not only as a great President but as one of the greatest Presidents of all."[100] In spite of Smith's unhappiness about American involvement in Vietnam, she fully supported the military effort. She criticized government officials who did not give top priority to winning the war, and journalists who underreported American victories. She could be numbered among the most influential of the group of politicians who kept the United States fighting.

But the war affected Maine as it did every part of the nation. When Smith's constituents expressed anxiety and criticism, she responded with a blend of concern and entrenched support for the military. In some ways she presented a sympathetic face to anxious citizens. She responded promptly to one mother who feared that the soldiers in Vietnam were being endangered by topless dancers.[101] When a New Brunswick woman accused Smith of failing "to differentiate between fringe groups and responsible dissent," the senator reminded her of her June 1950 Declaration of Conscience, and of her more recent defense of Senator Fulbright's right to dissent from the Vietnam War.[102] Yet in these responses, Smith seemed to be looking for inspiration to the distant days when she had been the "vice admiral," and to her best-remembered moment of glory, her confrontation with McCarthy. Like other politicians in the 1960s, she was finding it difficult to come to terms with the present.

Smith could see that the war was causing problems at home. In one long disquisition, she told the readers of the *Portland Sunday Telegram* "Why I Worry About the War in Vietnam." As usual, she said that entry into the war had been questionable, that surrender was now unthinkable, and that McNamara was a slippery politician. But she revealed that she was also worried about the effects of the war on domestic living standards.[103] At the same time she began to worry about the other representatives of Maine in Congress—all of them by now Democratic in a state that had formerly been solidly Republican. Would they waver in their support for the war effort, and where would that leave her politically?[104]

Within a year it was obvious that Maine party politics would not be immune from the debate over the Vietnam War. Five hundred delegates to the Democratic Issues Conference in Lewiston in March 1968 made it "the Day of the Doves." At the conference Representatives Peter N. Kyros and William D. Hathaway had to make strenuous appeals for party unity.[105] Smith felt obliged to restate her position. She now said that the Tonkin Gulf resolution enabling the president to run a war may have been based on McNamara's deceptive information policy. She thought the United States should fight on after Tet. She noted, however, that the war was bringing about a "decay of American life" that went beyond even the "hippies" and the "flower children." She worried: "While it may not be clear as to whether we are winning the war in Vietnam, it is crystal clear that we are losing it here at home and that Ho Chi Minh knows this and is banking heavily for it to continue that way."[106]

Anxious though she may have been, Senator Smith continued with her support for the war effort after the election to the presidency of her fellow Republican Richard M. Nixon. Smith was later to rate Nixon's presidential caliber below that of Johnson. But in the course of his presidency Nixon more than once had cause to express his particular appreciation of her support for his Vietnam policy. Loyal to the end, in the summer of 1972 Smith threw her weight against congressional war termination initiatives that passed narrowly at the time, but later bogged down as the president's forces maintained their political pressure on the doves. Nixon thanked Smith for her "vote against the fund cutoff proposal that finally passed the Senate" (it was overturned in September) and praised her "courage and statesmanship."[107]

But Smith had not escaped the traumatizing effect of the antiwar protest movements. On May 9, 1970, for example, she had appeared before a turbulent audience of students at Maine's Colby College in the wake of the war's extension into Cambodia. An ardent champion of the military draft—which she continued to advocate even during Nixon's "Vietnamization" program, designed to phase out the use of American ground combatants—she must have expected some criticism from members of the generation of draft age.[108] But the intensity of her reception at Colby was a shock to her, especially as she was at the time suffering the aftereffects of hip surgery. Her remarks transformed the audience mood from one of suspicious receptivity to one of rude resentment. For example, when she upheld Nixon's mendacious assertion that there had been no U.S. troops in Laos, she was accosted by Everett Carson, an ex-Marine who had been wounded and had seen half his platoon wiped out in that very country. Smith described the encounter as "the most unpleasant experience of my entire career" and thought the students had conspired to embarrass her. According to one newspaper report, Smith demonstrated an "essential lack of understanding of the reasons for the tumult of the young," and showed "just how far out of touch she is with her times."[109]

The perception that Smith was too warlike spelled her political doom, and in 1972 she lost her Senate seat. While her support for the Vietnam War was the critical factor in her defeat, other factors were at work as well. Perhaps the most important of these was the long-term trend in Maine politics that had transformed it from a bastion of Yankee Republicanism into a genuine two-party state. Non-Protestant immigration—notably from French Canada, Ireland, and Greece—helped to break the Republican stranglehold, as evidenced by the election in 1958 of the state's first Democratic Senator—Edmund Muskie was a Catholic of Polish descent.[110] Smith's defeat was a Democratic victory waiting to happen. Yet it was still remarkable in that the victor, William Hathaway, was not a major politician (and survived only one term), and in that it occurred in the year of a Republican landslide.

A further factor that supposedly militated against Smith was Bill Lewis's heart attack at Walter Reed Hospital on December 9, 1971. Early speculation that this would deter her from running gave way to the view that she would still run but would miss his sound judgment and financial backing. Yet the illness of her close aide may not have been such a great blow to her political prospects. Memories lingered of charges—ill founded but tenacious in their grip on local gossip—that Smith was having an affair with Lewis—an illusion that fed on the circumstance that she shared a house with the bachelor's affluent family in Washington. Lewis does not appear to have been a political asset locally. As for his advice, it was consistently hawkish, and his illness might have been a blessing in disguise, but for Smith's own stubborn support for the Vietnam War on her own count.[111]

Yet another aspect of the campaign that agitated Smith was what she regarded as a politically motivated campaign against her by the Ralph Nader Congress Project. The senator complained that Nader's researcher asked "a smutty question about my personal life."[112] But, in the event, the Nader organization produced a balanced and in some respects favorable account of her political career. For example, it computed her Senate voting record in a way that definitively discredited the charges of one Maine politician that she had absented herself from roll calls.[113] It is nevertheless evident that Smith had to put up with a renewed flurry of smears. It was alleged that she was eighty, too old to continue—in fact she was seventy-four, and remained very active into her nineties. It was falsely alleged that she was of French Canadian origin and ashamed of it, so had anglicized her name from Chasse to Chase. Reacting to the various smears, Bill Lewis said the 1972 campaign was "the dirtiest we've ever been through." But there was no comparison with the 1948 campaign, and a Bangor newspaper was probably correct when it dismissed his complaints as subjective and trivial.[114]

While some of the foregoing factors help to explain why Maine's long-term vote getter was at last vulnerable, it was her stance on the Vietnam War that finally toppled her. Smith's Democratic opponent, Hathaway, was a notable opponent of the war. (This had not always been the case: In 1966 he had confidently predicted U.S. victory in Vietnam, and had called for more troops to be sent. However, in those days the war was not a major issue—pride of place in the congressional race that year had gone to the question of the trade in potato futures.) The advent of a Republican president in 1969 gave Democrats a greater opportunity and incentive to criticize, and Hathaway moved steadily from a position of bipartisan support to being an outright critic of Southeast Asian policy and a champion of Congress's right to make informed decisions on foreign affairs. Smith's early suspicions that the prowar consensus in Maine might not hold were therefore well founded. The Vietnam issue alone could not have won Hathaway the 1972 election, but it was acknowledged on all sides to be a factor in ending Smith's long tenure in the Senate.[115]

Furthermore, there is some evidence to suggest that Smith had been overtaken by the tide of modern feminism, both on domestic issues and with respect to the Vietnam War. In June 1972 Ramona Barth, cofounder of the National Organization of Women (NOW) in Maine, denounced the Republican candidate as a "token woman" because of what she regarded as the pusillanimity of her stance on women's liberation.[116] As the election approached Smith became for the press the very symbol of antifeminism.[117] It no longer seemed sacrilegious for women to criticize Smith now that other women were running for Congress—some of them, like Bella Abzug and WILPF president Katherine L. Camp, strongly committed to ending America's presence in Vietnam. On the issue of the war, women simply did not warm to the incumbent senator. Fifty-nine percent of the mail she received on the war came from men. By her own account this was a departure from the usual pattern, for Smith believed that "women are more prone to write letters than men.

Men are callers. They tend to use the phone. Women write on behalf of the family." The relative silence of Maine's women on the Vietnam War suggests that they had abandoned faith in Smith.[118]

When Margaret Chase Smith advocated peace through security, she spoke for a substantial number of women throughout the United States. When, however, she supported the "hot" war in Vietnam, she began to alienate women, who had rallied to her side in 1948. On the Vietnam issue she appears to have alienated them even more than did the male commander in chief of the American armed forces, the president. According to nationwide samples of public opinion taken by the Harris organization in 1971, an equal number of men and women (60 percent) thought that President Nixon was making an "excellent/pretty good" effort to secure peace—a pointer to his success against the Democrats' peace candidate George McGovern in 1972. But on the identification of the peace challenge as a "very serious" problem, there was a gender gap, with 90 percent of women agreeing compared with 83 percent of men.[119] Smith's hyperloyalty to the war effort left her more exposed than her president to political disapproval in general, and to women's in particular. Her blunt rejections of feminism compounded her political problems with women, making her seem outmoded in a self-proclaimed age of women's liberation. Moreover, in spite of her advocacy of women's rights in the armed forces, she could draw no comfort from the support of women veterans of the war, who appeared to be even more shell-shocked than the men and took little part in the Vietnam debate.[120] The Vietnam War had left her stranded, a fish out of water at one of the lowest tides in American political history

Yet Margaret Chase Smith's career remains of undoubted significance in the context of a study of American women and foreign policy, furnishing evidence of the way in which a woman, in spite of enduring prejudice against the capabilities of her sex, could influence foreign and defense policy. Some of her achievements were controversial, but none of them can be dismissed. Smith improved naval morale in World War II. She helped to advance the status of women within the military. She fired one of the earliest shots against Joseph McCarthy, whose pronouncements were an embarrassment to U.S. foreign policy. She played a role in developing arms agreement verification procedures. She cracked the ice in bidding for the presidency—the job having the greatest impact of all on foreign policy formation. She boosted political support for America's longest war, the conflict in Vietnam. Less tangibly, but no less important in terms of inspiration, for thirty-two years she provided the role model of a respected woman at work in the nation's highest defense councils.

Smith's most notable congressional contribution was her support—discriminating but solid—for defense spending. Since pressure for such spending came from many sources, her voice was one among many, but her advocacy is significant because of her senior and influential position and because it was so consistent over a long period. Did higher defense spending provoke emulative conduct that broke the Soviet economy, thus bringing the Cold War to a peaceful conclusion on terms favorable to the United States and its cherished ideals of democracy and self-determination? Or did higher spending prolong the Cold War, weakening the U.S. economy and making it vulnerable to competition from countries like Japan and the former West Germany, which had relatively low military costs? The verdict on Smith's wisdom will in future years depend on the outcome of a wider debate on the history of U.S. defense strategy.

8 | BELLA ABZUG
Signpost to the Future

Margaret Chase Smith said of Eleanor Roosevelt, "Though I disagreed with her politics, I admired her." New York's congresswoman Bella Abzug lauded Smith in the same spirit, saying that she "was an outstanding Senator for twenty-four years." It is therefore striking that, in Abzug's case, the even tenor of mutual regard was sometimes quite savagely ruptured. To Smith, Abzug "was ineffective. One reason for this is that she was too loud." The senator's reaction illustrates that Bella Abzug had become one of the nation's most controversial politicians.[1]

There can be no doubt about Abzug's "loud" style, which was evident in visual terms. Though she was short but ample, her two conspicuous hallmarks were bright red lipstick and broad-brimmed hats. Aurally she was just as difficult to miss. Norman Mailer said that Abzug had a voice loud enough "to boil the fat off a taxi driver's neck."[2] Campaigning among Manhattan's apartment houses, she would not wait for people to come out but used a megaphone to boom her "Hi! I'm Bella!" greeting and its ensuing message directly at voters. Her language could be ripe as well as stentorian, as she demonstrated on her first day in Congress. On asking her to remove her hat in conformity with House rules, Doorkeeper Fishbait Miller elicited from her the celebrated retort, "Go fuck yourself."[3]

The political scientist Ruth B. Mandel notes that "Abzug's aggressive style has been held up as a symbol of bad behavior." But the same author thinks that Abzug "carries a record as an effective and courageous public official."[4] Perhaps indeed it should be remembered that Abzug was a crusader, and crusaders, be they Tom Paine or Betty Friedan, cannot remain effective and universally popular at the same time. Again, one must bear in mind the fact that those who criticized her for being ineffective were sometimes moved by mere prejudice. The language used against Abzug was less profane but sometimes more offensive than her own—what man would have been accused of "pouting" over Chile?[5]

Abzug shocked people because she was an apostle of the new feminism. Her style was that of the political fighter-climber—she did not reach Congress through a dynastic accident. But she felt no need to "pay a price" for being a successful woman. Certainly male privileges survived, and she knocked them over when they got in her way. Geraldine Ferraro recalls: "Bella made it easier for us, even down to taking a swim in the congressional swimming pool. When she was in Congress, the men had at first refused to let her take a dip, claiming it infringed on the delights of their swimming in the nude. Bella . . . made short shrift of that."[6] But Abzug did not suffer from breakthrough syndrome; she felt no need to clone herself to normative male conduct in order to ensure her political survival.

In foreign policy terms this meant that Abzug was free to be a herald of the emergent gender. Her stance on Vietnam incorporated the "old" female objection to "hot" wars, but, with other like-minded women, she brought a wholly new vitality to the antiwar campaign. Her approach to overseas military assistance, to foreign trade, and to nuclear issues signaled a departure from the foreign policy stances associated with women in the interwar years and the 1950s. Moreover, to a much greater extent than earlier congresswomen, Abzug consciously and confidently exploited the politics of the gender gap in relation to foreign policy.

Abzug was gifted with charisma and a sometimes irresistible driving force. By the time she came to politics, she had lived a life that honed her skills and toughened her resistance to setbacks and injustice. She was born Bella Savitski in the Bronx in 1920, the granddaughter of an Orthodox Jew who had emigrated from Russia. As a child she stood on street corners collecting pennies for the Zionist cause. Her Jewish upbringing taught her resistance, even to the ways of the resisters. On the death of her father, the proprietor of the Live and Let Live Meat Market on New York's Ninth Avenue, the thirteen-year-old feminist broke a traditional male monopoly by reciting kaddish for him. In World War II she crossed another time-honored gender demarcation by working in a shipyard. Then she discovered she could not go to Harvard Law School, which admitted no women. She graduated instead from Columbia, taking her LL.B. in 1945. It was at Columbia that she met Martin Abzug, who typed her term papers and persuaded her into an egalitarian matrimony.

In the next decade and a half Bella Abzug developed a reputation as a lawyer for the underdog, taking on labor cases and, in one trial of note, defending Willie McGee, a Mississippi black man accused of raping a white woman. (He was executed in 1951.) In a series of divorce cases she defended women who were in danger of getting a raw deal. Though she did not enter politics until she was in her fifties, she battled for social justice, especially for improved housing. She had a number of sources for inspiration: Her interest in Zionism gave her an internationalist perspective. Her contact with people of diverse social and ethnic backgrounds gave her a cosmopolitan outlook comparable to that of Jane Addams. It might be added that Abzug was conscious of the efforts of past feminists to make the world a more peaceful place. She described Jeannette Rankin as "one of the great ladies of the peace movement and the women's movement," and as "a source of strength and inspiration to all of us."[7]

According to Abzug, her major commitment to "the peace movement" began in 1961.[8] In that year the resumption of nuclear testing by the Soviet Union and the United States prompted the founding of a new peace organization. Abzug was a founding member of Women Strike for Peace (WSP), and for ten years remained its political action director. WSP officer and historian Amy Swerdlow recalled that the women of the new group "seemed to have emerged from nowhere."[9] To outward appearances the 1950s had been a quiet decade in the history of American feminism. Yet in Abzug's belief, the reason why women were 5 to 6 percent more supportive of President Eisenhower was that they thought he would bring peace in Korea, and approved of his peaceful mediation in the Suez war.[10]

WILPF had already declared itself against nuclear testing in 1956. In 1959 in New York City, there was an upsurge in protest against the annual nuclear air excercise, "Operation Alert." Feminist pacifists led by Dorothy Day had been sent to prison several times for defying the alert. Suddenly they found themselves reinforced by a substantial number of middle-class mothers who also refused to take shelter for the legally required ten minutes. In the face of continuing resistance, the Kennedy administration eventually had to cancel the alert.[11] Thus, although it surprised politicians at the time, the emergence of WSP took place against the backdrop of women's ever-resilient resistence to the more senseless aspects of militarism.

The Women's Strike for Peace took its name from an episode on November 1, 1961, when fifty thousand women all over the United States registered their protest against a radioactive cloud hanging over their country caused by a Soviet atmospheric test. In Swerdlow's words, the women "walked out of their kitchens and off their jobs in a one-day women's strike for peace."[12] This kind of spontaneous "direct action" was in the tradition of the extraparliamentary tactics that had been associated, in the Progressive Era, with the revolutionary Industrial

Workers of the World (IWW, or "Wobblies"). Direct-action tactics had more recently been used in the black struggle for civil rights in the South, and they were soon to be resurrected, discussed, and adopted on the nation's campuses. The influential radical scholar Frances Piven argued that organized reform movements such as labor unions soon acquired bureaucratic inertia and establishment attitudes, and that spontaneous direct action was one of the few recourses open to people outside traditional power structures. As Swerdlow saw it, WSP was a reaction against the fossilized attitudes of WILPF and a rebellion against a similar sluggishness, compounded by male domination, in the National Committee for a Sane Nuclear Policy (SANE). Its women were middle class and not impoverished like the Wobblies or the black people of Alabama, yet they appear to have been attracted to alternative tactics because, like earlier less affluent rebels, they conceived of themselves as being outside the political process. According to a survey of every eighth member of WSP, conducted by Elise Boulding of Ann Arbor, Michigan, the majority of WSP activists were well-educated mothers who remembered the more activist days of the feminist movement but had recoiled from politics in the McCarthyist-Stalinist atmosphere of the 1950s.[13]

Some of the women had radical backgrounds, and the House Un-American Activities Committee investigated. But in congressional hearings WSP's leader, Dagmar Wilson, ran circles around her interrogators. WSP survived as a significant pressure group.

In judging its effectiveness, one must allow for WSP's "outsider" status. By definition WSP did not gain access to the policy-making inner circle, or to the "network" of establishment women for whom Eleanor Roosevelt was still an eminence grise. She had persuaded President Kennedy to set up a women's task force in the executive department; she herself ended up in charge of it. The former first lady told Dagmar Wilson she could not support WSP or "help in any way unless you have consulted the President and the Secretary of State and have their consent."[14] Yet it was precisely in order to counter this kind of response that WSP had sprung to life in the first place. Its activities did contribute to the climate that produced the test ban treaty. President Kennedy publicly acknowledged his respect for the WSP picket and peace march outside the White House in January 1962, and later justified the treaty in terms that reflected the parental values of WSP mothers—he said he wanted a better world for his daughter, Caroline.[15]

Overradical though WSP may have been in Eleanor Roosevelt's view, its campaign seemed to some women to be just a beginning, and a timid one at that. Amy Swerdlow noted the role that "motherism" played in the early WSP. Motherism may have been politically effective in the Kennedy years, when the spectacle of toddler-toting, well-dressed mothers taking a break from their domestic routines proved to be quite disarming. But for Swerdlow motherism was unsatisfactory in the longer term. For her the WSP experience was a political awakening, and she became more self-consciously feminist. According to her account, she was not alone:

> WSP has been justifiably criticized for celebrating the sexual stereotypes that have kept women in secondary status, but I argue that although WSP did not transform American foreign policy, or American gender relations, the women of WSP transformed themselves.
>
> Finding their strength in fighting for a test ban treaty, and coming up against entrenched male power in government and in the peace movement, the women were forced to challenge traditional sex/gender power relations, if only in the area of foreign policy.[16]

Swerdlow further noted that the WSP experience brought home to its women the extent to which they and their international sisters were outsiders, and (whatever the achievements of direct action in the short run) the penalties of that status. Women had, for example, no representation on either the Russian or the American side in the 1962 Geneva negotiations. WSP women decided they needed to be on the inside, "and proceeded to elect their own legislative chairperson Bella Abzug to Congress."[17]

In agreeing to back Abzug for a legislative career, WSP had to undergo a change of philosophy, adopting parliamentary means of securing its objectives. Abzug, however, already had the requisite philosophy and did not need to change. In fact, her ambition and her feminism had made her an uneasy leader of WSP until that organization came around to her own way of thinking. Swerdlow noted that there had been "real tension" between Abzug and the prefeminist WSP. Abzug agreed: "I had difficulties with the WSP, because I was a feminist. They were not. They were mothers who worried about Strontium 90 in the milk for their kids. I wanted an end to nuclear testing for women, for us ourselves, not just for our kids." As Swerdlow aptly put it, Abzug was "a lawyer, not a housewife." Abzug was already a feminist. She was fitted to the task of entering a lawmaking assembly, to behave as an insider rather than as an extralegal, direct-action outsider.[18]

The entry of antiwar feminists into the mainstream of American politics was to be a significant phenomenon. Feminist opposition to American participation in the Vietnam War can take its place among the several factors that led to U.S. withdrawal from hostilities in 1973. The historian Charles DeBenedetti suggested that Abzug played a role in the "normalization" of protest against the war.[19] According to this theory the protesters came in from the cold and found a voice in Congress, so the nation's leaders had to listen to them. However, Abzug's normalization of protest was not achieved at the cost of "normalizing" women. Where war was concerned, Abzug wanted men to change, not women. In killing the Vietnam War, she brought to life the gender gap in ways that were to be important for future politics and foreign policy.

By late 1966 American casualties were beginning to mount in the Vietnam War, and WSP began to make opposition to the draft the main focus of its antiwar work. WSP was by no means alone in its campaigns over the next few years. By 1969 antiwar protest was at fever pitch across the nation. DeBenedetti described the activities of that fall as "the most potent and widespread antiwar protests ever mounted in a western democracy."[20] Bella Abzug pitched herself with some enthusiasm into this protest. For example, she was on hand at a confrontation between WSP pickets and the police at the White House gate, and—in lawyerly fashion—negotiated the deal whereby the women would be able to march at the White House in a continually moving circle with police acquiescence.[21] By now Abzug had acquired the taste for politics that was to make her a national figure. In 1970 she won election to the House of Representatives as a Democrat from New York's Nineteenth District. As she later put it, she "came to Congress from the peace movement."[22]

Had Abzug been entirely eccentric or radical she would not have achieved such prominence in American politics. Her reasons for opposing the Vietnam War were in some ways orthodox, differing little from those of male protesters. She believed that American democracy needed some restorative treatment. Her image was that of a "people's candidate."[23] She wanted the nation's leaders to be more accountable and honest. In 1971 she told a gathering in Pittsburgh: "Foreign policy has nothing to do with the people anymore, but only the military and experts. I don't believe that President Nixon wants to end the war. He has been lying to you."[24] As the Nixon administration persisted in secret with its attempts to swing things America's way in Southeast Asia, Abzug was in the forefront of those who tried to reassert congressional prerogatives in the foreign-policy-making field. She later recalled: "*Every*thing we did on Vietnam was a trauma. We were in constant trauma. The administration was shocked every time we asked for information. They never gave it. There was a stone wall."[25] Abzug's ability to articulate and publicize these viewpoints was exceptional—yet the viewpoints as such were not peculiar to her gender.

However, Abzug's opposition to the Vietnam War had other characteristics that did give it a gendered aspect. She developed a new philosophy on foreign assistance, yet its novelty does not disguise its feminist historical roots, for it was based on an antimilitarism that would have been instantly recognizable to the women who had backed Dorothy Detzer in the 1920s and 1930s. Even more pointedly, she attacked the sexual chauvinism of men who made a mess of foreign policy. Senior advisers to President Johnson, the "Wise Men," did not escape the scorn of LBJ's fellow Democrat. The adjective in the phrase "Wise Men" had already attracted some sarcasm, but Abzug focused her irony on the noun, referring to "the insulting spectacle of a President choosing, in time of crisis, a committee of Wise Men—usually the same men who got us into the crisis in the first place—to advise him and ignoring the wisdom and recommendations of women."[26] She had equally scant respect for the Republican appointee Henry Kissinger, who served President Nixon as national security affairs adviser and as secretary of state. She contemptuously noted Kissinger's remark: "For me, women are only amusing, a hobby. Nobody spends too much time on a hobby."[27] A significant part of Abzug's opposition to the Vietnam War came from her conviction that men had got the United States into it, and that women could reverse the commitment.

In her first year in Congress Abzug confirmed her feminist credentials when she helped to found the National Women's Political Caucus (NWPC). The NWPC sprang from the groundwork prepared by Abzug and two other leading feminists, Gloria Steinem and Betty Friedan. Following its establishment in Washington in July 1971, the organization grew over the next dozen years to a membership of seventy thousand women. The NWPC addressed the issues of equal opportunity, abortion, and day care—and opposed the war in Vietnam. Furthermore, one of the NWPC's chief goals was the appointment and election of more women to public office, a change that would, of course, give them a greater say in foreign policy.[28]

But the dominant feature of Abzug's opening year in Congress was her campaign to extricate the United States from Vietnam. In publicizing this campaign she wasted neither time nor photo opportunities. On her inaugural day in the House, she won public attention not only through her exchange with House Doorkeeper Miller, but also, after being officially sworn in, by taking a second, "people's oath" on the Capitol steps. A cheering crowd of supporters from Manhattan attended the ceremony. Shirley Chisholm—a representative from Brooklyn and the first black woman to serve in Congress—administered the oath. A champion of social causes domestically, she also shared some of Abzug's main foreign policy concerns: opposition to the draft, reductions in defense spending, and opposition to British arms sales to South Africa.[29]

Abzug's defiance of convention did not stop with the administration of the people's oath. Just in case there were Americans obtuse enough to miss the message behind that symbol, the "freshman" congresswoman introduced a bill on the opening day of the new session. The bill called for withdrawal of American troops from Vietnam within six months. It was the beginning of an unremitting Abzug campaign on Capitol Hill. In April 1972 she told a constituent: "I have sponsored and co-sponsored every House measure which would set a firm date for complete U.S. withdrawal from Vietnam in return for all American prisoners of war, and shall continue to speak out against this illegal involvement."[30]

Not content with her activities in the national legislature, Azbug took her campaign to the people. On February 23 the charismatic new congresswoman invited her colleagues to take part in "a proposed 'Peace and Priorities' barnstorming trip around the U.S. by a bipartisan group of members of Congress." Twenty-seven members of Congress responded, including some well-known personalities and peace campaigners, such as Democrats Don Edwards (California), Edward I. Koch (New York) and Michael Harrington (Massachusetts) and Republican Paul McCloskey (California). The antiwar campaigners spoke in sixty meetings and on thirty radio and television programs, concentrating initially on Cleveland, Ohio; Pittsburgh, Pennsylvania; and various communities in Connecticut.[31]

Abzug received the kind of attention that later led to her being accused of "preoccupation with the vertical pronoun."[32] The newspapers dubbed her "Fiery Bella," and journalists made comments infused with gender prejudice: In Cleveland, for example, Robert Crater noted "her stocky figure," compared her effectiveness with that of "a well-aimed howitzer," and noted that she had held up "the whole schedule so that she could buy fresh lipstick." Yet none of this prejudice was harmful to publicity, and it was neither the intention nor the effect of the journalists to hurt the latest object of public fascination. Crater reminded his readers that Abzug was a champion of the underdog and was, in spite of appearances, a wife and the mother of two daughters, both at college. He thought Bella Abzug was "the most exciting member of the 92nd Congress."[33]

The Abzug campaign in the spring of 1971 marked the passage of the antiwar movement into the realm of respectable politics. In DeBenedetti's words the rebellion by congressional Democrats in which she played a leading role constituted "the first commitment from a responsible body . . . to a full and final U.S. pullout."[34] Having achieved this, Abzug kept up the pressure. While the war in Vietnam continued, she never relinquished her increasingly telling pressure on the administration. In May, for example, along with neighboring Manhattan representative William F. Ryan, she set an important precedent when she introduced impeachment proceedings against the president—for "high crimes and misdemeanors in conducting a war against the peoples and nations of Indochina in the absence of a Declaration of War as required by the United States Constitution."[35]

Abzug made enemies even among her own kind, and to a certain extent this may have modified her effectiveness as an antiwar campaigner. For she proved herself to be a troublemaker even by the turbulent standards of Manhattan politics. After an upstate Republican committee had gerrymandered the Nineteenth District out of existence, leaving her without a constituency, she challenged Ryan in the Twentieth's Democratic primary. This challenge seemed inappropriate to some because Ryan shared Abzug's political outlook and had been the first member of Congress to come out publicly against the Vietnam War. Abzug was bitterly criticized for the further reason that Ryan was seriously ill with cancer. But the redrawn Twentieth contained a portion of Abzug's old Nineteenth, and, as Abzug had said on the announcement of the gerrymander: "I did not win election by making deals with politicians, and I don't intend to lose my seat in Congress by becoming the sacrificial victim of male deals."[36] Ryan beat Abzug but then died, whereupon she inherited his seat and was able to continue her peace crusade.

In the 1972 presidential election, Nixon inflicted a heavy defeat on the Democrats' peace candidate, George McGovern. However, in the course of the campaign Kissinger had been obliged to assure Americans that peace was "at hand," and, after the election, it was incumbent upon the administration to deliver.[37] In January 1973 the North Vietnamese and the Americans at last agreed on peace terms. To the degree that Nixon had been forced to accede to the demands of the antiwar protesters, Abzug could claim to have contributed to the ending of a war.

While Bella Abzug's impact on the Vietnam debate reflected her personal qualities, it also derived from the efforts of others who provided her with support. Opposition to the war took many forms and came from a great variety of people who formed a collective backdrop to the efforts of any individual. But the degree and the particular nature of Abzug's backing may be appreciated by looking at two special groups, her local New York constituents and women nationwide.

Although Wall Street was a bastion of world capitalism, the city in which it was located had long been the repository of every conceivable kind of radicalism. Stimulated by the Vietnam War, politically motivated groups directed much of their attention, during Abzug's years in Congress, to the peace issue. Among the organizations involved in New York City were the People's Peace Treaty, Vietnam Peace-Parade Committee, Lower Eastside Mobilization for Peace Action, Bronx Citizens for Peace, Friendshipment People-to-People Aid to Vietnam, World Congress for Peace, U.S. Preparatory Committee, War Resisters League, Catholic Peace Fellowship, Coalition for International Cooperation and Peace, and Continental Walk for Disarmament and Peace.[38]

Abzug was, in Swerdlow's words, "a real politician," and as such she cultivated the antiwar activists.[39] In April 1971, for example, she asked an assistant to locate seventeen people with addresses in Greenwich Village who had petitioned her with antiwar postcards, to invite them "to work with us on the Lower East Side."[40] Abzug was furthermore aware that influential feminists were active in their support for certain New York peace organizations. Gloria Steinem had endorsed the United Women's contingent; Ruth Gage-Colby of WILPF was one of the three coordinators of the New York Peace Action Coalition; Betty Friedan backed the same movement. Good politics and the politics of conviction went hand in hand: It made sense for Abzug to cultivate Manhattan's peace seekers, including the feminists among them.

The second group of Abzug constituents under consideration is antiwar women nationwide. Some activists, it is true, were disenchanted with the nation's women. Jeannette Rankin could not disguise her disappointment at women's failure to take action over Vietnam: "They've been worms. They let their sons go off to war because they're afraid their husbands will lose their jobs in industry if they protest."[41] The evidence does suggest that, in some ways, women were able to accomplish little. For example, Swerdlow noted that young women were browbeaten into silence in Boston antiwar meetings by men who told them to remain in the background because it was only men who were threatened by the draft.[42] In a similar vein, a student of the Berkeley movement against the Vietnam War observed that women "routinely cooked, cleaned, typed, and filed, while men held meetings and made crucial decisions." Gloria Steinem recalled: "There was this idea, 'Women say Yes to men who say No.' Women were not meant to do only the mimeography but supply the sex besides. At least in the Republican Party you only had to do the mimeographing."[43]

But the phenomenon of women in opposition to the Vietnam War bears closer examination. The undiscouraged Steinem opposed the war, as did Friedan, Chisholm, Swerdlow, and Rankin. Other committed feminists like Robin Morgan (a critic of Leftist sexism) and Bernadine Dohrn (who with Mark Rudd led the Weathermen) shared their conviction, to a degree that suggests a firm link between the new feminism and the antiwar movement. In taking their stand, these feminists were supported by a solid bedrock of female public opinion. One guide to the strength of that opinion is the number of women who participated in peace marches—a historian of the Californian protest movement has asserted that "the Vietnam War was especially loathsome to women, as evidenced by the large number of women who marched."[44] Polls are another clue to how women felt about the war. For when support for the war shriveled, women led the defection: "Gallup discovered that in May 1965, 58 percent of white men indicated support for the war, but only 48 percent of white women did; in April 1968 the figures were 48–40; and in April 1970, 41–30."[45] As indicated in the last chapter, Harris polls in the run-up to the 1972 presidential election revealed that women placed a higher priority than did men on ending the war. One Harris poll conducted in 1971 confirmed the perception among respondents of both genders that women were peacemakers, in that 58 percent of the men thought that "women in public office" could do "just as good" or a "better job than men" in "getting us out of the war in Vietnam." Women were even more confident of their capabilities, registering 64 percent on that item.[46]

Perhaps because of the rarity of women's contributions to politics, women who opposed the war attracted attention. They supplied the movement with some of its stars, and therefore with some of its charisma. Few of the Berkeley agitators were better known than Bettina Aptheker. One quip attributed to her—"Q: What's a nice girl like you doing mixed up with communism? A: Who says I'm a nice girl?"—referred to the fact that her father was a member of the Communist party. But in spite of Herbert Aptheker's distinction as a Marxist historian, his daughter was considered more dangerous than he, and largely because of her assertiveness as a woman.[47] Most influential politicians were at least subliminally affected by the activities of Bettina Aptheker and her like. In his 1966 campaign for the governorship of California, Ronald Reagan chose to put it this way: "The preservation of free speech does not justify letting beatniks, and advocates of sexual orgies, drug usage and filthy speech disrupt the academic community and interfere with our universities' purpose."[48]

Though more mature, the women of WSP continued to match the activities of the student generation. In 1971, for example, Swerdlow went on a three-woman peace mission to Hanoi, returning with messages from the Communist leadership and letters from thirty-two prisoners of war.[49] A much older woman, too, contributed to the charisma of the movement, and not only through the inspiration of past example. On a bitterly cold January day in 1968 Jeannette Rankin, eighty-seven, led her "Jeannette Brigade" of five thousand WILPF women, each one symbolizing an American who had fallen in Vietnam, in a protest march on Capitol Hill.[50] The following year the indomitable Rankin was still participating in moratorium marches in Georgia and South Carolina.[51]

Women of star quality opposed the war: Joan Baez was possibly the best exponent of the antiwar song, but other talented singers not known for their repertoire in that genre also made their position clear. Eartha Kitt was invited to a White House social function and seized the opportunity to sing a protest song before Lady Bird Johnson. Barbra Streisand declared her opposition to the war. Leading film actresses joined the crusade as well. The Oscar-winning Donna Reed (*From Here to Eternity*, 1953) supported Another Mother for Peace, an organization whose newsletter reached an estimated 240,000 women. In 1971 she confronted Henry Kissinger at a Hollywood party; the press reported his remark that she was "ridiculous."[52] Jane Fonda's contribution to the antiwar campaign so worried the Nixon administration that the FBI ran a disinformation campaign against her.[53] And feminist Shirley MacLaine, another of Hollywood's leading actresses, campaigned for McGovern in 1972 and was one of several stars who supported Abzug in her New York electoral battles.[54]

Women made a substantial literary contribution, too. Among the earliest was that of veteran Communist Anna Louise Strong, whose book *Cash and Violence in Laos and Vietnam* (1962) attacked American policy in Southeast Asia. The Pulitzer Prize–winning journalist Marguerite Higgins and the novelist Joan Didion wrote history, commentary, and fiction critical of the war. On the basis of visits to both South and North Vietnam, Mary McCarthy wrote disapprovingly of the war. She brought glimpses to her narrative that reflected her gender and appealed to other women: On flying to Hanoi, "It was funny to see a hostess on a military plane," and the division of the country meant that the "theme of separation" meant a great deal to Vietnamese women. A similar point could be made about Frances FitzGerald, who also wrote extensively on the war. Her 1972 book *Fire in the Lake*, which won the Pulitzer and Bancroft Prizes, attempted to explain Vietnamese culture and the Vietnamese idea of what kind of peace might be achieved.[55]

Seventy American women worked as war correspondents in Vietnam, and two of the sixteen U.S. journalists killed in action were women. In quantitative terms women war correspondents were evenly divided on the merits of the conflict.[56] In qualitative terms, however, the "stars" were on the side of protest. McCarthy, FitzGerald, Didion, and Higgins had no peers among the war supporters. Many millions of literate American women were exposed to their subtly gendered views and were drawn to them in a special way.

Abzug was aware of the importance of female support. By her own account she could rely on a woman's network in Congress. In opposing the Vietnam War, she worked with Ella Grasso of Connecticut; Shirley Chisholm of New York, and Patsy Mink of Hawaii—all Democrats.[57] Unlike some earlier women in Congress, Abzug had no cause to feel isolated. She was also fully aware of the support she had among women across the nation—though disappointed with the quality of McGovern's peace candidacy in 1972, she thought it was significant that women voted for him in appreciably greater numbers than did men.[58]

The nationwide women's peace constituency was an asset at Abzug's disposal. Unlike Margaret Chase Smith, she was prepared to appeal to the peace instincts of the woman voter, and she seems to have succeeded both nationally and locally in New York City. The point may be illustrated locally in the case of the write-in campaign that prompted Greenwich Village dwellers to mail protest postcards. These standardized cards were used widely and sent to several House members, opening with the phrase "Dear Congressman" even when addressed to Abzug. But 65 percent of those received by Abzug came from women.[59] It will be recalled that only 41 percent of a comparable batch of letters to Smith came from women.

In summary Abzug helped to normalize the protest against the Vietnam War instead of, conversely, normalizing herself by subscribing to perceived male norms in foreign policy. In this respect the support of other women was important to her psychologically, in that it gave her the confidence to pursue her foreign policy goals. Finally Abzug emphasized the gender gap on foreign policy and exploited it from her earliest days with WSP.

Once the main struggle over Vietnam had ended, Abzug renewed her efforts to exploit that gender gap and to mobilize women. The degree to which she could hope to succeed was limited by the relative powerlessness of any one individual, however forceful in personality. Abzug was specifically disappointed at the outcome of her bid to become the first woman since 1948 (when Smith left for the Senate) to sit on the House Armed Services Committee, which she described as "an occult male domain that functioned as a blank-check committee for the Pentagon." In spite of Abzug's frontal attack on the committee seniority system, she had to settle for places on the Committee on Government Operations and the Committee on Public Works. Yet Abzug's efforts were not unrewarded. According to her account, she had to be bought off the Armed Services job with the appointment of two male liberals, the black Californian Ron Dellums and Wisconsin's Les Aspin. Abzug's stand also prepared the way for the appointment to the committee of the Colorado feminist Patricia Schroeder on her election in 1972 to what was to be to a long term in Congress.[60]

Yet Abzug did not exploit the gender gap merely as a means to power for herself and other women. Concerned with issues and principles, she defined a modern, feminist foreign policy in three areas: military assistance, trade, and peace-and-nuclear matters.

In the realm of military assistance, Abzug took up some of the issues raised by Helen Douglas before Nixon and McCarthy snuffed them out along with her career. She shared Douglas's opposition to confrontational Cold War policies, and her faith in the UN as the proper vehicle for solving international problems. She thought that the United States had a duty to provide nonmilitary foreign assistance, but had strong reservations about military aid, especially when it had strings attached, and when it supported oppressive regimes. Like Douglas she insisted on democracy.

In August 1971 Abzug complained in the House that, as a donor of foreign assistance, the United States ranked only eleventh out of fifteen developed countries. Most of the assistance was military in character, and the the bulk of it went "to countries who should be anathema," including fascist Spain and Portugal.[61] Later in the same year she sponsored a bill concurrently introduced in the Senate by McGovern, "to redesign U.S. programs of foreign assistance and help build a new era in world affairs." She believed that the American military involvement in Vietnam had "crystallized" the foreign aid crisis. For American military aid to South Vietnam was more than double the amount given for peaceful economic development, and was increasing year by year. Abzug said that "as the era of the Cold War comes to an end," an opportunity existed to move from a policy funding repressive regimes and containing communism, to a policy of supporting the work of UN agencies.[62]

But Israel caused Abzug problems in a way that threatened her authority as a foreign aid reformer, for she was tempted to go along with military assistance to that country. Israel was a democracy, treated its women relatively well, and had a female prime minister, Golda Meir. As a Jew Abzug was subject to the emotions and loyalties of two thousand years of exile and of the Holocaust. Furthermore she had to consider the views and possible voting intentions of her constituency's numerous Jews. Abzug was undoubtedly under both personal and political pressure to respond to Israel's pleas for American military help, endangering the code of nonmilitary assistance she so ardently demanded.

Abzug's response was to support arms for Israel but only on a modest scale and on an exceptional-case basis. In 1971 she endorsed the sale of Phantom jets to Israel—as an emergency measure and in light of Israel's status as a democracy under imminent threat of attack. She took care to balance her plea by asking simultaneously for money to be spent to help a distressed group of Muslims, the ten million refugees who entered India during Pakistan's civil war.[63] She continued with her support for Israel but, on September 13, 1972, voted against a $500 million military credit for Israel because it was a part of a $21 billion military procurement authorization against which other New York liberals like Koch and Chisholm also voted. This was during an election campaign, and Swerdlow recalls that Abzug's enemies within the Jewish community seized the opportunity to denounce her, dubbing her the "no arms to Israel" candidate. Abzug survived this assault. Then, in opposing the sale of nuclear capability to Egypt in 1974, she made it clear that she wished the prohibition to extend to Israel as well. Thus, while Israel was a difficult case for Abzug, she kept as closely as possible to her antimilitarist stance.[64]

One of the distinctive attributes of Abzug's approach to the assistance problem was her appreciation of people's desire to run their own lives. From the perspective of the recipient, aid sometimes seemed to arrive in incomprehensible ways: "To drop sacks of rice on some Cambodians, and tons of bombs on others, is not only hypocritical but self-defeating."[65] In July 1973 Abzug supported a bill that sought to export the 1960s Great Society reform principle that poor people should have a say in their own destiny, the bill's stated purpose being "to encourage the developing countries to allow the poorest people to participate more effectively in the development process."[66]

Through its militarization of aid, Abzug said, the United States had played into the hands of despised local power elites and encouraged "cynicism at home and abroad" about American motives. Showing a degree of sensitivity that belied her "howitzer" image, Abzug noted that "a policeman handing out lollipops is still a policeman, and no one can ignore the gun in [his] holster."[67] Her view differed from that of Margaret Chase Smith, who recalled taking five hundred lollipops to Germany: "I would throw them out at the children. That was quite a satisfaction. It was my way of showing them a little bit of understanding and friendship."[68] Abzug wanted assistance to be linked to indigenously directed democratic development.

In carrying through her commitment to vote against military aid to particular countries, for example, to the Chilean junta in 1976, Abzug sometimes despaired of being effective.[69] Yet it could be argued that, in the long term, she contributed to the international climate of opinion that increasingly favored a swing to democracy. Elections did eventually resume in Chile, and democracy was also restored to Spain and Portugal. All three countries had been right-wing dictatorships. Whereas at the height of the Cold War the United States had pressed for elections only in Communist autocracies, a change in emphasis had occurred by the late 1970s. Democracy everywhere, and with it women's rights, seemed to have a better chance. A reappraisal of military assistance played a part in the process, and Abzug had contributed to that reappraisal.

Abzug's approach to the problems of international trade distinguished her from the free-trade feminists of the 1920s. She inclined to the policy that came to be known as "managed trade." This was consistent with her belief in a strong role for governments, and was a pragmatic response to America's changing circumstances. For, by the 1970s, there were signs that the United States was about to lose the omnipotence hitherto associated with its role as an economic superpower. Spending on the Vietnam War, the exactions of the Organization of Petroleum-Exporting Countries (OPEC), and the Arab oil boycott following U.S. help to Israel in 1973, all created inflationary pressures. America became less competitive, and jobs were threatened when multinational corporations exported factories and work to countries with low wages—in 1970, American multinationals' investments abroad amounted to about $100 billion, about 40 percent of it in Great Britain. Abzug deplored this tendency and favored government intervention to curtail the free movement of capital: In 1971 she introduced legislation to try to curb the export of jobs.

In doing so she noted that while she concurred in other respects with the views of the AFL-CIO's counsel, Ray Denison: "The one significant point on which we disagree—at least for the present—is that of blanket quotas [which] could lead to a tariff war reminiscent of the disastrous Smoot-Hawley period of the 1930s . . . which undoubtedly prolonged the Depression for several additional years."[70] But Abzug did not believe that the pursuit of peace through international free trade and economic interdependency was "a major concern" of a significant number of modern feminists.[71] She was never prepared to sacrifice American jobs on the altar of free trade. In 1973 she assured a union official in the New York needle trades that she would oppose the latest trade reform bill and all similar measures until the multinationals were restrained from exporting jobs, until provision was made for alternative employment at home, and until restructuring had been devised to cope with the effects of U.S. transition "from a manufacturing economy to a service oriented economy." It would be necessary, she thought, to arrive at "a new definition of free trade."[72]

In 1974 Abzug responded to a call from the New York State labor movement for what was virtually a new mercantilism reminiscent of English trade regulations in the seventeenth century. The AFL-CIO's Raymond Corbett asked her to support a flagship bill requiring at least 25 percent of oil imports to arrive in American vessels—stimulating shipbuilding, reducing U.S. dependence on foreign shipping, and improving the balance of payments. Abzug replied that she was in fact cosponsoring the legislation: "In view of the Arab boycott on oil exports to the United States, we can no longer depend on foreign flagships to carry our oil imports."[73]

Yet this outlook was by no means the product of blind nationalism. Bella Abzug was a vigorous internationalist. Whether in her opposition to the Marcos dictatorship in the Philippines, her support for UN sanctions against the illegitimate white minority regime in Rhodesia, or in her castigation of U.S. complicity in Chilean torture, her stance was with very few exceptions cosmopolitan and humanitarian.[74] One of the exceptions was, perhaps, her objection to wheat deals with the Soviet Union. She explained her wheat position by saying the U.S. exports would probably have an inflationary effect on domestic prices. She hoped for "a revision of the arrangement to prevent it from operating to the detriment of the American consumer."[75] Perhaps there is visible here a vestigial feminist concern for consumer welfare, though it is notable that her concern was far removed from the 1920s insistence on free trade. It may be that Abzug was wary of the wheat deal for the further reason that the Soviets appeared to be as unsympathetic as ever to the aspirations of East European Jews. But it would be quite wrong to infer from any of this that Abzug was an isolationist or a Cold Warrior. She was simply an internationalist without free-trade dogma.

Abzug's stance on trade was not influenced by her gender. In defining her policy, she perhaps helped to eliminate the issue from the feminist agenda. However, by the 1970s, for reasons discussed in chapter 6, women were in any case disposed to think along the same lines as men where trade was concerned. She was more an archetype than an architect of change. In feminist terms her statements on trade are a counterpoint to her more gendered approach to assistance, with its typically feminist antimilitary, prodemocracy character.

In a further contrast Abzug's stance on nuclear issues casts her unmistakably in the role of aggressive feminist peacemaker. WSP had in the course of its commitment to the anti–Vietnam War crusade lost little of its passionate opposition to nuclear testing. When the Atomic Energy Commission (AEC) planned a nuclear test in the Pacific, WSP's annual conference dubbed President Nixon "the mad bomber who lives in the White House."[76] Abzug rarely missed an opportunity to assure her constituents she was "vitally concerned with the issue of peace."[77] In 1974 she reported to one of them that she was introducing a bill to stop all nuclear bomb testing, and was also calling for a moratorium on the construction of nuclear power stations: "I feel that we are entering a very dangerous period with the proliferation of nuclear weapons and materials and feel that we need an active peace movement more than ever before."[78]

The principles of social feminism underlay Abzug's defense stance. In March 1973 she distributed a questionnaire to her constituents in the Twentieth Congressional District. In a covering letter she declared:

> The President's proposed budget reveals all too clearly his deference to the rich and his disdain for the rest of us. He has ordered a $12 billion cut in the services we need most—housing, health, aid to senior citizens, veterans, and the handicapped, school lunches, child care, education, pollution control, legal assistance to the poor, community action programs. He is even insisting that the elderly pay *more* for Medicare.
>
> The President says we cannot afford these programs without a big increase in taxes. But at the same time, he is raising the military budget $4 billion to an all-time high and has dropped tax reform, leaving intact loopholes whereby the rich can shortchange the Treasury of some $29 billion.[79]

Yet Abzug was aware that arms reductions would have social costs. In opposing the B-1 bomber program, which she dubbed "the most expensive weapons development in history," she proposed a "conversion which would utilize both skilled and unskilled workers in civilian industries."[80] She realized that she would need to deploy persuasion in addition to solutions. Like other politicians she used the circular letter device—thinking out her position carefully, then sending the same reply to a number of constituents. One such letter went out on September 4, 1974, and explained her position on the "ever-increasing military budget." She called for "drastically" different budgetary priorities, for a $15 billion cut in military spending, and for more expenditure on health, welfare, and education. But, she further noted, "our challenge is now to educate the American public and the members of the Congress" on the dangers of a renewed arms race that would undermine détente.[81]

Having helped to focus the attention of WSP and the women's movement on the Vietnam War in the mid-1960s, Abzug was in the mid-1970s trying to redirect attention to the nuclear disarmament question. At a time when SALT I was being criticized and SALT II's consummation and ratification seemed distant prospects, she helped to stiffen the faltering demands for détente that finally came to fruition in the latter half of the 1980s. In this effort, as in the case of her opposition to U.S. policy in Vietnam, Abzug appears to have sparked a special response from women: She had to send the antimilitarist letter mentioned in the previous paragraph to twice as many women as men.[82]

Abzug had interacted with other women and especially feminists in opposing the Vietnam War. After Vietnam her campaign to reshape foreign assistance helped to redefine the feminist outlook; in discarding the "housewife's" approach to trade, she reflected the new status of women; in her opposition to nuclear proliferation and support for arms limitation, she continued American feminists' long-term foreign policy campaign. All in all Abzug did much to define women's approach to foreign policy in the last quarter of the twentieth century.

In January 1977 Bella Abzug's six-year spell in Congress came to an end when she was defeated in an attempt to enter the senate. But from the mid-1970s into the 1990s, she continued to define and comment on the feminist foreign policy agenda. She saw a need for the achievement of more power for women, for example, through financial changes that would improve their prospects of being elected to political office. She continued her attack on the arms race, linking it to the disproportionate spread of poverty amongst women. She articulated and publicized the politics of the gender gap. None of these issues was entirely new to the women's movement, but Abzug managed to infuse them with urgency and intellectual and political credibility.

In 1975 Abzug found a new platform on which to air her views on campaign finances. In that year, she became the congressional representative on the Women in Power Committee of the National Commission on the Observance of International Women's Year. At the committee's first meeting, Abzug noted, its members "agreed that the real problem confronting women in American society this International Women's Year is a lack of power. It is clear that few women are in the positions where policy is either made or implemented." The committee resolved to look into such issues, including the question of "campaign finance laws as they affect female candidates."[83]

It is worth pausing to consider the basis of Abzug's reservations about large-scale donations to male (especially conservative) candidates. Compared with male candidates, Abzug depended to a disproportionate degree on small contributions. Political observer Ruth Mandel notes that this was consistent with her image as a "people's candidate." She further observes that women respect hard-earned small amounts of money and are suspicious of easily given larger sums that may be tainted with corruption.[84] It is indeed noteworthy that few women politicians, in the United States or worldwide, have been involved in corruption, a product no doubt of the gender's need to prove its worth in the process of political breakthrough, and also of its lack of exposure to the temptations of power. Abzug was well aware that her philosophy on campaign contributions would appeal to her own sex, and she accordingly used special mailing lists to solicit funds from sympathetic women. Her gender was significant at the polls, too. In 1976 she entered the Democratic primary for the New York Senate race. According to a survey by the *New York Times,* she attracted the votes of four in ten women, compared with three in ten men. In the case of her male rival, Daniel Patrick Moynihan, the ratio was reversed.[85]

As these ratios suggest, the contest was close. Out of 916,000 votes cast, only 10,000 separated the candidates. But in the event it was Moynihan who went on to enjoy a distinguished career in the Senate, and Abzug who found herself out of office. This was in fact the end of her career in elective public positions. She lost in her 1977 bid for the New York mayoralty. She then failed to win the congressional seat vacated by the victor in the mayoralty race, Ed Koch. She had no better luck in subsequent campaigns up to and including her 1986 attempt to win back the redrawn Twentieth District on an anti-nuclear-arms-race ticket. Why did she fail to make a comeback? Did this signify that her brand of feminism, with its peace ingredient, was doomed to ineffectiveness in the American context?

In comparison with other countries, the United States has in some ways been relatively barren ground for peace feminism. Abzug's self-distancing from machine politics was a dangerous ploy in the American context, especially as she embraced radical views that invited political enmity. At the same time Abzug's poor relations with the Carter administration diminished her prospects. Like President Wilson and like Eleanor Roosevelt, Jimmy Carter at first aspired to lead the peace campaign, including its feminist component. But, again like his Democratic predecessor, Carter deserted his own cause—or so it seemed to his erstwhile supporters. Division ensued, and Abzug, like Carter himself, suffered from the in-fighting.

At first all seemed well. The new president appointed women to an unprecedented 14 percent of his top policy positions in 1977 (twenty-two percent by 1979).[86] In 1975 the United Nations sponsored an International Women's Year, which soon evolved into the Decade for Women. Responding to this and to legislation introduced earlier by Abzug, President Carter expanded the membership and prolonged the activities of the U.S. National Commission on the Observance of International Women's Year. He appointed Abzug presiding officer of the commission.[87] When the commission's term ended in 1978, he replaced it with a forty-member National Advisory Committee for Women. He made Abzug cochair of that, too.

The activities of the Carter-Abzug axis had the effect of publicizing new questions about foreign policy. Female students of world politics were beginning to ask whether bilateral, country-to-country relations were, after all, an acceptable framework within which to perceive and influence the workings of the global community. If a rich country, say the United States, gave aid to a poor country, the terms of the aid were important—it could be used to reinforce the ascendancy of one group at the expense of a weaker one within the target nation. The women of the world should where necessary unite, disregarding national boundaries. Specifically women demanded that aid be given in a way that helped women as well as men in the receiving countries.[88]

Though Carter seemed to be making the right public gestures, relations between him and Abzug soured. According to Abzug, the first lady turned the White House against her. Abzug heard through a friend of Rosalynn Carter's remark that "the women in Georgia wear pinafores and Bella doesn't wear a pinafore." In her memoir Abzug commented: "If I had known about Mrs. Carter's views at the time, I could have pointed out that I usually wear a hat, but I had taken off my gloves a long time ago."[89]

On January 12, 1979, President Carter fired Abzug. The parting was abrasive, with neither side in the mood to issue emollient statements or to gloss over the differences between the chief executive and the feminist. One of Carter's initial objectives, to the early pleasure of the peace feminists, had been to promote détente with the Soviet Union, especially through the medium of the proposed SALT II treaty, limiting the nuclear arms race. But increasing tensions with the Soviet Union and a concerted attack on his policies by domestic hawks persuaded Carter to trim his principles in what he fondly hoped would be a politically advantageous manner. He withdrew SALT II from the Senate and dropped his opposition to increases in U.S. defense expenditure. The effect of this was inflationary at a time when price levels were already increasing at an alarming rate. So Carter decided, in a move that had the apparent advantage of further appeasing political conservatives, to cut back on social programs—programs that would have helped women in particular because, as a report by Abzug's new committee noted, women made up 63 percent of the sixteen million Americans living below the poverty line. Shortly before Abzug and her committee met with the president on January 12, the women issued a press release deploring the $15 billion cuts in domestic expenditure at a time when defense spending was being increased. It was in response to this attack that the annoyed president dismissed Abzug.[90]

If the first lady was correct, if Abzug was unrepresentative of American women, then the president's decision was politically well judged, and Abzug-style feminism lacked a powerful constituency in the United States. The hope within the Carter administration was that her "social feminism," embracing a broad outlook that linked military expenditure and women's welfare, was a minority tendency within the feminist movement. After Abzug's dismissal Carter appealed to her cochair, Marjorie Bill Chambers, to continue her work within the "pure feminist" sphere, including the advocacy of the Equal Rights Amendment (ERA), which Carter was still prepared to support. In the words of his press secretary Jody Powell, "Our idea is that if you want to get ERA passed, you don't do it by kicking your friends in the face." The president was prepared to allow the women's commission its independence, provided it stuck to women's issues narrowly defined.[91]

But Abzug was closer to the mainstream than Carter and his coterie imagined. However robust her public statements, she was no peripheral politician. She had parted with Betty Friedan, for example, over the latter's early-1970s antimale stance.[92] Abzug's linkage of women's welfare and the arms race was neither new nor marginal. The link to welfare regardless of gender had been a staple of left-wing political discourse in the 1930s and 1960s. Then Shirley MacLaine and Gloria Steinem had taken George McGovern to task when, in spite of their efforts on behalf of his nomination, he had shunted aside women's welfare issues in his 1972 anti–Vietnam War candidacy.[93]

Steinem was highly critical of Abzug's dismissal in what she dubbed the "Friday night massacre."[94] Twenty-four of the forty-member National Advisory Committee for Women resigned immediately in sympathy with Abzug. Women's organizations threatened that they would make an issue of the firing in the 1980 presidential election campaign. Five weeks after the incident an ABC News-Harris survey estimated that Americans regardless of gender gave the president a 52–29 percent negative rating over the dismissal. In his vain pursuit of pragmatism, Carter had made compromises that lost him support in a significant quarter.[95]

Carter could not hope to benefit from the undiluted enthusiasm of feminists in his 1980 campaign for reelection. Not only did he seem to question the right of women to have an independent voice in politics, he gave further offense in trying to preempt the political appeal of the hawks. As Abzug later put it:

His 1981 budget called for another $17 billion in domestic cuts and a 12.8 percent increase in military spending. His image as a peacemaker was being replaced by that of a hawk as he gave up on SALT II, pushed for the new MX and Cruise missiles, and made militaristic threats in the Persian Gulf area.[96]

It would be a mistake to assume that Abzug and other peace-oriented feminists had an impact on the outcome of the 1980 presidential election. They did not campaign against Jimmy Carter. Nor could they have, in an election in which the Republican candidate, Ronald Reagan, was running on a hawkish ticket. It would have meant being against a president who had appointed a black man (Andrew Young) to be ambassador to the UN, restored the Canal Zone to Panama, opened full diplomatic relations with China, induced Israel and Egypt to conclude a historic peace at Camp David, and—in spite of his tactics in the Senate—authorized, in tandem with the Soviets, a de facto compliance with the terms of SALT II. Even if they had come out against Carter, it is arguable that their campaign would have been futile. As in so many elections, the state of the economy appeared to be an overriding issue. With a 5.3 percent drop in purchasing power in 1979, the economy was doing badly and the president seemed destined for defeat on this count alone. According to the Harris poll just cited, the economy was chiefly responsible for Carter's 63 percent overall negative rating in February 1979.[97]

Abzug thought that if Carter had matched his actions to his words, women might have saved him from defeat at the hands of his Republican challenger in 1980. Even as it was, a gender gap opened in favor of the Democrats in the election, with Carter enjoying an 8 percent advantage over Reagan with women.[98] In the 1980s the extent, nature, and significance of the party-political gender gap generated heated discourse.[99] As in the 1920s and in the presidential election of 1932, politicians feared the female vote, even if its precise nature could not always be established. Feminists interested in foreign policy had an opportunity to command an attentive audience.

The voting pattern of 1980 certainly encouraged Abzug to keep the gender gap on the political agenda and to press on with her agitation for a women-oriented international program. Statistics on the gender gap, Abzug noted, could be misleading. Sometimes the gap narrowed because "men listened to their wives, daughters, and sisters and decided to change their votes, the reverse of what had been believed to be the traditional pattern." But, she insisted in her 1984 book *Gender Gap*, the difference was still in evidence in the 1982 elections.[100]

Yet in spite of the vice presidential candidacy of Geraldine Ferraro, Democratic expectations of a gender windfall were disappointed in the election of 1984. Fifty-five percent of women voted for Reagan. Abzug pleaded special circumstances. The Republican machine direct-mailed seventy categories of women on specific issues; presidential candidate Walter Mondale "declared himself for women's rights, but had no policy;" Ferraro had sound policies "on Nicaragua and generally" but the press smeared her husband's business reputation and she became "a victim of sexism." In spite of the 1984 result, therefore, Abzug still found it possible to believe that the underlying gender gap remained about "a constant eight to nine percent."[101]

Abzug warned in 1984 that a "feminization of poverty" was occurring in the United States. Women and children would "account for almost all of the nation's poor by the year 2000."[102] Her argument that the United States could no longer afford the social cost of the Cold War perhaps formed part of the consensus that forced Reagan and Bush to respond to peace overtures from Gorbachev. If so, her predictions promise to be analytically self-defeating. Because of the crumbling of the Cold War and the dissipation of the Soviet threat from the later 1980s, her grim gender-military prognosis may never be put to the test. But she did not allow such brighter prospects to dim her enthusiasm for feminist-inspired directions on foreign policy. In 1985 she formed the Women's Foreign Policy Council, having as its aim increased visibility for women in the foreign-policy-making process. The council compiled a directory of women who were expert on various aspects of foreign policy and were willing to appear in public forums. In the early 1990s Abzug's main concerns included North-South and international environmental issues.[103]

The political analyst Hope Chamberlin observed in 1973 that Bella Abzug's only real political achievement was "a traffic light on Rivington and Columbia."[104] One could belittle the achievements of any reformer that way: In democracies especially, political advances are collective. After all, Frederick Douglass did not force the abolition of slavery singlehandedly, nor did Senator Robert F. Wagner personally persuade Americans to accept the principle of social security.

Of Abzug it can be said that she was determined to discover and define the role of women in foreign policy. She was a feminist pioneer who, in her own words, took the "gloves off"—yet she did not suffer from "breakthrough syndrome." She rejected the option of stereotypical male behavior. Her aggressive style did not translate into warlike action; on the contrary, she was a leading advocate of international peace. She wished to raise women's consciousness and "to educate the American public" on the nuclear arms race and its social implications. She played an inspiring role in two successful campaigns—to extricate the United States from Vietnam and to end the Cold War. She publicized the "gender gap" in foreign policy matters. Finally she helped to highlight a continuing problem for women, their "lack of power in American society." She can be said to have heralded America's emergent gender. But this latter observation invites international comparison, the subject of the next chapter.

9 | THE MYTH OF THE IRON LADY
An International Comparison

In 1929 Florence Boeckel noted that, on the international plane, women had scarcely broken through at all into the higher reaches of democratic government: "In only one instance has there been a woman cabinet member. Under the Socialist Government in Denmark Fru Nina Bang was Minister for Education from 1923 to 1926."[1] Another three decades passed before any significant change took place. But then the world witnessed a dramatic and accelerating trend. In the thirty years between 1960 and 1989, ten female prime ministers or presidents took office. From 1990 to 1994, no fewer than twelve further women achieved similar distinction.

Sirimavo Bandaranaike became the world's first female prime minister in 1960. Like all the women in the accompanying table, except Perón and Pascal-Trouillot, she was elected.[2] Furthermore she was a peaceful conciliator in the distinctly female mode. She inherited her assassinated husband's national prominence in the country then called Ceylon (now Sri Lanka). But, whereas her husband had stamped the name Bandaranaike into his nation's history as a zealous nationalist, his widow made her name as an anticonfrontational internationalist: She achieved world prominence as a nonalignment advocate.[3] She pioneered a way forward for women and established for them the important precedent of a nonconfrontational style.

The election of Sirimavo Bandaranaike was no flash in the pan but the precursor of a significant change. The table, which illustrates the point, is restricted to top officeholders, prime ministers, and presidents. But there would be little difficulty in expanding the roster of women who have projected themselves onto the international political scene since 1960. Some women have been among the more prominent also-rans, for example, Sheikh Hasima, who lost the 1991 Bangladesh election to another woman, Begum Khaleda Zia. An expanded list might

Women Prime Ministers and Presidents, 1960–1994[4]

	Country	Office	Office First Assumed
Sirimavo Bandaranaike	Ceylon (Sri Lanka)	P.M.	1960
Indira Gandhi	India	P.M.	1966
Golda Meir	Israel	P.M.	1969
"Isabel" Perón*	Argentina	Pres.	1974
Margaret Thatcher	United Kingdom	P.M.	1979
Vigdís Finnbogadóttir	Iceland	Pres.	1980
Eugenia Charles	Dominica, West Indies	P.M.	1980
Gro Harlem Brundtland	Norway	P.M.	1981
Maria Corazon Aquino	Philippines	Pres.	1986
Benazir Bhutto	Pakistan	P.M.	1988
Violetta de Chamorro	Nicaragua	Pres.	1990
Kazimiera Prunskiene	Lithuania	P.M.	1990
Mary Robinson	Republic of Ireland	Pres.	1990
Aung San Sun Kyi†	Burma (Myanmar)	P.M.	1990
Ertha Pascal-Trouillot	Haiti	Pres.	1990
Begum Khaleda Zia	Bangladesh	P.M.	1991
Edith Cresson	France	P.M.	1991
Hanna Suchoka	Poland	P.M.	1992
Kim Campbell	Canada	P.M.	1993
Tansu Ciller	Turkey	P.M.	1993
Agathe Uwilingiyimana	Rwanda	P.M.	1993
Chandrika Bandaranaíke Kumaratunga	Sri Lanka	P.M.	1994

*María Estela Martínez de Perón
†On her party's victory at the polls, the Burmese military imprisoned Aung San Sun Kyi and prevented her from taking office.

include the British Labour cabinet minister and member of the European Parliament, Barbara Castle; the controversial international campaigner against South African apartheid, Winnie Mandela; the rejuvenator of the Japanese Socialist party and antimilitary campaigner, Takako Doi; the leader of Greece's left alliance, Maria Damanaki; Germany's global "Green" leader, the late Petra Kelly; and the reviled but powerful Chinese Communist oligarch Qiang Qing. Women have "arrived" in ways that give them extensive and diverse influence on international politics.[5]

This chapter offers an overview and general analysis of the recent, spectacular rise of international stateswomen—a digression undertaken for reasons that nonetheless have a bearing on U.S. women. One such reason is that female leaders in foreign countries are beginning to shape the international context within which American diplomats have to formulate their policies. It could even be argued that they have had more influence on U.S. foreign policy than have American women. A second reason is that some U.S. female ambitions are being realized vicariously or by proxy, abroad. Aquino, Bhutto, Ciller, Brundtland, Meir, and Robinson all studied in the United States. American women and their brand of feminism to varying degrees exercise a hidden influence through such women, as well as through others educated in English-speaking countries susceptible to U.S. ideological currents—Aung San, Campbell, Charles, Gandhi, and Thatcher all fall into that category.

A third reason for digression into the international sphere has to do with the remarkable fact that, although the advance of women worldwide seems clearly related to the spread of democracy, and although the United States is upheld as the world's leading example of democracy, U.S. women nevertheless seem to have been left behind. Through an international comparison one can attempt to identify or eliminate some factors bearing on U.S. tardiness. A fourth reason has to do with standard social-science methodology: Through a comparative survey it may be possible to isolate factors bearing on women's advancement and behavior that are, respectively, local variables and cross-national constants. Doing so should raise some pertinent questions about the foreign policy aspirations of contemporary American women. The fifth and final reason for studying non-American women leaders is that the comparative approach helps to compensate methodologically for the absence of female leaders in the United States. Although it is impossible to study nonexistent American women leaders, it is reasonable to estimate how they might behave by studying those of other countries.

In this chapter the emergence of the international stateswoman will be examined within the context of a theoretical framework that has to do with the notion of the self-made woman and the attributes stereotypically associated with her. This idea is related to the concepts of "breakthrough" and "normalization" already discussed in relation to Carrie Chapman Catt and Margaret Chase Smith: In order to enter the male world, some women have appeared to sacrifice the attributes of their gender, becoming just like the "normative" men, who were tough and aggressive and who habitually resorted to war. The idea of the "transformational" woman who surrenders her gender characteristics and often eschews feminist goals has gained currency even among informed observers.[6] It has become a worldwide gibe to say that a particular woman leader is "the only man in the cabinet." Such a woman is said to be every bit as aggressive and warlike as her male peers, and an explanation is readily at hand: Because of male antiwoman prejudice, she had to fight twice as hard to get to the top, so she was twice as tough once she got there. The woman thus popularly depicted would have more in common with the "Iron Duke," Wellington, vanquisher of Napoleon at the Battle of Waterloo, than with Sirimavo Bandaranaike. She is a fighter-climber, a hawk, an "iron lady."

Susan Crosland, the American widow of British Foreign Secretary Anthony Crosland and one of numerous journalists who subscribe to the iron lady notion, set forth some of its characteristics in an article in 1993. Explaining that Tansu Ciller and Kim Campbell won election over aspiring male politicians in Turkey and Canada, respectively, "by being deadlier," she went on to declare that "the woman who achieves public power plays the game the same way male leaders do." She poured scorn on the "great cry" of the 1960s "that if only women ruled the world we would have no more war." She articulated an oft-repeated dimension of the iron lady image: "Margaret Thatcher was the quintessential woman leader whose manhood became conspicuous: helmet for hair, and so abrasive she might have been wearing Y-fronts [British male underwear] under her skirt."[7]

The image of a woman who could be tough, aggressive, and even war-like was striking and newsworthy in the same sense that other "man bites dog" stories make the headlines. But men do not bite dogs often enough to offer a basis for generalization about changes in diet. To what extent can the iron lady concept be sustained as a generalization about the conduct of female foreign policy leaders?

The logic of the iron lady concept demands that two corollaries be true: One is that there should be a complementary phenomenon, the dynastic dove. This refers to the woman who rises on the wings of a man's reputation, the widow or daughter of a famous-but-departed husband or father. According to the iron lady thesis, a dynastic woman, who has not had to fight her way to the top, can be expected to be correspondingly gentle and peaceful. The second corollary is that there should be no such thing as an iron dove. The iron dove has been largely ignored by the popular media on the principle that when a dog bites a man it is not news. She is a woman who has reached the top by dint of hard struggle and personal toughness—yet shows peaceful tendencies. If fighting gender-based prejudice requires and fans an aggressive spirit, how could such a woman escape the warlike instincts ascribed to some of her international sisters?

The main argument in this chapter is that the concept of an iron lady defined as a bloodthirsty self-made woman is a myth based on a fiction. There has been no convincing example, in the contemporary democratic age, of such an iron lady. Dynastic women in politics have shown just as much aggression in international relations as self-made women. Moreover, the world has witnessed some stirring examples of iron doves at work.

The international comparisons that follow further suggest how certain mythologies grow from local cultures, illuminating not only the mythology of the iron lady but also how certain regional cultural attributes can make it easier for women to rise to positions of national and international leadership, or to articulate and advocate openly the goals of international peace.

An examination of the proposition that the self-made female leader is likely to be a knee-jerk hawk confirms its fictitious and rhetorical nature. The political scientist Patricia Lee Sykes examines the case of Margaret Thatcher. She notes that the press, not Thatcher herself, applied to her the term "iron lady" (the Soviet news agency TASS appears to have invented the phrase for her in 1976). Sykes questions the view that women leaders themselves carry "responsibility" for their tough images and styles.[8]

Margaret Thatcher's aggressive reputation does in some ways reveal more about the culture of the beholders than about the reality of the perceived. British Conservative prime minister from 1979 to 1991, she is a significant figure for the study of American women because she became the stereotypical iron lady, because she came to give a high priority to foreign policy, and because her image was formed within the framework of the English-speaking world, which contained the United States.[9] The argument here—and it will be controversial in European circles—is that Thatcher was not a particularly warlike leader. She only seemed so because she was a woman operating in the context of Anglo-American culture, a culture that postulated that any woman tough enough to break through must be at least as aggressive as a man.

There can be no question about the challenge Margaret Thatcher faced in striving to win her country's greatest political prize. She had to overcome the real and psychological obstacles in the path of the first woman to attain such prominence in British politics. Thatcher overcame another kind of barrier too: She did not come from the governing classes. Her father was a grocer who became a minor local politician. In order to succeed Alfred Roberts's daughter therefore had to triumph over the Conservative party's class prejudice as well as its gender prejudice.

Margaret Thatcher did succeed, but, one could argue, she paid a heavy price for her breakthrough within the Conservative party, and for her victories at three successive general elections. She conformed. The Conservatives pride themselves on being a bulwark against socialism. Accordingly Thatcher became a Red-baiter.[10] The Conservatives pride themselves on being the party of patriotism. Accordingly Thatcher was, in her responses to plans for European integration, nationalistically "patriotic" to the point of serious obstruction. The Conservatives pride themselves on being the party of law and order. Accordingly Thatcher blamed the soaring crime rate, which so inconveniently characterized her tenure as prime minister, on "the professional progressives among broadcasters, social workers and politicians, who have created a fog of excuses in which the mugger and the burglar operate."[11] In all these ways Thatcher conformed to the well-worn tenets of populist conservatism.

Her adoption of some of the staples of male-dominated politics led not a few commentators to assume that Margaret Thatcher had given up being a woman. Her own rhetoric encouraged this perception. Indeed, her rhetoric is so convincing that it is clear that she was less an opportunist than a person who had come to believe passionately in what she said. In 1983 she offered the image makers a readymade discourse when she toured North America delivering, in the words of Canadian journalist John Hay, "a seamless and self-assured assault on the Soviet Union." She warned a Toronto gathering that the "mother figure" of the state "can so easily end up not succouring but suffocating." Hay recalled that this was the politician who had abolished free milk handouts to British children, earning her the epithet "Milk Snatcher Thatcher."[12] Thatcher thus distanced herself from actions and words associated with "nurturant motherhood."

But journalists went further in their attempts to build up a Boadicean image for Margaret Thatcher. Writing for the *Washington Monthly* in 1988, British reporter Polly Toynbee asked, "Is Margaret Thatcher a Woman?" Toynbee noted that Thatcher had done nothing for women—the prime minister was avowedly antifeminist and was the only British leader since 1945 to appoint no women to her cabinet. Taking issue with British feminists who in her opinion over-criticized Thatcher, Toynbee argued that Thatcher had no alternative to making herself into "an imitation man." She had to be "twice as tough," like those women business executives with "padded power-dressing shoulders" who sacrificed family life to ambition. Toynbee warned against feminist fatalism, the creed that there was no point in campaigning to place women in office as a means to ending hierarchy, war, and ambition. The creed was based on the expectation that they would always end up like Thatcher. But women would not need to outmacho the men forever. "Gradually, there will be changes, when there are enough women at the top to prevent them all having to turn themselves into Mrs Thatchers."[13] However, Thatcher herself remained, for Toynbee, the archetypal imitation male.

Those who believed Thatcher to be exceptionally belligerent pointed to her record. She traumatized domestic politics by the ruthlessness of her use of state power to defeat the 1984 coal miners' strike. But she was above all renowned for her aggressive stances in foreign policy. She was an acerbic critic of the Soviet Union. She supported high defense spending, notably the purchase of U.S. Trident II missiles to boost the British independent nuclear deterrent. She supported President Reagan's Strategic Defense Initiative. She fought a successful war against Argentina in 1982. In defiance of European opinion, she sanctioned the use of British bases for the U.S. air strike against Libya in 1986. It seemed self-evident that Thatcher deserved the epithet "hawk."

Is it, then, correct to assume that Thatcher was "an imitation man" who did not represent the foreign policy wishes of the majority of her countrywomen? According to public opinion polls, a "gender gap" was opening up in Britain, with women more opposed to military expansion than men.[14] Whether this made Thatcher yesterday's woman or the precursor of a "mature," undifferentiated foreign policy outlook might be open to question, but it did make her rhetoric stand out for its belligerent tone.

Yet the real question is: Was Thatcher an iron lady in the sense that so many journalists imagined? Here there is a need for a distinction that is fundamental to an understanding not only of Thatcher but also of other women leaders. For a confusion arises from the fact that the term "iron lady" is used interchangeably to mean, on the one hand, a stateswoman who is eager to resort to war and, on the other, a female leader with a "virago" disposition. Without question Margaret Thatcher met the latter criterion. Her "iron lady" reputation stemmed in large part from her personality: her strength of character, will-power, tone of voice, and domineering treatment of senior colleagues who were all male and who had never had to contend with women on equal terms in their single-sex private boarding schools. Thatcher could and would not play the game as the boys played it, and in this respect was indeed a woman of iron.

However, this does not mean that Thatcher was a bloodthirsty leader of her nation. The assertion that she was belligerent in that manner needs to be quantified. While many have made the leap linking virago personality with gory foreign policy, the English novelist and freelance journalist Julian Barnes is one of the few to have attempted to supply any evidence. Commenting on the Falklands/Malvinas War, he wrote:

> Mrs. Thatcher, with her shopping-basket view of the world, likes to assure us that she does her sums. But it's odd that she doesn't mention the basic statistic of the war. One thousand eight hundred islanders were liberated from the Argentines (who brought not torture

and death but color TV sets to cheer the crofters' firesides), at a cost of just over a thousand deaths, two hundred and fifty-five of them British, plus countless modern maimings. Try doing the same sum on a different war: imagine that the reinvasion of France in 1944 had cost twenty-three million lives, six million of them Allied. Would we rejoice so much and praise our leaders?[15]

But it would be quite wrong to extrapolate from such figures a generalization about Margaret Thatcher's propensity to indulge in force. Reputable authorities on the statistics of deadly quarrels such as Lewis Fry Richardson and David Wilkinson use more reliable measures of warfare. They compare the magnitude of a given war with that of other wars, judging its intensity in relation to the size of the populations of the warring countries, not just of a small, disputed area like the Falklands—or Normandy. The war studies specialist Lawrence Freedman points out that fewer British servicemen were killed in the Falklands than in Korea, Kenya, and Malaya a few years earlier, and that contemporaneously more bloody conflicts were taking place in Lebanon, Afghanistan, Iran/ Iraq, and Kampuchea.[16]

Thatcher's bellicose image is beyond dispute, but the record of her actions is less conclusive. She never launched an aggressive war. The word "defense" in relation to armed action is, of course, subject to daily and often cynical abuse. But, whatever the merits of the background debates, there is no dispute over Argentina's initiation of the Falklands/ Malvinas War, and there is even some evidence to suggest that Thatcher tried to pull out of that confrontation at the last minute.[17] Nor would there be any serious dissent from the view that Libya's leader Colonel Gadhafi had been conducting an aggressive international terrorist campaign. Adopting the Richardson criterion, British casualties were light in the campaign to recapture the Falklands, and they were nonexistent in the case of the Libyan raid. Furthermore, it could be argued that Thatcher showed restraint in international confrontations where armed conflict might otherwise have ensued. She recalls in her memoir that China, mindful of Thatcher's action against Argentina, feared the worst in negotiations over the decolonization of Hong Kong. But she believed that "international law should prevail over the use of force," and used other means to put pressure on Beijing to respect British interests.[18]

Using the objective criterion of the ratio of British war deaths to British population, the Iron Lady's eleven years as prime minister appear to have been one of the most peaceful eras in British history. To illustrate this point, it is pertinent to review the list of "great" British prime ministers. Only two, Sir Robert Walpole and Clement Attlee, had peace records to compare with Margaret Thatcher's—and Walpole's ministry, tragically in his eyes, ended at arms with Spain.[19] Some of Britain's "great" and "brilliant" leaders, William Pitt the Elder and Winston Churchill among them, showed their abilities primarily as war leaders or, as in the case of Pitt the Younger, survived as "greats" in spite of questionable war records. Historians accept as normal the bloody deeds of men, and even disregard them in passing judgement. The Liberal leader David Lloyd George is sympathetically remembered for his social reforms, not as one of those responsible for the carnage of World War I. To suggest otherwise would seem blasphemous to British historians. This is a clear case of double standards, by comparison with Thatcher's treatment.

As for the "Pax Britannica" of the nineteenth century, it can be said to describe most fittingly the stability of the center at the expense of the periphery—just like Pax Romana before and Pax Americana after.[20] Yet, in terms of image making, there has been little recognition of this. Viscount Palmerston's reputation, it is true, is blemished by the horrors of the Crimean War. But it is customary to hail Sir Robert Peel, Benjamin Disraeli, and William Ewart Gladstone as great exponents of the art of British parliamentary politics—forgetting the gory depredations of the Empire. During the tenures of these revered statesmen the Indians, the Afghans, the Zulus, and the Boers all felt the weight of imperial "retribution" for standing in the way of white Anglophone expansion. Nor did the British always escape lightly. In just one attack in 1841, the Afghans massacred a column of sixteen thousand British soldiers and camp followers—only one man escaped to tell the tale. Adjusted to fit present-day population figures, that would be a massive loss of life, yet it is trivial compared with the uncounted toll of the Indian Mutiny of 1857 and the retribution that followed. Nothing even remotely similar occurred in the Thatcher administration. Yet, because she flew in the face of certain expectations of female conduct, Thatcher was represented as a leader with blood on her hands.

It must, then, be borne in mind that the archetypal iron lady conducted her foreign military policy with some restraint. This is important in a direct sense, in that Thatcher and Thatcherite imagery have been so influential. France's first woman premier, the socialist Edith Cresson, proved to have but a fragile grip on power, yet was dubbed a Thatcher-type iron lady.[21] Poland's first woman premier, Hanna Suchoka, courted conservative opinion with her antiabortion stance and declared that Margaret Thatcher was her model.[22] When Tansu Ciller became her country's first female prime minister, the London *Times* dubbed her "Turkey's Thatcher."[23] In these cases the intended comparisons were to Thatcher's style, but there was always the implied danger of emulation of Thatcher the warrior queen.

Yet it would be too easy to forget, under the spell of Thatcher's more recent eminence, that she was neither the only nor the first woman prime minister with a belligerent reputation. Blurred perceptions of the proclivities of tough women may have been acute in the Thatcher era, but they were already endemic. Golda Meir, Israel's prime minister from 1969 to 1974, seemed to fit the iron lady stereotype. In some significant ways, for example, in being a socialist and a feminist, she was very different from Thatcher. Yet there is no end to the stream of jokes about Golda Meir's being "the only man in the Israeli cabinet." During her premiership a store on Harvard Square married this perception to contemporary campus culture and sold "genuine Israeli women paratroopers' boots."[24] Meir could be portrayed as one of those women who represent a dangerous transition stage in the female ascent, and is here of special interest because she operated beyond, as well as within, the confines of Anglophonic culture.

Meir's self-perception and early career were at variance with her later depiction as a hawk. She had been an active leader of women's groups, and in her autobiography she hinted at her role as a peace advocate of the nurturant-motherhood variety. She stressed the point that she had made diplomatic efforts to avert the use of force: In 1948, for example, she tried to dissuade King Abdullah of Jordan from joining the Arab invasion of Israel.[25]

But in spite of this retrospective self-perception, it was as a tough war leader that Meir made an enduring impression. After a long spell as Israel's foreign minister (1956–1966), she became prime minister in the wake of the 1967 Six-Day War. As premier she proved reluctant to surrender Israel's war gains. Israeli moderates took her to task for opposing the return of the Sinai and the Golan Heights to the Arabs, and because she was instrumental in denying the West Bank Palestinians local autonomy within the Kingdom of Jordan. Then, in 1973, Meir established her warrior capabilities in an unmistakable manner. When Israel's neighbors launched the Yom Kippur War, she proved equal to the task of leading her nation to victory.

Yet even here it must be noted that the image outran the reality. Meir was criticized for not having made proper preparations for the 1973 attack—her alleged neglect of war preparations was surely more characteristic of a peace-loving than of a warmongering person. Second, whatever one thinks of her intransigence, the 1973 war was not started by Israel—like Thatcher, Meir fought a defensive war. Finally, the 1973 war was not an exceptional event in the history of Israel's relations with its neighbors. It only seemed so because the attack almost succeeded, and because the person in charge was a woman. The woman of iron resolve who fights her way to the top and proves equal to dealing with military aggression tends to be regarded as a warmonger, but as a matter of historical record she is not.

The self-made women leaders of the present democratic age are less belligerent than their male equivalents. But are they, nevertheless, more belligerent than women who did not have to fight to achieve power, finding themselves in high office through dynastic accident? The following review will suggest that dynastic women leaders are not more "dovish" than those women who have made their own way to the top. In some significant cases, they have acquired a reputation, at least, for being tough and even "hawkish"—a reputation that is balanced, nevertheless, by some conspicuous peaceful traits.

Indira Gandhi of India is an example of a dynastic woman who acquired a reputation for toughness—she is said to have been the only female leader whom Thatcher admired.[26] Gandhi was the daughter of Jawaharlal Nehru, who had led his nation from independence in 1947 until his death in 1964. She was prime minister of India from 1966 to 1977, and from 1980 to her assassination in 1984. Freed from the obligations of marriage by her husband's death in 1960, Gandhi concentrated on the task for which she had been prepared by background and upbringing—politics. Her biographer Nayantara Sahgal noted that, in the Lal Bahadur Shastri premiership of 1964–1966 (ending with Shastri's death and Gandhi's selection), she "remained, as daughter of the charismatic Nehru, a figure whom his party could not comfortably ignore in the emotional aftermath of his death."[27] Yet, while she proved a diligent political assistant to her father, she was still not, when chosen to be leader of the governing Congress party, a member of the national legislature. To allow her to exercise her prime ministerial office, party managers had to make available her late husband's constituency, Rae Bareli. Hoping to insulate herself from charges of ruthless self-promotion, Gandhi continued to play on her dynastic provenance—sitting under a portrait of Nehru, she received an incredulous British journalist and told him she was the "housewife" India needed.[28] Gandhi was not a self-made woman, and she exploited the fact.

But if Gandhi was a dynastic beneficiary, she was by no means timid. She had physical courage, as she proved when she was bombarded and injured by stone-throwing crowds, and when she approached the front lines to boost the morale of Indian troops. Furthermore, she was the subject of discourse comparable to that concerning Margaret Thatcher and Golda Meir. Her visit to the front lines at Kashmir during the Indo-Pakistan war of 1965 prompted the remark that she was "the only man in the cabinet," possibly the first application of that phrase.[29] In 1964 *U.S. News & World Report* launched an all-out attack on the martial leanings of "India's Autocratic Woman of Iron":

Although Gandhi often preaches nonviolence to the rest of the world, she oversaw India's uninvited annexation of the Himalayan kingdom of Sikkim. She fought a war with Pakistan in 1971, which resulted in the truncation of that Moslem nation and led to the birth of Bangladesh. She inherited border disputes with China and Pakistan. She has dealt summarily with the long-simmering rebellion among the Sikhs as well as with communal fighting between the Hindus and Moslems and between the native tribespeople and immigrating Hindus in remote Assam.

She embraced nonalignment yet has tilted India toward Moscow in order to build a powerful, well-equipped army, 1.2 million strong.[30]

This perception was by no means unusual. A columnist in *Mademoiselle* said she would have voted against both Thatcher and Gandhi, but at least they had established one thing about women: "The strongest among us take bombs and bullets, and don't squeal."[31]

However, the American columnist's language contained a subliminal nuance. Her use of the word "take" implies courage in defense. The record of Gandhi's foreign policy does not suggest she was a warmonger. The fighting that took place in her lengthy periods in office was modest in extent compared with the turbulence in the half decade immediately preceding her accession to the premiership, when India fought two wars with Pakistan and one with China. The 1971 defense treaty with the Soviet Union was not an aggressive pact—it made good sense. India was relatively weak militarily, and feared another attack from China. The United States was out of the running as a defense partner because of its ties with Pakistan. Thus India had to look elsewhere for the ally it needed. The buildup of India's armed forces by a woman prime minister was an instance of the female preference for security and defense, as distinct from wars of aggression. The test would be not the increase in military strength but the uses to which the new army was put.

No sooner was the Soviet treaty signed than India went to war with Pakistan, securing in a short campaign the independence from Pakistan of its former eastern province, which became the new nation of Bangladesh. But the war came too soon to have formed part of the military buildup plan. It was a response, rather, to the problem of almost ten million refugees who fled to India from East Pakistan during the revolutionary civil war, bringing with them problems of disease and social tension that could have destabilized India itself. Gandhi's intervention was prophylactic, supported by international opinion, and relatively bloodless. In her critical study Sahgal argues that Gandhi's policies were bloody and intolerant internally but concedes that in foreign policy she succeeded, in the long run, in establishing "a pattern of cordial relations."[32]

One conspicuous feature of dynastic female leadership is its clean sweep of the Indian subcontinent. This affords an opportunity to examine the iron lady notion free of cluttering interregional variables. The picture presented by the subcontinent's women would appear to be one of conciliation, military toughness when occasion demands, and vulnerability to sexist hyperbole.

The cases of India's tough yet nonconfrontational Indira Gandhi and of Sri Lanka's conciliatory Bandaranaike have already been noted. (It is of further interest here that Sri Lanka has become not only the first nation to elect a woman prime minister, but also the first to elect a second, and the first to practice matriarchal dynasticism: Chandrika Bandaranaike Kumaratunga, who became prime minister in 1994, is Sirimavo Bandaranaike's daughter.) Begum Khaleda Zia, who in 1991 became the first democratically elected leader of Bangladesh, was the daughter of a former president. Pakistan's Benazir Bhutto is likewise a dynastic figure who wore her father's political mantle—Zulfikar Bhutto was the prime minister of Pakistan from 1971 to his overthrow by the military in 1977 and execution two years later. She struggled to restore domestic harmony both during her brief term as premier from December 1988 to her dismissal by President Ishaq Khan in August 1990, and after her return to power in 1993 upon the defeat of the Moslem League.

Like Gandhi, Bhutto acquired a virago reputation. The novelist Salman Rushdie's 1983 characterization of her as "Virgin Ironpants" was incongruous in a way. The prime minister had participated in anti–Vietnam War marches while a student at Harvard, stopped short of war with India, and gave the lie to Rushdie's assessment by giving birth during her term in office. Yet she was unyielding in her handling of the Kashmir border dispute with India, and resisted U.S. pressure in insisting on Pakistan's right to develop its own atomic weapon. If it is true that the "daughters of the East" were peace-loving conciliators inappropriately calumnified for their aggressive tendencies, it is also true that they could be as tough as their self-made sister leaders in the West.[33]

Looking beyond the subcontinent of India, there are further cases of women acting as conciliators. The international policies of Burma's Aung Sang (the daughter of a revolutionary hero) remain a subject of speculation; she has been a prisoner of the military since her election to the premiership in 1990. Corazon Aquino was the widow of the heir apparent to the Filipino presidency, who was murdered by the Marcos dictatorship. As president she tried to tame the violent factionalism of the Philippines while at the same time curbing the power of the military.[34] "Non-violence," she told a Harvard audience in 1986, is "the key to peace."[35] Nicaragua's Violetta de Chamorro is not, strictly speaking, a dynastic figure, in that she first won election in her own right. However, the Chamorros have been the country's leading political family for most of the twentieth century.[36] Chamorro's election marked the end of her country's civil war, an end to confrontation with the United States, and the restoration of peaceful relations with Nicaragua's neighbors. It must be conceded that all this was largely because the United States ended its destabilizing policies of the Iran-Contra era. Nevertheless one might argue that a dynastic woman presided over the reconciliation process in Nicaragua.

Yet, while there is widespread evidence of the conciliatory behavior of dynastic women, the cases of Gandhi and Bhutto demonstrate that when occasion demanded, they could be "iron ladies" in the military sense of the word. Moreover, as shown above through the example of Margaret Thatcher, restraint was not the exclusive property of the dynastics. Finally, it is surely significant that there is no historical rule linking male dynastic provenance to peaceful ways. Most men acquire power through unfair competition, if not through outright dynasticism or nepotism—and there is no suggestion that nephews of prime ministers or sons of kings are less aggressive in foreign policy than the men who have exceptionally risen from poverty or obscurity to lead their countries. Dryden's words were about class, but are equally true of gender: "War is the trade of kings." Dynastic women were peaceful because they were women, not because they were privileged.

To complete the demolition of the myth that self-made women who break through to become national leaders are likely to be iron ladies of the belligerent variety, it is appropriate to turn to politicians who have won power in their own right and are noted not just for their peaceful ways but for their advocacy of peace.

Scandinavia offers two examples of the "iron dove." Vigdís Finnbogadóttir of Iceland made it to the top strictly in her own right. She established her peace credentials in the 1960s and 1970s by opposing the continued presence of the U.S. base at Keflavík. In one sense her opposition was an instance of small-nation indulgence: Given Iceland's strategic position in the North Atlantic, the United States was going to afford the protection of its nuclear umbrella whether or not it continued to have a base on the island. In another sense, though, her opposition was a radically pacifist stance, for Iceland had no standing army of its own with which to replace the Americans: the three-thousand-strong Icelandic Defense Force consisted of American soldiers. Be that as it may, in 1980, with the help of socialists and feminists, Finnbogadóttir narrowly won election to the presidency of Iceland. She became, in the proud words of official publicists, "the first woman in World history to be elected a constitutional Head of State."[37]

In 1984 Finnbogadóttir was returned unopposed for a second presidential term. Her enthusiasm for feminism and peace remained undiluted. In spite of the fact that Iceland's president is supposed to be apolitical, she joined the 1985 women's twenty-four-hour strike protesting against male privilege—one of the very few occasions when a head of state has joined a strike instead of suppressing it. On that occasion Finnbogadóttir also threatened to use the presidential veto for the first time in the forty-one years since Iceland gained its independence from Denmark: she opposed a bill ordering air hostesses back to work.[38] In 1986 this ardent and successful feminist confirmed her commitment to peace by hosting the Reykjavík summit between Reagan and Gorbachev. Though disappointing in itself, this meeting established a pathway toward future arms-reduction agreements.

Gro Harlem Brundtland is the second example of a Scandinavian woman who became a leader on merit and espoused the peace cause. Brundtland entered politics with academic credentials, having written her Harvard School of Health doctoral dissertation on the subject of first menstruation. Unlike the divorcée Finnbogadóttir, Brundtland was married, but she was equally independent of male support—in fact her husband did not share her political persuasion, which was distinctly antimilitarist. Brundtland supported NATO, but in February 1981 she became Norway's prime minister on the crest of a bitterly fought campaign against the stockpiling of U.S. nuclear weapons on Norwegian soil. In September of the same year the Socialists lost to the Conservatives, who formed a government for the first time since 1928, but in 1986 Brundtland was able to return to the premiership at the head of a minority Labor government.

Brundtland had the power and inclination to go further than Iceland's president. The Norwegian socialists had a long-standing commitment to the policy that 40 percent of civil service jobs at all levels should be occupied by women. In May 1986 Brundtland appointed an exceptionally youthful eighteen-member Council of Ministers, eight of whom were women. The prime minister was not only supportive of women but in debt to the feminist movement and perhaps even its prisoner: Left to her own devices, she would have been more accommodating to the Americans on the nuclear issue. But regardless of the reason, she is an example of the "iron dove," a tough self-made woman devoted to peaceful ideals, the very antithesis of the proposition that self-made women will be warlike in foreign policy.[39]

Hitherto this chapter has concentrated on the question of war and peace. The evidence reviewed makes it plain from several perspectives that the idea of the "iron lady" as a self-made warhawk is a myth based on fiction. Yet the emergence of world stateswomen raises other another issue, too. This is the cultural context within which certain women may become outspoken peace advocates, as distinct from those women who were, like Thatcher, restrained in action but aggressive in tone.

The case of Gro Harlem Brundtland is of further interest here, in that her commitment to the peace cause was just one aspect of a wide-ranging portfolio of "caring" issues. Notably she was committed to the environmental, or "green" cause. Still prime minister of Norway in the 1990s, she chaired the United Nations–sponsored Commission on Environment and Development, known in her honor as the Brundtland Commission. The commission worked for some time to set up an Earth Summit in Rio de Janeiro in June 1992. With America's President Bush dragging his heels on environmental issues on the eve of the summit, Brundtland tried to concentrate his mind. She said that the United States would have to pay a higher price for stronger environmental controls, for it was the world's prime offender, especially in its consumption of fossil fuels—these fuels accounted for rising emissions of carbon dioxide, the most serious of the climate-changing "greenhouse gases."

The outspoken Norwegian appealed for a curb on consumption as well as production. There were too many people consuming the limited food supplies now being further threatened by climatic change. Thus, Brundtland felt, population control through family planning was essential to the reduction of poverty. Brundtland bluntly took issue with the opponents of birth control, including the Vatican. The Norwegian prime minister was not just an "iron dove" but a woman with a broad sense of international commitment.[40] In that respect she could be likened to Bella Abzug and described as a fellow herald of the emergent gender.

Yet it would be unwise to generalize too unguardedly about the type of culture likely to produce women who are successful and who are outspoken advocates of international peace. The women leaders of the subcontinent of India are different from their counterparts in Scandinavia not just because they are dynastic but in other ways, too. Here it is appropriate to return to the case of Indira Gandhi. As *U.S. News & World Report* observed, Gandhi often preached nonviolence. Also she was prominent in the nonalignment movement with its rejection of Cold War confrontation, and campaigned for the limitation and control of nuclear weapons.[41] What were the regional cultural factors that led to her acceptance as national leader and gave her such a peaceful outlook?

One of these factors might be expressed as a negative: Chivalry, an artifact of medieval European culture that still circumscribes Western women, has not held back their Eastern sisters. Certain other cultural-religious factors, though, might by their presence be imagined to hold back millions of non-Western women: In the 1920s, the American-born Katherine Mayo, in her controversial book *Mother India,* stirred up a storm when she opposed Indian independence on the ground that the subcontinent's women were not ready for it.[42] Two traditions, the first Muslim and to a lesser extent Hindu, and the second purely Hindu, may even today be significant in their impact on secular attitudes toward widows. Purdah requires women to retire from public life during their childbearing years. Suttee, the consignment of a Hindu widow to the funeral pyre on the death of her husband, implies that a woman derives her worth exclusively from her association with a man. However, these traditions need to be considered carefully. That purdah is a tradition of fluctuating intensity is plain from Bhutto's childbearing while in office (no other prime minister has ever produced babies). Purdah could, moreover, be said to encourage women to live their lives with special intensity before and after their childbearing years. As for the idea of suttee, it could be said to put moral pressure on widows, in the absence of committal to the flames, to live worthy lives, for example by performing public duties.

Turning to the effects of Indian culture on women's discourse on war and peace, there is, on the one hand, no disposition to believe, like the "chivalrous" West, in myths about the physical incapacities of women. India's gods include females as well as males, and they invoke destruction as well as creation. A heroine of the 1857 Indian Mutiny, Rani Jhansi, was revered for her part in killing numerous Englishmen. On the other hand India has a strong male pacifist tradition, a tradition moreover with a proven practical side—nonviolence was the tactic that had won independence from Britain. Women have not challenged that tradition; indeed, in the democratic era, they have upheld it firmly. In conclusion it could be said that the experience of India demonstrates the diversity of factors likely to enhance the rise of women, and supplies an example of a region where militarism is not a male norm to which women might be tempted to conform.[43]

Scandinavian societies offer some similarities, yet some differences, too. In a study of Swedish politics, Joyce Gelb used the suggestive phrase "feminism without feminists."[44] In one sense the phrase is inappropriate because organized feminism was very much in evidence in Iceland and Norway. In another sense, though, it may be true that strident "feminists" were rare in Scandinavia, because women were pushing on an already open door. Confident, peace-oriented feminism may well have flourished because of its cultural context. One might be tempted to take this argument further, for the entrenched position of the male as well as female peace activists, notably those opposed to the stationing of foreign nuclear weapons on national territory, is a feature of the political culture of both Iceland and Norway—and a cultural factor shared with India. Given the residual asexual support for antimilitary policies, Scandinavian women of the 1980s did not need to appear on the world stage in drag. On the other hand on peace issues they were still equipped to supply a lead. The gender gap flourished in Norway in spite of the general tendency to favor peace. A 1982 poll showed 76 percent of women opposed to the stationing of U.S. cruise missiles in Europe, compared with 46 percent of men.[45]

Another feature of Scandinavian political culture is its socialist traditions, and the links between those traditions and recent feminism. In her study *Women in Western Political Thought* (1979), Susan Moller Okin noted the disposition of both classical and modern conservative philosophers to treat women as property; she further noted the rejection of this notion, along with other ideas about property, by some socialist thinkers.[46] Perhaps in part because socialist philosophy helped to sustain them, Scandinavian women's movements flourished in the 1970s and 1980s by comparison with those in more conservative countries like the United States and Britain.[47] In Iceland, for example, the Women's Alliance commanded, in the 1987 election, about 10 percent of the popular vote and won, in consequence, six of the sixty-three seats in the national parliament.

In spite of the spectacular rise of female leadership worldwide, the numbers of women presidents and prime ministers are still too small for the historian to offer authoritative generalizations. Such an effort would be bedeviled by exceptions. In February 1994, for example, another Scandinavian country, Finland, almost chose a woman president— but the defeated candidate, Defense Minister Elisabeth Rehn, was no dove. She promised she would "give the Finnish people security," in other words stand up to the Russians.[48] Scandinavian women are clearly variable in outlook.

Another complex comparison is provided by the case of Canada, which has a political culture similar in some ways to that of Scandinavia. Canadian politics, like that of its transatlantic Nordic counterparts, is substantially to the left of that in the United States or Britain, and Canadian foreign policy is strongly committed to international peacekeeping. Canadian women have broken through politically to a greater extent than have their counterparts south of the border. In the 1993 election, for example, 23.8 percent of the House of Commons candidates overall were women, ranging from 38 percent in the case of the left-wing National Democratic Party to 11 percent in the case of the far-right Reform Party. Yet in spite of this "sympathetic" culture, the first Canadian woman prime minister, Kim Campbell, was a Tory with no special peace agenda: indeed, she opposed a proposal by Norway's defense minister that a UN college should be set up in Canada for the purpose of training peacekeeping forces.[49]

These qualifications confirm that women are different from men not just in ways that change over time but also in different ways in different cultures. In spite of this complication, however, it is possible to generalize both about similarities and about the nature of differences. The similarity between diverse regional cultures is that the notion of the bloodthirsty "iron lady" is a myth based on fiction: Women show a uniform disposition to be peaceful. What varies according to different cultures is not so much the degree to which women practice peace, as their willingness to advocate it.

10 | AMERICAN WOMEN AND CONTEMPORARY FOREIGN POLICY

When Bill Clinton entered the White House in 1993, the debate over gender politics was as vibrant as ever. On the one hand there was the idea that a female candidate should "run as a woman." Implicit in this outlook were pride in gender difference, and the tendency to view women candidates as "politically correct," meaning that they were feminists, liberals in domestic affairs, and advocates of peaceful options in foreign policy.[1] On the other hand there was the idea that as women matured politically through experience in high office, they would tend to adopt opinions that made them no different from men—including some hawkish views on foreign policy.[2]

While this debate is of intrinsic interest to any student of feminism, its practical implications depend on the degree to which women have empowered themselves to influence foreign policy. Clearly, American women have failed to break through on the executive level. In other words there has been no female president, vice president, or secretary of state. Even when this situation is rectified, as surely it must be in due course, the record will show that, by comparison with a number of other countries, the United States was slow to recognize the claims and talents of its female half. This is particularly ironic when one considers that the United States took the lead in terms of organized feminism, produced the first women's peace party, and developed a liberal education system that cradled the intellects of a significant proportion of those women who went on to lead other nations.

Even when one turns to less elevated echelons of the executive branch, the picture is not reassuring to those who would wish to see women take a greater part in the construction of foreign policy. President Reagan appointed Jeane Kirkpatrick American ambassador to the UN in 1981. But she remarked how out of place she felt in his administration's foreign policy meetings, such as those held in the "Situation Room": "I don't think there had ever been a woman in that room before [because] the male monopoly of foreign policy had been so complete."[3] President Clinton has appointed another woman, Madelaine Albright, to the same job. In light of Eleanor Roosevelt's earlier service at the UN, and of President Nixon's appointment of Shirley Temple as a delegate to the General Assembly, one could portray this as reconfirmation of a bipartisan determination to give women a greater role. On the other hand the UN ambassador merely explains policy, as distinct from making it, and, as the Kennedy–Adlai Stevenson relationship illustrated at the time of the Bay of Pigs fiasco, even he or she is sometimes not adequately briefed. With the United States now the world's only superpower, and the UN threatened with client status, one could adapt Susan Jeffords's language to say that the UN ambassadorship is a "feminized space," a disempowered job in which two women have been placed.

The slow emergence of American women is curious because, starting in Sirimavo Bandaranaike's time, American feminism underwent a renaissance that seemed to complement the international trend and to promise major advances. But to committed feminists the renaissance seemed increasingly empty. Women in the 1960s were blocked on the legislative, as well as the executive front. Between 1961 and 1969, the number of women in Congress declined from twenty to eleven. Matters did improve thereafter. Yet in 1989 Rutgers University's Center for the American Woman and Politics estimated that, at the then-current rate of progress, it would take 410 years for the percentage of women in congress to match their proportion of the entire population.[4] At the start of the Clinton presidency, female House representation rose from twenty-eight to forty-eight. Although this made 1992 the "Year of the Woman" in politics, the rise to 11 percent of membership was eclipsed in the following year by the 18 percent achieved by women in the Canadian House of Commons. The Senate, with its special foreign policy powers, never until 1993 had more than three female members, and from 1960 to 1992, women comprised only between 0 and 2 percent of that chamber's hundred-strong membership. No woman has ever chaired the Senate Foreign Relations Committee.[5]

Turning from the formulation to the administration of policy, there has been a similar scarcity of women in responsible positions. Homer Calkin remarked in his 1978 study for the U.S. Department of State that, in spite of the considerable time lapse since the appointment of Ruth Bryan Owen as the first U.S. woman ambassador in 1933, "no woman career Foreign Service officer has been appointed as Ambassador to one of the major (Class I) diplomatic posts."[6] Between 1957 and 1970 the percentage of women foreign service officers actually declined, from 8.9 to 4.8 percent—another indicator of the darker side of the "new feminism" of the 1960s. The number of women in senior State Department positions was 3.3 percent of the total by 1977, low when one considers that 15 percent is considered the threshold for moving beyond "token status." At the time, 76.9 percent of the employees in the State Department as a whole were women.[7]

The picture must, however, be balanced. The rise of American women in foreign policy circles has been slow but steady. The point can be illustrated in several ways. First, individual contributions threaten to make nonsense of the statistics. Women outside politics and the civil service have come to exert influence on the policy process. The film stars and other women who protested the Vietnam War fall into this category, as do those who are members of feminist, peace, and other radical organizations. The socialist publicist Agnes Smedley is an example of the latter; she continued in the tradition of pre–World War II women in trying to increase American tolerance of China, even after the Communist takeover in 1949. The rise of women in influential professions like journalism has also created a better forum for individuals like Freda Kirchwey, the editor of the liberal journal *The Nation*, who opposed McCarthyism and international fascism and espoused an array of international causes. No account of foreign policy formation that does not take cognizance of the contributions of such influential outsiders can be complete. It is they who, collectively with many others, make up the public opinion that is the inescapable driving force behind many political decisions.[8]

Turning to the insiders, the picture is not so gloomy as the statistics might suggest. From the 1950s on some well-known women showed the way by accepting posts with the foreign service and Department of State. In December 1952 Eleanor Lansing Dulles was appointed special assistant to the German Bureau within the State Department. She assumed responsibility for Berlin and made some appreciable progress, helping, for example, toward the success of the Free University in that city.

Eleanor Dulles's brothers headed, respectively, the State Department and the CIA, which meant that she could simply not be overlooked. Clare Boothe Luce enjoyed a similar advantage. Luce was appointed American ambassador to Rome in 1953—at a time when the CIA was busily, if not particularly effectively, suborning the workings of Italian democracy. Her good looks and her marriage to media mogul Henry Luce made her, too, a conspicuous figure. The aforementioned Shirley Temple, who went on to become U.S. ambassador to Ghana, was similarly in the public eye: She had been a famous actress, the child prodigy of such often-saccharine Hollywood movies as *Bright Eyes, Curly Top,* and *Poor Little Rich Girl.* Although "PC" feminists might not find such women to their taste, the publicity they attracted was the oxygen of future ambition.[9]

An aroused awareness of the issue of female representation in the foreign service has become a feature of Washington politics. One indication of that awareness is the fact that Americans go to the trouble of compiling statistics indicating the gender of the public servants involved. At the root of this practice is not so much the opinion that women might be more peaceful and caring than men, or that they might perform as well as or better than men, as the strong feeling that women have the right to be properly represented. By 1970 there existed within the State Department an ad hoc committee to improve the status of women in foreign affairs agencies. One of its members was Mary S. Olmstead, who had been in 1945 one of the first six women admitted to the foreign service. Olmstead was a talented woman who became America's first ambassador to Papua New Guinea. But she found within the State Department "an appalling array of discriminatory attitudes and policies against women." In her experience, for example, women had to accept lower-grade jobs than men with identical qualifications. Olmstead became president of the Women's Action Organization, which in the 1970s campaigned for women and helped to restore morale in a foreign service that needed new blood.[10]

Alison Palmer was another woman who ran into sex discrimination in the State Department, and campaigned effectively against it. Though she was a graduate of Brown University, she was at first assigned to a secretarial job. In the foreign service oral examination, she was denied the opportunity to display her gifts, being obliged instead to answer obscure questions such as, "What states does the Suwannee River flow through?"[11] She interpreted this as an attempt to make her fail the oral and went on to file several lawsuits against the State Department. In 1987 the United States District Court for the District of Columbia found in her favor in a class action suit backed by the Women's Action Organization. The State Department was found to have engaged in gender discrimination in violation of the provisions of the 1964 Civil Rights Act. By August 1992 financial compensation had been paid to more than two hundred women whose careers had been affected by discrimination.[12]

The Palmer case and its outcome were symptomatic of a long-term change in the gender climate. By the 1980s self-made women were beginning to secure appointments in senior State Department positions. Rozanne L. Ridgeway, for example, was assistant secretary of state for European and Canadian affairs from 1985 to 1989. In the early 1990s, the same desk was again occupied by a woman, Avis T. Bohlen. Being in charge of such a regional bureau "is what really matters," according to one close observer of women in the foreign service.[13] To be sure, women were still in a small minority, and fortune did not always smile on them. For example, in a meeting in July 1990, American ambassador to Baghdad April C. Glaspie was held to have misled Iraqi dictator Saddam Hussein into believing that the United States would not object to his takeover of Kuwait—a miscalculation that led directly to the Gulf War. Glaspie's defenders had to protest that her "soft" approach accurately reflected U.S. policy on Iraq, and that being a woman made her a convenient scapegoat for American nonanticipation of the invasion.[14] But in spite of slow progress and occasional setbacks, the recent trend is unmistakable and is confirmed by the figures: By 1990 women made up 24.3 percent of America's foreign service officers.[15]

Finally, while American women may in some ways be the missing sisters of international politics, that picture can be misleading. There is some evidence to support the view that women's progress in America is relatively broad based. In fact, according to one comparative study of gender status, the United States has lagged behind only Sweden and Finland in terms of women's general progress toward equality.[16] Broad-based advances perhaps hold forth steadier prospects for the future of women's power than may exist in countries where women from privileged social strata have begun their ascent of the political ladder at or near its topmost rung.

Furthermore, the United States is by no means the only omission from the roster of countries that have yet to cast a woman in the role of national leader. If Canada, its neighbor to the north, has forged ahead, Mexico, its other contiguous neighbor, has never produced a woman leader. It is true that there have been women leaders south of the Rio Grande: Argentina's Perónist women, Evita and Isabel, and the Caribbean's Eugenia Charles and Ertha Pascal-Trouillot. But they have been few in number and marginal or undistinguished in their contribution to foreign affairs.[17] Huge areas of the world are entirely bereft of female leadership, and in others female politicians have had a limited and checkered history. In 1988 Uganda's ambassador to Washington, Princess Elizabeth of Toro, caused a stir precisely because she was a curiosity, as Africa was then so lacking in women leaders.[18] The first African woman prime minister, Rwanda's Agathe Uwilingiyimana, was assassinated in 1994, just as she was attempting to steer her country toward tribal reconciliation and democracy. Africa's most charismatic woman leader, Winnie Mandela, became a member of South Africa's first multiracial cabinet in 1994, but she had already been discredited because of involvement in serious crimes.

It is therefore no sterile exercise to inquire which factors have shaped the fortunes and actions of contemporary American women aspiring to make their mark on foreign policy. There is a case for looking in turn at general cultural factors, at the contemporary state of consumer consciousness, at recent aspects of Red-baiting, and at the gender gap as a phenomenon in political culture.

Cultural factors that determine the rate at which women rise to become leaders of international prominence are in several ways similar to those which explain the rate at which they emerge in domestic politics: for example, the availability of role models and the prevailing sense of public duty. Others have a more special bearing on international affairs. In the United States one of the latter factors is the "nuclear family." The spatially dispersed, two-generational family makes greater demands on women who find, in the words of the historian Carl Degler, that in contemporary society "the future of the family and the fulfilment of women as persons are at odds as never before."[19] Because active participation in foreign policy so often involves extensive travel, an even greater strain is placed on family-conscious women with ambitions in that field. This, and the problems anticipated for female diplomats in patriarchies such as those in the Muslim world, was for decades used as an argument against the promotion of women in the foreign service.[20] Quite apart from this male-generated discrimination, the prospect of family-disruptive travel may have deterred some women from foreign service careers. Foreign service officers have never been very well paid in any case, and in a gender-conscious age, private business has actively sought to recruit talented women who might otherwise become ambassadors abroad or serve in the State Department.

Yet one can set against these factors certain considerations that potentially qualified women in a special way for foreign policy work. One is that women of a certain social status have tended to be more proficient at foreign languages than men, who, for career promotion reasons, tend to study such subjects as law, business, and engineering—disciplines conducive to careers that do not take them abroad. U.S. attachés overseas in the 1920s usually could not speak the language of the local people, whereas their wives were expected to. In spite of a 1930s upgrading of language tuition for foreign service officers, no great progress was made amongst this overwhelmingly male cadre: In 1959 William Lederer and Eugene Burdick complained bitterly about Americans' linguistic limitations in the factual epilogue of their renowned novel about Vietnam, *The Ugly American*. Ironically, parents who dismissed their daughters to finishing schools thereby ensured that they often picked up the skills to become better qualified ambassadors than the men they were intended to marry.[21]

More broadly, educated women may have been better attuned to foreign cultures. In 1955 the anthropologist Margaret Mead published a biting indictment of male intellectuals' "isolationism."[22] Though these are impressionistic points whose potential effects on the conduct of diplomacy are probably unquantifiable, they nevertheless cannot be dismissed dogmatically.

It is time now to turn from general cultural factors affecting women's fate and outlook to the more specific problem of the contemporary state of consumer and job consciousness. Female consumerism was still, in the second half of the twentieth century, a phenomenon of some interest. But it was no longer rooted in the laissez-faire doctrine of the 1920s, and, in terms of its foreign policy impact, it was no longer exclusively associated with the tariff issue.

A comparison with India suggests, in one way, that price consciousness is less the product of an ideology such as laissez-faire than of womanly prudence. The Anti Price Rise Movement (APRM) of Bombay had strong support from women in India until its suppression during the state of emergency declared by the Indira Gandhi government in 1975. Its American equivalent in the 1920s and 1930s was clearly different from the APRM of Bombay; the latter was communist and socialist led, not laissez-faire in philosophy; the Indian movement aimed at changing the complexion of the government, but the American movement had just wanted to change policy. Yet women were heavily involved in both movements.[23]

The Indian comparison encourages the notion that gender differences exist yet can be deceptive in their connotations, and can change according to circumstances. In the United States trade-oriented price consciousness among women declined after the 1940s. It did not disappear entirely: Helen Douglas, Persia Campbell, and Carla Hills all supported free trade and believed in its function as a bolster to world peace. Other influential women, for example NCL general secretary Sarah Newman, expressed similar views. But the myth of the housewife as an engine of free trade had all but disappeared. Opinion polls made it clear that women were not especially prone to worrying about the inflationary effects of the Vietnam War. They were still aware of the economic aspects of foreign and defense policy, it is true, but instead of reacting as consumers, they began to incline toward views such as those expressed by Bella Abzug. They believed that money can be spent on better things than weapons, and that foreign assistance should support economic reconstruction, not military hardware.

If the consumer culture has changed to such a degree that it no longer affects women's outlook on foreign policy, is that change a factor that affects their fate? It could be argued that American women did not benefit from their nation's change from having a production-oriented economy to being, from the 1950s, an increasingly services- and consumer-oriented society. According to this argument women had been consigned before World War II to a weaker, "feminized" function of consumption and then chose (or were made to choose) the wrong moment to change to the job-seeking, production mode: They were disempowered by falsely predicated ambitions at a time of change in consumer culture. But in reality the picture is more complicated: Consumer politics in the interwar years were based on shaky foundations, and it would be a distortion of post-1945 social relationships to say that power is now divorced from job status. Nevertheless the expectation that woman at work is a prelude to woman in the White House and woman as global leader falls short of being a sustainable truism.

The decline of Red-baiting has had an effect on the political opportunities and outlook of women seeking to influence foreign policy. In the first few decades after women achieved the vote, Red-baiting and its accompanying sexual smears retarded women's political progress and tempted women to ward off potential right-wing attacks by adopting anti-Communist stances on foreign policy. In the 1920s there had been the "Pink Sisters" calumny. Margaret Chase Smith and Helen Douglas suffered from "Marcantonio" smears. The atmosphere remained repressive in the 1950s.

More recently, though, there have been some changes. The "New Left" of the 1960s never won numerous converts, but it did make itself less objectionable, and less vulnerable to attack, by rejecting old Marxist rigidities. Since then the gradual thawing of the Cold War followed by the collapse of the Soviet empire has diminished the potency of the communist bogeyman.[24] Some women, indeed, see a great opportunity for their gender in the ending of the Cold War.[25]

Sexual attitudes may also be changing—a substantial portion of the electorate forgave Governor Bill Clinton his alleged amatory peccadillos and voted him into the White House, and such magnanimity may to a certain degree herald the decline of the sexual smear as a political tactic. Partly in consequence of these developments, women appear to be prospering politically and are displaying distinctly "liberal" and dovelike tendencies. Several studies of women in public office support this generalization. For example, a survey of women in the Carter administration (an unprecedented 22 percent of President Jimmy Carter's appointees were women) indicated that they were more "liberal" than male appointees, and more opposed to military buildup.[26]

It remains to be seen how significant will be the effects of the decline of the culture of the Red scare. It is still possible to browbeat and straitjacket opponents with the dictates of right-wing ideology. In 1982 the Reaganite State Department issued a report depicting WILPF as an international Communist front. Members of the WILPF had offended the Right by making trips to the Soviet Union. Even after accession to power in Russia of the conciliatory Mikhail Gorbachev, East-West contacts remained unacceptable to some conservatives. In 1988 Guenter Lewy, who had been one of the intellectual forces behind the Reagan presidential campaign a decade earlier, attacked the peace movement for having sold out to Moscow, singling out women in particular: "Of the four major pacifist organizations, the WILPF has developed the most pronounced pro-Soviet outlook."[27] In the 1988 presidential campaign, the Bush camp "smeared" Democratic candidate Michael Dukakis as a "liberal," and a minority on the Right continued to be unforgiving of Clinton in terms of both his political goals and his alleged sexual conduct. Nor is it by any means clear, given the prevalence of double standards, that sexual smears against women, as distinct from men, will become a thing of the past. In 1993 the authors of one well-researched study observed that "sexual innuendo still follows women candidates and officeholders like an ominous shadow."[28]

In considering the gender gap as a phenomenon in political culture, there is a case for establishing its salience as well as its reality. Perceptions of women's political attitudes have been important ever since the 1920s. But the particular salience of the gender gap on foreign policy is a relatively recent phenomenon, the product of exit-poll analyses and opinion sampling—and of effective feminist propaganda.

Since the 1960s there has been a concerted campaign to increase the visibility and power of women in American politics. Politically active feminists have capitalized on the gender gap by organizing support for female candidates for office—through, for example, NOW (established in 1966), the National Women's Political Caucus (NWPC, 1971), the Women's Campaign Fund (WCF, 1973), the Republican Women's Task Force (RWTF, 1975), and the Democratic Women's Task Force (DWTF, 1974).[29] Even if the number of successful female candidates has remained relatively small, male candidates have had to accommodate their policies to meet the challenge. In particular, analysts have alerted them to the need to meet women's preferences in foreign policy. For example, in his study of the 1980 and 1984 elections, Arthur Miller concluded that "the vote among women appears more sensitive to concerns about war and defense spending than is true for men."[30] This point was not lost on the White House. One of President Reagan's advisers noted in November 1981 that the Republicans were worried about women's fear that "he might be reckless about war and peace."[31]

The publication of opinion poll findings in the 1980s continued to confirm and publicize the foreign policy gender gap. *Glamour* magazine in 1983 revealed that women were heavily critical of America's war-like policy in Central America: Evidently the popular antipathy to "hot" wars continued unabated. Then, in 1986, the same magazine published figures indicating that a majority of women wanted Star Wars (SDI) to be discontinued. However, by the following year, women were evenly divided on the issue. The suggestion here is that women favored not just peace but peace with security—as had been their preference ever since the start of the Cold War. Yet the general assumption continued to be that women were more reliably behind peace efforts than men. In fact, faith in this aspect of the gender gap may have been increasing. In 1983, 48 percent of a mixed-gender group polled by the *New York Times* thought that men were better at war-and-peace decisions than women (only 42 percent disagreed). But in a Virginia Slims poll in 1989, 91 percent of women and 98 percent of men thought that women in public office would do just as well as men or would do better than them in "working for peace in the world." While these questions and answers are not strictly comparable, they could only have reinforced in the public mind the notions that men are better at making war, and women are better at making peace.[32]

The gender gap on foreign policy had become a political consideration not just because it was real but because it was a perceived and salient cultural phenomenon. It has replaced the interwar mythology of the housewife's preference for free trade. It is an antidote to the Red-scare, sexual smear tactics previously directed against women. The political culture of the gender gap has bolstered the confidence of women, encouraged them to stick to their beliefs, affected the attitudes of politicians, boosted the number of female appointees to public office, and affected foreign policy at a critical juncture in East-West relations.

The arrival in politics of the self-made woman, and the commensurate decline of dynastic politics and "the widow's game," have had a potential influence on the nature and extent of women's impact on foreign policy. Some figures on widows appeared in a report called "Women in the United States Congress," released by the Congressional Research Service (CRS) in 1991. Up to and including the 102d Congress of 1991–1993, according to the CRS report, 120 women were elected or appointed to serve in the House of Representatives, of whom 32 "were elected to fill vacancies caused by the death of their husbands."[33] Thus the political widows have over the long period made up a substantial 27 percent of the women who have served in the lower house.

However, the phenomenon of the congressional widow is in decline. Political scientist Kathleen Frankovic found that there were only three widows in Congress by 1974, 20 percent of the total of women. She believed that widows in the United States never had been responsible for peace campaigns and liberal politics. She thought it might be significant that, "through 1974, the older, traditional women in Congress were being replaced by younger, more liberal Congresswomen, and particularly by nonwidows."[34] The statistical trend to which she alluded strengthened with the passage of time. In the 102d Congress, only three of the twenty-nine House women were political widows, making up a mere 10 percent of female membership—and neither of the woman senators was a widow.

The decline of the political widow is self-evidently consistent with democratic and republican principles, and feminists might well enthuse about the rise of the self-made woman representative and senator. Yet the trend raises several debating points. One concerns the degree of impact self-made as distinct from dynastic women may have. Another is the question of how peaceful the new women will be in their attitudes to foreign policy questions: the "iron lady" issue is as alive in the United States as it is in other countries. Finally there is the matter of expertise. Just as some maintain that the CIA enjoyed its finest hour when dominated by a thoroughly undemocratic Ivy League elite, so it could be argued that privileged, dynastic women can bring to bear on foreign policy the traditional know-how of the governing classes.[35]

In terms of impact it is perfectly true that political widows have produced few "stars": Margaret Chase Smith was a House widow but a self-made senator. The spectacle of a grief-torn widow taking her husband's seat was, party managers once assumed, good for a few votes, and her short-term selection could buy time to allow the politicos to make a "real" choice of candidate. But, even if several of them took their sponsors by surprise, widows were not expected to shine. As revealed in their reactions to foreign royalty, Americans regard dynastic arrangements with a mixture of fascination and contempt. The expectation that politicians should be self-made is sternly applied to women, even if it is relaxed in the case of rich men.

Nor does the presidential arena hold out any pronounced hope for the phenomenon of dynastic politics. Presidential wives, it is true, have sometimes exerted influence. In his memoir of his days as secretary of state, George P. Shultz recalled Nancy Reagan's encounter, in September 1984, with Soviet foreign minister Andrei Gromyko:

> Gromyko took Nancy to one side and whispered to her, "Does your husband believe in peace?"
> Nancy replied, "Yes, of course."
> "Then whisper 'peace' in his ear every night," Gromyko said.

In another memoir former secretary of the treasury Donald Regan recalled Nancy Reagan's formidable management of her husband, and her resentment at what she regarded as overexpenditure by the Department of Defense. The story that Nancy Reagan made her husband reconsider his support for the Nicaraguan Contras and for Star Wars is not so whimsical as one might think.[36] Yet, the distinction between wives and widows is important in the case of the presidency, because of the workings of the U.S. Constitution. Mao and Perón left powerful widows behind them, but if President Reagan had expired in office, his job would have gone to Vice President George Bush.

On the other hand, the confinement of one's definition of dynastic women to widows threatens to be one of those statistical conveniences that obscures reality. Indira Gandhi and Benazir Bhutto were not the widows of famous men, but their daughters. By the same token one can broaden one's definition of an American dynastic politician. Representative Ruth Bryan Owen (Dem., Fla., 1929–1933) was not a political widow. But it is of course significant that she was the daughter of three-time presidential candidate William Jennings Bryan; she benefited from his prominence and inherited his anti-imperialist and antimilitarist outlook. Nor did Millicent Hammond Fenwick (Rep., N.J., 1975–1983) occupy a dead husband's seat. But it seems probable that her work on the House Foreign Affairs Committee and on behalf of the Helsinki Commission on Human Rights may have drawn inspiration and know-how from her father's diplomatic career—at the age of fifteen, for example, she had accompanied him when he served as U.S. ambassador to Spain.

Dynastic politics does have a long arm if one considers immediate ancestry as well as marital circumstance. Moreover, while the dynastic process has not produced visibly powerful women, the historical evidence suggests that it has produced women who were relatively interested in foreign affairs, and adept at obtaining positions of influence. Thirteen of the 120 women who served in congress have been members of the House Foreign Affairs Committee. This makes women as a whole only slightly under-represented on that committee in proportion to their numbers.[37] No fewer than eight of these thirteen, or 62 percent, had a dynastic background. Thus, historically, dynastic women have been heavily, even disproportionately represented on the committee that holds the foreign policy purse strings.[38]

The proposition that dynastic women tend to be doves does not hold true historically. As indicated in chapter 6, Congresswomen Byron, Rogers, and Smith, as well as Senator Caraway, were all political widows and all strongly supportive of World War II preparedness. Turning to the 102d Congress of 1991–1993, there is the same need to qualify the supposition that dynastic women are distinctively peaceful. Using the expanded definition, five of the congress's 31 members were dynastic. But it is plain that members of the nondynastic contingent made the running as opponents of the Cold War.

One of these was Barbara Boxer (a Democrat from California elected to the House in 1982 and then to the Senate in 1992). As a member of the House Armed Services Committee, Boxer agitated for stronger congressional oversight of defense spending. She won national prominence when she exposed some Pentagon procurement scandals, notably the purchase of an Air Force coffeepot for $7,622. Then, in 1992, she won election to the Senate. The other dynamic opponent of Cold War policies was Congress's longest-serving female legislator, Patricia S. Schroeder (Dem., Colo.). She first won election in 1972 on an anti–Vietnam War ticket, then won a seat on the Armed Services Committee, where she campaigned for responsible defense spending and better conditions for military personnel. She was known as a feminist and witty debater—coining the phrase "the Teflon president" to describe the politically impervious Reagan—but above all she won recognition as a leading advocate of arms control. As peace seekers, Boxer and Schroeder outshone the dynastic contingent.

The voting behavior of the group of 1990s congressional women as a whole, irrespective of dynastic or other provenance, would appear to uphold the reputation of female legislators as doves with liberal-left opinions. To be sure, the pattern is not unrelieved. Information is available on fourteen of the group who had been in Congress in 1986 and had voted on key foreign policy issues that year. On one "hot-war" issue, so-called "covert" aid to antileft rebels in Angola, seven voted in favor with one abstention (here treated for statistical purposes as a half vote), making 54 percent in favor of military action compared with the overall House vote of 55 percent. However, in other cases, the women diverged from the congressional norm. Eight voted against aid to the Contras, 57 percent compared with the House's 51. Nine voted to limit spending on SDI with one abstention—69 percent to the House's 58. Thirteen voted for sanctions against the racist regime in South Africa, 93 percent to the House's 79. Such percentages are crude measures because of the small numbers involved, but the cumulative weight of the evidence suggests that, regardless of dynastic provenance, women were prone to oppose war and oppression.

A closer examination of the congressional group tends to bear this out. The dynastics in the 102d Congress were not more dovelike or liberal than the nondynastics. As only four voted in the foregoing 1986 divisions, the comparative figures must be treated with caution: the dynastics were more warlike than the peer group in their voting on Angola and Nicaragua, but were 100 percent opposed to supplementing SDI and 100 percent supportive of sanctions on South Africa. Within the limitations of the evidence, it would appear that they were roughly in line with the dove-liberal outlook of the other women.

There is, however, a significant difference between the broadly defined dynastic group and the nondynastics. The twenty-six non-dynastics supplied three members of the House Armed Services Committee and one member of the Foreign Affairs Committee. But, reflecting a long-term historical trend, the dynastic women without exception had foreign policy commitments. One of these did so for a compelling political reason. Susan Molinari (Rep., N.Y.), who had taken over her father's congressional seat in 1990, fought for naval appropriations to support shipbuilding in her native Staten Island, which made up the bulk of her constituency.

The other four dynastics were all on foreign policy committees. Olympia J. Snowe succeeded her husband to a seat in the Maine House of Representatives before entering Congress on the Republican ticket in 1979. A member of the House Foreign Affairs Committee, she inspected the Moscow embassy when it became known that it was compromised by Soviet listening devices, and—reflecting her Greek ethnic origin—spoke against military aid to Turkey. Barbara Kennelly (Dem., Conn., 1982–) was the daughter of John Bailey, who had chaired the Democratic National Committee between 1961 and 1968. She became the first woman to serve on the Permanent Select Committee on Intelligence. Beverly Byron (Dem., Md., 1979–) inherited her seat from her husband; she served on the Armed Services Committee and chaired the House Special Panel on Arms Control and Disarmament, 1983–1986.

In the Senate, Nancy Landon Kassebaum (Rep., Kans., 1979–) sat on the Foreign Relations Committee. She was the daughter of Alfred M. Landon, the liberal Republican who was overwhelmingly defeated by the FDR landslide in 1936. Kassebaum favored restraint in Central America, took a skeptical line on military procurement, and in the Reagan years chaired the Foreign Relations Subcommittee on African Affairs. In the latter capacity she was the architect of the policy of imposing limited economic sanctions on South Africa, an attempt to force that republic to end its policies of apartheid and racial discrimination.

In the United States women from families with political and international experience do seem to gravitate to foreign policy work. They would appear to benefit from family tradition and expertise, not just from the political fixing that goes hand in hand with widow politics. In this they resemble men—from the Adams, Roosevelt, and Dulles dynasties, and from numerous lesser ones. There is a gender difference in that, on the whole, they reflect the dovish and liberal leanings of their sex. But they are not more dovish than other women. Again, while they may have performed a pioneering role in terms of political breakthrough, they have not, barring rare exceptions like Kassebaum, been among the more forceful role models. Moreover, they are losing their prominence as a constituent of the whole. In the United States the dynastic factor still operates, for women as for men, but it is no longer distinctively important as a means of projecting women to the top, and it has never determined what women do to foreign policy when they get there.

Turning to U.S. self-made women, the need to consider their roles as iron ladies of the hawkish variety is less pressing than the need to consider why and with what consequences they are portrayed in that way. Nevertheless, it is appropriate to mention two studies which suggest that self-made women do gravitate to male norms in foreign policy. The first of these, by Nancy McGlenn and Meredith Reid Sarkees, notes the consistent 8–9 percent gender gap that has made women as a whole more peaceful than men in their approach to foreign policy since the 1950s. But, on the basis of their survey of women's views within the departments of state and defense, the authors concluded that the gender gap was much less evident in the case of insiders. They suggested that "traditional" women preferred peace, but empowered women were prepared to play the same game as men.[39]

Of course, women appointees in the State and Defense Departments in the Reagan and Bush year may have been influenced by loyalty to their patrons. Elected women politicians were different in that they responded to voters, not just to the power elite. However, according to one study of female politicians in the 1980s, they, too, as they matured politically, drew closer to men's views. On the one hand this study showed that "women in public office are more liberal" than men. On the other it portrayed the difference as transitional:

> There is . . . no assurance that these differences will persist as more women enter the political élite. For example, the voting gap between men and women in the U.S. House of Representatives decreased steadily between 1972 and 1982. . . . A decrease in male-female differences can . . . be produced by women exercising stronger influence on the political agenda and the thinking of male colleagues. Thus we might see women moving in a more conservative direction and men moving in a more liberal one.[40]

This raises the intriguing possibility that the foreign policy gender gap will end with the demise of the male-driven Cold War. The best-selling postcard at the 1992 International Feminist Book Fair proclaimed: "I'll be a post feminist in post patriarchy."[41] It remains to be seen whether the gender gap will close, and in what manner.

More certain is the fact that the iron lady exists in the United States as a myth, if not a reality. The habit of commenting on the loud or attention-grabbing characteristics of women politicians is widespread. For example, in the respected reference book, *The Almanac of American Politics*, women are presented as strident and aggressive. In general the authors of the *Almanac* are even-handed in their judgments, and they are not prejudiced against women on political grounds, for example on the ground that they took an antiwar stance. But the authors do persist in dwelling on certain characteristics of women in Congress. The 1974 edition's treatment of the thirty-eight members of Congress from the State of New York illustrates the tendency. The three female members were judged on their vocal abilities. Elizabeth Holtzman was a "dogged" campaigner but could be partially absolved for being "not so vocal as Abzug." Bella Abzug indulged, of course, in "loud rhetoric." Capitol Hill's first black woman legislator, Shirley Chisholm, had such a weakness for the "glamour of the lecture circuit" that she had to "quietly" apply herself to legislating in order to restore the confidence of the voters.

One could be forgiven for regarding this as fair comment on women who had had to battle their way to the top, usually with less than full support from party political machines. But it is revealing that the same criteria are not applied to the thirty-five male legislators. Congressman Samuel S. Stratton, it is true, is "pesky," but most of the men attract no comments on their style unless it is to say that they rose "quietly" in the House (James Grover) or gained respect while generating "little attention" (John W. Wydler). Otis G. Pike, surely one of the most aggressive legislators of the decade, is just a "maverick," while there is no mention of Edward I. Koch's abrasive style. These double standards persisted over the years. Chisholm's talk of retiring in 1980 was "an effort to get people to pay more attention." According to the 1988 edition, Senator Barbara Mikulski (Dem., Md., 1987–   ) was "loud and brash," while Representative Pat Schroeder was "aggressive." The international stirrings of a predominantly peaceful female leadership might have called such judgments into question but had left the *Almanac* untroubled by curiosity.[42]

Women themselves, perceiving a need to appear tough, have sometimes contributed to their own hard images. Dianne Feinstein, elected to the Senate from California in 1992, tempered her liberal image by supporting the death penalty. In Texas, another aspiring liberal Democrat, future Governor Ann Richards, ran "television ads wearing hunter's camouflage and toting a shotgun to show she is just as much a good ol' boy as any other Texan." Welcoming the 1993 Austin premiere of Clint

Eastwood's gory and locally shot film *A Perfect World*, she declared, "This is the kind of film we like to make in Texas."[43] The image of the female politician as tough fighter-climber derives from several sources and is firmly implanted in the discourse of American politics.

Jeane Kirkpatrick was a particularly prominent political figure who attracted the image of a self-made hawk. Kirkpatrick had been a successful career woman before she shot into diplomatic prominence in the 1980s. She had gained a scholarly reputation on the basis of her studies of right-wing figures—the British fascist Oswald Mosley and the Argentinian dictator Juan Perón—and of the political behavior of women. In 1979 she published a much-discussed essay called "Dictatorships and Double Standards," in which she recommended a distinction between totalitarian regimes such as those of the Communist world, and right-wing authoritarian regimes worthy of American support. In this sense she seemed to depart from many feminists' unflagging insistence on democracy as a means of advancing women's cause. Kirkpatrick, however, thought that right-wing dictatorships, such as those of the shah in Iran and the Somozas in Nicaragua, carried a potential for democratic reform.[44] On the strength of her contribution, President Reagan appointed her American ambassador to the United Nations. According to her admirers, Kirkpatrick was a successful envoy—indeed, on the wings of her enhanced reputation she was to be discussed as a presidential aspirant in 1988, and as a possible vice presidential candidate in 1992.[45]

Kirkpatrick complained that her hard-line public image was an invention of the press.[46] This complaint was not entirely justified, for she contributed appreciably to her own tough image. Her defense of the whites-only South African regime put her in the conservative camp and alerted her left-wing critics to the possibility of other failings. Amongst those they detected were her membership in the Committee on the Present Danger, a lobby for stronger national defense. Moreover, she seemed to be all too ready to perceive a Soviet threat where none existed. For example, in the January 1981 issue of the magazine *Commentary*, she attacked Cuba over the already-discredited story that it had hosted "a Soviet combat brigade" in 1979. In the same article she poured scorn on those who depicted the Vietnam experience as the beginning of the end of the Cold War. In fact, she claimed, the Soviet Union was still a real menace to the United States. She appeared to be unaware that there were serious doubts about the Soviet Union's ability and willingness to continue with the arms race.[47] Kirkpatrick seemed prepared to take a hard line regardless of the evidence.

But the ambassador was correct in saying that she was not so tough as some of the commentators imagined. On the personal level the evidence is mixed. After all, as a political appointee, she was not a fighter-climber in the democratic sense of having won her way to the top via bruising election campaigns. The historian Joan Hoff thinks she was a tough academic careerist, but cautions that government in-fighting is tougher than its academic equivalent, and notes that Kirkpatrick professed a distaste for bureaucratic politics.[48] The future ambassador also took time out to nurture her three sons, her main activity in the years 1957–1962. It is possible that this time out softened her, indeed made her too soft for the "rat race." Here, though, one might note that some male politicians of renowned toughness also took career breaks— Theodore Roosevelt to engage in dude ranching and African safaris, Franklin D. Roosevelt to fight against polio; furthermore, some ethnologists suggest that women tough enough to handle family problems find little difficulty in managing male politicians. What is more telling on the personal level is that Kirkpatrick regarded women as deficient in staying power. She commented on "the number of women who make it, make it to high levels and who quit," adding that although she could not prove it, "the percent[age] of women who say at some point, 'I've had enough of this,' is . . . probably significantly higher than men."[49]

Kirkpatrick displayed some of the hallmarks of a peacefully inclined woman. Like Margaret Chase Smith, and like the 1950s women whose preferences she had described in her own book, she supported strong defense as a means of ensuring national security—but she had reservations about "hot" wars. She had favored American withdrawal from Vietnam. She supported politically risky peace initiatives in Lebanon. When she defended past U.S. military interventions in Latin America, an area on which she professed academic expertise, it was on the ground that such interventions had preserved peace and stability. When she explained her country's 1983 invasion of the tiny Caribbean island of Grenada as a response to "unique" circumstances, she seemed to be implying that otherwise the era of the bullet solution should be considered obsolete. In the course of the British-Argentine war over the Falklands/Malvinas islands, she risked a break with the Reagan administration's pro-British policy by abstaining on a UN cease-fire resolution instead of voting against it. She added that she personally favored the cease-fire resolution as an "attempt to substitute reason for force, negotiation for violence, words for bombs and bullets."[50] While even the most bellicose of politicians tend to pay lip service to peace, Kirkpatrick's record would seem to indicate a discernible commitment to it.

Jeane Kirkpatrick fails on more than one count to live up to her image as a tough hawk. What is significant about the image is its place in American political discourse, not its reflection of reality. The utility of the iron lady/breakthrough hypothesis is not upheld in her case.

Moreover, the breakthrough hypothesis is discredited in the of the United States, as in other countries, by the phenomenon of the iron dove. There have been several significant examples of tough, self-made doves in contemporary American history, including the whole of the 1974 female New York delegation mentioned earlier, and Bella Abzug in particular. But on the national, executive, level, there has only been one case, the 1984 Democratic vice presidential candidate, Geraldine A. Ferraro. There can be little doubt about Ferraro's fighter-climber credentials. Because her Italian immigrant father died when she was eight, she was brought up by her mother, who scraped a living doing beadwork in the Bronx. Though she was helped financially by marriage to the businessman John A. Zaccaro, Ferraro fought her own way to national prominence, raising three children while she qualified to practice law, and she won a seat in Congress in her own right. In spite of the ritual invocation of slogans like "log cabin to White House" and "rags to riches," few male presidential aspirants have in reality come from a background as impoverished as Ferraro's.

Ferraro considered herself to be rugged: "You had to be tough to be a female member of Congress." She looked up to earlier pioneers, especially Bella Abzug, who had broken through "the first lines of defense" in Congress. Ferraro saw Abzug as "a fighter for women and their concerns," which included "the environment, the budget, and the arms race." Just as, in Ferraro's view, "Bella had made it far easier for us," Jeane Kirkpatrick, in the spirit of female freemasonry, noted that Ferraro herself was a pioneer: Her vice presidential candidacy "put women forward. . . . I think that every time a barrier like this is broken, it moves women forward."[51]

Ferraro saw herself as a gender-gap candidate. She noted that President Reagan did not command the confidence of women voters, that women had swayed the results in a number contests in the elections of 1982, and that the Democrats were hunting for a woman candidate. Reviewing similar evidence, Abzug raised expectations and fears in her book *Gender Gap,* predicting that "nineteen eighty-four could be a watershed year in American political history."[52] The Reagans were worried. The president had already preemptively appointed two women to his cabinet—Elizabeth Dole as secretary of transportation and Margaret Heckler as secretary of health and human services. When the Democrats made their vice presidential choice, he thought "it was obvious Mondale picked Geraldine Ferraro simply because he believed there was a 'gender gap' where I was concerned and she was a *woman*."[53] Nancy Reagan, according to her biographer, was not worried about Mondale's presidential challenge, but when he picked Ferraro as his running mate, she "agonized that the Democrats would capture the female vote."[54]

Geraldine Ferraro took peace as her main electoral theme, believing she was at her "best" dealing with "foreign policy questions" and criticizing the buildup of nuclear weaponry as well as United States intervention in Nicaragua and Grenada. There can be no doubt that she spoke for the majority of American women on these issues. From the beginning of Reagan's term, as already noted, the Republicans worried about women's fear that "he might be reckless about war and peace." The foreign policy gender gap was still a factor in 1984, the year of Ferraro's vice presidential campaign, as the University of Michigan's National Election Studies unit found in a study devoted to the matter. There can be no doubt about Ferraro's credentials as a iron dove; she was a living refutation of the iron lady/breakthrough hypothesis.[55]

But America was not yet ready for a Geraldine Ferraro, and her political opponents were able to exploit the prejudice still inherent in political discourse about women. At the instigation of Nancy Reagan, sleaze specialists began to unearth allegations about Ferraro's father being involved in the numbers racket, and about her husband's business dealings.[56] The political analyst Susan Carroll gave the following synopsis of Ferraro's treatment:

At many points in the campaign, Ferraro was treated differently because she was a woman. Ferraro was asked if she could bake blueberry muffins, called "bitchy" by her opponent's press secretary and a "four-million-dollar—I can't say it, but it rhymes with rich" by her opponent's wife, "patronized" by Vice-President Bush before millions of viewers of the vice-presidential debate, and asked on national television if she could bring herself to push the button to fire nuclear weapons.[57]

While not so viciously smeared as Helen Douglas and Margaret Chase Smith, Ferraro was still subjected to harsh treatment. The Mondale-Ferraro ticket made a poor showing in the election, and Reagan won a plurality of the female vote. American women failed to produce another White House candidate in the course of the next decade. For these reasons one might be tempted to argue that Ferraro supplied American women with an unsuitable role model. In fact, one outcome of the election result was the emergence of a popular perception that Ferraro had played the gender card and failed.[58]

However, one should not dismiss Ferraro too hastily. A number of circumstances beyond Ferraro's control help to explain the Democrats' defeat. Ferraro could not work wonders as a vice presidential candidate. Democratic party tacticians allowed themselves to be forced onto the defensive in handling the nuclear button issue, and thus, in the view of their critics, "nixed every attempt she made to reach out to the legions of women voters who were overjoyed that a women had finally made it onto the ballot."[59] Another problem was that Mondale was a lackluster running mate: It has been suggested that Ferraro had an adverse effect on the Democratic campaign because her personality and policy stances showed him up. It may well be that her forcefulness enhanced the long-term standing of women in politics more than it helped her immediate vice presidential prospects. Perhaps most important of all, Ferraro and Mondale could not fight the effects of what seemed at the time to be good economic news. While her emphasis on the foreign policy issue may have had some potential as a way of recruiting female support (the gender gap appears to have been more significant in years when foreign policy becomes an issue), elections are notoriously won on domestic, especially economic issues—and in 1984 the majority of Americans were prospering.[60]

In retrospect Ferraro's redeeming features seem impressive. She attracted more money to the campaign than is usual for a vice presidential candidate. The sleaze people failed to score a direct hit. As Kirkpatrick, Carroll, and others remarked, Ferraro set a precedent for other women to follow. Finally she defined foreign policy issues in such a way that, in Reagan's second term, some account was taken of American women's overwhelming desire for better relations with the Soviet Union.

The gender gap survived as a factor in American politics in spite of the 1984 election result. Vice President George Bush won the 1988 election at a time when gender issues were not prominent. But, with the end of the Cold War, he could no longer with such urgency appeal to women on the issue of national security. He fought a "hot" war in the Persian Gulf that seemed to make him popular at the time, but it did not uphold his long-term credentials with women. A dramatic "gender gulf" opened up on a wide variety of issues connected with hostilities against Iraq.[61] He came to be seen as unsympathetic to women on the domestic gender issues that predominated in the post–Cold War climate: health care, welfare, family leave, and abortion. With women making up 54 percent of the electorate, this was a perception he could ill afford. In the 1992 presidential election, the Democrats' Bill Clinton won 45 percent of the women's votes cast, compared with 41 percent of the male vote, and compared with 38 percent of women who supported Bush (the remaining 17 percent of the female vote went to independent candidate Ross Perot). Women could claim to have put Clinton into the White House. The gender gap was still alive—thanks in part to women like Ferraro.[62]

A merican women have been slow to produce leaders of international prominence. Their one White House candidate, Geraldine Ferraro, did reflect the distinctive foreign policy values of the female half of the population—but failed to win election. On the other hand the underlying trend in the United States—and here it compares more favorably with the international community—is toward a greater measure of women's emancipation and equality. Additionally, promising developments have taken place in the realm of political culture. The culture of the Red scare, with its sinister overtones of international confrontation and misogyny, appears to be in decline. The culture of the gender gap, defined not just as an arid statistic, but as a consciously perceived and exploited phenomenon, appears to have shouldered aside that of anti-Communism.

Against this encouraging background more women are participating in the political process. In the United States as elsewhere, there has been speculation about the personalities and outlook of the women who break through into the "male world" of politics and, by extension, international affairs. As in other countries, commentators in the United States have treated as salient and unusual, when they appear in women, those characteristics of toughness that are necessarily a part of the makeup of the successful politician. The idea that only those women who are masculine, aggressive, and hawkish are likely to succeed threatens to take root in the United States as in Britain, France, Israel, and other countries where prejudiced discourse thrives on gender matters. But the actions and thoughts of so-called hawks like Kirkpatrick show that no great distinction can be made between them and "dynastic" women who did not have to struggle so hard to get to the top. Nor, as Ferraro's case confirms, did every dove ascend the easy way. In the United States as elsewhere, the idea that the woman of iron is a woman of violence is a baneful myth.

11 | CONCLUSION

Who ended the Cold War? Historians will no doubt debate this question with just as much vigor as they do the question of who started it. But amongst the claimants to the honor, American women must feature to a discernible degree. It is no coincidence that precisely at the moment of East-West thaw, women have taken forty-eight seats in the House and six in the Senate, and almost a quarter of foreign service posts. Thus it can be argued that détente encouraged the rise of women to political prominence; equally, however, women's pressure contributed to the improvement in the international climate. Their pressure took the form of not only an increased presence in powerful circles in Washington but also mass lobbying. As both Margaret Chase Smith and Bella Abzug have attested, women influence men politically. The end of East-West confrontation does owe something to the millions of deflating conversations in which women have told men exactly what they thought of their macho war games.

This impact of American women on foreign policy is no novel phenomenon. They were a force behind the Washington naval conference and agreements of 1921–1922. They helped to shape the climate of support for the Kellogg-Briand nonaggression pacts of the late 1920s; demanded and obtained the improvement in U.S.–Latin American relations sealed in President Roosevelt's Good Neighbor policy; and contributed substantially to the political underpinnings of the Reciprocal Trade Agreements Act of 1934. It is doubtful whether the far-reaching Nye investigation of the munitions industry in 1934–1935 would have taken place without the lobbying activities of women. The United Nations Universal Declaration of Human Rights of 1948 owed both its shape and its adoption to an individual American woman, Eleanor Roosevelt, and to the women who backed her.

In the 1950s women were observably not just part of, but ahead of, the consensus supporting a U.S. security policy based on the adoption of the nuclear shield and on the eschewing of "hot" wars. But a radical minority was already agitating against the nuclear defense exercise Operation Alert, in this way forging a new women's movement. In 1963 this new movement proved to be an irresistible force in demanding an end to the atmospheric testing of nuclear devices—though an individual woman, Senator Smith, successfully proposed the proviso that Soviet compliance with the terms of the resultant treaty should be monitored. American withdrawal from the Vietnam War in 1973 stemmed from a variety of factors—of which not the least significant was women's protest both in the mass and individually, especially in Congress. In so far as one can ascribe concrete achievements to particular groups in a sophisticated and pluralistic democracy, women were doing well even before their more obvious breakthrough in the 1990s.

At the same time they achieved international influence through other less concrete but still significant means. From Lady Astor to Prime Minister Brundtland, American-educated women have had a major impact on the international policies of foreign countries. Women in the United States have prided themselves on their ability to be caring, cooperative, and understanding. They have contributed not only to peace intitiatives and human rights campaigns, but also to reconcilitation between nations: From Pearl Buck to Agnes Smedley, a small band of informed women strove to improve American understanding of China. Other American women have been conscious of the obligations of international sisterhood and have exploited their country's wealth and dominance of the media to raise consciousness on the issue of the oppression of women in nations less egalitarian than the United States.

But if women have achieved a measurable degree of success, it has not been without a struggle. They have had to overcome sexism of various types, notably the belief that a woman cannot possibly do a job as well as a man, and the conviction amongst a waning but troublesome old guard that it is dangerous to confer foreign policy powers on women who are emotionally averse to war and cannot be trusted with national defense. Unfair means have been used to obstruct the progress of women. Two tactics have been particularly prominent. One is the Red smear, used against several insurgent groups but particularly potent against women in the Cold War era, when Communist Russia was the foe, as women were deemed too weak to "push the nuclear button."

The other tactic used to obstruct the progress of women is the sexual smear. This has rested on double standards stemming from the Victorian tendency to debase women by placing them on a moral pedestal in a way that made them much more vulnerable than men to scandal. In the 1990s various ideological and practical ploys of a sexual nature were still being used to keep women in the home: for example, the rhetoric on "family values" and the campaign against abortion. Of its nature, involvement in the foreign policy process means travel away from home, so women who are ambitious in the diplomatic sphere find themselves under particular pressure from the sleazier promoters of involuntary domesticity.

The resistance power of American patriarchy affected the attitudes some people held about the role of women who broke through into policy-making circles. Such people came to fear that it is too hard for women to break through, so that those who do succeed are likely to be akin, in temperament, to Britain's archetypal "iron lady," Margaret Thatcher. More broadly, they fear that women will in political terms become men, either as part of the price they have to pay for achieving equality or because of the excessively toughening effects of the struggle. Some commentators welcome this postulated process of "normalization," which they regard as a maturing process that sets modern women apart from and above their more archaic sisters. All these perceptions suggest a paradoxical contingency, whereby women will preach peace and start wars.

Yet it seems unlikely that such expectations will be realized. An examination of Thatcher and other leaders with aggressive reputations shows the need to distinguish between women with iron temperaments and women who start wars. Amongst the "ladies," there has so far been no "iron hawk" of bloodthirsty disposition. On the contrary, there have been several examples of "iron doves," women who fought their way to the top and demanded peace. An examination of America's female leadership confirms that picture very strongly. And where the rank and file is concerned, the foreign policy "gender gap" showing that women are more peaceful than men appears to be long-term, not just a protest gesture that will disappear when women win greater power.

Another doubt about the impact of American women is that they appear to have become the "missing sisters" of the international scene, failing to produce national leaders in the style of other countries like Israel, India, Canada, and Britain. This doubt is negated, to a large degree, by the list of achievements just noted. But one can still speak of underachievement in relation to expectations, and this prompts the question, which factors seem to stimulate the rise of female leaders, and in turn, govern their behavior? The findings in this book are in part universal, in part cultural. It seems incontrovertible that the emergence of women after 1960 was connected with the spread of the peaceful processes of democracy. However, women respond to different cultural stimuli in different parts of the world. In America, it would appear that politically-aspiring women have hitherto thrived mainly in the context of an antimilitaristic, broad left, or "PC" culture.

Finally, American feminists have consistently addressed the question of whether and how women and men are different. The history of women's attempts to influence foreign policy shows how women, over time, embraced several, changing types of difference. These changing differences affected economic, humanitarian, and other concerns, as well as the debate over war-and-peace issues. They sometimes occurred because of domestic developments: notably, the perception that women had become wage earners as much as shoppers contributed to the decline of their low-price-driven free-trade thrust in foreign policy. At other times international events determined which features of the women's agenda should be prominent. The rise of the Cold War, with the Soviets' military posturing and abuse of civil liberties, stimulated their human rights campaign and their pronounced support for nuclear-based national security. The prospect of the Cold War's demise brought forth their renewed demand, again pronounced by comparison with what men wanted, for curbs on the arms race.

In the 1990s women are empowered as never before to implement their foreign policy preferences: Four of the fourteen members of President Clinton's first cabinet were women, not to mention the special powers vested in his wife, Hillary. American women will now be able to participate in the shaping of their own destiny—and with it that of their nation and of the world beyond it. What will this mean? If history is a guide, the only constant feature of the difference between women and men over foreign policy would appear to be that it is rarely constant: Clearly gender differences in this sphere are neither innate nor immutable. It does seem likely that women will remain more peaceful than men until well into the twenty-first century. Yet that will reflect not an unchangeable law of nature but a conscious choice made by women.

NOTES

1. INTRODUCTION

1. The meaning of words like "pacifist," "peace loving," and "dove" has been open to interpretation. Elihu Root was secretary of war from 1899 to 1903, yet the award to him in 1912 of the Nobel Peace Prize was by no means incongruous by the precepts of the day, when anyone who worked toward peace, even through military means or saber rattling, could be labeled a pacifist. Root was also secretary of state from 1905 to 1909. He was a successful campaigner for the legal resolution of international disputes, and served as president and chairman of the board of the Carnegie Endowment for International Peace—established by the philanthropist Andrew Carnegie, who had made some of his money by manufacturing the steel for America's new navy in the 1890s. For an assessment of Root's work, see Sondra R. Herman, *Eleven Against War: Studies in American Internationalist Thought, 1898–1921* (Stanford, Calif.: Hoover Institution Press, 1969), 22–54. Presidents Theodore Roosevelt (1901–1909), William Howard Taft (1909–1913), and Woodrow Wilson (1913–1921) all interacted with the organized peace movement, yet Roosevelt and Wilson in particular embraced war as a way of advancing their country's diplomatic objectives. For an appraisal of their activities, see David S. Patterson, *Toward a Warless World: The Travail of the American Peace Movement, 1887–1914* (Bloomington: Indiana University Press, 1976).

In World War I the term "pacifist" tended to be strictly applied, as a term of opprobrium, to those who opposed war under any circumstances. The historian Charles Chatfield suggested that the narrowing in the meaning of the word "pacifist" was a phenomenon particularly associated with that conflict: "The word *pacifist* changed under the pressure for patriotic conformity in 1917–18. Having had the benign connotation of one advocating international cooperation for peace, it was narrowed malevolently to mean one who would not support even a 'war to end war.'" Chatfield, *For Peace and Justice: Pacifism in America 1914–1941* (Knoxville: University of Tennessee Press, 1971), 4.

The terminology has over the years been further confused by the incongruous inclusion, in the ranks of "peace lovers," of certain people. Among the unlikely proclaimers of their enthusiasm for peace have been Hitler and Saddam Hussein. Others have in all sincerity claimed they were pursuing peace through deterrence systems with names like "Mutually Assured Destruction" and "Star Wars." In light of these distortions, it is hardly surprising that loose definitions have been applied to the outlook of women. In particular, women who claim to be working in favor of peaceful solutions but have not entirely abjured the use of force have tended to be judged by the yardstick of strict pacifism and therefore found wanting. Some women are celebrated for their aggression only because of the application of double standards, whereby one has to be doubly peaceful to be a female "dove."

2. Anna Graves quoted in Harriet Hyman Alonso, *Peace as a Women's Issue: A History of the U.S. Movement for World Peace and Women's Rights* (Syracuse, N.Y.: Syracuse University Press, 1993), 146. Emphasis in the original.

3. See Geoffrey S. Smith, "Commentary: Security, Gender, and the Historical Process," *Diplomatic History* 18 (Winter 1994), 79.

4. For a summary of these episodes, see Linda Witt, Karen M. Paget, and Glenna Matthews, *Running as a Woman: Gender and Power in American Politics* (New York: Free Press, 1993), 70–71.

5. Quotations, facts, and opinions not sourced in the introduction's endnotes are documented later in the book.

6. An influential exposition of the idea of "difference" is Carol Gilligan, *In a Different Voice: Psychological Theory and Women's Development* (Cambridge, Mass.: Harvard University Press, 1982); in the 1993 edition of this work, the author adds a "Letter to Readers" (pp. ix–xxx), in which she comments on difference literature since 1982. For some reservations about "difference," as well as for a convenient summary of some of the main points in the debate, see Nancy E. McGlen and Meredith Reid Sarkees, *Women in Foreign Policy: The Insiders* (New York: Routledge, 1993), 3–12. Diana Fuss, *Essentially Speaking: Feminism, Nature and Difference* (New York: Routledge, 1989) cautions against attempts to "discredit closet essentialists," appeals for a more analytical approach, and offers various definitions of essentialism—which deals with what is "constitutive of a given person or thing," or the belief that "woman is born not made," xii, 2, 3.

7. Emily Greene Balch, "The Effect of War and Militarism on the Status of Women," *Publications of the American Sociological Society* (1915): 39.

8. Mary R. Beard, *Women as Force in History* (New York: Macmillan, 1946), 37.

9. Balch, "Effect of War," 43. For more recent remarks on the linkage between violence against women and the international peace movement, see Alonso, *Peace as a Women's Issue*, 8. For an exposition of the relationship between male hegemony and world insecurity, see J. Ann Tickner, *Gender in International Relations: Feminist Perspectives on Achieving Global Security* (New York: Columbia University Press, 1992), 128.

10. Patricia Hill, *The World Their Household: The American Women's Missionary Movement and Cultural Transformation, 1870–1920* (Ann Arbor: University of Michigan Press, 1985), 3; C. Roland Marchand, *The American Peace Movement and Social Reform, 1898–1918* (Princeton, N.J.: Princeton University Press, 1972), 184–185; Barbara J. Steinson, "'The Mother Half of Humanity': American Women in the Peace and Preparedness Movements in World War I," in Carol R. Berkin and Clara M. Lovett, eds., *Women, War, and Revolution* (New York: Holmes and Meier, 1980), 259–260; Charles DeBenedetti, *Origins of the Modern American Peace Movement, 1915–1927* (Millwood, N.Y.: KTO Press, 1978), 90.

11. Steinson, "Mother Half," 259.

12. Alonso, *Peace as a Woman's Issue*, 11.

13. Antonia Fraser, *Boadicea's Chariot: The Warrior Queens* (London: Weidenfeld & Nicolson, 1988), 10.

14. Kate Muir, *Arms and the Woman* (London: Hodder and Stoughton, 1992), 83. The books by Fraser and Muir appear to have been a response to Margaret Thatcher's premiership. A third contribution to this British genre is Tim Newark, *Women Warlords: An Illustrated Military History of Female Warriors* (London: Blandford, 1989). Newark's book surveys in popular style the period between the Amazons of antiquity and the women of the Hundred Years' War, but its author's motives appear to have been mixed. Its narrative opens (on page 9) with an account of the defeat of the Amazons at the hands of Heracles, and its color illustrations represent, inter alia, the capture of Joan of Arc and humiliation of Zenobia, who is depicted before the Emperor Aurelian's chariot in chains and a sexy black dress.

15. Emily S. Rosenberg, "Gender," one of ten contributions to "A Round Table: Explaining the History of American Foreign Relations," *Journal of American History* 77 (1990), 116–124.

16. Edward P. Crapol, ed., *Women and Foreign Policy: Lobbyists, Critics, and Insiders*, 2d ed. (Wilmington, Del.: Scholarly Resources, 1992). In this collection a group of scholars supplies chapters on Lydia Maria Child, Jane M. Cazneau, Anna Ella Carroll, Lucia True Ames Mead, Eleanor Roosevelt, Eleanor Lansing Dulles, Jane Fonda, and Jeane Kirkpatrick.

17. See Rosenberg, "Gender," 116–124.

18. Lloyd S. Etheredge, *A World of Men: The Private Sources of Foreign Policy* (Cambridge, Mass.: MIT Press, 1978), xv, 1, 62.

19. Quoted in Susan Jeffords, *The Remasculinization of America: Gender and the Vietnam War* (Bloomington: Indiana University Press, 1989), 172. The film referred to is *Full Metal Jacket* (1987).

20. Carol Cohn, "Emasculating America's Linguistic Deterrent," in Adrienne Harris and Ynesta King, eds., *Rocking the Ship of State: Toward a Feminist Peace Politics* (Boulder, Colo.: Westview, 1983), 156.

21. Fraser, *Boadicea's Chariot*, 9.

22. Eisenhower quoted in Blanche Wiesen Cook, *Eleanor Roosevelt* (New York: Viking, 1992), 18.

23. Charles DeBenedetti, *An American Ordeal: The Antiwar Movement of the Vietnam Era* (Syracuse, N.Y.: Syracuse University Press, 1990), 313.

2. A MOMENTARY SILENCE: THE SURVIVAL OF GENDER DISTINCTION IN WORLD WAR I

1. These are Fowler's words quoted in Eric Foner and John A Garraty, eds., *The Reader's Companion to American History* (Boston: Houghton Mifflin, 1991), 153–156. See also Robert Booth Fowler, *Carrie Catt: Feminist Politician* (Boston: Northeastern University Press, 1986), 4, 9.

2. A student of a women's movement having some affinity with its American counterpart has observed: "It is generally supposed that women won the vote in Britain by first making a tremendous nuisance of themselves to the government and their fellow-citizens down to the outbreak of the war, and by then, on the instant and with one accord, turning into loyal and unquestioning supporters of the

government and throwing themselves wholeheartedly into helping to win the war, thus showing they could be as sensible and productive as the men and so deserved a part in ruling the country": Jo Vellacott Newberry, "Anti-War Suffragists," *History* 62 (October 1977): 411.

3. J. Stanley Lemons, *The Woman Citizen: Social Feminism in the 1920s* (Urbana: University of Illinois Press, 1973), 4.

4. Addams quoted in Linda Kay Schott, "Women Against War: Pacifism, Feminism, and Social Justice in the United States, 1915–1941" (Stanford University Ph.D. diss., 1985), 2.

5. Jane Addams, *Newer Ideals of Peace* (New York: Macmillan, 1907), 235. Addams's ideals are discussed in John C. Farrell, *Beloved Lady: A History of Jane Addams' Ideas on Reform and Peace* (Baltimore: Johns Hopkins University Press, 1967), 17, 140, in Sondra R. Herman, "Jane Addams: The Community as Neighborhood," in Herman, *Eleven Against War: Studies in American Internationalist Thought, 1898–1921* (Stanford, Calif.: Hoover Institution Press, 1969), 114–149, and in Allen F. Davis, *American Heroine: The Life and Legend of Jane Addams* (New York: Oxford University Press, 1973), 145–147.

6. Addams, *Newer Ideals of Peace*, 236.

7. Gerard T. Rice notes that the views of the philosopher William James on a moral equivalence to war (see note 24) were an antecedent to Peace Corps thinking but were unpopular because they involved conscription—an element of compulsion absent from the writings of Addams, which Rice does not discuss: Gerard T. Rice, *The Bold Experiment: JFK's Peace Corps* (Notre Dame, Ind.: University of Notre Dame Press, 1985), 7.

8. Addams, *Newer Ideals of Peace*, 208.

9. Addams quoted in Charles Chatfield, *For Peace and Justice: Pacifism in America 1914–1941* (Knoxville: University of Tennessee Press, 1971), 10. See also Neil A. Wynn, *From Progressivism to Prosperity: World War I and American Society* (New York: Holmes and Meier, 1986), 29; David S. Patterson, "Woodrow Wilson and the Mediation Movement, 1914–17," *Historian* 33 (1971), 539–540.

10. Women had the vote in New Jersey until 1807, and were in that state considered to be a peaceful foreign policy force: Augusta Genevieve Violette, *Economic Feminism in American Literature Prior to 1848* (1925; reprint, New York: Burt Franklin, 1971), 37. See also Merle Eugene Curti, *The American Peace Crusade 1815–1860* (1929; reprint, New York: Octagon, 1965), 23–24, and, for a discourse on the stimuli supplied by the antislavery crusade, the Civil War, the temperance movement, and other nineteenth-century factors to the growth of "feminist-pacifist consciousness," Harriet Hyman Alonso, *Peace as a Women's Issue: A History of the U.S. Movement for World Peace and Women's Rights* (Syracuse, N.Y.: Syracuse University Press, 1993), 20–55.

11. Though it was edited by a man, Henry B. Blackwell, *The Woman's Journal* criticized the Philippines war; the poet and essayist Abbie Morton Diaz also opposed the conquest. See Richard E. Welch, Jr., *Response to Imperialism: The United States and the Philippine-American War, 1899–1902* (Chapel Hill: University of North Carolina Press, 1979), 128, 130–131, who also supplies an account of torture and other American maltreatment of the Filipinos, pp. 133–149.

12. For further details concerning the women discussed in this section, and for guidance on sources for studying them, see Edward T. James et al., eds., *Notable American Women 1607–1950*, 4 vols. (Cambridge, Mass.: Belknap Press of Harvard University Press, 1971, 1980).

13. Wald quoted in Schott, "Women Against War," 27.

14. C. Roland Marchand, *The American Peace Movement and Social Reform, 1898–1918* (Princeton, N.J.: Princeton University Press, 1972), 183.

15. Paul's reminiscence of exhortation to Rankin, in "Conversations with Alice Paul: Woman Suffrage and the Equal Rights Amendment," an oral history conducted by Amelia R. Fry, Suffragists Oral History Project, Bancroft Library, University of California, Berkeley, 1976, 175.

16. Alice Paul died in 1977.

17. Paul oral history, 175.

18. Paul's comments at the time of the Washington naval conference quoted in Joan Hoff Wilson, "'Peace is a woman's job . . . ': Jeannette Rankin and American Foreign Policy: The Origins of Her Pacifism," *Montana* 30 (Winter 1980): 35.

19. Joan Hoff Wilson entry on Rankin in *Notable American Women*, vol. 4, 568. See also Carol Hymowitz and Michaele Weissman, *A History of Women in America* (New York: Bantam, 1978), 283. Rankin died in 1973.

20. On the rise and decline of women's foreign policy consciousness from 1898, see Judith Papachristou, "American Women and Foreign Policy, 1898–1905," *Diplomatic History* 14 (1990): 493–509. See also Wynn, *Progressivism and Prosperity*, 26.

21. Davis, *American Heroine*, 214–218; Alonso, *Peace as a Women's Issue*, 63–69.

22. Arthur S. Link, *Wilson the Diplomatist: A Look at his Major Foreign Policies* (Baltimore: Johns Hopkins Press, 1957), 93; Marchand, *Peace Movement*, 183, 221; Catherine Foster, *Women for All Seasons: The Story of the Women's International League for Peace and Freedom* (Athens: University of Georgia Press, 1989), 10; Alonso, *Peace as a Women's Issue*, 83.

23. See Elaine Tyler May, *Homeward Bound: American Families in the Cold War Era* (New York: Basic Books, 1988), 135 ff.

24. The philosopher William James, an admirer and supporter of Addams's views on peace, published an essay in 1910 called "The Moral Equivalent for War," suggesting a peacetime army to sublimate aggressive instincts. The historian Allen Davis called the James essay "famous" and "dramatic" (*American Heroine*, 143–144). One could argue that it was a more influential expression of Addams's philosophy than her own book, which had a mixed reception. But that would be to discount the impact of her charismatic personality, compared with that of James, the remote and ailing Boston Brahmin by 1910 in the last year of his life. The capitalist-philanthropist Andrew Carnegie had medals struck for peacetime heroism. He declared: "Civilization, not barbarism, is the mother of true heroism": Carnegie, *War as the Mother of Valor and Civilization* (London: The Peace Society, 1910). But Carnegie was already being subjected to ridicule, for example by the Chicago-Irish newspaper sage "Mr. Dooley": "I've heard Andhrew Carnaygie called a hayro but I don't believe it. . . . If he was a stable boy, he'd find that he'd have to catch runaway horses or lose his job": Finley Peter Dunne, *Mr. Dooley on Mr. Carnegie's Hero Fund* (London: McClure, Phillips, 1904).

25. Nancy C. M. Hartsock, "Masculinity, Heroism, and the Making of War," in Adrienne Harris and Ynesta King, eds., *Rocking the Ship of State: Toward a Feminist Peace* (London: Westview, 1989), 134.

26. Willa Cather, *One of Ours* (1922; reprint, Boston: Houghton Mifflin, 1937), 513.

27. Balch, "Effect of War on Women": 43.

28. Christine Bolt has told the story of how women organized in the Loyalty League supported the Union in the Civil War and collected petitions against slavery, only to find themselves bypassed in favor of the freedmen after Appomattox: Bolt, *The Women's Movements in the United States and Britain from the 1790s to the 1920s* (New York: Harvester Wheatsheaf, 1993), 119.

29. Marchand, *Peace Movement*, 199.

30. All quotations from Barbara J. Steinson, *American Women's Activism in World War I* (New York: Garland, 1982), 237–239, 315.

31. Tumulty to Equal Suffrage League of Baltimore, April 24, 1917, Presidential Papers of Woodrow Wilson, Library of Congress, Washington, D.C.

32. Steinson, *Women's Activism*, 317. See also Sally Hunter Graham, "Woodrow Wilson, Alice Paul, and the Woman Suffrage Movement," *Political Science Quarterly* 98 (Winter 1983–1984), 673.

33. Alonso, *Peace as a Women's Issue*, 74.

34. Gardener to the President, July 19, 1917, Records of the National American Woman Suffrage Association (henceforth NAWSA Papers), Library of Congress, Washington, D.C.

35. Gardener to Wilson, June 17, 1918, NAWSA Papers.

36. Wilson to Shields, two letters, n.d., sent in June 1918, Wilson to David Baird (N.J.), July 31, 1918; copies of all three letters in NAWSA Papers.

37. Catt to the President, Sept. 18, 1918, Wilson Papers.

38. Wilson to Catt, Sept. 18, Catt to Wilson, Sept. 29, 1918, Wilson Papers.

39. Lloyd E. Ambrosius, *Woodrow Wilson and the American Diplomatic Tradition: The Treaty Fight in Perspective* (Cambridge, England: Cambridge University Press, 1987), 47.

40. Catt to Wilson, Sept. 29, 1918, Wilson Papers.

41. Wilson to Catt, Sept. 30, 1918, Wilson Papers.

42. Quoted in Eleanor Flexner, *Century of Struggle: The Women's Rights Movement in the United States* (Cambridge, Mass.: Harvard University Press, 1959), 294.

43. Andrews quoted in Bolt, *Women's Movements*, 255.

44. See Alonso, *Peace as a Women's Issue*, 81–82. Presidents Harry Truman and Lyndon Baines Johnson both stirred up fears of radicalism, which played into the hands of their opponents.

45. Betty Boyd Caroli, *First Ladies* (New York: Oxford University Press, 1987), 151.

46. Wilson to Catt, Feb. 10, 1920.

47. Rosemary Rainbolt, "Women and War in the United States: The Case of Dorothy Detzer, National Secretary WILPF," *Peace and Change* 4 (Fall 1977), 20.

48. Fowler, *Catt*, 32, 96.

49. There is an account of the determined but mostly frustrated efforts of American women in Geneva in Carol Miller, "Feminists, Pacifists, and Internationalists: American Women at the League of Nations, 1919–1939," draft consulted by kind permission of its author; to be published in Martin David Dubin, ed., *Women, War and Peace: American Women's Experience with War from the First World War to the Cold War.*

50. "Like most politicians, Wilson was capable of transforming political necessity into personal advocacy": Christine Lunardini and Thomas Knock, "Woodrow

Wilson and Woman Suffrage: A New Look," *Political Science Quarterly* 95 (Winter 1980–1981), 670.

51. William Gibbs McAdoo was secretary of the treasury until January 1919. See Lunardini and Knock, "Wilson and Suffrage," 657 n7. In one well-known book it is claimed that Wilson was heavily influenced by his mother and by his second wife, but the influence is described for its effect on his personality, not on his policy— perhaps a commentary on the authors as much as the object of their study: Sigmund Freud and William C. Bullitt, *Thomas Woodrow Wilson: Twenty-Eighth President of the United States: A Psychological Study* (London: Weidenfeld & Nicolson, 1967).

52. For the facts of the case, see Graham, "Wilson, Paul," 676–678.

3. FROM PEACE TO PRICES IN THE TARIFF DECADE

1. As, for example, in the case of the enactment of the Sheppard-Turner bill on infant care. See William H. Chafe, *The Paradox of Change: American Women in the 20th Century* (New York: Oxford University Press, 1991), 27. For a summary of the earlier view that "the feminist movement reached its apogee" with the Nineteenth Amendment, see Andrew Sinclair, *The Better Half: The Emancipation of American Woman* (New York: Harper & Row, 1965), 343 ff.

2. Harriet Hyman Alonso, *The Women's Peace Union and the Outlawry of War, 1921–1942* (Knoxville: University of Tennessee Press, 1989), xvi.

3. Arthur S. Link, *Wilson the Diplomatist: A Look at His Major Policies* (Baltimore: Johns Hopkins University Press, 1957), 93.

4. See Charles Forcey, *The Crossroads of Liberalism: Croly, Weyl, Lippmann and the Progressive Era, 1900–1925* (New York: Oxford University Press, 1961), x and passim.

5. Harriet Hyman Alonso identified the four major groups as WILPF, the WPS, the WPU, and the National Committee on the Cause and Cure of War, with WILPF as the "mother organization" of the other three: Alonso, *Peace as a Women's Issue: A History of the U.S. Movement for World Peace and Women's Rights* (Syracuse, N.Y.: Syracuse University Press, 1993), 90.

6. Charles Chatfield, *For Peace and Justice: Pacifism in America, 1914–1941* (Knoxville: University of Tennessee Press, 1971), 94.

7. Florence Brewer Boeckel, "Women in International Affairs," *Annals of the American Academy of Political Sciences* 143 (1929): 230–232; Nancy F. Cott, *The Grounding of American Feminism* (New Haven: Yale University Press, 1987), 66, 72.

8. Robert Gordon Kaufman, *Arms Control During the Pre-Nuclear Era: The United States and Naval Limitation Between the Two Wars* (New York: Columbia University Press, 1990), 23.

9. Chatfield, *Peace and Justice*, 147.

10. Robert H. Ferrell, *Peace in Their Time: The Origins of the Kellogg-Briand Pact* (New Haven: Yale University Press, 1952), 15.

11. See Kaufman, *Arms Control*, 24.

12. Ibid., 30.

13. C. Leonard Hoag, *Preface to Preparedness: The Washington Disarma-*

ment Conference and Public Opinion (Washington, D.C.: American Council on Public Affairs, 1941), 74, 89–90.

14. Hoag, *Preface*, 89.

15. Chatfield, *Peace and Justice*, 147.

16. Quoted in Hoag, *Preface*, 94.

17. The correspondence took place in October 1921: quoted in ibid., 81.

18. For an assessment of the secretary of state's tactics, see John Chalmers Vinson, "Charles Evans Hughes (1921–1925)," in Norman A. Graebner, ed., *An Uncertain Tradition: American Secretaries of State in the Twentieth Century* (New York: McGraw-Hill, 1961), 138–139. According to one recent assessment, the advantages conferred by code breaking were relatively unimportant: Robin Denniston, "Yardley on Yap," *Intelligence and National Security* 9 (January 1994), 115–116.

19. One group that proved to be "hesitant" in 1921, though it was better organized by the 1930s, was the WILPF, according to Hoag, *Preface*, 93.

20. Walter Lippmann reflected the contemporary concern in his book *Public Opinion* (New York: Harcourt Brace, 1922), in which he accepted that the press was, quite rightly, coming to be viewed as an imperfect vehicle for public opinion, and advocated a greater role for political science. Lippmann thought that the suffragists had been effective because they had a simple, concrete objective, but that feminists' motivations and objectives were "extremely subtle": see pp. 31–32, 346.

21. Both quotations from Dexter Perkins, *Charles Evans Hughes and American Democratic Statesmanship* (Boston: Little, Brown, 1956), 111–113. Perkins's view appears to be that public opinion did constrain Hughes, that the conference did leave the United States weakened in the Pacific, but that the experiment was worthwhile. According to Robin Denniston, the hoodwinking of Japan was not an important precipitant of the Manchurian conflict, which later ended the Republicans' dream of peace: Denniston, "Yardley's Diplomatic Secrets," *Cryptologia* 18 (April 1994), 95.

22. Joan M. Jensen, "All Pink Sisters: The War Department and the Feminist Movement in the 1920s," in Lois Scharf and Joan M. Jensen, *Decades of Discontent: The Women's Movement, 1920–1940* (Westport, Conn.: Greenwood, 1983), 201, 210.

23. Quoted in Martin Gruberg, *Women in American Politics: An Assessment and Sourcebook* (Oshkosh, Wis.: Academia Press, 1968), 13.

24. Jensen, "Pink Sisters," 209.

25. See, for example, AAUW Executive Secretary Memorandum to Branches, reporting resolutions of the Committee on Legislative Policies, January 21, 1924, Mic. Reel 110, File 487, Legislative Committee Records, Papers of the American Association of University Women, AAUW headquarters, Washington, D.C. Child labor was also regarded as an "emergency" matter.

26. Carol Miller, "Feminists, Pacifists, and Internationalists: American Women at the League of Nations, 1919–1939," draft consulted by kind permission of its author, to be published in Martin David Dubin, ed., *Women, War and Peace: American Women's Experience with War from the First World War to the Cold War.*

27. Ferrell, *Peace in Their Time*, 18–19, 28–29, 118–119. Ferrell offers a mixed appreciation of WILPF's impact on the Kellogg-Briand process.

28. Boeckel, "Women in International Affairs," 238–243.

29. "Two-thirds of those who served in Congress from 1920 to 1930 succeeded their husbands, most for only a single term": Chafe, *Paradox*, 32. Chafe should

have written "almost one-third" and is correct only in the sense that widows were relatively prominent in the first few postfranchise decades. It might be added that one of the widows, Florence Prag Kahn, served in the House from 1925 to 1937. Another, Edith Nourse Rogers, became the longest-serving congresswoman (1925–1960). See Mildred L. Amer, comp., *Women in the United States Congress* (Washington, D.C.: Congressional Research Service, 1991), 23, 37, 60.

30. Moskowitz organized and managed New York City mayor John Purroy Mitchell's Committee of Women on National Defense from October 1917, but does not appear to have taken a major interest in foreign policy. Elisabeth Israels Perry, *Belle Moskowitz: Feminine Politics and the Exercise of Power in the Age of Alfred E. Smith* (New York: Routledge, 1992), ix, 113.

31. For a summary of these views, see Chafe, *Paradox*, 29.

32. Sinclair, *Better Half,* 343–44; Chafe, *Paradox*, 30; Paul F. Lazarsfeld, Bernard Berelson, and Hazel Gaudet, *The People's Choice: How the Voter Makes Up His Mind in a Presidential Campaign*, 2d ed. (New York: Columbia University Press, 1948), 141.

33. See chapter 6.

34. The observations of, respectively, Senator Margaret Chase Smith and Representative Bella Abzug: see chapters 7 and 8.

35. John L. Hayes, *Protection a Boon to Consumers* (Boston: John Wilson, 1867), 7.

36. On the historical background to the phenomenon, see Richard Wightman Fox and T. J. Jackson Lears, eds., *The Culture of Consumption, Critical Essays in American History, 1880–1980* (New York: Pantheon, 1983). For a discussion of women's prominence in advertising discourse and its effect on international relations, see Cynthia Enloe, *Bananas, Beaches and Bases: Making Feminist Sense of International Politics* (London: Pandora, 1989), 197 and passim.

37. The words are those of one of the five hundred women surveyed in 1927 by the Consumers' League of New York, and quoted illustratively in Alice Kessler-Harris, *Out to Work: A History of Wage-Earning Women in the United States* (New York: Oxford University Press, 1982), 217.

38. Victoria Hattam distinguishes between the wage-earning and productive mentalities of different groups of nineteenth-century workers; the ambitious modern woman does have a more positive approach to the intrinsic worth and rewards of work. See Hattam, *Labor Visions and State Power: The Origins of Business Unionism in the United States* (Princeton, N.J.: Princeton University Press, 1993), x.

39. Thorstein Veblen, *The Theory of the Leisure Class: An Economic Study of Institutions* (1899, reprint, London: George Allen & Unwin, 1922), 179.

40. Richardson quoted in Julie A. Matthaei, *An Economic History of Women in America: Women's Work, the Sexual Division of Labor, and the Development of Capitalism* (New York: Schocken, 1982), 164–165; Wesley C. Mitchell's essay reproduced in Wesley C. Mitchell, *The Backward Art of Spending Money, and Other Essays* (New York: McGraw-Hill, 1937), 3–19, especially 6.

41. Costigan to Mary Sumner Boyd, chairman of the National League of Women Voters' Research Standing Committee, July 28, 1919, Costigan to state chairmen NLWV, October 22, 1920, both in Records of the National League of Women Voters, Library of Congress, Washington, D.C. (henceforth LWV).

42. *New York Times*, September 3, 1929.

43. See M. W. Reder, "Chicago School," in John Eatwell et al., eds., *The New*

Palgrave: A Dictionary of Economics (London: Macmillan, 1987), vol. 1, 413–418.

44. Hazel Kyrk, *A Theory of Consumption* (Boston: Houghton Mifflin, 1923), 20, 292.

45. Theresa S. McMahon, *Social and Economic Standards of Living* (Boston: D.C. Heath, 1925); Jessica B. Peixotto, *Getting and Spending at the Professional Standard of Living: A Study of the Costs of Living of Academic Life* (New York: Macmillan, 1927) and *Cost of Living Studies. Vol. 2. How Workers Spend a Living Wage: A Study of the Incomes and Expenditures of Eighty-two Typographers' Families in San Francisco* (Berkeley: University of California Press, 1929); Elizabeth E. Hoyt, *The Consumption of Wealth* (New York: Macmillan, 1928).

46. "Women and the Tariff, No. 1" (typed leaflet. Racine, Wis.: FTL, April 26, 1922), LWV.

47. *Corsets and the Tariff* (Racine, Wis.: FTL, 1922), LWV.

48. "Women and the Tariff, No. 2" (typed leaflet. Racine, Wis.: FTL, May 10, 1922), LWV.

49. *The National Cyclopedia of American Biography/White's Conspectus of American Biography* (St. Clair Shores, Mich.: Scholarly Press, 1972), vol. 26, 236–237.

50. *New York Times*, September 22, 1922. Emphasis added.

51. *Detroit Free Press*, September 13, 22, 1922; *New York Times*, September 18, 24, November 9, 10, 1922; Theodore Saloutos and John D. Hicks, *Agricultural Discontent in the Middle West 1900–1939* (Madison, Wis.: University of Wisconsin Press, 1951), 348–349; Theodore Saloutos, "Lynn Joseph Frazier," *Dictionary of American Biography*, supplement 4 (New York: Scribner's, 1974), 308–309; Eleanor Flexner, *Century of Struggle: The Woman's Rights Movement in the United States*, rev. ed. (Cambridge, Mass.: Belknap/Harvard University Press, 1975), 322. The WPU had roots in the Woman's Peace Party, and had split from WILPF in October 1919 under the leadership of Fanny Garrison Villard, an absolute pacifist disgruntled with the moderation of WILPF (itself sometimes regarded as radical): Chatfield, *Peace and Justice*, 143.

52. Ann Dennis Bursch, "Living Costs," *The Woman Voter's Bulletin* 5 (June 5, 1925), 3. Also: Mason to Maud Wood Park (president, LWV), April 11, 1922, and Marion Parkhurst to Mason, June 6, 1922, both in LWV; Basil M. Manly, "The High Cost of Sugar—Why?" *Woman Citizen*, June 2, 1923.

53. Raymond T. Bye, "The Tariff and the Consumer" (broadcast over 24 stations on March 19, 1929, and released by the LWV press department on March 20, 1929), LWV.

54. *New York Times*, September 3, 1929.

55. Ibid.

56. On the social composition of the LWV, see Chafe, *Paradox*, 48–49.

57. Paxton, 46; *Women in Congress*.

58. Quoted in Hope Chamberlain, *A Minority of Members: Women in the U.S. Congress* (New York: Praeger, 1973), 30. See also *Women in Congress* and *The Atlanta Constitution*, October 4, 5, 1922. Felton was, however, opposed to the League of Nations and refused to express her view on the tariff.

59. Edward T. James, ed., *Notable American Women 1607–1950* (Cambridge, Mass.: Belknap Press of Harvard University Press, 1971).

60. *Minneapolis Tribune*, October 16, 1929.

61. Persia Campbell, *Consumer Representation in the New Deal* (1940; reprint, New York: AMS Press, 1968), 24. George found it difficult to make progress in the 1930s, too, in part because he obstructed some of President Franklin D. Roosevelt's plans, for example his scheme to "reform" the Supreme Court: George Wolfskill, *The Revolt of the Conservatives: A History of the American Liberty League, 1934–1940* (Boston: Houghton Mifflin, 1962), 250.

62. Anne Hard, "Am I Blue? The Housewife's Interest in National Legislation that Enters the Kitchen," *Ladies Home Journal*, December 1929, 13, 14, 190, 193.

63. Ibid., 14, 190.

64. *New York Times*, October 16, 1932; Sidney Ratner, *The Tariff in American History* (New York: Van Nostrand, 1972), 52.

65. *New York Times*, May 5, 1932.

66. *New York Times*, May 24, October 10, 1932.

67. Charles S. Peterson, *Utah: A Bicentennial History* (New York: Norton, 1977), 176.

68. *New York Times*, November 20, 1932.

69. Joan Hoff Wilson has discussed the nature of business's influence on foreign policy in the period 1920–1933, though she questions the view that "the economic power of the business community was automatically translated into political power": *American Business and Foreign Policy, 1920–1933* (Lexington, Ky.: University of Kentucky Press, 1971), xv. Lloyd E. Ambrosius has described President Wilson's nonresponsiveness to Irish American pressure at the Versailles peace conference on the question of Irish independence, and further argues that such pressure did not affect the Senate's stance on the League: "Contrary to the claims of professional Irish-Americans and the accusations of Wilson and other advocates of the League, ethnic politics exerted only a marginal impact": Ambrosius, *Woodrow Wilson and the American Diplomatic Tradition: The Treaty Fight in Perspective* (Cambridge, England: Cambridge University Press, 1987), 143–144, 248. For a discussion of the constraints that affected the Irish American lobby in a key state, see Rhodri Jeffreys-Jones, "Massachusetts Labor and the League of Nations Controversy," *Irish Historical Studies* 19 (September 1975): 90–106. Francis M. Carroll argues that Irish American agitation had a greater impact in Ireland (in that it produced financial support), and in England (in that it produced neurosis), than in the United States (where neither political party endorsed the Irish cause in the 1920 presidential election): Carroll, *American Opinion and the Irish Question 1910–23: A Study in Opinion and Policy* (Dublin: Gill & Macmillan, 1978), 192.

4. PRESIDENTIAL RECOGNITION OF THE FEMALE VOTE, 1932

1. Joan Hoff Wilson, *Herbert Hoover: Forgotten Progressive* (Boston: Little, Brown, 1975), 8, 19, 136.

2. Herbert Hoover, "What I Would Like Women to Do," *Ladies Home Journal*, August 1917, 25.

3. Herbert Hoover, "Thrift and American Women," *Ladies Home Journal*, August 1920, 3, 100.

4. Hoff, *Hoover*, 76.

5. *The Woman Citizen* 7 (April 21, 1923), 7.

6. Hoff, *Hoover*, 131.

7. Quoted in Walter LaFeber, *The American Age: United States Foreign Policy at Home and Abroad Since 1750* (New York: Norton, 1989), 337.

8. Dorothy Detzer, *Appointment on the Hill* (New York: Henry Holt, 1948), 91.

9. Detzer, *Appointment on the Hill*, 107. Rosemary Rainbolt describes a bruising encounter, in December 1931, between Detzer and Assistant Secretary of State James Grafton Rogers, after the journalist Drew Pearson warned her that Woolley's name was not on the list of delegates. Detzer told Rogers that "elections come with fair regularity in this country," and that one million women had backed the Woolley nomination. Rogers conveyed her sentiment to the president and, within the hour, the list had been amended: Rainbolt, "Women and War in the United States: The Case of Dorothy Detzer, National Secretary WILPF," *Peace and Change* 4 (Fall 1977), 20.

10. Hugh Hawkins, "Mary Emma Woolley," in Edward T. James, ed., *Notable American Women 1607–1950* (Cambridge, Mass: Belknap Press/Harvard University Press, 1971), vol. 3, 660–663.

11. Robert H. Ferrell quoting from the diary of the colleague in question, Jay Pierrepont Moffat, in Ferrell, *American Diplomacy in the Great Depression: Hoover-Stimson Foreign Policy, 1929–1933* (New Haven: Yale University Press, 1957), 206 n30.

12. Mabel Vernon, "Speaker for Suffrage and Petitioner for Peace," an oral history conducted in 1976 by Amelia R. Fry, Suffragists Oral History Project, Bancroft Library, University of California, Berkeley, 1976, 103.

13. Vernon oral history, 198; Ferrell, *American Diplomacy*, 207 n33.

14. Hawkins, "Woolley," 660–663; Detzer, *Appointment on the Hill*, 112.

15. According to the 1930s secretary of state in *The Memoirs of Cordell Hull* (London: Hodder and Stoughton, 1948), vol. 1, 308.

16. Jim Potter, *The American Economy between the Wars* (London: Macmillan, 1974), 98.

17. Peter Fearon, *War, Prosperity and Depression: The U.S. Economy 1917–1945* (Oxford, England: Philip Allan, 1987), 130.

18. Fearon, *War, Prosperity and Depression*, 140, table 8.3.

19. Frank W. Taussig, *The Tariff History of the United States*, 8th ed. (New York: Capricorn, 1964), 516–17.

20. Idella Gwatkin Swisher, *An Introduction to a Study of the Tariff* (Washington, D.C.: Committee on Living Costs, LWV, 1931), 8, 101.

21. Louise G. Baldwin, *Study Questions on the Tariff* (Washington, D.C.: LWV, 1931), 4, 6, 7.

22. Mrs. Harris T. [Louise G.] Baldwin, "A Tariff Luncheon" ("a suggested program for college leagues," December 1931), Records of the National League of Women Voters (henceforth LWV), Library of Congress, Washington, D.C.

23. *New York Times*, October 16, 1932. According to the *Times*, Roosevelt's low-tariff campaign was one of his key attractions. Yet, on September 20, 1932, the Democratic candidate had announced he favored high tariffs: Elliot A. Rosen, *Hoover, Roosevelt, and the Brains Trust: From Depression to New Deal* (New York: Columbia University Press, 1977), 346. As the campaign entered its final stage, the Democratic candidate explained that he favored agricultural protection but also reciprocal reductions. Hoover complained on October 28 of "the most startling shift in opinion by a Presidential candidate in the midst of a political campaign in all

recent political history": *The Memoirs of Herbert Hoover: The Great Depression, 1929–1941* (London: Hollis and Carter, 1953), 299. Martin L. Fausold contrasts Roosevelt's eve-of-election comments with the "vehemence with which he attacked the Smoot-Hawley Tariff early in the campaign": Martin L. Fausold, *The Presidency of Herbert C. Hoover* (Lawrence: University Press of Kansas, 1985), 208.

24. Hoover, "Radio Address to the Women's Conference on Current Problems," September 29, 1932, *Public Papers of the Presidents: Herbert Hoover, 1932–1933: Herbert Hoover: Containing the Public Messages, Speeches, and Statements of the President, January 1, 1932 to March 4, 1933* (Washington, D.C.: U.S. Government Printing Office, 1977), 446.

25. Women's Division, Republican National Committee, *The What Why and How of the Tariff* (Washington, D.C.: 1932): one-page leaflet.

26. Livermore to Ritchie, September 23, 1932, Papers of French Strother, folder on "Republican Women, 1932," Box 14, Herbert Hoover Presidential Library, West Branch, Iowa.

27. Strother to Hoover, telegram relaying text of speech, October 4, 1932, Strother Papers, "Republican Women" folder.

28. For information on Strother's drafting of the speech, I am grateful to Dwight D. Miller, senior archivist at the Hoover Library: Miller letter of February 5, 1992.

29. Hoover, "Radio Address to the Women of America, October 7, 1932," *Public Papers*, 492. Also: notes on the speech, and Hebert to Hoover, September 26, 1932, both in Strother Papers, "Republican Women" folder.

30. Poole to Hoover, September 27, 1932, in Strother Papers, "Republican Women" folder.

31. Rosen, *Hoover, Roosevelt*, 244, 341.

32. Ibid., 346.

33. "Radio Address to the Women of America, October 7, 1932," 491 ff.

34. List of radio programs, Presidential Subject File, Women's Division Republican National Committee, Box 269, Hoover Library.

35. Rogers speech, October 27, 1932, Presidential Subject File, Women's Division Republican National Committee, Box 269, Hoover Library.

36. Catt address, November 2, 1932, Presidential Subject File, Women's Division Republican National Committee, Box 269, Hoover Library.

37. Emphasis in the original.

38. Woolley speech, November 3, 1932, Presidential Subject File, Women's Division Republican National Committee, Box 269, Hoover Library.

39. Address from St. Paul, Minnesota, November 5, 1932, *Public Papers*, 765.

40. *New York Times*, November 8, 1932.

41. Ibid.

42. Transcript of sound recording of Hoover's address of November 8, 1932, *Public Papers*, 795–799.

43. Vernon oral history, 111.

5. DOROTHY DETZER AND THE MERCHANTS OF DEATH

1. Detzer did little to discourage the assessment after World War II, for she devoted herself to married life—in contrast to Eleanor Roosevelt, who, after her

husband's death in 1945, devoted herself with renewed energy to public activities, became a major inspirational figure for fellow American women, and captured the attention of historians. Further reasons for Detzer's neglect include: Detzer's association with "appeasement," a concept that was anathema to post–World War II Cold Warriors, and her inclusion in the ranks of the interwar "left," which removed her from serious consideration in an age of postwar scholarly McCarthyism whose end date has yet to be determined.

2. Charles Chatfield, *For Peace and Justice: Pacifism in America 1914–1941* (Knoxville: University of Tennessee Press, 1971), 321.

3. *New York Times* quoted in Rosemary Rainbolt, "Women and War in the United States: The Case of Dorothy Detzer, National Secretary WILPF," *Peace and Change* 4 (Fall 1977), 18.

4. Rainbolt, "Women and War," 18. Rainbolt (p.21, n5) lists some of the texbooks which note this achievement.

5. Rainbolt, "Women and War," 19; Harriet Hyman Alonso, *Peace as a Woman's Issue: A History of the U.S. Movement for World Peace and Women's Rights* (Syracuse, N.Y.: Syracuse University Press), 122–123.

6. Russell J. Clinchy, "The Plight of the Du Ponts," *The Christian Century* (October 3, 1934), 1234; Dorothy Detzer, *Appointment on the Hill* (New York: Henry Holt, 1948), 7–8. Detzer married only when her main career was over, indicating, possibly, a confidence in the durability of her charm. A photograph of Detzer taken in her lobbying days suggests an intent and determined personality, but also reveals vivacious and mischievous eyes, a prominently displayed ring on her engagement finger, and an unmistakably attractive overall appearance: I. K.Sundiata, *Black Scandal: America and the Liberian Labor Crisis, 1929–1936* (Philadelphia: Institute for the Study of Human Issues, 1980), between pages 50 and 51.

7. Detzer, *Hill*, 3, 9, 33, 35; Rainbolt, "Women and War," 18.

8. Detzer, *Hill*, 49.

9. Detzer, *Hill*, 43–44.

10. Joan M. Jensen, "All Pink Sisters: The War Department and the Feminist Movement in the 1920s," in Lois Scharf and Joan M. Jensen, eds., *Decades of Discontent: The Women's Movement, 1920–1940* (Westport, Conn.: Greenwood, 1983), 206, 217.

11. Rainbolt, "Women and War," 19.

12. Chatfield, *Peace and Justice*, 159. See also Rainbolt, "Women and War," 19, and Alonso, *Peace as a Woman's Issue*, 100.

13. Detzer, *Hill*, 38. Augusto Sandino's guerrilla campaign against U.S. Navy counterinsurgency forces occasioned a Senate inquiry in February 1928. See Larry E. Cable, "The Banana Wars, 1915–1934," in Cable, *Conflict of Myths: The Development of American Counterinsurgency Doctrine and the Vietnam War* (New York: New York University Press, 1986), 96–110.

14. *Nation*, n.d., opinion cited in Gertrude Bussey and Margaret Tims, *Women's International League for Peace and Freedom, 1915–1965: A Record of Fifty Years' Work* (London: George Allen & Unwin, 1965), 130.

15. Detzer, *Hill*, 140.

16. In 1926 WILPF considered sending Detzer on an anti-Hitler speaking tour of the United States, a venture Detzer later said would have been futile: Detzer, *Hill*, p. 78. In being antifascist so early, she was in advance of American public opinion and even further in advance of opinion in the rest of the English-speaking

world. John P. Diggins notes that Boston's *Lantern* (1927–1929) was "the first periodical in English devoted to the anti-Fascist cause": Diggins, "The Italo-American Anti-Fascist Opposition," *Journal of American History* 54 (December 1967), 581–582.

17. Chatfield, *Peace and Justice*, 225, 227.

18. "Memorandum," p. 6. In exposing the activities of Gulf Oil, Detzer drew on the research of journalist Ludwell Denny. In 1954 she became Denny's second wife.

19. "Memorandum," 7, 10.

20. *The Good Earth* (London: Methuen, 1931), was by 1936 in its 33d printing (*National Union Catalog of pre-1956 Imprints*). See also Harold R. Isaacs, *Images of Asia: American Views of China and India* (New York: Capricorn, 1962), 155 n, 162–163, cited in Kenneth E. Shewmaker, *Americans and Chinese Communists, 1927–1945: A Persuading Encounter* (Ithaca and London: Cornell University Press, 1971), 58. Nym Wales (the pseudonym of Helen Foster Snow) wrote *Inside Red China* (New York: Doubleday, Doran, 1939), which was factually supplementary to the book by her husband Edgar Snow, *Red Star Over China* (London: Victor Gollancz, 1938), second in influence only to Buck's novel, according to the Isaacs study. Agnes Smedley, Anne Louise Strong, Joy Homer, and Ilona Ralf Sues also helped shape American opinion on China in the interwar years and subsequently.

21. "Memorandum," 13. The Vinson-Trammel bill, sponsored by Representative Carl Vinson (Georgia) and Senator Park Trammel (Florida), did become law. It provided for the construction of 102 new ships, bringing the United States up to the limits set by the Washington and London naval treaties of 1922 and 1930. While it supplied a framework for naval expansion and a politically valuable promise of more jobs, it did not furnish the appropriation necessary to its purposes.

22. Robert Dallek, *Franklin D. Roosevelt and American Foreign Policy, 1932–1945* (New York: Oxford University Press, 1979), 66.

23. Miller to Howe, May 2, 1933, Detzer to Miller, May 25, 1933, Detzer to Howe, May 29, July 18, 1933, Howe to Detzer, June 26, 1933, all in PPF 28, Franklin D. Roosevelt Library, Hyde Park, New York. The suggestion that Roosevelt was unreceptive to Detzer is not meant to imply that Howe received her with open arms. When Miller complained to him about Detzer's treatment, Howe scrawled on her letter the initialed remark "forget": Miller to Howe, May 29, 1933, PPF 28, Roosevelt Library.

24. Detzer statement, final draft, enclosed with Detzer to Seldes, April 11, 1934, Dorothy Detzer Papers, Swarthmore College Peace Collection, Swarthmore, Pennsylvania. Seldes was about to publish his book *Iron, Blood and Profits: An Exposure of the World-Wide Munitions Market* (New York: Harper, 1934), a publication which reinforced the message of the book that overshadowed it, H. C. Engelbrecht and F. C. Hanighen's *Merchants of Death: A Study of the International Armament Industry* (New York: Dodd, Mead & Company, 1934). Fascism and Red-baiting were among the targets of Seldes's later books.

25. Detzer statement, above.

26. Detzer to Roosevelt, April 4, 1934, PPF 28, Roosevelt Papers.

27. Seldes to Detzer, April 10, 1934, and Detzer to Seldes, April 11, 1934, both in Detzer Papers.

28. Detzer's handwritten amendments to the typescript of the prepared statement she had originally sent Seldes, in Detzer Papers.

29. "Memorandum," 4; Paul A. C. Koistinen, *The Military-Industrial Complex: A Historical Perspective* (New York: Praeger, 1980), 54–55.

30. Warren I. Cohen, *The American Revisionists: The Lessons of Intervention in World War I* (Chicago and London: University of Chicago Press, 1967), 161; Wayne S. Cole, *Roosevelt and the Isolationists, 1932–45* (Lincoln: University of Nebraska Press, 1983), 168.

31. Cohen, *Revisionists*, 144.

32. "Arms and the Men," *Fortune*, March 1934. Although this exposé came under attack for being sensationalist, it largely exonerated the U.S. manufacturers, portraying them as "small fry" and an "open book" compared with their secretive European competitors: pp. 53, 55. The information on Borah is in Drew Pearson and Robert S. Allen, "The Washington Merry-Go-Round," syndicated column appearing in various newspapers, including the *Philadelphia Record*, on September 4, 1934—clipping in Detzer Papers.

33. Detzer, *Hill*, 152.

34. Susan Ware, *Beyond Suffrage: Women in the New Deal* (Cambridge, Mass.: Harvard University Press, 1981), 8–9. A Jewish member of the New York City branch of WILPF complained to Detzer in 1934 about the "Mayflower complex" of the local leadership: Alonso, *Peace as a Women's Issue*, 103.

35. Susan Ware, *Partner and I: Molly Dewson, Feminism, and New Deal Politics* (New Haven: Yale University Press, 1987), xii–xiii and passim.

36. Ingrid Winther Scobie, *Center Stage: Helen Gahagan Douglas, A Life* (New York: Oxford University Press, 1992; paperback reprint, New Brunswick, N.J.: Rutgers University Press, 1995), 161.

37. In the 73rd Congress, the following women served in the House of Representatives: Marian Williams Clarke, Isabella Selmers Greenway, Virginia Ellis Jenckes, Florence Prag Kahn, Kathryn O'Loughlin McCarthy, Mary Teresa Norton, and Edith Nourse Rogers; Hattie W. Caraway served in the Senate. Clarke and Kahn had inherited their husbands' seats. (Julius Kahn had authored the Selective Draft Act of 1917.) See Mildred L. Amer, comp., *Women in the United States Congress* (Washington, D.C.: Congressional Research Service, 1991), 59, and, for biographical sketches of women legislators, *Women in Congress, 1917–1990* (Washington, D.C.: U.S. Government Printing Office, 1991).

38. Blanche Wiesen Cook, "Eleanor Roosevelt and Human Rights: The Battle for Peace and Planetary Decency," in Edward P. Crapol, ed., *Women and American Foreign Policy: Lobbyists, Critics and Insiders* (New York: Greenwood, 1987), 97; Jason Berger, *A New Deal for the World: Eleanor Roosevelt and American Foreign Policy* (New York: Social Science Monographs/Columbia University Press, 1981), 7–9.

39. Mabel Vernon, "Speaker for Suffrage and Petitioner for Peace," an oral history conducted in 1976 by Amelia R. Fry, Suffragists Oral History Project, Bancroft Library, University of California, Berkeley, 1976, 107.

40. Vernon oral history, 107.

41. *Women in Congress.*

42. Charles Chatfield suggested that Detzer, Rankin, and Sternberger were amongst the top five lobbyists pressing for the Nye investigation: Chatfield, *Peace and Justice*, 165.

43. Quotations from Susan Ware, *Still Missing: Amelia Earhart and the Search for Modern Feminism* (New York: Norton, 1993), 24, 120.

44. Helmuth C. Engelbrecht, *Revolt Against War* (London: T. Werner Laurie, 1938), 21, 153.

45. Edwin Williamson, *The Penguin History of Latin America* (Harmondsworth, England: Penguin, 1992), 274. For a more extended account of "one of the most senseless wars in history" (p. 314) and the failure of the League's attempts at embargo, see Harris Gaylord Warren, *Paraguay: An Informal History* (Norman: University of Oklahoma Press, 1949), 298–314.

46. "Memorandum," 10.

47. Amended typescript, above.

48. Ware, *Beyond Suffrage*, 9, 92, 93, 153.

49. Cole, *Roosevelt and the Isolationists*, 45.

50. Hull, quoted in Cole, *Roosevelt and the Isolationists*, 147.

51. Dallek, *Roosevelt and American Foreign Policy*, 76.

52. Detzer, *Hill*, 38–40. The passages occur in the chapter "The Lion and the Tiger," 34–42. Cf. her praise for the "skillful and shrewd parliamentary tactician" Senator Nye in ibid., 158.

53. Detzer, *Hill*, 156; Wayne S. Cole, *Senator Gerald P. Nye and American Foreign Relations* (Minneapolis: University of Minnesota Press, 1962), 233.

54. "Memorandum," 13.

55. Dallek, *Roosevelt*, 86.

56. Pearson and Allen, "Washington Merry-Go-Round"; Pennsylvania Branch WILPF *Newsletter* 7 (October 1934): 1; Clinchy, "Plight of the Du Ponts," 1234; Gerald P. Nye to "Miss Arne," January 8, 1935, copy in Detzer Papers. Drew Pearson was a Quaker journalist who specialized in international affairs. He won renown for his "Washington Merry-Go-Round" syndicated column, which appeared regularly from 1931 to his death in 1969.

57. Detzer took credit for a number of reforms. For example, in her memoir she quoted from a letter she received in the 1930s from L. A. Grimes, Liberian secretary of state: "I sincerely feel the modified view of the American government . . . is due more to your efforts than to those of any other single individual." Detzer, *Hill*, 137.

58. See Dallek, *Roosevelt*, 85–86, 551 n9 and Cole, *Roosevelt and Isolationists*, 143. Cole credited Detzer's influence in spite of Nye's reservation, noted below.

59. Nye read Wayne S. Cole's book *Senator Gerald P. Nye and American Foreign Policy* in the fall of 1962. At the time Cole was a Fulbright lecturer at the University of Keele in England. Nye drafted a letter to his biographer, but did not polish or mail it, possibly because he had just emerged from a four-week hospital stay, or because he was unsure of Cole's address. On December 2, 1963, he did enclose the 1962 draft in another letter to Cole. Here is Cole's account of the matter:

> His full reference to Dorothy Detzer in the draft letter he sent me (undated but written either near the end of November or before December 19 in 1962) was as follows: "Again, I think you have let Dorothy Detzer in for more credit than she really deserves for bringing about the inventigation [sic] of the munitions committee. I never criticized her book on the subject though I felt she was taking much more credit unto herself and others for the conception of the investigation and the legislative steps to bring it about. But these are quite minor criticisms in my weighing of the overall merit of your presentation." That constitutes

in full the only written reference I have seen from Senator Nye on her role. If I recall correctly, I later queried him on the subject in personal conversation, and he essentially restated the comment he had made in his draft letter and did not elaborate more fully than that. (Cole to author, October 8, 1989)

In his 1962 book Cole had depicted Detzer as the "key figure" in the agitation for the enquiry: *Nye*, 67. According to the historian John E. Wiltz, "It took much prodding by Dorothy Detzer before he [Nye] even agreed to offer a resolution for an arms inquiry": Wiltz, *In Search of Peace: The Senate Munitions Inquiry, 1934–36* (Baton Rouge: Louisiana State University Press, 1963), 229.

60. On one occasion when Detzer was waiting in an anteroom to see Lord Cecil, chairman of the League of Nations Liberia Commission, she overheard his secretary: "Sir, I should warn you; for she is not like most of the peace ladies who come to see you. She is under seventy years of age; has bought a hat since 1900; but talks like a Bolshevik." On greeting Cecil, Detzer enlightened him: "I don't talk like a Bolshevik, I only talk like a good middle-western American." Detzer, *Hill*, p. 128.

61. William L. Langer and Everett S. Gleason, *The Challenge to Isolation: The World Crisis of 1937–1940 and American Foreign Policy.* (New York: Harper & Row, 1952), vol. 1, 14, 89, 682, 772. Robert A. Divine thought that "the United States abdicated its responsibilities and became a creature of history rather than its molder. . . . In the last analysis the United States was saved only by the Japanese miscalculation in attacking Pearl Harbor": Divine, *The Reluctant Belligerent: American Entry into World War II* (New York: John Wiley, 1965), 158. Selig Adler was of like mind in his searing account of the Nye investigation's analyses and effects: Adler, *The Uncertain Giant, 1921–1941: American Foreign Policy between the Wars* (New York: Collier, 1965), chapter 7. According to John E. Wiltz, "The Nye Committee failed to prove munitions makers an important cause of war." Wiltz regretted the fact that the isolationists had continued to "restrict policy" until 1938: "The best the government could hope for was that in time Americans and their representatives in Congress would see the flaws in isolationist logic and liberate diplomacy from the bonds of isolationist legislation." But Wiltz defended the munitions inquiry because its hearings on neutrality came too late to influence the outcome of the debate on the first Neutrality Act, as well as on the unusual ground that, by exposing its flaws, it made the arms industry serve the national interest more efficiently, thus contributing to the success of the war effort in 1941–1945. Wiltz, *From Isolation to War, 1931–1941* (London: Routledge & Kegan Paul, 1967), 50, 66, 231–232.

62. Nye himself took a broader view than did his committee. For an authoritative account of the committee's work and findings, see Cole, *Roosevelt and the Isolationists*, 147–162. For the broader view taken by the New Left variant of the revisionist school, see LaFeber, *American Age*, 364.

63. In his critical study of the munitions committee, John E. Wiltz praises its impartiality and its careful handling of testimony: *In Search of Peace: The Senate Munitions Inquiry, 1934–36* (Baton Rouge: Louisiana State University Press, 1963), 222–223.

64. Raymond Leslie Buell had fanned fears of this nature in his book *The Native Problem in Africa*, 2 vols. (New York: Macmillan, 1928).

65. Detzer, *Hill*, pp. 124–125. For information on Anna Melissa Graves and her activities, see Sundiata, *Black Scandal*, 90–91, 101, 104.

66. Graves to Detzer, July 27, 1933, Detzer Papers. According to one authority, the State Department was by 1937 impeding German mineral investment in Liberia in a manner suggestive of "aggressive opposition to Hitler's regime": Lloyd N. Beecher Jr., "The State Department and Liberia, 1908–1941: A Heterogeneous Record" (University of Georgia Ph.D. dissertation, 1970), 152.

67. Detzer memoir, 167; "Statement made by Dorothy Detzer before Nye Munitions Investigating Committee, April 10, 1935," in Detzer Papers.

68. Chatfield, *Peace and Justice*, 245, 274. For information on Detzer's reactions to the Spanish Civil War, I am indebted to Carol Miller of the UN Research Institute for Social Development, Geneva: Miller to author, 22 Sept. 1993.

69. Detzer paraphrased by William J. Gross of the Fort Wayne *News-Sentinel*, in Gross to Herbert Hoover, October 5, 1939, in Post-Presidential Files, Box 344, Herbert Hoover Library, West Branch, Iowa.

70. Chatfield, *Peace and Justice*, 321; Rainbolt, "Women and War," 20.

71. Detzer to Eleanor Roosevelt, March 7, 1944, enclosed with Paul Grosjean (of the Belgian Red Cross) to Herbert Hoover, Post-Presidential Files, Box 343, Hoover Library.

6. A TALE OF TWO WOMEN: HARRIET ELLIOTT, ELEANOR ROOSEVELT, AND CHANGING DIFFERENCES

1. Elliott to Dewson, Jan. 15, Dewson to L. L. McCorliss (Democratic National Committeewoman, Honolulu), Jan. 18, Dewson to Farley, Jan. 18, Dewson to Elliott, Jan. 18, May 1, all 1936, all in Mary W. Dewson Papers (henceforth MWD), Franklin D. Roosevelt Library, Hyde Park, New York; Susan Ware, *Partner and I: Molly Dewson, Feminism, and New Deal Politics* (New Haven: Yale University Press, 1987), 202–203.

2. *Complete Presidential Press Conferences of Franklin D. Roosevelt* (New York: Da Capo, 1972), vol. 1, May 26, 1933.

3. Caner to Roosevelt, May 7, 1933, Presidential Papers of Franklin D. Roosevelt (henceforth FDR) , Franklin D. Roosevelt Library/OF.

4. Morgan to Caner, May 19, 1933, FDR/OF.

5. Arthur M. Schlesinger, Jr., *The Age of Roosevelt*, vol. 2, *The Coming of the New Deal* (Boston: Houghton Mifflin, 1959), 129, 134.

6. Quoted in Schlesinger, *Coming of the New Deal*, 255.

7. See Lucy B. Creighton, *Pretenders to the Throne: The Consumer Movement in the United States* (Lexington, Mass.: D.C. Heath, 1976), 22.

8. Paul H. Douglas, "Rules and Regulations Governing the Relationship of the Consumers' Council Section to the NEC," enclosed with Douglas to Dewson, February 23, 1934, Records of the Democratic National Committee, Women's Division (henceforth DNC/WD), Franklin D. Roosevelt Library, Hyde Park, New York. Paul Douglas was the author of *Wages and the Family* (Chicago: University of Chicago Press, 1925), and *Real Wages in the United States, 1890–1926* (Boston: Houghton Mifflin, 1930).

9. I. M. Destler notes that "Smoot-Hawley was the last general tariff law ever enacted by the United States Congress." From the mid-1930s, representatives wanted to protect themselves, not industry: In the new climate of opinion, they did not want to have to take responsibility for "bad trade law" fostered by "one-sided

pressure from producer interests": Destler, *American Trade Politics*, 2d ed. (Washington, D.C.: Institute for International Economics, 1992), 11, 14.

10. *New York Times*, October 8, 1936.

11. Corwin D. Edwards (economist, Consumers' Advisory Board, NRA) to L. W. Moore (administrative officer, U.S. Tariff Commission), Jan. 18, 1934, and Sidney Morgan to Edwards, Jan. 23, 1934, both in Records of the U.S. Tariff Commission, National Archives, Washington, D.C..

12. Quoted in Susan Ware, *Beyond Suffrage: Women in the New Deal* (Cambridge, Mass.: Harvard University Press, 1981), 93.

13. Hamilton to Dewson, August 26, 1935, DNC/WD.

14. *Complete Press Conferences*, vol. 6, July 31, 1935; circular issued by the Consumers' Division of the Department of Labor, Jan. 10, 1936, DNC/WD; Creighton, *Pretenders*, 25.

15. Statement on Sept. 1, 1937, in "Excerpts from Statements by the President Regarding the Price Level and Structure," a compilation in FDR/PPF.

16. Perkins, *Roosevelt*, 285.

17. Robert E. Sherwood, *Roosevelt and Hopkins: An Intimate History* (New York: Harper, 1948), 158.

18. Perkins, *Roosevelt*, 285.

19. *Complete Press Conferences*, vol. 15, May 30, 1940.

20. Elliott to Grady, July 12, 1940, in Department of State, Decimal file (henceforth SDF), National Archives.

21. Tasca memorandum to Ben W. Lewis, July 31, 1940, in Records of the Consumer Division, Office of Price Administration (henceforth OPA/CD), National Archives.

22. Samuel I. Rosenman, comp., *The Public Papers and Addresses of Franklin D. Roosevelt. 1942: Humanity on the Defensive* (New York: Harper, 1950), 325, 327.

23. Ware to Elliott, Aug. 6, Elliott to Harriman, Aug. 19, and Harriman to Elliott, Aug. 27, all 1940, all in OPA/CD.

24. Lewis memorandum for Leon Henderson (the NDAC's price custodian), "Proposed Inter-American Coffee Treaty" (September 11, 1940), p. 2 in SDF.

25. All the penciled comments were hostile: Elliott to Harriman, Nov. 4, 1940, SDF.

26. Elliott to Dewson, Jan. 2, 1941, MWD.

27. Elliott to Dewson, Jan. 2, 1941, MWD; Astor to Eleanor Roosevelt, 29 December 1940, FDR/PPF 192.

28. FDR to Astor, Feb. 19, 1941, FDR/PPF 192.

29. Elliott to Eleanor Roosevelt, Nov. 21, 1941, in FDR/OF; Elliott to FDR, Nov. 22, 1941, in FDR/PPF; Donald M. Nelson (War Production Board chief) to Elliott, Nov. 24, 1941, in FDR/OF.

30. FDR to Elliott, December 10, 1941, in FDR/PPF.

31. Andrew H. Bartels, "Office of Price Administration," in Donald R. Whitnah, ed., *Government Agencies* (Westport, Conn.: Greenwood, 1983), 421–426.

32. On this aspect of the Elliott-Roosevelt differences, see Joseph P. Lash, *Eleanor and Franklin: The Story of Their Relationship Based on Eleanor Roosevelt's Private Papers* (New York: Signet, 1973), 808–809.

33. Office of War Information (OWI), Bureau of Intelligence, Report no. 31,

"Women and the War," Record Group 44, Entry 164, Box 1798, National Archives, Washington, D.C., 25. The report was declassified on August 31, 1945.

34. George H. Gallup, *The Gallup Poll: Public Opinion 1935–1971* (New York: Random House, 1972), vol. 1, 273, 522.

35. Elaine Tyler May, *Homeward Bound: American Families in the Cold War Era* (New York: Basic Books, 1988), 165–166.

36. Claudia Goldin, *Understanding the Gender Gap: An Economic History of American Women* (New York: Oxford University Press, 1990), 55–57.

37. In more recent years, there has been concern that women have retained a good proportion of family spending power yet continued to be prey to the demands of a selfish, materialistic culture. According to Linda Witt, Karen M. Paget, and Glenna Matthews, "[unspecified] studies have shown that women spend 70–80 percent of the family income," but "few have had any inclination to spend it politically, let alone on women candidates": *Running as a Woman: Gender and Power in American Politics* (New York: Free Press, 1994), 24.

38. Campbell to Long, October 25, 1967, Records of the National Consumers' League (henceforth NCL), Box C-48, Library of Congress; "Statement of National Retail Merchants Association presented to Senate Finance Committee Hearings on Import Quotas by Thomas Bowers October 20, 1967," enclosed with W. Wilson Young (Associated Merchandising Corporation, Washington representative) to Sarah Newman (Executive Secretary, National Consumers' League), October 24, 1967, NCL, Box C-48; Hills speech, September 6, 1991, quoted in the *Gerald R. Ford Foundation Newsletter* (Fall 1991), 2–3.

39. 1972 Virginia Slims American Women's poll, conducted by Louis Harris and Associates, accessed via the DIALOG/POLL computer facility.

40. Smith quoted in Frank Graham, Jr., *Margaret Chase Smith: Woman of Courage* (New York: John Day, 1964), 36.

41. Jason Berger, *A New Deal for the World: Eleanor Roosevelt and American Foreign Policy* (New York: Columbia University Press, 1981), 5. Another close student of Mrs. Roosevelt's policies on peace and foreign relations asserted that she merely "believed in power. She understood power, sought power, and, more than any other contemporary woman in public life, influenced policy from positions of power": Blanche Wiesen Cook, "'Turn Toward Peace:' Eleanor Roosevelt and Foreign Affairs," in Joan Hoff Wilson and Marjorie Lightman, eds., *Without Precedent: The Life and Career of Eleanor Roosevelt* (Bloomington: Indiana University Press, 1984), 108.

42. Berger, *New Deal for the World*, 2, 21; Cook, "Peace," 108, 113, 114; Ware, *Beyond Suffrage*, 16.

43. William H. Chafe, *The Paradox of Change: American Women in the Twentieth Century* (New York: Oxford University Press, 1991), 60.

44. Deborah E. Lipstadt argues that, for a variety of opportunistic reasons, there was a virtual conspiracy of silence on the extermination of Jews: the American press, in particular, proved unequal to the task of following up ample clues about the true state of affairs in Germany and Poland: Lipstadt, *Beyond Belief: The American Press and the Coming of the Holocaust 1933–1945* (New York: Free Press, 1986), 135–158, 278.

45. Roosevelt responded to Dewson's pleas by appointing Florence Jaffray "Maisy" Harriman, yet another of Edward Henry Harriman's progeny, minister to a neutrality-minded nation, Norway. The quotation is Susan Ware's paraphrase in *Partner and I*, 191.

46. Dispatch dated 1 Feb. 1940, enclosed with Lothian to Halifax, Feb. 3, 1940. Private Papers of Lord Halifax, Public Record Office, London (FO 800/324, H XXXVII/46).

47. Ratio extrapolated from figures in Linda Kay Schott, "Women against War: Pacifism, Feminism, and Social Justice in the United States, 1915–1941" (Ph.D. diss., Stanford University, 1985), 108–109.

48. Patricia Lochridge, "The Mother Racket," *Woman's Home Companion* (July 1944), 20, 21, 72; Laura McEnaney, "He-Men and Christian Mothers: The America First Movement and the Gendered Meanings of Patriotism and Isolationism," *Diplomatic History* 18 (Winter 1994), 47, 48, 51.

49. Emphasis added. Quotations from Robert D. McFadden's obituary of Rankin in the *New York Times*, May 20, 1973. See also Joan Hoff Wilson, "'Peace Is a Woman's Job . . .': Jeannette Rankin and American Foreign Policy: Her Lifework as a Pacifist," *Montana* 30 (Spring 1980), 44–46.

50. OWI, "Women and the War," 1. In Appendix 2b, it is explained that tables based on the surveys and appended to the report "were planned to show uniformly for each question the responses for different occupational and age groups of men and women in parallel form."

51. OWI, "Women and the War," 1–2, 8, and supporting tables.

52. OWI, "Women and the War," 1, 3, 4, 5, 7, 14, and supporting tables. On the basis of extrapolations from similar OWI data, D'Ann Campbell wrote: "Two months after Pearl Harbor, 57 percent of the men, but only 36 percent of the women, favored all-out war against Japan, 'even if our cities would be bombed'": Campbell, *Women at War with America* (Cambridge, Mass.: Harvard University Press, 1984), 7.

53. Mary R. Beard, *Woman as Force in History: A Study in Traditions and Realities* (New York: Persea, 1987 [1946]), 37–38; Robert Booth Fowler, *Carrie Catt: Feminist Politician* (Boston: Northeastern University Press, 1986), 32–33; Harriet Hyman Alonso, *Peace as a Women's Issue: A History of the U.S. Movement for World Peace and Women's Rights* (Syracuse, N.Y.: Syracuse University Press, 1993), 152.

54. The exception was Jessie Sumner of Illinois, who was critical of proposals for postwar international structures. The women in the 77th Congress were, with their spans in office:

Frances P. Bolton	House	Rep.	Ohio	1940–1969
Katharine E. Byron	House	Dem.	Md.	1941–1943
Hattie W. Caraway	Senate	Dem.	Ark.	1931–1945
Mary T. Norton	House	Dem.	N.J.	1925–1951
Caroline L. G. O'Day	House	Dem.	N.Y.	1935–1943
Jeannette Rankin	House	Rep.	Mont.	1917–1919, 1941–1943
Edith Nourse Rogers	House	Rep.	Mass.	1925–1960
Margaret Chase Smith	House	Rep.	Me.	1940–1949
Jessie Sumner	House	Rep.	Ill.	1939–1947

Unless otherwise stated the data on women of the 77th Congress, here as in earlier passages, are drawn from Annabel Paxton, *Women in Congress* (Richmond, Va.: Dietz, 1945), and from *Women in Congress, 1917–1990* (Office of the Historian, House of Representatives, 1991).

55. Ingrid Winther Scobie, *Center Stage: Helen Gahagan Douglas, A Life*

(New York: Oxford University Press, 1992; paperback reprint, New Brunswick, N.J.: Rutgers University Press, 1995), 214.

56. Susan Ware, *Still Missing: Amelia Earhart and the Search for Modern Feminism* (New York: Norton, 1993), 25.

57. Eleanor Roosevelt in 1933, quoted in Lois Scharf, "Eleanor Roosevelt and Feminism," in Joan Hoff Wilson and Marjorie Lightman, eds., *Without Precedent: The Life and Career of Eleanor Roosevelt* (Bloomington: Indiana University Press), 236. Emphasis in the original.

58. Mrs. Roosevelt may have enjoyed at least subliminal lesbian attachments; if so, this would make a nonsense of the suggestion that she remained forever a matrimonial victim. For a summary of the Franklin–Eleanor relationships, see Shelley Ross, *Washington Babylon: Sex, Scandal, and Corruption in American Politics from 1702 to the Present* (London: W.H. Allen, 1989), 172–179.

59. See McEnaney, "He-Men," 55.

60. On Mrs. Roosevelt's family background, see Lash, *Eleanor and Franklin*, 27–47.

61. Although Mrs. Roosevelt's humanitarianism was to win through decisively, in 1939 she still bordered on sympathy with German attempts to curtail "the ascendency of the Jewish people": Blanche Wiesen Cook, "Eleanor Roosevelt and Human Rights: The Battle for Peace and Planetary Decency," in Edward P. Crapol, ed., *Women and Foreign Policy: Lobbyists, Critics, and Insiders*, 2d ed. (Wilmington, Del.: Scholarly Resources, 1992), 98–99.

62. Many years later, in an influential book on the concept of just war heavily influenced by World War II, Michael Walzer gave focus to modern concerns with the morality of "human rights": *Just and Unjust Wars: A Moral Argument with Historical Illustrations* (New York: Basic Books, 1977), xvi.

63. Blanche Wiesen Cook, *Eleanor Roosevelt* (New York: Viking, 1992), 17.

64. Scharf, "Eleanor Roosevelt and Feminism," 244. Elsewhere, my account of Eleanor Roosevelt's UN work is mainly drawn from Cook, "Eleanor Roosevelt and Human Rights": 91–118.

65. Cook, "Eleanor Roosevelt and Human Rights," 100.

66. Kim Salomon, *Refugees in the Cold War: Toward a New International Refugee Regime in the Early Postwar Era* (Lund, Sweden: Lund University Press, 1991), 112–114.

67. Eisenhower quoted in Cook, *Eleanor Roosevelt*, 18.

68. For a discussion of some of these issues, see A. Glenn Mower, *The United States, the United Nations, and Human Rights: The Eleanor Roosevelt and Jimmy Carter Eras* (Westport, Conn.: Greenwood, 1979), x, 98ff.

7. MARGARET CHASE SMITH AND THE FEMALE QUEST FOR SECURITY

1. Margaret Chase Smith, *Declaration of Conscience* (New York: Doubleday, 1972), 205, 251, 257.

2. Geoffrey S. Smith, "National Security and Personal Isolation: Sex, Gender, and Disease in the Cold-War United States," *International History Review* 14 (May 1992), 310, 329, 335.

3. She took over Clyde Smith's candidacy in the 1940 election, when he was on his deathbed. Of the 120 women elected to the House by 1991, 32 had filled vacancies caused by the death of their spouses: Mildred L. Amer, *Women in the United States Congress* (Washington, D.C.: Congressional Research Service, 1991), 1.

4. Cora E. Edgerly, leaflet, "Why I Shall Not Vote for Margaret Chase Smith" n.d./1948: Elections, 1948/Correspondence. Unless otherwise specified, manuscript citations in this chapter are to the Margaret Chase Smith Papers, Skowhegan, Maine. The name of the file is given, followed, in the cases of subdivided files, by the name of the folder within the file.

5. Author's conversation with an elderly acquaintance of the Smith family on the evening of July 31, 1991. Clyde Smith's first marriage was to Edna Page, 1907–1914.

6. Rebecca L. Felton, Hattie W. Caraway, Rose M. Long, Gladys Pyle, Dixie B. Graves, and Vera Bushfield had all been elected or appointed to fill a vacancy. The next woman to be elected to the Senate in her own right would be Nancy L. Kassebaum, in 1978: Amer, *Women in Congress*, 50–60.

7. Clyde Smith correspondence with various high-school girls, notably Mary Eldina Pratt, apparently in the late 1890s: Smith, Clyde H./Personal Material. A charismatic young man, Smith was elected sheriff of Somerset County in 1897 at the age of twenty-one: Alberta Gould, *First Lady of the Senate: A Life of Margaret Chase Smith* (Mt. Desert, Me.: Windswept House, 1990), 21.

8. Clyde to Margaret, then in Skowhegan, n.d., in envelope postmarked The Hotel Manchester, Middletown, Ohio, December 7, 1932: Smith, Clyde H./Voting Record. At the time of their marriage in 1930, Clyde Smith was fifty-four years old, Margaret Chase thirty-three.

9. Unheaded, undated chronology discounting Margaret's relationship to Clyde's divorce: Elections, 1948/"Smear Charges" and Reply.

10. Author's interview with Margaret Chase Smith on "Defense and Foreign Policy," Skowhegan, Maine, July 29, 1991, 3. The agreed text of this interview is on deposit at the Smith Library.

11. Smith, *Declaration of Conscience*, 85. Dennis L. Morrison believes that Smith's mistreatment in 1948 motivated her to stand up to McCarthyism in her famous "Declaration of Conscience Speech" two years later: Morrison, "Margaret Chase Smith's Declaration of Conscience Speech," *Maine Historical Society Quarterly* 32 (Summer 1992), 14.

12. Janann Sherman, "'They Either Need These Women or They Do Not': Margaret Chase Smith and the Fight for Regular Status for Women in the Military," *Journal of Military History* 54 (January 1990): 51.

13. Author's interview, 9.

14. Author's interview, 5–6.

15. Transcript, Margaret Chase Smith oral history interview, August 20, 1975, by Joe B. Frantz for the Lyndon Baines Johnson Presidential Library, Smith Library, 5.

16. Sherman, "Regular Status": 49 n5, 70 n69, 76, 77; Navy surgeon-general quoted in Jeanne Holm, *Women in the Military: An Unfinished Revolution* (Novato, Calif.: Presidio, 1982), 113.

17. Smith, Frantz interview, 3–4.

18. Author's interview, 2.

19. *Lewiston Journal*, October 1, 1927.

20. Four-page typescript, dated "1944" in pencil, but possibly compiled later to protect Smith against charges that she was a leftist: Labor Organizations/International Labor Organization (ILO).

21. Interview with Margaret Chase Smith, Northeast Archives of Folklore and Oral History (University of Maine, Orono), Accession 2026, Cassette 505, June 6, 1988, 2.

22. Northeast Oral, A 2026, C 504, 23; "Significance of Maine Election," *U.S. News & World Report*, September 24, 1948, 15.

23. Author's interview, 2; Philip Taft, *Organized Labor in American History* (New York: Harper & Row, 1964), 557.

24. *Portland Press Herald*, May 23, 1948.

25. *Washington Post*, June 24, 1948.

26. Smith, *Declaration of Conscience*, 107.

27. Dorothy Sabin Winslow to State of Mainer, circular letter, n.d. : Elections, 1948/"Smear Charges" and Reply. For the background to the smear letter, see the *Portland Press Herald*, May 23, 1948. On Marcantonio's support for the outlawry resolution, see Harriet Hyman Alonso, *The Women's Peace Union and the Outlawry of War, 1921–42* (Knoxville: University of Tennessee Press, 1989), 148. Marcantonio led the American Labor Party which, in the estimate of historian David Shannon, "worked hand in glove with the Communists": Shannon, *The Decline of American Communism: A History of the Communist Party of the United States Since 1945* (London: Atlantic Books, 1959), 3.

28. The Skowhegan archives contain extensive refutations of the charges leveled against Smith. These were issued to the press, a selection appearing, for example, in the *Portland Press Herald* of May 25, 1948.

29. On Catt, see Nancy F. Cott, *The Grounding of Modern Feminism* (New Haven: Yale University Press, 1987), 60.

30. Lee Agger, *Women of Maine* (Portland: Guy Gannett Publishing Company, 1982), 204–206. The Guy Gannett papers were the *Portland Press Herald*, the *Portland Evening Express*, the *Portland Sunday Telegram*, the *Waterville Morning Sentinel*, and the *Augusta Daily Kennebec Journal*.

31. Responses to a questionnaire sent on June 8, 1948 by Edward D. Talberth of Gannett Newspapers: Elections, 1948/Guy Gannett Questionnaire.

32. Campaign notes and postcard: Elections, 1948/Election Statistics and Materials.

33. *Washington Post*, June 24, 1948; *Portland Press Herald*, June 24, 1948.

34. Text of NBC radio broadcast, November 1, 1948.

35. *Christian Science Monitor*, October 25, 1948.

36. The first of thirteen points made on the invitation of the *Bangor Daily Commercial*, March 12, 1948.

37. Responses to Talberth.

38. Text of NBC radio broadcast, November 1, 1948: Elections, 1948/General Material.

39. *Bangor Daily Commercial*, March 12, 1948.

40. Smith, *Declaration of Conscience*, 17–18.

41. But her immediate political impact was limited because so few of her colleagues had the courage to support her. For a political assessment, see David M. Oshinsky, *A Conspiracy so Immense: The World of Joe McCarthy* (New York: Free Press, 1983), 165.

42. Ingrid Winther Scobie suggests that Douglas might have lost the 1950 election to Nixon even if he had not resorted to smear tactics: Scobie, "Helen Gahagan Douglas and Her 1950 Senate Race with Richard M. Nixon": *Southern California Historical Quarterly* 55 (Spring 1976), 113–126. Cf. Stephen Ambrose's view below.

43. Helen Gahagan Douglas, "Congresswoman, Actress, and Opera Singer," an oral history conducted in 1973, 1974, and 1976 by Amelia R. Fry, Suffragists Oral History Project, Regional Oral History Office, University of California, Berkeley, 1982, 52; Ingrid Winther Scobie, "Helen Gahagan Douglas and the Roosevelt Connection," in Joan Hoff Wilson and Marjorie Lightman, eds., *Without Precedent: The Life and Career of Eleanor Roosevelt* (Bloomington: Indiana University Press, 1984), 153; Ingrid Winther Scobie, *Center Stage: Helen Gahagan Douglas, A Life* (New York: Oxford University Press, 1992; reprint, New Brunswick, N.J.: Rutgers University Press, 1995), 150.

44. Helen Gahagan Douglas speech in the House, May 1947, quoted in her autobiography, *A Full Life* (Garden City, N.Y.: Doubleday, 1982), 256.

45. Douglas oral history, 154.

46. The "Pink Sheet," headed "Douglas-Marcantonio Voting Record," was issued by the official Nixon for U.S. Senator Campaign Committee: copy in Helen Gahagan Douglas Collection, Carl Albert Congressional Research and Studies Center, Congressional Archives, University of Oklahoma at Norman, Box "Outsized, Misc." The historian Stephen E. Ambrose has revealed that although Douglas coined the enduring term of opprobrium "Tricky Dick" to describe her opponent in 1950, it was she herself who first invoked the Marcantonio ploy. She complained that Nixon had voted with Marcantonio to cut aid to Europe and to Korea. Therefore she helped to dig her own political grave by inviting the Republicans' devastating counterattack. According to Ambrose, the ploy was pointless anyway, for Nixon was already well known for his early warnings on Korea, to such a degree that the outbreak of war virtually assured him of victory in the election: Ambrose, *Nixon: The Education of a Politician, 1913–1962* (New York: Simon & Schuster, 1987), 214–215. Douglas's biographer Ingrid Scobie defends her subject on the moral ground that she was accusing Nixon of foreign policy incompetence, not of being a "Communist or fellow traveler": Scobie, *Center Stage*, 280. On the penny postcards see Oshinsky, *Conspiracy so Immense*, 177.

47. *Portland Press Herald*, February 11, 1950; September 27, 1951.

48. Smith to Lilla Chiavelli, October 26, 1951: Korean War 1950–1953/Atomic Bomb.

49. Unidentified newspaper clipping dated August 13, 1953: Korean War 1950–1953/Atomic Bomb.

50. "An Old Police State Custom," *I. F. Stone's Weekly*, 2 (February 1, 1954), 4.

51. William Manchester, *The Glory and the Dream: A Narrative History of America 1932–1972* (London: Michael Joseph, 1975), 704–705.

52. Oshinsky notes that Smith had devoted much of her time to combating McCarthy, and had been deserted by most of her supporters—even as early as January 1952, she "probably needed a rest" from the anti-McCarthy battle: *Conspiracy so Immense*, 224–225.

53. Author's interview, 10–11.

54. Richard Arens, Director, HUAC, to Smith, July 30, 1957: Communism/ Women's International League for Peace and Freedom.

55. Vinson to Smith, June 4, 1945: Georgia Congressional Delegation/Vinson, Carl.

56. Vinson to Gurney, December 6, 1948: Georgia Congressional Delegation/ Vinson, Carl.

57. Quoted in Arthur H. Vandenberg, Jr., ed., *The Private Papers of Senator Vandenberg* (Boston: Houghton Mifflin, 1952), 516–517.

58. Smith was on the District of Columbia and Expenditures in the Executive Departments Committees in 1949–1950, and on the Expenditures and Rules and Administration Committees in 1951–1952.

59. See Jeane J. Kirkpatrick's analysis of 1972 Gallup Poll data in *Political Woman* (New York: Basic Books, 1974), 139–140.

60. Smith was generally supportive of the CIA, but was critical of one of its directors, John McCone, for being insufficiently alert to the Communist menace in Cuba: Typescript of Smith questions to McCone, March 12, 1963: Armed Services Committee; Cuban Missile Crisis/General Material. On her opposition to active oversight of the CIA: Smith to Richard R. Wood, Sr., July 22, 1966: Central Intelligence Agency/Correspondence.

61. Lady Bird Johnson, *A White House Diary* (New York: Holt, Rinehart & Winston, 1970), 51.

62. Hazel Hempel Abel, Eva Kelly Bowring, and Elaine Edwards all served in the Senate during the period in question, but only for very short spells in emergency situations. Maurine Brown Neuberger (Dem., Oregon) served from November 1960 to January 1967 and played a more active role, contributing to debate and policy on consumer affairs, foreign trade, tourism, and U.S.–Canadian relations.

63. Smith concluded that her election to the Senate "didn't mean as much to [her mother] as perhaps it should have": Northeast Oral, A 2026, C 506, 19. This must have been disappointing, as her mother had been the "formative influence" on her in her youth. On this and on Margaret Chase's escape from family chores, see Northeast Oral, A 2026, C 504, 5, 10. Cf. Frank Graham, Jr., *Margaret Chase Smith: Woman of Courage* (New York: John Day, 1964), 15–23.

64. On these events and on the diverse elements of the peace movement since the mid-1950s, see Charles DeBenedetti, *An American Ordeal: The Antiwar Movement of the Vietnam Era* (Syracuse, N.Y.: Syracuse University Press, 1990), 14, 27.

65. Address at Lindenwood College, St. Charles, Missouri, May 27, 1961, in "Statements, Speeches, Monthly Report," 42 vols., 1941–1976, XXII.

66. Smith, *Declaration of Conscience*, 257, 273.

67. Ibid., 281. Emphases in the original.

68. Ibid., 285. Lewis wrote some sections of Smith's memoir, including this one.

69. Text of Smith's Senate speech just before the roll call, in ibid., 322–326 at 322.

70. Ibid., 317.

71. McNamara to Smith, September 19, 1963: Armed Services Committee; Nuclear Test Ban Treaty/Correspondence.

72. See Allan M. Winkler, *Life Under a Cloud: American Anxiety About the Atom* (New York: Oxford University Press, 1993), 4, 108. Winkler believes that antinuclear protest has been effective only in fits and starts.

73. Smith speech, *Declaration of Conscience*, 323.

74. *Portland Press Herald*, September 27, 1963.

75. "Statements, Speeches," October 20, 1964, XXIX.

76. Smith to Guy Gannett, January 28, 1949: Press Relationships: Guy Gannett Publishing Company/Gannett, Guy P.; Smith, *Declaration of Conscience*, 21. The year 1952 may well have been a better opportunity for her than occurred in 1964. Bill Lewis explained why she held back on that occasion:

> A week before the Republican National Convention, her mother underwent serious surgery for cancer. Shortly thereafter her mother's condition was such that she was expected to die at any moment. At the same time a strong movement was started at the National Convention to nominate Margaret Smith Vice President. There were demands that Margaret come out to help the drive and frantic calls that certain elements such as the Dewey forces would knife her in the back and block her nomination. Margaret not only refused to go out but she refused to talk with anyone at the convention. Instead she stayed at the bedside of her mother 24 hours a day having had a bed for herself put in the hospital room with her mother. (William C. Lewis, Jr., to Frances F. Bolton, December 10, 1953: Smith, Margaret Chase, Biographical Materials/Lewis, Outstanding Qualities of Margaret Chase Smith.)

77. Martin Gruberg, *Women in American Politics: An Assessment and Sourcebook* (Oshkosh, Wis.: Academic Press, 1968), 128.

78. Smith, *Declaration of Conscience*, 363.

79. Text for Maine speeches to Republicans, October 13, 26, 30, 1964: "Statements, Speeches," XXIX.

80. Excerpt from the transcript of a hearing before the Senate Preparedness Investigating Subcommittee, March 1, 1965, and copy of Smith statement in the Senate, August 11, 1967: both in Armed Services Committee, Secretary of Defense/McNamara, Robert.

81. For a discussion of the phenomenon of black protest against the war, in which black women were to the fore, see David W. Levy, *The Debate over Vietnam* (Baltimore: Johns Hopkins Press, 1991), 110–113.

82. Smith to McNamara, August 14, 1967: Armed Services Committee, Secretary of Defense/McNamara, Robert.

83. *Portland Sunday Telegram*, April 2, 1967.

84. Smith, *Declaration of Conscience*, 396.

85. Edward L. Schapsmeier and Frederick H. Schapsmeier, *Dirksen of Illinois: Senatorial Statesman* (Urbana: University of Illinois Press, 1985), 224.

86. Standard letter to various correspondents, for example to Fred W. Lowell, May 14, 1969: Armed Services Committee; Missile Systems; Anti-Ballistic Missile/Correspondence L–M.

87. Smith, *Declaration of Conscience*, 400, 418.

88. See Henry Kissinger, *White House Years* (Boston: Little, Brown, 1979), 535; Robert D. Schulzinger, *Henry Kissinger: Doctor of Diplomacy* (New York: Columbia University Press, 1989), 56, 118, 121; John Prados, *The Soviet Estimate: U. S. Intelligence Analysis and Soviet Strategic Forces* (1982; reprint, Princeton, N.J.: Princeton University Press, 1986), 230 ff; Stephen E. Ambrose, *Nixon: The Triumph of a Politician 1962–1972* (New York: Simon & Schuster, 1989), 615–616; Rhodri Jeffreys-Jones, *The CIA and American Democracy* (New Haven: Yale University Press, 1989), 188.

89. Smith replies to form letters of protest against the Vietnam War, for example to Mrs. David Gallup, September 15, 1967: Vietnam War. Cf. Smith in the *Portland Sunday Telegram*, April 16, 1967.

90. *White House Diary*, 414.

91. Transcript, corrected in her own hand, of former Senator Smith's contribution, in November 1977 at the Lyndon Baines Johnson Library, to a symposium on "The Presidency and the Congress: A Shifting Balance of Power," 59, 61.

92. *Portland Press Herald*, May 19, 1964.

93. Ibid., June 4, 1964.

94. For a contemporary criticism of the American stance, see I. F. Stone, "International Law and the Tonkin Bay Incidents (August 24, 1964)," reproduced in Marcus Raskin and Bernard B. Fall, eds., *The Viet Nam Reader: Articles and Documents on American Foreign Policy and the Viet Nam Crisis* (New York: Random House, 1965). A Senate hearing in 1967–1968 cast doubt on the Johnson administration's version of events, and furnished the basis for Joseph C. Goulden's book *Truth Is the First Casualty: The Gulf of Tonkin Affair—Illusion and Reality* (Chicago: Rand-McNally, 1969).

95. *Portland Evening Express*, October 6, 1964; press release concerning the address to the Pierian Club, together with the text of the address itself, both October 5, 1964: "Statements, Speeches," XXIX. For a discussion of the international context and of the shortfalls of information concerning it, see R. B. Smith, *An International History of the Vietnam War. Vol. 2, The Struggle for South-East Asia 1961–65* (London: Macmillan, 1985), 3–4, 233.

96. *Congressional Record*, February 23, 1967, S2498.

97. *Congressional Record*, March 20, 1967, S4078.

98. *Congressional Record*, March 21, 1967, S4176.

99. See William C. Westmoreland, *A Soldier Reports* (Garden City, N.Y.: Doubleday, 1976), in which America's military commander in Vietnam takes issue with politicians and the media back home, and the "neoconservative" study *America in Vietnam* (New York: Oxford University Press, 1978), in which author Guenter Lewy is critical of American tactical errors, but, on relativist grounds, defends the moral record of U.S. troops in Vietnam. Daniel C. Hallin has argued that the press did not so much initiate criticism of the U.S. prosecution of the war in Vietnam, as report it: Hallin, *The "Uncensored War": The Media and Vietnam* (New York: Oxford University Press, 1986). However, historians have made a powerful case for the effectiveness of the wider domestic campaign against the Vietnam War. Melvin Small states that "the antiwar movement succeeded in capturing the attention of Johnson and Nixon and affecting their policies in Vietnam": Small, *Johnson, Nixon, and the Doves* (New Brunswick, N.J.: Rutgers University Press, 1988), 233. DeBenedetti notes that "as a political force it remained embarrassingly weak," yet "Movement leaders helped to rally a shattering rebellion that altered the course of American politics and foreign policy": *American Ordeal*, 4.

100. Transcript, corrected in her own hand, of former Senator Smith's contribution, in November 1977 at the Lyndon Baines Johnson Library, to a symposium on "The Presidency and the Congress: A Shifting Balance of Power," 61: Oral History Project.

101. Doris Letourneau to Smith, March 7, 1967; Brig. Gen. William W. Berg, deputy assistant secretary of defense, to Smith, March 16, 1967: both in Vietnam Correspondence.

102. Elizabeth B. May to Smith, June 4, 1967; Smith to May, June 7, 1967: Vietnam War.

103. Margaret Chase Smith, "Why I Worry About the War in Vietnam," *Portland Sunday Telegram*, April 16, 1967.

104. Smith to Professor C. Douglass McGee, chair of the department of philosophy, Bowdoin College, May 1, 1967: Vietnam War.

105. *Portland Press Herald*, March 18, 1968.

106. *Maine Sunday Telegraph*, March 24, 1968.

107. Nixon to Smith, August 3, 1972; also November 10, 1969: Nixon Administration/Nixon-Smith Correspondence. 91–109–26. DeBenedetti, *American Ordeal*, 340.

108. On Smith's continuing defense of the draft, see *Bangor News*, September 15, 1971.

109. Dale Pullen, *Margaret Chase Smith: Republican Senator from Maine* ([Washington, D.C.?]: Ralph Nader Congress Project, 1972), 12; *Maine Times*, May 15, 1970.

110. See Michael Barone and Grant Ujifusa, *The Almanac of American Politics 1988* (Washington, D.C.: National Journal, 1987), 505.

111. *Boston Sunday Globe*, January 9, 1972. On the sexual slurs concerning her and Lewis, see the correspondence between Smith and Robert B. Beith, who had become an influential director at the Guy Gannett Publishing Company: Beith to Smith, January 19, 1959, Smith to Beith, January 21, 1959, Beith to Smith, January 26, 1959: all in Press Relationships: Guy Gannett Publishing Company/Beith, Robert B. Subsequently Lewis recovered sufficiently to help Smith with some aspects of her campaign.

112. Undated press release: "Senator Smith's Comments on Nader Profile on Her": Nader-Smith Correspondence/Correspondence.

113. Pullen, *Smith*, 15; charges of former Representative Stanley Tupper reported in the *Maine Sunday Telegraph*, June 18, 1972.

114. *Portland Press Herald*, October 7, 1972; clipping from an unidentified Bangor newspaper, October 10, 1972: "Scrapbooks/Clippings," vol. 360, p. 51.

115. *Congressional Record*, July 12, 1966, December 1, 2, 1969, May 11, 1970, November 17, 1971; memorandum on Hathaway's statements in the *Congressional Record*, Sam Bouchard of the Senate Republican Conference to William C. Lewis, Jr., July 25, 1972, 45–62–15; *Portland Press Herald*, August 20, 1966, June 2, November 17, 1972.

116. *Portland Press Herald*, June 28, 1972.

117. *York County Coast Star*, October 11, 1972; *Portland Press Herald*, October 11, 1972.

118. Author's interview, 6. The percentage is based on the first 130 letters in the Vietnam/Cambodia files (54 from women, 76 from men), being rather more than one quarter of the total in the Smith Library. Only a portion of the letters received by Smith were retained in the library, and the criterion for retention is unknown. However, as Smith readily acknowledged on several occasions, the letter writers were overwhelmingly against the Vietnam War.

119. 1972 Virginia Slims American Women's polls, conducted by Louis Harris and Associates, accessed via the DIALOG/POLL computer facility.

120. Rose Sandecki, "Women Veterans," in Tom Williams, ed., *Post-Traumatic Stress Disorders: A Handbook for Clinicians* (Cincinnati: Disabled American Vet-

erans, 1987), 159–168, paraphrased in Joe P. Dunn, "The Vietnam War and Women," in Dunn, *Teaching the Vietnam War: Resources and Assessments* (Los Angeles: Center for the Study of Armament and Disarmament, California State University, 1990), 47–67.

8. BELLA ABZUG: SIGNPOST TO THE FUTURE

1. Author's interview with Margaret Chase Smith on "Defense and Foreign Policy," Skowhegan, Maine, July 29, 1991, 14; Bella Abzug, *Gender Gap* (Boston: Houghton Mifflin, 1984), 156.

2. Mailer quoted in Hope Chamberlin, *A Minority of Members: Women in the U.S. Congress* (New York: Praeger, 1973), 336.

3. Author's interview with John Laitin, a former Abzug campaign helper, Skowhegan, Maine, July 25, 1991; Susan Tolchin and Martin Tolchin, *Clout—Womanpower and Politics* (New York: Coward, McCann and Geoghegan, 1974), 174.

4. Ruth B. Mandel, *In the Running: The New Woman Candidate* (Boston: Beacon Press, 1981), 47, 48.

5. Leland Smith to Abzug, July 4, 1976, Box 174, Bella Abzug Papers, Rare Book and Manuscript Library, Columbia University, New York. Other documentary items cited in this chapter are also located in the Abzug collection.

6. Geraldine A. Ferraro, *Ferraro: My Story* (New York: Bantam, 1985), 41–42.

7. Abzug was speaking in the House on the occasion of Rankin's death, when she called for the printing of a commemorative postage stamp: *Congressional Record*, May 21, 1973. The biographical information is drawn from: Abzug, *Gender Gap*, 158–159, Chamberlin, *Minority*, 335, and *Women in Congress, 1917–1990* (Office of the Historian, House of Representatives, 1991), 4.

8. Abzug to Lottie Fairbrook, July 25, 1974, Box 499.

9. Amy Swerdlow, "Ladies' Day at the Capitol: Women Strike for Peace versus HUAC," *Feminist Studies* 8 (Fall 1982), 494. Swerdlow was the WSP's publicity officer, and for a period edited the organization's publication, *Memo*: author's interview with Swerdlow, Baltimore, November 2, 1991.

10. Abzug cited Gallup's analysis as the source of her view: Abzug, *Gender Gap*, 90 n. Cf. John E. Mueller's finding that "liberated" women were more likely to support the Korean war: Mueller, *War, Presidents and Public Opinion* (New York: John Wiley, 1973), 146–147.

11. Charles DeBenedetti, *An American Ordeal: The Antiwar Movement of the Vietnam Era* (Syracuse, N.Y.: Syracuse University Press, 1990), 27; summary of Dee Garrison, "'Our Skirts Gave Them Courage': The Civil Defense Protest Movement in New York City, 1955–1961," a paper delivered at the Council on Peace Research in History (now the Peace History Society)—Society for Historians of American Foreign Relations panel meeting in Charlottesville, Virginia, June 1993, in *CPRH News* 29 (Summer–Fall 1993), 11–12.

12. Swerdlow, "Ladies' Day," 493.

13. Frances Fox Piven and Richard A. Cloward, *Poor People's Movements: Why They Succeed, How They Fail* (New York: Pantheon Books, 1977), xii; Swerdlow, "Ladies' Day," 495, 513; Swerdlow interview. For more extensive discus-

sions of the WSP, see Amy Swerdlow, *Women Strike for Peace: Traditional Motherhood and Radical Politics in the 1960s* (Chicago: University of Chicago Press, 1993) and Harriet Hyman Alonso, *Peace as a Women's Issue: A History of the U.S. Movement for World Peace and Women's Rights* (Syracuse, N.Y.: Syracuse University Press, 1993), especially chapter 7, "From Civil Rights to the Second Wave of the Feminist Movement, 1960–1975," 193–226.

14. Quoted in Amy Swerdlow, "The Tactics of the Outsider: Women Strike for Peace and the Test Ban Treaty of 1963," paper presented at the annual conference of the Society for Historians of American Foreign Relations, June 27, 1986, and made available by kind courtesy of its author, p. 5.

15. Ibid., 7, 12.

16. Ibid., 16.

17. Ibid., 17.

18. Swerdlow interview, 1; author's telephone interview with Bella S. Abzug, November 1, 1991, 2.

19. DeBenedetti, *American Ordeal*, 313, in the chapter on "Normalizing Dissent."

20. DeBenedetti, *American Ordeal*, 248.

21. Amy Swerdlow, *Women Strike for Peace: Traditional Motherhood and Radical Politics in the 1960s* (Chicago: University of Chicago Press, 1993), 179.

22. Abzug to Lottie Fairbrook, July 25, 1974, Box 499.

23. Mandel, *In the Running*, 198.

24. *Pittsburgh Post-Gazette*, May 11, 1971.

25. Abzug interview, 1. The emphasis was in Abzug's voice, after she had been asked about a particular trauma.

26. Abzug, *Gender Gap*, 13.

27. Text of Kissinger interview with the Italian journalist Oriana Fallaci, n.d., early 1970s, marked up by Abzug, Box 275.

28. Abzug, *Gender Gap*, 22–25; Tolchin and Tolchin, *Clout*, 172. The other main NWPC goal was to campaign for the Equal Rights Amendment. For a sketch of the organization, see Mandel, *In the Running*, 209–214.

29. *Women in Congress*, 43; Chamberlin, *Minority*, 334.

30. Abzug to Luise Bell, April 19, 1972, Box 274.

31. Abzug circular, February 23, 1971, and undated report on the "Congressional Barnstorming Tour," both in Box 499; *New York Times*, April 30, 1971.

32. Irving Faust article in *New York* magazine, quoted in Chamberlin, *Minority*, 337.

33. *Cleveland Plain Dealer*, May 8, 1971; *Pittsburgh Post-Gazette*, May 11, 1971.

34. DeBenedetti, *American Ordeal*, 313, in the chapter on "Normalizing Dissent."

35. Ibid. 331; Tolchin and Tolchin, *Clout*, 173.

36. Press release, February 16, 1972, quoted in Tolchin and Tolchin, *Clout*, 158.

37. Kissinger quoted in Robert D. Schulzinger, *American Diplomacy in the Twentieth Century* (New York: Oxford University Press, 1984), 301.

38. Gleaned from Abzug's correspondence, Box 499.

39. Swerdlow interview, 1.

40. Abzug to Dora Friedman, April 26, 1971, Box 499.

41. *New York Times*, May 20, 1973.

42. Swerdlow, *Women Strike for Peace*, 160.

43. W. J. Rorabaugh, *Berkeley at War: The 1960s* (New York: Oxford University Press, 1989), 132; Gloria Steinem, interviewed by Andrew Billen, *Life: The Observer Magazine*, May 15, 1994, 112. Cf. Swerdlow's wording: "Gals Say Yes to Guys Who Say No": Swerdlow, *Women Strike for Peace*, 160.

44. Rorabaugh, *Berkeley at War*, 132; Steinem interview with Billen, 12.

45. David W. Levy, *The Debate over Vietnam* (Baltimore: Johns Hopkins University Press, 1991), 109.

46. 1972 Virginia Slims American Women's polls, conducted by Louis Harris and Associates, accessed via the DIALOG/POLL computer facility.

47. The relationship between Herbert Aptheker and his FBI tail was so cosy that they used to baby-sit for one another: Author's conversation with Aptheker in the spring of 1966, on the occasion when Aptheker became the first American Communist since McCarthyism to speak at Harvard University.

48. Reagan quoted in Reagan for Governor Committee press release, April 10, 1966, in Ronald Reagan Gubernatorial Collection, Hoover Institution Library, Stanford, California.

49. Santa Anna, California, *Evening Register*, October 29, 1971.

50. DeBenedetti, *American Ordeal*, 207. The number of marchers was 10,000 according to the *Buffalo Evening News*, May 21, 1973.

51. *New York Times*, May 20, 1973.

52. Report by Mary McGrory in the *Philadelphia Evening Bulletin*, March 9, 1971. See also DeBenedetti, *American Ordeal*, 207.

53. Tom Hayden, *Reunion: A Memoir* (New York: Random House, 1988), 441.

54. Abzug, *Gender Gap*, 37; Tolchin and Tolchin, *Clout*, 172.

55. Anna Louise Strong, *Cash and Violence in Laos and Vietnam* (New York: Mainstream, 1962); Mary McCarthy, *Hanoi* (London: Weidenfeld & Nicolson, 1968), 21, 88; Frances FitzGerald, *Fire in the Lake: The Vietnamese and Americans in Vietnam* (Boston: Little, Brown, 1972). Some of Joan Didion's themes were summed up later in her novel *Democracy* (New York: Simon & Schuster, 1984). Marguerite Higgins had won the Pulitzer Prize in 1950 for her reporting on the Marines' landing at Inchon in the Korean War. For her disaffection in the 1960s, see her book *Our Vietnam Nightmare* (New York: Harper & Row, 1965). For further works by the writers mentioned and by numerous other women, see Deborah A. Butler, comp. and ed., *American Women Writers on Vietnam: A Selected Annotated Bibliography* (New York: Garland, 1990).

56. Virginia Elwood-Akers, *Women War Correspondents in the Vietnam War* (Metuchen, N.J.: Scarecrow, 1988), 1–2.

57. Abzug, *Gender Gap*, 163.

58. Abzug, *Gender Gap*, 39.

59. Eleven received from women, six from men: Box 499.

60. Abzug, *Gender Gap*, 164; *Women in Congress*, 4.

61. *Congressional Record*, 92 Cong., 1 sess., August 3, 1971.

62. *Congressional Record*, 92 Cong., 1 sess., November 4, 1971. The following figures show the discrepancy between civilian and military assistance, in millions of dollars, following the "Vietnamization" of the war from 1968, and illustrate

the dramatic effect of the eventual congressional cutback in funding due to the efforts of Abzug and like-minded legislators:

Year	Civilian Aid	Military Aid
1967	666.6	662.5
1968	651.1	1,243.4
1969	560.5	1,534.0
1970	655.4	1,577.3
1971	778.0	1,945.6
1972	587.7	2,602.6
1973	531.2	3,349.4
1974	657.4	941.9

Figures extracted from a table, based on U.S. Agency for International Development data, in Douglas C. Dacy, *Foreign Aid, War, and Economic Development: South Vietnam, 1955–1975* (Cambridge, England: Cambridge University Press, 1986), 200.

63. *Congressional Record*, 92 Cong., 1 sess., August 3, November 4, 1971.

64. "[Abzug's] Votes on Israel/Soviet Jews," memorandum dated October 26, 1972, Abzug to Mike Havenar, January 3, 1975, both Box 274; Swerdlow interview, 2.

65. Text of Abzug's House speech on the Mutual Development and Cooperation Act, July 25, 1973, Box 276.

66. Ibid.

67. Ibid.

68. Interview with Margaret Chase Smith, Northeast Archives of Folklore and Oral History (University of Maine, Orono), Accession 2026, Cassette 504, June 6, 1988, 5, Smith Papers, Skowhegan, Maine.

69. Abzug to Donald S. Harrington (chairman of the Liberal Party of New York State), April 6, 1976.

70. Abzug's speech on her introduction of the Foreign Investment and Multinational Corporation Control Act, *Congressional Record*, 92 Cong., 1 sess., November 16, 1971.

71. Abzug interview, 2.

72. Abzug to Douglas Levin (Manager, Local 99–ILGWU), December 18, 1973, Box 278.

73. Corbett (President, New York State AFL-CIO) mailgram to Abzug, January 9, 1974; Abzug to Corbett, January 23, 1974, both Box 278.

74. Abzug to Alita Aquino Fagan, May 30, 1973 and to Henry M. Murray, July 16, 1976, both Box 274, and to Edgar Lockwood and Christine Root of the Washington Office on Africa, July 9, 1974, Box 278.

75. Abzug to Sigmund Andersen, November 20, 1975, Box 278.

76. *Chicago Sun-Times*, October 11, 1971.

77. Abzug to John S. Leopold, May 1, 1973, Box 428.

78. Abzug to Lottie Fairbrook, July 25, 1974, Box 499.

79. Box 428.

80. Abzug to Edward J. Garrett, President, Instrument System Corporation, Huntington, N.Y., September 4, 1974, Box 428.

81. Abzug to Michele Mooney, September 4, 1974, Box 428.

82. Men: seven; women: fourteen; sex unspecified: one. Box 428.

83. Notes, Box 620.

84. Mandel, *In the Running*, 197–198.

85. Ibid., 199, 245.

86. Susan J. Carroll and Barbara Geiger-Parker, *Women Appointed to the Carter Administration: A Comparison with Men* (New Brunswick, N.J.: Center for the American Woman and Politics, Rutgers, 1983), ix.

87. Abzug, *Gender Gap*, 56.

88. For a summary of literature on this theme, see Emily S. Rosenberg, "Gender," one of ten contributions to "A Round Table: Explaining the History of American Foreign Relations," *Journal of American History* 77 (1990), 122.

89. Abzug, *Gender Gap*, 65.

90. *New York Times*, February 3, 1979; *Detroit News*, February 8, 1979; Abzug interview, WCBS-TV, Channel 2 [New York City], January 18, 1979, transcript in Box 988.

91. *New York Times*, February 3, 1979.

92. Abzug also criticized Friedan for claiming too much credit as the founder of modern feminism. Materials on the parting of the ways are in Box 616. Friedan had revised her anti-male stance by 1983, when she published a new edition of her famous book: Betty Friedan, "Twenty Tears After," in *The Feminine Mystique* (New York: Dell, 1983), xxvii–xxviii.

93. Tolchin and Tolchin, *Clout*, 54–56.

94. Abzug, *Gender Gap*, 69.

95. *Detroit News*, February 8, 1979; *Detroit Free Press*, January 31, February 20, 1979.

96. Abzug, *Gender Gap*, 79.

97. *Detroit Free Press*, February 20, 1979.

98. The candidacy of the independent, John B. Anderson, complicated the "gender gap" analysis. See Abzug, *Gender Gap*, 89–92.

99. For a discussion of some of the issues, see Nancy E. McGlen and Meredith Reid Sarkees, *Women in Foreign Policy: The Insiders* (New York: Routledge, 1993), chapter 5, "Gender Gap in Attitudes Toward the Foreign Policy Process?": 221–255. See also chapter 10 of this book.

100. Abzug, *Gender Gap*, 104. Alice Rossi noted that the gender gap on militarism had existed since the 1950s; the new development in the 1980s was that women candidates were beginning to take advantage of the gap. Susan Welch observed that women in Congress were more "dovish" than men, but she thought that the gender gap was closing. See Alice C. Rossi, "Beyond the Gender Gap: Women's Bid for Political Power," *Social Science Quarterly* 64 (December 1984), 718–719, and Susan Welch, "Are Women More Liberal than Men in the U.S. Congress?" *Legislative Studies Quarterly* 10 (February 1985), 127.

101. Abzug interview, 2.

102. Abzug, *Gender Gap*, 114.

103. Abzug interview, 2–3; McGlen and Sarkees, *Women in Foreign Policy*, 3.

104. Chamberlin, *Minority*, 338.

9. THE MYTH OF THE IRON LADY: AN INTERNATIONAL COMPARISON

1. Florence Brewer Boeckel, "Women in International Affairs," *Annals of the American Academy of Political and Social Sciences* 143 (1929), 238.

2. Though Isabel Perón was not elected president, she had been elected vice president on her famous husband's presidential ticket in 1973. She took over as president when he died the following year.

3. It should be noted that the distinction is one of emphasis. Sirimavo Bandaranaike's husband had also been an advocate of nonalignment, but his chief contribution to his country's history had been as a nationalist. See D. M. Prasad, *Ceylon's Foreign Policy Under the Bandaranaikas (1956–65): A Political Analysis* (New Delhi: S. Shand, 1973), 35–37, 414.

4. The list and some of the remarks based on it are based on my collection of newspaper clippings. Details may be confirmed or amplified by consulting the indexes and files of major newspapers.

5. Perhaps a special qualification is in order here. Possibly because women distrust the traditionally male-dominated ideas and structures of diplomacy, they have comparatively rarely been in charge of foreign policy portfolios. Golda Meir served as Israel's Labor foreign minister from 1956 to 1966, Alva Myrdal was Sweden's Social Democrat minister in charge of disarmament in 1966–1973 with cabinet status in the last four years, and there is another, more recent exception in Flora MacDonald, the Canadian Progressive Conservative who was for a few months her country's minister of state for foreign affairs. In the early 1990s the French Socialist Elisabeth Guigon was minister for European affairs, Ursula Seiler Albring served as a state minister in the German Foreign Ministry, and the Palestinians' Hanan Ashrawi negotiated with Israel and with several other countries. Still, these are exceptional cases—it would appear that women have preferred to treat foreign policy as a means to an end, not just as a career. But the relatively small number of official female foreign ministers does not detract from the point that, judged by the yardstick of political eminence, women have had an increasing say in international affairs.

6. For a critical discussion of this assumption, see Patricia Lee Sykes, "Women as National Leaders: Patterns and Prospects," in Michael A. Genovese, ed., *Women as National Leaders* (Newbury Park, Calif.: Sage, 1993), 220–225.

7. Susan Crosland, "Leading Ladies," *Style and Travel* (a section of the London *Sunday Times*), June 27, 1993, 12–13. Crosland credited Gandhi with leading the "bloody war against Pakistan," Meir with "waging fearless battle," Aquino with being "ferocious in putting down coups," Bandaranaike with leading "a great civil war," Bhutto with being "vengeful," and Finnbogadóttir with launching a "cod war."

8. Sykes, "Women as National Leaders," 225; Margaret Thatcher, *The Downing Street Years* (New York: Harper Collins, 1993), 65.

9. According to a British estimate in *U.S. News & World Report*, she came to occupy "center stage" in the West's dealings with the Soviet Union: Simon D. Jenkins, "Now at Center Stage, NATO's Leading Lady," *U.S. News & World Report* (April 6, 1987), 33. Jenkins later became editor of the London *Times*.

10. Thatcher saw, or at least portrayed, the Labour party opposition in her own country as disloyalty-tainted Marxists cast in the same mold as Communists in totalitarian countries. Addressing fellow Conservative members of Parliament in

1989 she remarked with typical belligerence: "The Marxists said they would bury us. Well, we are burying them": London *Daily Telegraph*, May 4, 1989.

11. London *Observer*, March 20, 1988.

12. John Hay, "Thatcher's Cold War Crusade," *Maclean's*, October 10, 1983, 24, 25, 27.

13. Polly Toynbee, "Is Margaret Thatcher a Woman? No Woman If She Has to Make It in a Man's World," *Washington Monthly* 20 (May 1988), 34, 36, 37.

14. Beatrix Campbell, *The Iron Ladies: Why Do Women Vote Tory?* (London: Virago, 1987), 121–122, 130–132.

15. Julian Barnes, "The Maggie Years," *The New Yorker*, November 15, 1993, 87.

16. Lewis Fry Richardson, *Statistics of Deadly Quarrels* (Pittsburgh: Boxwood Press, 1960), 133, 167; David Wilkinson, *Deadly Quarrels: Lewis F. Richardson and Statistical Study of War* (Berkeley: University of California Press, 1980), 132–143; Lawrence Freedman, *Britain and the Falklands War* (Oxford, England: Basil Blackwell, 1988), 2, 106.

17. The British ambassador at the UN, Sir Anthony Parsons, viewed Thatcher's final offer of May 19, 1982, as a major and surprising concession to the Argentine position, which should have obviated, even at the eleventh hour, the need for armed conflict: Parsons' statement on "The Falklands War," part 3, a Fine Arts program produced for Channel 4 TV by Denys Blakeway and first shown in Britain in January–February 1992. For further comments on Thatcher's final negotiating position from diverse perpectives, see Paul Eddy and others, *The Falklands War* (London: Warner, 1982), 174, Max Hastings and Simon Jenkins, *The Battle for the Falklands* (London: Pan, 1983), 200–201, Lawrence Freedman and Virginia Gamba-Stonehouse, *Signals of War: The Falklands Conflict of 1982* (London: Faber & Faber, 1990), 292–319, and *Britain and the Falkland Islands* (London: Her Majesty's Stationery Office, 1993), 40–41.

18. Thatcher, *Downing Street Years* , 173, 259.

19. Even Attlee, who was trying to decolonize the British Empire peacefully, had to contend with violence in Palestine, Malaya, and Korea. For an account of the emergencies in Palestine and Malaya, see Brian Lapping, *End of Empire* (London: Granada, 1985), 116–119, 122–134.

20. Perhaps it is a telling comment on the historiography of the British Empire that there never seems to have been a proper accounting of "native" casualties. Nevertheless, in the volume of *The Cambridge History of the British Empire* devoted to India in the years 1818–1918, four out of thirty-three chapters, or just under 10 percent of the text are entirely devoted to military matters or warfare: H. H. Dodwell, ed., *The Cambridge History of the British Empire*, vol. 5, *The Indian Empire* (Cambridge, England: At the University Press, 1932). The historian Donald C. Gordon has paraphrased the British colonial attitude as follows: "India was a conquered land, and what had been obtained by the sword must be kept by the sword": Donald C. Gordon, *The Moment of Power: Britain's Imperial Epoch* (Englewood Cliffs, N.J.: Prentice-Hall, 1970), 65.

21. Serge July, "La Dame de Fer," reprinted in translation from *Libération*, *Guardian*, May 17, 1991.

22. "La Dame de Fer Polonaise," *Paris-Match*, July 23, 1992.

23. London *Times*, June 15, 1993.

24. Author's observation.

25. Golda Meir, *My Life* (New York: G. P. Putnam's Sons, 1975), pp. 437, 461.

26. Michael A. Genovese, "Margaret Thatcher and the Politics of Conviction Leadership," in Genovese, *Women as National Leaders*, 205.

27. Nayantara Sahgal, *Indira Gandhi: Her Road to Power* (New York: Frederick Ungar, 1982), 7.

28. Bruce Chatwin, *What Am I Doing Here?* (London: Jonathan Cape, 1989), 323.

29. Sahgal, *Indira*, 29.

30. "India's Autocratic Woman of Iron," *U.S. News & World Report*, June 24, 1984, 9.

31. Barbara Grizzuti Harrison, "The Women You Hate to Love," *Mademoiselle*, March 1985, 120.

32. Sahgal, *Indira*, 85.

33. Nancy Fix Anderson, "Benazir Bhutto and Dynastic Politics: Her Father's Daughter, Her People's Sister," in Genovese, *Women as National Leaders*, 46, 57, 64.

34. See Lucy Komisar, *Corazon Aquino: The Story of a Revolution* (New York: George Braziller, 1987), 139–150, 163–174. Cf. Jeanne-Marie Col's aptly titled essay "Managing Softly in Turbulent Times: Corazon C. Aquino, President of the Philippines," in Genovese, *Women as National Leaders:* 13–40.

35. Aquino, "Non-Violence: The Key to Peace," address in Saunders Theater, Memorial Hall, Harvard University, September 22, 1986, reprinted in Corazon C. Aquino, *Democracy by the Ways of Democracy* (Manila: Republic of the Philippines Policy Statements, 1986), p. 95.

36. According to one study that examined Violetta de Chamorro's initial rise to prominence under the Sandinistas, "she was probably selected more for her late husband's reputation rather than in her own right": Helen Collinson et al., *Women and Revolution in Nicaragua* (London: Zed, 1990), 165. Pedro Joaquín Chamorro had been a leading critic of the right-wing Somoza regime until his assassination in 1978.

37. Publicity statement (1988) distributed by the Office of the President of Iceland and entitled "Vigdis Finnbogóttir, President of Iceland."

38. *Guardian*, October 2, 1986; *The Women's Alliance in Iceland* (leaflet, ca. 1987); *Kvenna Listinn: The Women's Alliance Policy Statement 1987*, pp. 42–43.

39. London *Times*, May 5, 1986.

40. London *Independent*, April 25, 1992. Left-feminist culture may not prove to be the sole inspiration of peaceful foreign policy conduct, especially if the world's democracies continue their early 1990s tendency in a conservative direction. Canada's Kim Campbell and Turkey's Tansu Ciller are both conservative, and not particularly feminist leaders, yet neither has shown any special aggressive tendency—though Campbell served an apprenticeship as defense minister, and Ciller is uncompromising in her support for her army's operations against the movement for Kurdish independence.

41. One occasion on which she expressed her views was when the magazine *Trialogue* put out a special issue on "Security and Disarmament" (Summer/Fall 1982), insert. Here she outlined her own contributions to UN discussions on the subject, attacked the notion of "winnable" nuclear wars, and expressed the special economic interest of non-aligned nations in securing reductions in arms-manufacturing programs.

42. For a critique of Katherine Mayo's *Mother India* (New York: Harcourt Brace, 1927), see Mrinalini Sinha, "Gender in the Critiques of Colonialism and Nationalism: Locating the 'Indian Woman,'" in Ann-Louise Shapiro, ed., *Feminists Revision History* (New Brunswick, N.J.: Rutgers University Press, 1994), 246–275

43. I am grateful to my Edinburgh University colleague Crispin Bates for supplying me with some informed speculation on these points. See also Doranne Jacobson and Susan S. Wadley, *Women in India: Two Perspectives* (1977; reprint, New Delhi: Manahar, 1986), 38–39, 133.

44. Joyce Gelb, *Feminism and Politics: A Comparative Perspective* (Berkeley: University of California Press, 1990). Chapter 5 is titled "Sweden: Feminism Without Feminists?" Gelb argues that, in the case of Sweden, "militant feminism was unacceptable in a consensus-orientated society": 146.

45. Birgit Brock-Utne, *Educating for Peace: A Feminist Perspective* (New York: Pergamon, 1985), 34.

46. Susan Moller Okin, *Women in Western Political Thought* (Princeton, N.J.: Princeton University Press, 1979), 8–9.

47. The Norwegian psychologist Berit Ås demonstrated in one article the way in which left-feminist thought combined in discussions of war and property. She complained that, in the past, "in our part of the world," women have been taken and sold as spoils of war, and that residual attitudes of this type remained. Her viewpoint epitomized the Scandinavian reaction against such attitudes: Ås, "A Materialistic View of Men's and Women's Attitudes Towards War," *Women's Studies International Forum* 5 (1982), 363. While the linkage of left and feminist theory may be pronounced in Scandinavia, it is by no means exclusive to that region. For some speculation and a review of the literature, see John Tosh, *The Pursuit of History: Aims, Methods and New Directions in the Study of Modern History,* 2d ed. (London: Longman, 1991), 179–182. Historians have further explored, perhaps under the influence of Lenin, the respective impacts of worldwide imperialism and decolonization on women. Some of these historians have held that decolonization is important in three ways: it has modified the depressive effects of male-serving Western legal structures, it has opened the prospect of democratic government to peoples previously under imperial sway, and it has invited women to apply the principle of *national* self-determination to their own *gender:* See Carol A. Christy's review of the scholarship pertaining to British colonial rule in India and Nigeria: Christy, *Sex Differences in Political Participation: Processes of Change in Fourteen Nations* (New York: Praeger, 1987), 8–9. The Conservative politician Winston Churchill confirmed the judgment of those on the Left, for he opposed the vote for women on the ground that they could not be entrusted with the defense of the British Empire: Paul Addison, *Churchill on the Home Front, 1900–1955* (London: Jonathan Cape, 1992), 313–314.

48. Rehn quoted in the London *Independent,* January 18, 1994. Rehn received 46 percent of the vote in her runoff against Martti Ahtisaari.

49. This was when Campbell was in charge of Canada's Ministry of Defence. See Robert Fife, *Kim Campbell: The Making of a Politician* (Toronto: Phyllis Bruce/Harper Collins, 1993), 172. When Campbell led the Tories and her nation, the New Democratic Party (Canada's socialists) had as its leader Audrey McLaughlin, the first woman to head a North American political party. McLaughlin was an avowed feminist and a peace advocate in the Canadian internationalist tradition: see Audrey

McLaughlin, *A Woman's Place: My Life and Politics* (Toronto: Macfarlane, Walter, and Ross, 1992), 132–159, 189, 195–223. In the 1993 election Campbell and McLaughlin went down to defeat with their parties, both of which fared very badly. But McLaughlin's contention that "women in politics are beginning to make a difference" (*Woman's Place*, 195) was supported by the substantial number of new women elected, as well as by recent history: Flora MacDonald and Margaret McDougall had served as foreign affairs minister, Louise Frechette had been the Canadian ambassador to the United Nations, and Sheila Copps was deputy leader of the Liberal party, which formed the new government in 1993. The figures on candidates in the 1993 election are taken from the St. Johns (Newfoundland) *Evening Telegram*, October 5, 1993.

10. AMERICAN WOMEN AND CONTEMPORARY FOREIGN POLICY

1. Linda Witt, Karen M. Paget, and Glenna Matthews, *Running as a Woman: Gender and Power in American Politics* (New York: Free Press, 1993), 220–221. The historian John Patrick Diggins offers the following definition of "political correctness": "As the decade of the nineties got under way, some remaining Academic Leftists took up the cause of multiculturalism, a new orthodoxy on the campus that the press described as 'PC' (politically correct). To be PC was to denounce Western culture from the top down. . . . Identifying with every color but white, multiculturalists attacked racism, sexism, and DWEMism—partiality to dead, white European males who wrote most of the books on a course's reading list": *The Rise and Fall of the American Left* (New York: Norton, 1992), 297. But the term "PC" has come to have a wider meaning and application than this, and is, perhaps, a successor to words like "socialism" and "liberalism," which have passed out of the American political vocabulary as a result of assaults from the Right.

2. This idea is articulated but not endorsed in Nancy E. McGlen and Meredith Reid Sarkees, *Women in Foreign Policy: The Insiders* (New York: Routledge, 1993), 186.

3. Quoted in Joan Hoff Wilson, "Conclusion: Of Mice and Men," in Edward P. Crapol, ed., *Women and American Foreign Policy: Lobbyists, Critics, and Insiders*, 2d ed. (Wilmington, Del.: Scholarly Resources, 1992), 173.

4. Mildred L. Amer, *Women in the United States Congress* (Washington, D.C.: Congressional Research Service, 1991), 67; CAWP study cited in Dorothy Cantor and Toni Bernay, *Women in Power: The Secrets of Leadership* (Boston: Houghton Mifflin, 1992), 6. The six women senators in the 103rd Congress of 1993–1995 are Barbara Boxer (Democrat, California), Carol Moseley Braun (Democrat, Illinois), Dianne Feinstein (Democrat, California), Nancy Landon Kassebaum (Republican, Kansas), Barbara A. Mikulski (Democrat, Maryland), and Patty Murray (Democrat, Washington).

5. Amer, *Women in Congress*, 67; *Facts on File 1992*, 825; Canadian figures supplied by kind courtesy of the Library of Parliament, Ottawa.

6. Homer L. Calkin, *Women in the Department of State: Their Role in American Foreign Affairs* (Washington, D.C.: Department of State, 1978), 234.

7. Calkin, *Women in the Department of State*, 150; McGlen and Sarkees, *Women in Foreign Policy*, 76.

8. For sympathetic studies, see, respectively, Janice R. and Stephen R. MacKinnon, *Agnes Smedley: The Life and Times of an American Radical* (Berkeley: University of California Press, 1988), and Sara Alpern, *Freda Kirchwey: A Woman of "The Nation"* (Cambridge, Mass.: Harvard University Press, 1987).

9. See Lynne K. Dunn, "Joining the Boys' Club: The Diplomatic Career of Eleanor Lansing Dulles," in Edward P. Crapol, ed., *Women and American Foreign Policy: Lobbyists, Critics, and Insiders*, 2d ed. (Wilmington, Del.: Scholarly Resources, 1992), 119–135, and, as an example of how glamour can endure, Wilfrid Sheed, *Clare Boothe Luce* (New York: Dutton, 1982)

10. Olmstead interview in McGlen and Sarkees, *Women in Foreign Policy*, 16–20.

11. Palmer interview in ibid., 114.

12. McGlen and Sarkees, *Women in Foreign Policy*, 65.

13. Jenonne Walker interview, in ibid., 260. Walker had worked for the CIA, the State Department, and the Carnegie Endowment for International Peace.

14. See William Ney, "Glaspie Speaks," *The New Combat* (Summer/Autumn 1991), 27–32.

15. McGlen and Sarkees, *Women in Foreign Policy*, 76.

16. The findings of Sharon L. Camp, ed., *Country Rankings of the Status of Women: Poor, Powerless, and Pregnant* (Washington, D.C.: Population Crisis Committee, 1988), summarized in Arvonne S. Fraser, "Women and International Development: The Road to Nairobi and Back," in Sara E. Rix, ed., *The American Woman 1990–91: A Status Report* (New York: Norton, 1990), 287.

17. On the American subsidization of Dominica's Charles in return for favors, see Bob Woodward, *Veil: The Secret Wars of the CIA, 1981–1987* (London: Simon & Schuster, 1987), 290. Jean-Bertrand Aristide, a priest who championed the cause of the poor and eventually restored democracy to Haïti, remarked of Pascal-Trouillot: "She was chosen by American power and groups loyal to [the dictator Papa Doc] Duvalier. She is a puppet in the hands of those people": London *Observer*, July 8, 1990.

18. Rudy Maxa, "Elizabeth of Toro," *Vogue*, February 1988, 214, 216.

19. Carl N. Degler, *At Odds: Women and the Family in America from the Revolution to the Present* (Oxford, England: Oxford University Press, 1980), 473.

20. Calkin, *Women in the Department of State*, 233.

21. Rhodri Jeffreys-Jones, *American Espionage: From Secret Service to CIA* (New York: Free Press, 1977), 138; Frederic L. Propas, "Creating a Hard Line Toward Russia: The Training of State Department Soviet Experts, 1927–1937," *Diplomatic History* 8 (Summer 1984), 218, 226; William J. Lederer and Eugene Burdick, *The Ugly American: A Novel; with a Factual Epilogue* (London: Victor Gollancz, 1959), 273.

22. Margaret Mead's attack on Richard Hofstadter, Nathan Glazer, and David Riesman was not couched in feminist terms but made use of female discourse—with admonitions against dogma on breast-feeding in Italy, and on U.S. familial attitudes to nationalism—in a manner that places it within the construct of gendered cultural politics: Mead, "The New Isolationism," *The American Scholar* (Summer 1955), 378–382.

23. Nandita Gandhi, "The Anti Price Rise Movement," in Ilina Sen, ed., *A Space Within the Struggle: Women's Participation in People's Movements* (New Delhi: Kali for Women, 1990), 50–81.

24. Michael J. Heale suggests that another reason for the decline of anti-Communism has been the reduction in class conflict in the postindustrial United States: Heale, *American Anticommunism: Combating the Enemy Within, 1830–1970* (Baltimore: Johns Hopkins University Press, 1990), 192.

25. Witt et al., *Running as a Woman*, 220–221.

26. Susan J. Carroll and Barbara Geiger-Parker, *Women Appointed to the Carter Administration: A Comparison with Men* (New Brunswick, N.J.: Center for the American Woman and Politics, Eagleton Institute of Politics, 1983), ix, 49–51. For a summary of research and surveys which confirm the liberal and propeace tendency amongst contemporary American women, see Alice B. Rossi, "Beyond the Gender Gap: Women's Bid for Political Power," *Political Science Quarterly* 64 (December 1983), 718–719. Expectations of "dovish" and "liberal" behavior amongst female legislators are discussed in Susan Welch, "Are Women More Liberal than Men in the U.S. Congress?" *Legislative Studies Quarterly* 10 (February 1985), 127.

27. Guenter Lewy, *Peace and Revolution: The Moral Crisis of American Pacifism* (Grand Rapids, Mich.: Wm. B. Eerdmans, 1988), 202, 218. A circle of intellectuals had given the conservative cause renewed respectability in the few years preceding the election of Ronald Reagan in 1980. Lewy's influential book *America in Vietnam* (New York: Oxford University Press, 1978) had corrected the view that only the Americans committed atrocities in the Vietnam War and opened the way for a restoration of faith in American morality and military prowess.

28. Witt et al., *Running as a Woman*, 25.

29. For concise descriptions of these groups and their activities, see Ruth B. Mandel, *In the Running: The New Woman Candidate* (Boston: Beacon Press, 1981), 209–215.

30. Arthur Miller, "Gender and the Vote: 1984," in Carol M. Mueller, ed., *The Politics of the Gender Gap: The Social Construction of Political Influence* (Beverly Hills, Calif.: Sage, 1988), 279–280.

31. Kathy Bonk, "The Selling of the 'Gender Gap': The Role of Organized Feminism," in Ibid., 91.

32. From 1983, 1986, and 1987 *Glamour* magazine "Women's Attitudes Polls," conducted by Mark Clements Research, and 1983 *New York Times* Women's Survey, conducted by the *New York Times*, all accessed via the DIALOG/POLL computer facility.

33. Only one woman preceded her husband in Congress; a further seven female representatives were the daughters of representatives; another three were congressional granddaughters: Amer, *Women in Congress*, 1. Unless otherwise stated, the congressional analysis in the following paragraphs is abstracted from Amer, from *Women in Congress, 1917–1990* (Washington, D.C.: Office of the Historian, U.S. House of Representatives, 1991), and from Michael Barone and Grant Ujifusa, comps., *The Almanac of American Politics 1988* (Washington, D.C.: National Journal, 1987).

34. Kathleen A. Frankovic, "Sex and Voting in the U.S. House of Representatives 1961–1975," *American Politics Quarterly* 5 (July 1977), 323.

35. See Robert E. Spears, "The Bold Easterners Revisited: The Myth of the CIA Elite," in Rhodri Jeffreys-Jones and Andrew Lownie, eds., *North American Spies: New Revisionist Essays* (Lawrence: University Press of Kansas, 1991), 202–217.

36. George P. Shultz, *Turmoil and Triumph: My Years as Secretary of State*

(New York: Charles Scribner's, 1993), 484; Donald T. Regan, *For the Record: From Wall Street to Washington* (London: Hutchinson, 1988), 177; Kitty Kelley, *Nancy Reagan: The Unauthorized Biography* (New York: Simon & Schuster, 1991), 448.

37. The ratio of women serving on the Foreign Affairs Committee was 1:9.23. The overall Foreign Affairs membership ratio for the 102d Congress, with 52 out of 435 Representatives sitting on the committee, was 1:8.36.

38. A further seven gained places on the House Armed Services Committee, of whom four (57 percent) were dynastic. It must of course be remembered that women were badly underrepresented in Congress as a whole, so these figures have to be considered in a relative light.

39. McGlen and Sarkees, *Women in Foreign Policy*, 186, 190, 192.

40. R. Darcy, Susan Welch, and Janet Clark, *Women, Elections, and Representation* (New York: Longman, 1987), 154. For an earlier version of this argument, see Ole R. Holsti and James N. Rosenau, "The Foreign Policy Beliefs of Women in Leadership Positions," *Journal of Politics*, 43 (May 1981), 329, 347.

41. Cynthia Enloe, *The Morning After: Sexual Politics at the End of the Cold War* (Berkeley: University of California Press, 1993), 252.

42. Michael Barone, Grant Ujifusa, and Douglas Matthews, comps., *The Almanac of American Politics 1974* (London: Macmillan, 1974); Michael Barone, Grant Ujifusa, and Douglas Matthews, comps., *The Almanac of American Politics 1980* (New York: Dutton, 1979); Barone and Ujifusa, *Almanac 1988*.

43. Martin Walker, "Democrats Turn to Roots," *Guardian*, October 24, 1990; author's notes on Governor Richards's remarks at the premiere at the Paramount theater, Austin, November 22, 1993.

44. The article appeared in the November 1979 issue of *Commentary* and was reprinted in Jeane J. Kirkpatrick, *Dictatorships and Double Standards: Rationalism and Reason in Politics* (New York: Simon & Schuster for the American Enterprise Institute, 1982), 23–52 (at p. 33).

45. According to Allan Gerson, her counsel at the UN, Kirkpatrick exercised "greater influence over the formulation and articulation of U.S. foreign policy than any other U.S. Permanent Representative to the United Nations": Gerson, *The Kirkpatrick Mission: Diplomacy without Apology: America at the United Nations* (New York: Free Press, 1991), xvi. Judith Ewell, an authority on South America, was more critical, citing a *New York Times* finding that the U.S. "voted with the majority only 14 percent of the time in 1984 as compared with 21 percent in 1983," suggesting that Kirkpatrick increasingly lacked the ability to persuade: Judith Ewell, "Barely in the Inner Circle: Jeane Kirkpatrick," in Edward P. Crapol, ed., *Women and American Foreign Policy: Lobbyists, Critics, and Insiders*, 2d ed. (Wilmington, Del.: Scholarly Resources, 1992), 165.

46. Jeane Kirkpatrick, "Pardon Me, But Am I That 'Hard-Liner' the Anonymous Sources Are Talking About?" *Washington Post*, June 20, 1983, referred to in Ewell, "Barely," 162.

47. By 1982 Russian expert Robert Gates, later director of the CIA, was openly questioning inflated assumptions about the potential Soviet rate of weapons production. See Kirkpatrick's article "U.S. Security and Latin America" reprinted in *Dictatorships and Double Standards*, 53, 56, and Jeffreys-Jones, *CIA and American Democracy*, 242–243.

48. Hoff Wilson, "Conclusion: Of Mice and Men," in Crapol, *Women and American Foreign Policy*, 183.

49. Kirkpatrick quoted in Ronna Romney and Beppie Harrison, *Momentum: Women in American Politics Now* (New York: Crown, 1988), 163; conversations in Edinburgh, August 1993, with Elizabeth Warnock Fernea, author of *Guests of the Sheik: An Ethnography of an Iraqi Village* (New York: Doubleday, 1965).

50. Gerson, *The Kirkpatrick Mission*, 129, 171, 229. See also Ewell, "Barely," 156; Kirkpatrick, "U.S. Security and Latin America," 68.

51. Geraldine A. Ferraro, *My Story* (New York: Bantam, 1985), 41–43; Kirkpatrick quoted in Romney and Harrison, *Momentum*, 164.

52. Ferraro, *Story*, 60–61; Bella Abzug, *Gender Gap* (Boston: Houghton Mifflin, 1984), 198.

53. Ronald Reagan, *An American Life* (London: Hutchinson, 1990), 327. Emphasis in the original. For a contemporary account of Reagan's attempt "to prove he [was] not a male chauvinist," see Sara Fritz, "The President Tackles his 'Gender Gap,'" *U.S. News & World Report*, November 8, 1982, 52–53.

54. Kelley, *Nancy Reagan*, 411.

55. Ferraro, *Story*, 20, 116, 119, 124, 127; Miller, "Gender," 274–275.

56. Ferraro quoted in Romney and Harrison, *Momentum*, 121; Kelley, *Nancy Reagan*, 421.

57. Susan J. Carroll, *Women as Candidates in American Politics* (Bloomington: Indiana University Press, 1987), xiii–xiv.

58. Nancy Woloch, "Geraldine Ferraro," in Eric Foner and John A. Garraty, eds., *The Reader's Companion to American History* (Boston: Houghton Mifflin, 1991), 398.

59. Witt et al., *Running as a Woman*, 216.

60. Miller, "Gender," 266, 281.

61. For a summary of the polls, see McGlen and Sarkees, *Women in Foreign Policy*, 191.

62. London *Times*, October 26, 1992; *Guardian*, December 22, 1992.

BIBLIOGRAPHY

MANUSCRIPT SOURCES

Locations

AAUW	American Association of University Women headquarters, Washington, D.C.
FDR	Franklin D. Roosevelt Library, Hyde Park, New York
HHL	Herbert Hoover Library, West Branch, Iowa
HILS	Hoover Institution Library, Stanford, California
HUAP	Harvard University Archives, Pusey Library, Cambridge, Massachusetts
LC	Library of Congress, Washington, D.C.
MCS	Margaret Chase Smith Library, Skowhegan, Maine
NA	National Archives, Washington, D.C.
PRO	Public Record Office, London
RBMC	Rare Book and Manuscript Library, Columbia University, New York, New York
SCPC	Swarthmore College Peace Collection, Swarthmore, Pennsylvania

Collections

Abzug, Bella, Papers of, RBMC
American Association of University Women, Legislative Committee Records in the Papers of, AAUW
Bureau of Intelligence, Office of War Information, Record Group 44, NA
Consumer Division, Office of Price Administration, Records of the, NA
Detzer, Dorothy, Papers of, SCPC
Dewson, Mary W., Papers of, FDR
Halifax, Private Papers of Lord, PRO
Hoover, Herbert, Post Presidential Files, HHL
Labor Policy Committee, Office of Price Administration, Records of the, NA
National American Woman Suffrage Association, Records of the, LC
National Consumers' League, Records of the, LC
National League of Women Voters, Records of the, LC
Reagan, Ronald, Gubernatorial Collection, HILS

Roosevelt, Franklin D., Presidential Papers of, FDR
Smith, Margaret Chase, Papers of, MCS
State Department, Decimal file, NA
Strother, French, Papers of, HHL
Tariff Commission, Records of the U.S., NA
Taussig, Frank W., Papers of, HUAP
Women's Division Democratic National Committee, Records of the, FDR
Women's Division Republican National Committee, Records of the, in Presidential Subject File, HHL
Wilson, Woodrow, Presidential Papers of, LC

UNPUBLISHED ITEMS

Abzug, Bella S. Telephone interview with author, November 1, 1991.
Anderson, James Russell. "The New Deal Career of Frances Perkins, Secretary of Labor, 1933–1939." Case Western Reserve University, Ph.D. dissertation, 1968.
Beecher, Hoyst N., Jr. "The State Department and Liberia, 1908–1941: A Heterogeneous Record." University of Georgia, Ph.D. dissertation, 1970.
Douglas, Helen Gahagan. "Congresswoman, Actress, and Opera Singer." An oral history conducted in 1973, 1974, and 1976 by Amelia R. Fry, Women in Politics Oral History Project, Bancroft Library, University of California, Berkeley, 1982.
Gallant, Gregory P. "Margaret Chase Smith, McCarthyism and the Drive for Political Purification." University of Maine, Ph.D. dissertation, 1972.
Laitin, John. Interview with author, Skowhegan, Maine, July 25, 1991.
Miller, Carol. "Feminists, Pacifists, and Intermediates: American Women at the League of Nations, 1919–1939." Manuscript of chapter for inclusion in the projected publication, Martin David Dubin, ed. *Women, War and Peace: American Women's Experience with War from the First World War to the Cold War.*
Paul, Alice. "Conversations with Alice Paul: Woman Suffrage and the Equal Rights Amendment." An oral history conducted in 1976 by Amelia R. Fry, Suffragists Oral History Project, Bancroft Library, University of California, Berkeley, 1976.
Schott, Linda Kay. "Women against War: Pacifism, Feminism and Social Justice in the United States, 1915–1941." Stanford University, Ph.D. dissertation, 1985.
Smith, Margaret Chase. "Defense and Foreign Policy." Interview with author in Skowhegan, Maine, July 29, 1991; agreed text on deposit in the Smith Library.
———. Oral history interview, August 20, 1975, by Joe B. Frantz for the Lyndon Baines Johnson Presidential Library, in Smith Library.
———. Interviews with Pam Warford, May 9, June 6, 1988, for Northeast Archives of Folklore and Oral History (University of Maine, Orono), Accession 2026.
———. "Statements, Speeches, Monthly Report," 42 vols., 1941–1976, in Smith Library.
Swerdlow, Amy. Interview with author, Baltimore, Maryland., November 2, 1991.
Vernon, Mabel. "Speaker for Suffrage and Petitioner for Peace." An oral history conducted in 1976 by Amelia R. Fry, Suffragists Oral History Project, Bancroft Library, University of California, Berkeley, 1976
Watt, Donald Cameron. "Women in International History." Manuscript by kind courtesy of its author, October 1991.

MEMOIRS, PUBLISHED PAPERS, AND ADDRESSES

Abzug, Bella, with Mim Kelber. *Gender Gap: Bella Abzug's Guide to Political Power for American Women.* Boston: Houghton Mifflin, 1984.

Aquino, Corazon C. *Democracy by the Ways of Democracy.* Manila: Republic of the Philippines Policy Statements, 1986.

Bhutto, Benazir. *Daughter of the East: An Autobiography.* London: Mandarin, 1989.

Carter, James E. *Public Papers of the Presidents of the United States.* Vol. 2. Washington, D.C.: U.S. Government Printing Office, 1978.

Cott, Nancy E., ed. *A Woman Making History: Mary Ritter Beard Through Her Letters.* New Haven: Yale University Press, 1991.

Detzer, Dorothy. *Appointment on the Hill.* New York: Henry Holt, 1948.

Douglas, Helen Gahagan. *A Full Life.* Garden City, N.Y.: Doubleday, 1982.

Ferraro, Geraldine, with Linda Bird Francke. *Ferraro: My Story.* New York: Bantam, 1985.

Gandhi, Indira. "A Special Statement." Special Issue on Security and Disarmament, *Trialogue* 30 (Summer/Fall 1982): insert between pp. 26 and 27.

Hoover, Herbert. *The Memoirs of Herbert Hoover: The Great Depression, 1929–1941.* London: Hollis and Carter, 1953.

———. *Public Papers of the Presidents: Herbert Hoover, 1932–1933: Herbert Hoover: Containing the Public Messages, Speeches, and Statements of the President, January 1, 1932 to March 4, 1933.* Washington, D.C.: U.S. Government Printing Office, 1977.

Hull, Cordell. *The Memoirs of Cordell Hull.* 2 vols. London: Hodder and Stoughton, 1948.

Johnson, Lady Bird. *A White House Diary.* New York: Holt, Rinehart & Winston, 1970.

McLaughlin, Audrey, with Rick Archbold. *A Woman's Place: My Life and Politics.* Toronto: Macfarlane, Walter, and Ross, 1992.

Meir, Golda. *My Life.* New York: G. P. Putnam's Sons, 1975.

Perkins, Frances. *The Roosevelt I Knew.* London: Hammond and Hammond, 1947.

Regan, Donald T. *For the Record: From Wall Street to Washington.* London: Hutchinson, 1988.

Rosenman, Samuel I., comp. *The Public Papers and Addresses of Franklin D. Roosevelt. 1942: Humanity on the Defensive.* New York: Harper, 1950.

Roosevelt, Eleanor. *The Autobiography of Eleanor Roosevelt.* New York: Harper, 1961.

Roosevelt, Franklin D. *Complete Presidential Press Conferences of Franklin D. Roosevelt,* 25 vols. New York: Da Capo, 1972.

Shultz, George P. *Turmoil and Triumph: My Years as Secretary of State.* New York: Charles Scribner's, 1993.

Smith, Margaret Chase. *Declaration of Conscience.* Garden City, N.Y.: Doubleday, 1972.

Thatcher, Margaret. *The Downing Street Years.* New York: Harper Collins, 1993.

Todd, John M. *Reminiscences of John M. Todd: A Sketch of the Life of John M. Todd (Sixty-Two Years in a Barber Shop) and Reminiscences of his Customers.* Portland, Maine.: William W. Roberts, 1906.

Vandenberg, Arthur H., Jr., ed. *The Private Papers of Senator Vandenberg.* Boston: Houghton Mifflin, 1952.

REFERENCE SOURCES

Agger, Lee. *Women of Maine.* Portland, Maine: Guy Garrett Publ. Co., 1982.

Amer, Mildred, comp. *Women in the United States Congress.* Washington, D.C.: Congressional Research Service, 1991.

Bacon, Donald C., Roger H. Davidson, and Morton Keller, eds. *The Encyclopedia of the United States Congress.* 4 vols. New York: Simon & Schuster, 1995.

Barone, Michael, Grant Ujifusa, and Douglas Matthews. *The Almanac of American Politics 1974.* London, Macmillan, 1974.

———. *The Almanac of American Politics 1980.* New York: Dutton, 1979.

Barone, Michael, and Grant Ujifusa. *The Almanac of American Politics 1988.* Washington, D.C.: National Journal, 1987.

Chamberlin, Hope. *A Minority of Members: Women in the U.S. Congress.* New York: Praeger, 1973.

Center for the American Woman and Politics. *Women in Public Office: A Biographical Directory and Statistical Analysis.* New York: Bowker, 1976.

DIALOG/POLL computer facility.

Gallup, George H. *The Gallup Poll: Public Opinion 1935–1971.* 3 vols. New York: Random House, 1972.

James, Edward T., ed. *Notable American Women 1607–1950.* Cambridge, Mass.: Belknap Press of Harvard University Press, 1971.

National Cyclopedia of American Biography. St. Clair Shores, Mich.: Scholarly Press, 1972.

Opfell, Olga S. *The Lady Laureates: Women Who Have Won the Nobel Peace Prize.* 2d ed. Metuchen, N. J.: Scarecrow, 1986.

Paxton, Annabel. *Women in Congress.* Richmond, Va.: Dietz Press, 1945.

Robinson, Alice M., et al., eds. *Notable Women in the American Theatre.* London: Greenwood, 1989.

Smith, Margaret Chase, and H. Paul Jeffers. *Gallant Women.* New York: McGraw-Hill, 1968.

Women in Congress, 1917–1990. Office of the Historian, House of Representatives, 1991.

BIBLIOGRAPHIC SOURCES

Alonso, Harriet, and Melanie Gustafson. "Bibliography on the History of Women in Movements for Peace." *Women's Studies Quarterly* 12 (Summer 1984): 46–50.

Burns, Richard Dean, comp. *Guide to American Foreign Relations since 1700.* Santa Barbara, Calif.: ABC-Clio, 1983.

Butler, Deborah. *American Women Writers on Vietnam, Unheard Voices: A Selected Annotated Bibliography.* New York: Garland, 1990.

Dunn, Joe P. *Teaching the Vietnam War: Resources and Assessment.* Los Angeles:

California State University, Center for the Study of Assessment and Disarmament, 1990.

———. "Women and Vietnam: A Bibliographic Review." *Journal of American Culture* 12 (Spring 1989): 79–86.

Hinding, Andrea. *Women's History Sources: A Guide to Archives and Manuscript Collections in the United States.* 2 vols. New York: Bowker, 1979.

Loytved, Dagmar, and Hanna-Beate Schöpp-Schilling, comps. and eds. *A Bibliographic Guide to Women's Studies (based on the holdings of the John F. Kennedy-Institut library).* 2 vols. Berlin: John F. Kennedy-Institut für Nordamerikastudien, Freie Universität Berlin, 1976.

Loytved, Dagmar, comp. and ed. *A Bibliographic Guide to Women's Studies, Supplement One (based on the holdings of the John F. Kennedy-Institut library).* Berlin: John F. Kennedy-Institut für Nordamerikastudien, Freie Universität Berlin, 1980.

Manning, Beverley, comp. *We Shall Be Heard: An Index to Speeches by American Women, 1978–1985.* London: Scarecrow, 1988.

"Resources for the Study of Women at the Library of Congress." *Special Collections* 3 (Spring/Summer 1986).

OTHER BOOKS AND ARTICLES

Addams, Jane. *Newer Ideals of Peace.* 1907 Reprint, New York: Macmillan, 1915.

———. *Peace and Bread in Time of War.* New York: Macmillan, 1922.

Alonso, Harriet Hyman. *The Women's Peace Union and the Outlawing of War, 1921–1942.* Knoxville: University of Tennessee Press, 1990.

———. *Peace as a Woman's Issue: A History of the U.S. Movement for World Peace and Women's Rights.* Syracuse, N.Y.: Syracuse University Press, 1993.

Alpern, Sara. *Freda Kirchwey: A Woman of "The Nation."* Cambridge, Mass.: Harvard University Press, 1987.

Ambrose, Stephen E. *Nixon: The Education of a Politician, 1913–1962.* New York: Simon & Schuster, 1987.

———. *Nixon: The Triumph of a Politician, 1962–1972.* New York: Simon & Schuster, 1989.

Ambrosius, Lloyd E. *Woodrow Wilson and the American Diplomatic Tradition: The Treaty Fight in Perspective.* Cambridge, England: Cambridge University Press, 1987.

"Arms and the Men." *Fortune,* March 1934, 53–57, 113–126.

Ås, Berit. "A Materialistic View of Men's and Women's Attitudes Towards War." *Women's Studies International Forum* 5 (1982): 355–364.

Atholl, Katharine, Duchess of. *Women and Politics.* London: P. Allan, 1931.

Balch, Emily Greene. "The Effect of War and Militarism on the Status of Women" *Publications of the American Sociological Society* (1915): 39–55.

Baldwin, Louise G. *Study Questions on the Tariff.* Washington, D.C.: National League of Women Voters, 1931.

Baker, Paula. "The Domestication of Politics: Women and American Political Society, 1780–1920." *American Historical Review* 89 (June 1984): 593–647.

Bauer, Raymond A., Ithiel de Sola Pool, and Lewis Anthony Dexter. *American*

Business and Public Policy: The Politics of Foreign Trade. New York: Atherton Press, 1964.

Beard, Charles A. *President Roosevelt and the Coming of the War 1941: A Study in Appearances and Realities.* New Haven: Yale University Press, 1948.

Beard, Mary Ritter. *Woman as Force in History.* New York: Persea, 1987 (1946).

Berger, Jason. *A New Deal for the World: Eleanor Roosevelt and American Foreign Policy.* New York: Social Science Monographs/Columbia University Press, 1981.

Berkin, Carol R., and Clara M. Lovett, eds. *Women, War, and Revolution.* New York: Holmes and Meier, 1980.

Bertelsen, Judy. "Political Interest, Influence, and Efficiency: Differences Between the Sexes and Among Marital Status Groups." *American Political Quarterly* 2 (October 1974): 412–426.

Boeckel, Florence Brewer. "Women in International Affairs." *The Annals of the American Academy of Political and Social Sciences* 143 (1929): 230–248.

Bolt, Christine. *The Women's Movements in the United States and Britain: From the 1790s to the 1920s.* New York: Harvester Wheatsheaf, 1993.

Brock-Utne, Birgit. *Educating for Peace: A Feminist Perspective.* New York: Pergamon, 1985.

Buck, Pearl. *The Good Earth.* London: Methuen, 1931.

Bullock, Alan. *Hitler and Stalin: Parallel Lives.* London: Harper Collins, 1991.

Burner, David. *Herbert Hoover: A Public Life.* New York: Alfred A. Knopf, 1979.

Bussey, Gertrude, and Margaret Tims. *Women's International League for Peace and Freedom, 1915–1965.* London: George Allen & Unwin, 1965.

Cagan, Leslie. "Women and the Anti-draft Movement." *Radical America* 14 (1980): 9–11.

Calkin, Homer L. *Women in the Department of State: Their Role in American Foreign Affairs.* Washington D.C.: Department of State, 1977.

Campbell, Beatrix. *The Iron Ladies: Why Do Women Vote Tory?* London: Virago, 1987.

Campbell, D'Ann. *Women at War with America.* Cambridge, Mass.: Harvard University Press, 1981.

Campbell, Persia. *Consumer Representation in the New Deal.* New York: AMS Press, 1968.

Carnegie, Andrew. *War as the Mother of Valor and Civilization.* London: The Peace Society, 1910.

Cantor, Dorothy W., and Toni Bernay with Jean Stoess. *Women in Power: The Secrets of Leadership.* Boston: Houghton Mifflin, 1992.

Caroli, Betty Boyd. *First Ladies.* New York: Oxford University Press, 1987.

Carroll, Susan J. *Women as Candidates in American Politics.* Bloomington: Indiana University Press, 1987.

Carroll, Susan J., and Barbara Geiger-Parker. *Women Appointed to the Carter Administration: A Comparison with Men.* New Brunswick, N.J.: Center for the American Woman and Politics, Eagleton Institute of Politics, 1983.

Cather, Willa. *One of Ours.* 1922. Reprint, Boston: Houghton Mifflin, 1937.

Chafe, William H. *The Paradox of Change: American Women in the Twentieth Century.* New York: Oxford University Press, 1991.

Chatfield, Charles. *For Peace and Justice: Pacifism in America 1914–1941.* Knoxville: University of Tennessee Press, 1971.

Chodorow, Nancy. *The Reproduction of Mothering.* Berkeley: University of California Press, 1978.

Christy, Carol A. *Sex Differences in Political Participation: Processes of Change in Fourteen Nations.* New York: Praeger, 1987.

Cohen, Warren I. *The American Revisionists: The Lessons of Intervention in World War I.* Chicago: University of Chicago Press, 1969.

Cohn, Carol. "Emasculating America's Linguistic Deterrent." In *Rocking the Ship of State,* edited by Adrienne Harris and Ynesta King, 153–170. Boulder, Colo.: Westview, 1983.

Cole, Wayne S. *Roosevelt and the Isolationists, 1932–45.* Lincoln: University of Nebraska Press, 1983.

———. *Senator Gerald P. Nye and American Foreign Relations.* Minneapolis: University of Minnesota Press, 1962.

Collinson, Helen, et al. *Women and Revolution in Nicaragua.* London: Zed, 1990.

Cook, Blanche Wiesen. *Eleanor Roosevelt.* New York: Viking, 1992.

———. "Eleanor Roosevelt and Human Rights: The Battle for Peace and Planetary Decency." In *Women and American Foreign Policy: Lobbyists, Critics, and Insiders,* edited by Edward P. Crapol, 91–118. New York: Greenwood, 1987.

———. "'Turn toward peace:' ER and Foreign Affairs." In *Without Precedent: The Life and Career of Eleanor Roosevelt,* edited by Joan Hoff and Marjorie Lightman, 108–121. Bloomington: Indiana University Press.

Cooper, Sandi. "The Work of Women in Nineteenth Century Continental European Peace Movements." *Peace and Change* 9 (1984): 11–28.

Cott, Nancy E. "Feminist Politics in the 1920s: The National Women's Party." *Journal of American History* 71 (June 1984): 43–68.

———. *The Grounding of Modern Feminism.* New Haven: Yale University Press, 1987.

Crapol, Edward P., ed. *Women and American Foreign Policy: Lobbyists, Critics, and Insiders.* 2d ed. Wilmington, Del.: Scholarly Resources, 1992 (1987).

Creighton, Lucy B. *Pretenders to the Throne: The Consumer Movement in the United States.* Lexington, Mass.: D.C. Heath, 1976.

Crosland, Susan. "Leading Ladies." *Style and Travel,* June 27, 1993, 12–13.

Crozier, Brian. "Thatcher and the World: The Protracted Conflict." *National Review,* July 22, 1983, 865.

Curti, Merle Eugene. *The American Peace Crusade, 1815–1860.* Durham, N.C.: Duke University Press, 1929.

Dallek, Robert. *Franklin D. Roosevelt and American Foreign Policy, 1932–1945.* New York: Oxford University Press, 1979.

Darcy, R., Susan Welch, and Janet Clark. *Women, Elections, and Representation.* New York: Longman, 1987.

Davis, Allen F. *American Heroine: The Life and Legend of Jane Addams.* New York: Oxford University Press, 1973.

DeBenedetti, Charles, with Charles Chatfield. *An American Ordeal: The Antiwar Movement of the Vietnam Era.* Syracuse, N.Y.: Syracuse University Press, 1990.

———. *Origins of the Modern American Peace Movement, 1915–1929.* Millwood, N.Y.: KTO Press, 1978.

Degen, Marie. *History of the Women's Peace Party.* Baltimore: Johns Hopkins University Press, 1939.

Degler, Carl N. *At Odds: Women and the Family in America from the Revolution to the Present.* New York: Oxford University Press, 1980.

Destler, I. M. *American Trade Politics,* 2d ed. Washington, D.C.: Institute for International Economics, 1992.

De Whitt, Bennie L. "A Wider Sphere of Usefulness: Marilla Ricker's Quest for a Diplomatic Post." *Prologue* 5 (1973): 203–207.

Didion, Joan. *Democracy.* New York: Simon & Schuster, 1984.

Diggins, John Patrick. *The Rise and Fall of the American Left.* New York: Norton, 1992.

Divine, Robert A. *The Reluctant Belligerent: American Entry into World War II.* New York: John Wiley, 1965.

Donahue, Francis. "Feminism in Latin America." *Arizona Quarterly* 41 (1985): 38–60.

Dunn, Lynne K. "Joining the Boys' Club: The Diplomatic Career of Eleanor Lansing Dulles." In *Women and American Foreign Policy: Lobbyists, Critics, and Insiders,* edited by Edward P. Crapol, 119–135. New York: Greenwood, 1987.

Dworkin, Andrea. *Right-Wing Women.* New York: G. P. Putnam's Sons/Pedigree, 1983.

Echols, Alice. "Women Power and Women's Liberation: Exploring the Relationship Between the Antiwar Movement and the Women's Liberation Movement." In *Give Peace a Chance: Exploring the Vietnam Antiwar Movement,* edited by Melvin Small and William D. Hoover, 159–170. Syracuse, N.Y.: Syracuse University Press, 1992.

Elshtain, Jean Bethke. *Women and War.* Brighton, England: Harvester, 1987.

Elwood-Akers, Virginia. *Women War Correspondents in the Vietnam War, 1961–1975.* Metuchen, N.J.: Scarecrow, 1988.

Engelbrecht, Helmuth C. *Revolt Against War.* London: T. Werner Laurie, 1938.

Engelbrecht, Helmuth C., and Frank C. Hanighen. *Merchants of Death: A Study of the International Armament Industry.* New York: Dodd, Mead, 1934.

Enloe, Cynthia. *Bananas, Beaches, and Bases: Making Feminist Sense of International Politics.* Berkeley: University of California Press, 1990.

———. *The Morning After: Sexual Politics at the End of the Cold War.* Berkeley: University of California Press, 1993.

Etheredge, Lloyd S. *A World of Men: The Private Sources of American Foreign Policy.* Cambridge, Mass.: MIT Press, 1978.

Ewell, Judith. "Barely in the Inner Circle: Jeane Kirkpatrick." In *Women and American Foreign Policy: Lobbyists, Critics, and Insiders,* edited by Edward P. Crapol, 153–171. New York: Greenwood, 1987.

Farrell, John C. *Beloved Lady: A History of Jane Addams' Ideas on Reform and Peace.* Baltimore: Johns Hopkins University Press, 1967.

Fausold, Martin L. *The Presidency of Herbert C. Hoover* (Lawrence: University Press of Kansas, 1985).

Fearon, Peter. *War, Prosperity and Depression: The U.S. Economy, 1917–45.* Oxford, England: Philip Allan, 1987.

Fernea, Elizabeth Warnock. *Guests of the Sheik: An Ethnography of an Iraqi Village.* New York: Doubleday, 1965.

Ferrell, Robert H. *American Diplomacy in the Great Depression: Hoover-Stimson Foreign Policy, 1929–1933.* New Haven: Yale University Press, 1957.

————. *Peace in Their Time: The Origins of the Kellogg-Briand Pact.* New Haven: Yale University Press, 1952.

Fife, Robert. *Kim Campbell: The Making of a Politician.* Toronto: Harper Collins, 1993.

FitzGerald, Frances. *Fire in the Lake: The Vietnamese and Americans in Vietnam.* Boston: Little, Brown, 1972.

Fleming, Alice. *The Senator from Maine: Margaret Chase Smith.* New York: Thomas Y. Crowell, 1969.

Flexner, Eleanor. *Century of Struggle: The Women's Rights Movement in the United States.* Cambridge, Mass.: Harvard University Press, 1959.

Foot, Rosemary. "Where Are the Women?" *Diplomatic History* 14 (Fall 1990): 615–622.

Forcey, Charles. *The Crossroads of Liberalism: Croly, Weyl, Lippmann and the Progressive Era, 1900–1925.* New York: Oxford University Press, 1961.

Foster, Catherine. *Women for all Seasons: The Story of the Women's International League for Peace and Freedom.* Athens: University of Georgia Press, 1989.

Fowler, Robert Booth. *Carrie Catt: Feminist Politician.* Boston: Northwestern University Press, 1986.

Fox, Richard Wightman, and T. J. Jackson Lears, eds. *The Culture of Consumption: Critical Essays in American History, 1880–1980.* New York: Pantheon, 1983.

Frankovic, Kathleen A. "Sex and Voting in the U.S. House of Representatives 1961–1975." *American Politics Quarterly* 5 (July 1977): 315–330.

Fraser, Antonia. *Boadicea's Chariot: The Warrior Queens.* London: Weidenfeld & Nicolson, 1988.

Fraser, Arvonne S. "Women and International Development: The Road to Nairobi and Back." In *The American Woman 1990–91: A Status Report,* edited by Sara E. Rix, 287–300. New York: Norton, 1990.

Fraser, Nicholas, and Marysa Navarro. *Eva Perón.* New York: Norton, 1981.

Freedman, Lawrence. *Britain and the Falklands War.* Oxford, England: Basil Blackwell, 1988.

Friedan, Betty. *The Feminine Mystique.* 1963. Reprint, New York: Dell, 1984.

Fuchs, Victor R. *Women's Quest for Economic Equality.* Cambridge, Mass.: Harvard University Press, 1988.

Fuss, Diana. *Essentially Speaking: Feminism, Nature, and Difference.* New York: Routledge, 1989.

Gatlin, Rochelle. *American Women Since 1945.* Jackson: University Press of Mississippi, 1987.

Gelb, Joyce. *Feminism and Politics: A Comparative Perspective.* Berkeley: University of California Press, 1989.

Genovese, Michael A., ed. *Women as National Leaders.* Newbury Park, Calif.: Sage, 1993.

Gerson, Allan. *The Kirkpatrick Mission, Diplomacy Without Apology: America at the United Nations, 1981–1985.* New York: Free Press, 1991.

Gilligan, Carol. *In a Different Voice: Psychological Theory and Women's Development.* Cambridge, Mass.: Harvard University Press, 1982.

Goldin, Claudia. *Understanding the Gender Gap: An Economic History of American Women.* New York: Oxford University Press, 1990.

Gould, Alberta. *First Lady of the Senate: A Life of Margaret Chase Smith.* Mt. Desert, Me.: Windswept House, 1990.

Graebner, Norman A., ed. *An Uncertain Tradition: American Secretaries of State in the Twentieth Century.* New York: McGraw-Hill, 1961.

Graham, Frank. *Margaret Chase Smith: Woman of Courage.* New York: John Day, 1964.

Graham, Sally Hunter. "Woodrow Wilson, Alice Paul, and the Woman Suffrage Movement." *Political Science Quarterly* 98 (Winter 1983–1984): 665–679.

Gruberg, Martin. *Women in American Politics: An Assessment and Sourcebook.* Oshkosh, Wis.: Academic Press, 1968.

Hallin, Daniel C. *The "Uncensored War": The Media and Vietnam.* New York: Oxford University Press, 1986.

Hamby, Alonzo L. "An American Democrat: A Reevaluation of the Personality of Harry S. Truman." *Political Science Quarterly* 106 (1991): 33–55.

Hard, Anne. "Am I Blue? The Housewife's Interest in National Legislation That Enters the Kitchen." *Ladies Home Journal*, December 1929, 13, 190, 193.

Harris, Adrienne, and Ynesta King, eds. *Rocking the Ship of State: Toward a Feminist Peace Politics.* Boulder, Colo.: Westview, 1983.

Harris, Lillian Craig. "Comrade Dowager Chiang Ch'ing." *Asian Affairs* 9 (1982): 163–173.

Harris, Louis. "Newsweek Poll: The Women's Vote." *Newsweek*, September 21, 1964, 32.

Harrison, Barbara Grizzuti. "The Women You Hate to Love." *Mademoiselle*, March 1985, 120.

Hay, John. "Thatcher's Cold War Crusade." *Maclean's*, October 10, 1983, 24–27.

Hayes, John L. *Protection a Boon to Consumers.* Boston: John Wilson, 1867.

Heale, Michael J. *American Anticommunism: Combating the Enemy Within, 1830–1970.* Baltimore: Johns Hopkins University Press, 1990.

"Helen Gahagan Douglas." *New Republic*, September 20, 1948, 10.

Herman, Sondra R. *Eleven Against War: Studies in American Internationalist Thought, 1898–1921.* Stanford, Calif.: Hoover Institution Press, 1969.

Higgins, Marguerite. *Our Vietnam Nightmare.* New York: Harper & Row, 1965.

Higonnet, Margaret Randolph, et al., eds. *Behind the Lines: Gender and the Two World Wars.* New Haven: Yale University Press, 1989.

Hill, Patricia. *The World Their Household: The American Women's Missionary Movement and Cultural Transformation, 1870–1920.* Ann Arbor: University of Michigan Press, 1985.

Hoag, C. Leonard. *Preface to Preparedness: The Washington Disarmament Conference and Public Opinion.* Washington D.C.: American Council on Public Affairs, 1941.

Hoff, Joan. *American Business and Foreign Policy, 1920–1933.* Lexington: University Press of Kentucky, 1971.

———. *Herbert Hoover: Forgotten Progressive.* Boston: Little, Brown, 1975.

———. "Conclusion: Of Mice and Men." In *Women and American Foreign Policy: Lobbyists, Critics, and Insiders*, edited by Edward P. Crapol, 173–188. New York: Greenwood, 1987.

———. "'Peace Is a Woman's Job . . .' Jeannette Rankin and American Foreign Policy: The Origins of Her Pacifism." *Montana* 30 (Winter 1980): 28–41.

————. "'Peace Is a Woman's Job . . .' Jeannette Rankin and American Foreign Policy: Her Lifework as a Pacifist." *Montana* 30 (Spring 1980): 38–53.

Hoff, Joan, and Marjorie Lightman, eds. *Without Precedent: The Life and Career of Eleanor Roosevelt.* Bloomington: Indiana University Press, 1984.

Holm, Jeanne. *Women in the Military: An Unfinished Revolution.* Novato, Calif.: Presidio, 1982.

Holsti, Ole R., and James N. Rosenan. "The Foreign Policy Beliefs of Women in Leadership Positions." *Journal of Politics* 43 (May 1981): 326–347.

Hoover, Herbert. "Pro-work and Anti-war." *Woman Citizen*, April 21, 1923, 7–8, 23.

————. "Thrift and American Women." *Ladies Home Journal*, August 1920, 3, 100.

————. "What I Would Like Women to Do." *Ladies Home Journal*, August 1917, 25.

Hoover, Herbert, and Hugh Gibson. "World Peace—Women Can Win It." *Woman's Home Companion*, February 1944, 26–27, 38.

Horne, A. D., ed. *The Wounded Generation: America After Vietnam.* Englewood Cliffs, N. J.: Prentice-Hall, 1981.

Horovitz, Daniel. *The Morality of Spending: Attitudes Toward the Consumer Society in America, 1875–1940.* Baltimore: Johns Hopkins University Press, 1985.

Hunt, Michael H. *Ideology and U.S. Foreign Policy.* New Haven: Yale University Press, 1987.

Hymowitz, Carol, and Michaele Weissman. *A History of Women in America.* New York: Bantam, 1978.

"Indira Gandhi: India's Autocratic Woman of Iron." *U.S. News & World Report*, June 25, 1984, 9.

Jacoby, Susan. "Women and the War." In *The Wounded Generation: America After Vietnam*, edited by A. D. Horne, 112–121. Englewood Cliffs, N.J. Prentice-Hall, 1981.

Jeffords, Susan. *The Remasculination of America: Gender and the Vietnam War.* Bloomington: Indiana University Press, 1989.

Jenkins, Simon. "Now at Center Stage, NATO's Leading Lady [Thatcher]." *U.S. News & World Report*, April 6, 1987, 33.

Jensen, Joan M. "All Pink Sisters: The War Department and the Feminist Movement in the 1920s." In *Decades of Discontent: The Women's Movement, 1920–1940*, edited by Lois Scharf and Joan M. Jensen, 200–222. Westport, Conn.: Greenwood, 1983.

Jessup, Josephine Lurie. *The Faith of Our Feminists: A Study in the Novels of Edith Wharton, Ellen Glasgow, Willa Cather.* New York: Richard R. Smith, 1950.

Joseph, Helen. *Side by Side.* London: Zed, 1986.

Katra, William H. "Eva Perón: Media Queen of the Perónist Working Class." *Revista Interamericana* [Puerto Rico] 11 (1981): 238–251.

Katz, Milton S. *Ban the Bomb: A History of SANE.* London: Greenwood, 1987.

Kaufman, Robert Gordon. *Arms Control during the Pre-Nuclear Era: The United States and Naval Limitation Between the Two World Wars.* New York: Columbia University Press, 1990.

Keller, Evelyn Fox. *Reflections on Gender and Science*. New Haven: Yale University Press, 1985.

Kelley, Kitty. *Nancy Reagan: The Unauthorized Biography*. New York: Simon & Schuster, 1991.

Kennedy, Paul. *The Rise and Fall of the Great Powers: Economic Change and Military Conflict from 1500 to 2000*. New York: Random House, 1988.

Kessler-Harris, Alice. *Out to Work: A History of Wage-Earning Women in the United States*. New York: Oxford University Press, 1982.

Kirkpatrick, Jeane J. *Dictatorships and Double Standards: Rationalism and Reason in Politics*. New York: American Enterprise Institute/Simon & Schuster, 1982.

———. *Political Woman*. New York: Basic Books, 1974.

Koistinen, Paul A. C. *The Military-Industrial Complex: A Historical Perspective*. New York: Praeger, 1980.

Komisar, Lucy. *Corazon Aquino: The Story of a Revolution*. New York: George Braziller, 1987.

Kraditor, Aileen S. *The Ideas of the Woman Suffrage Movement, 1890–1920*. New York: Columbia University Press, 1965.

Ku Yen. "Ching Ch'ing's Wolfish Ambition in Publicizing 'Matriarchal Society.'" *Chinese Studies in History* 12 (1972): 75–79.

Kyrk, Hazel. *A Theory of Consumption*. Boston: Houghton Mifflin, 1923.

LaFeber, Walter. *The American Age: United States Foreign Policy at Home and Abroad Since 1750*. New York: Norton, 1989.

Langer, William L., and S. Everett Gleason. *The Challenge to Isolation: The World Crisis of 1937–1940 and American Foreign Policy*. New York: Harper, 1952.

Lash, Joseph P. *Eleanor and Franklin: The Story of Their Relationship Based on Eleanor Roosevelt's Private Papers*. New York: Norton, 1971.

———. *Eleanor: The Years Alone*. New York: Norton, 1972.

Lazarsfeld, Paul F., Bernard Berelson, and Hazel Gaudet. *The People's Choice: How the Voter Makes Up His Mind in a Presidential Campaign*. 2d ed. New York: Columbia University Press, 1948.

Lemons, J. Stanley. *The Woman Citizen: Social Feminism in the 1920s*. Urbana: University of Illinois Press, 1973.

Levy, David W. *The Debate over Vietnam*. Baltimore: Johns Hopkins University Press, 1991.

Lewy, Guenter. *Peace and Revolution: The Moral Crisis of American Pacifism*. Grand Rapids, Mich.: Wm. B. Eerdmans, 1988.

Lilley, Charles R., and Michael H. Hunt. "On Social History, the State, and Foreign Relations: Commentary on 'The Cosmopolitan Connection.'" *Diplomatic History* 11 (Summer 1987): 243–250.

Link, Arthur S. *Wilson the Diplomatist: A Look at his Major Foreign Policies*. Baltimore: Johns Hopkins University Press, 1957.

Lippmann, Walter. *Public Opinion*. New York: Harcourt Brace, 1922.

Lipstadt, Deborah E. *Beyond Belief: The American Press and the Coming of the Holocaust 1933–1945*. New York: Free Press, 1986.

Lochridge, Patricia. "The Mother Racket." *Woman's Home Companion*, July 1944, 20–21, 72–73.

Lunardini, Christine A. *From Equal Suffrage to Equal Rights: Alice Paul and* the *Woman's Party 1910–1928*. New York: New York University Press, 1986.

McCarthy, Mary. *Hanoi*. London: Weidenfeld & Nicolson, 1968.

McEnaney, Laura. "He-Men and Christian Mothers: The America First Movement and the Gendered Meanings of Patriotism and Isolationism." *Diplomatic History* 18 (Winter 1994): 47–57.

McGerr, Michael. "Political Style and Women's Power, 1830–1930." *Journal of American History* 77 (December 1990): 864–885.

McGlen, Nancy E., and Meredith Reid Sarkees. *Women in Foreign Policy: The Insiders*. New York: Routledge, 1993.

MacKinnon, Janice R., and Stephen R. MacKinnon. *Agnes Smedley: The Life and Times of an American Radical*. Berkeley, University of California Press, 1988.

Madison, Christopher. "Betting on Aquino" *National Journal*, February 20, 1988, 456–461.

Mandel, Ruth B. *In the Running: The New Woman Candidate*. Boston: Beacon, 1983.

Marchand, C. Roland. *The American Peace Movement and Social Reform, 1898–1918*. Princeton, N.J.: Princeton University Press, 1972.

Matthaei, Julie A. *An Economic History of Women in America: Women's Work, the Sexual Division of Labor, and the Development of Capitalism*. New York: Schocken, 1982.

May, Elaine Tyler. *Homeward Bound: American Families in the Cold War Era*. New York: Basic Books, 1988.

Mayo, Katherine. *Mother India*. New York: Harcourt Brace, 1927.

Mead, Margaret. "The New Isolationism." *American Scholar* 23 (Summer 1955): 378–382.

Mitchell, Wesley C. *The Backward Art of Spending Money, and Other Essays*. New York: McGraw-Hill, 1937.

Morrison, Dennis L. "Margaret Chase Smith's 1950 Declaration of Conscience Speech." *Maine Historical Society Quarterly* 32 (Summer 1992): 2–29.

Mower, A. Glenn. *The United States, the United Nations, and Human Rights: The Eleanor Roosevelt and Jimmy Carter Years*. Westport, Conn.: Greenwood, 1979.

Mueller, Carol M., ed. *The Politics of the Gender Gap: The Social Construction of Political Influence*. Beverly Hills, Calif.: Sage, 1988.

Mueller, John E. *War, Presidents and Public Opinion*. New York: John Wiley, 1973.

Muir, Kate. *Arms and the Woman*. London: Coronet, 1993.

Naipaul, V. S. *The Return of Eva Perón*. 1974. Reprint, New York: Vintage, 1981.

Newberry, J. V. "Anti-War Suffragists." *History* 62 (October 1977): 411–425.

Ney, William. "Glaspie Speaks." *The New Combat* (Summer/Autumn 1991): 27–32.

Noer, Thomas. *Cold War and Black Liberation: The United States and Black Rule in Africa*. New York: Columbia University Press, 1985.

Norris, Pippa. *Politics and Sexual Equality: The Comparative Position of Women in Western Democracies*. London: Lynne Rienner, 1987.

Okin, Susan Moller. *Women in Western Political Thought*. Princeton, N.J.: Princeton University Press, 1979.

Oshinsky, David M. *A Conspiracy So Immense: The World of Joe McCarthy*. New York: Free Press, 1983.

Papachristou, Judith. "American Women and Foreign Policy, 1898–1905: Exploring Gender in Diplomatic History." *Diplomatic History* 14 (Fall 1990): 493–510.

Parker, Gail, ed. *The Oven Birds: American Women on Womanhood, 1820–1920.* Garden City, N.Y.: Anchor/Doubleday, 1972.

Patterson, David S. "Woodrow Wilson and the Mediation Movement, 1914–17." *Historian* [United States] 33 (1971): 335–356.

Peel, Roy V., and Thomas C. Donnelly. *The 1932 Campaign: An Analysis.* 1935. Reprint, New York: DaCapo, 1973.

Peele, Gillian. "The Changed Character of British Foreign and Security Policy." *International Security* 4 (Spring 1980): 185–198.

Perkins, Dexter. *Charles Evans Hughes and American Democratic Statesmanship.* Boston: Little, Brown, 1956.

Perry, Elisabeth Israels. *Belle Moskowitz: Feminine Politics and the Exercise of Power in the Age of Alfred E. Smith.* New York: Routledge, 1992.

Potter, Jim. *The American Economy Between the World Wars.* London: Macmillan, 1974.

Prasad, D. M. *Ceylon's Foreign Policy Under the Bandaranaikes (1956–65): A Political Analysis.* New Delhi: S. Chand, 1973.

Priest, Ivy Baker. "The Ladies Elected Ike." *American Mercury* 76 (February 1953): 23–28.

Pullen, Dale. *Margaret Chase Smith: Republican Senator from Maine.* Washington, D.C.: Ralph Nader Congress Project, 1972.

Rainbolt, Rosemary. "Women and War in the United States: The Case of Dorothy Detzer, National Secretary WILPF." *Peace and Change* 4 (Fall 1977): 18–21.

Randall, Vicky. *Women and Politics.* London: Macmillan, 1982.

Richardson, Lewis Fry. *Statistics of Deadly Quarrels.* Pittsburgh: Boxwood Press, 1960.

Rix, Sara E., ed. *The American Woman 1987–88: A Report in Depth.* New York: Norton, 1987.

———. *The American Woman 1990–91: A Status Report.* New York: Norton, 1990.

Robinson, Edgar Eugene, and Vaughn Davis Bornet. *Herbert Hoover: President of the United States.* Stanford, Calif.: Hoover Institution Press, 1975.

Romney, Ronna, and Beppie Harrison. *Momentum: Women in American Politics Now.* New York: Crown, 1987.

Roosevelt, Eleanor. *The Moral Basis of Democracy.* London: Hodder and Stoughton, 1941.

Rorabaugh, W. J. *Berkeley at War: The 1960s.* New York: Oxford University Press, 1989.

Rosen, Elliot A. *Hoover, Roosevelt, and the Brain Trust: From Depression to New Deal.* New York: Columbia University Press, 1977.

Rosenberg, Emily S. "Gender." *Journal of American History* 77 (June 1990): 116–124.

Ross, Shelley. *Washington Babylon: Sex, Scandal, and Corruption in American Politics from 1702 to the Present.* New York: Ballantine, 1988.

Rossi, Alice. "Beyond the Gender Gap: Women's Bid for Political Power." *Social Science Quarterly* 64 (December 1983): 718–733.

Rupp, Leila J. *Mobilizing Women for War: German and American Propaganda, 1939–1945*. Princeton, N.J.: Princeton University Press, 1978.

Sahgal, Nayantara. *Indira Gandhi: Her Road to Power*. New York: Frederick Ungar, 1982.

Scharf, Lois, and Joan M. Jensen. *Decades of Discontent: The Women's Movement, 1920–1940*. Westport, Conn.: Greenwood, 1983.

Scharf, Lois. *Eleanor Roosevelt: First Lady of American Liberalism*. Boston: Twayne, 1987.

Schlesinger, Arthur M., Jr. *The Age of Roosevelt*. Vol. 2, *The Coming of the New Deal*. Boston: Houghton Mifflin, 1959.

———. *The Age of Roosevelt*. Vol. 1, *The Crisis of the Old Order, 1919–1933*. Boston: Houghton Mifflin, 1957.

———. *The Vital Center: The Politics of Freedom*. Boston: Houghton Mifflin, 1949.

Schulzinger, Robert D. *Henry Kissinger: Doctor of Diplomacy*. New York: Columbia University Press, 1989.

Scobie, Ingrid Winther. *Center Stage: Helen Gahagan Douglas, A Life*. New York: Oxford University Press, 1992. Reprint, New Brunswick, N.J.: Rutgers University Press, 1995.

———. "Douglas, Helen Gahagan." In *Notable Women in the American Theatre*, edited by Alice M. Robinson, et al. 218–222. London: Greenwood, 1989.

———. "Helen Gahagan Douglas and the Roosevelt Connection." In *Without Precedent: The Life and Career of Eleanor Roosevelt*, edited by Joan Hoff and Marjorie Lightman, 153–175. Bloomington: Indiana University Press, 1984.

———. "Helen Gahagan Douglas and Her 1950 Senate Race with Richard Nixon." *Southern California Historical Quarterly* 55 (Spring 1976): 113–126.

Scott, Joan W. "Deconstructing Equality-Versus-Difference: Or, The Uses of Poststructuralist Theory for Feminism." *Feminist Studies* 14 (Spring 1988): 33–50.

Seldes, George H. *Iron, Blood and Profits: An Exposure of the World-Wide Munitions Market*. New York: Harper, 1934.

Sen, Ilina, ed. *A Space Within the Struggle: Women's Participation in People's Movements*. New Delhi: Kali for Women, 1990.

Shafer, Byron E. *The Changing Structure of American Politics*. Oxford, England: At the Clarendon Press, 1986.

Shannon, David. *The Decline of American Communism: A History of the Communist Party of the United States Since 1945*. London: Atlantic Books, 1959.

Shapira, Anita. "The Debate in Mapri on the Use of Violence, 1932–1935." *Zionism* 2 [Israel] (1981): 99–124.

Shapiro, Anne-Louise, ed. *Feminists Revision History*. New Brunswick, N.J.: Rutgers University Press, 1994.

Sheed, Wilfrid. *Clare Boothe Luce*. New York: Dutton, 1982.

Sherman, Janann. "'They Either Need These Women or They Do Not': Margaret Chase Smith and the Fight for Regular Status for Women in the Military." *Journal of Military History* 54 (Jan. 1990): 47–78.

Sherwood, Robert E. *Roosevelt and Hopkins: An Intimate History*. New York: Harper, 1948.

Shewmaker, Kenneth E. *Americans and Chinese Communists, 1927–1945: A Persuading Encounter*. Ithaca: Cornell University Press, 1971.

Silber, Norman Isaac. *Test and Protest: The Influence of Consumers Union.* New York: Holmes and Meier, 1983.

Sinclair, Andrew. *The Better Half: The Emancipation of American Woman.* New York: Harper & Row, 1965.

Sinha, Mrinalini. "Gender in the Critiques of Colonialism and Nationalism: Locating the 'Indian Woman'." In *Feminists Revision History,* edited by Anne-Louise Shapiro, 246–275. New Brunswick, N.J.: Rutgers University Press, 1994.

Small, Melvin. *Johnson, Nixon, and the Doves.* New Brunswick, N.J.: Rutgers University Press, 1988.

Small, Melvin, and William D. Hoover, eds. *Give Peace a Chance: Exploring the Vietnam Antiwar Movement.* Syracuse, N.Y.: Syracuse University Press, 1992.

Smith, Geoffrey S. "Commentary: Security, Gender, and the Historical Process." *Diplomatic History* 18 (Winter 1994): 79–90.

———. "National Security and Personal Isolation: Sex, Gender, and Disease in the Cold-War United States." *International History Review* 14 (May 1992): 221–240.

"Special Convention Guide" *Ms.,* (August 1988), 42–56.

Speth, James Gustave. "On the Road to Rio and to Sustainability." *Environmental Sciences and Technology* 26 (June 1992): 1075–1076.

Steinson, Barbara J. *American Women's Activism in World War I.* New York: Garland, 1982.

———. "'The Mother Half of Humanity': American Women in the Peace and Preparation Movements in World War I." In *Women, War, and Revolution,* edited by Carol R. Berkin and Clara M. Lovett, 259–284. New York: Holmes and Meier, 1980.

Stephenson, A. Jill R. *Women in Nazi Society.* London: Croom Helm, 1975.

Strong, Anna Louise. *Cash and Violence in Laos and Vietnam.* New York: Mainstream, 1962.

Sundiata, I. K. *Black Scandal: America and the Liberian Labor Crisis, 1929–1936.* Philadelphia, Pa.: Institute for the Study of Human Issues, 1980.

Swerdlow, Amy. "Ladies' Day at the Capitol: Women's Strike for Peace versus HUAC." *Feminist Studies* 8 (1982): 493–520.

———. *Women Strike for Peace: Traditional Motherhood and Radical Politics in the 1960s.* Chicago: University of Chicago Press, 1993.

Swisher, Idella Gwatkin. *An Introduction to a Study of the Tariff.* Washington, D.C.: Committee on Living Costs, NLWV, 1931.

Taussig, Frank W. *The Tariff History of the United States,* 8th ed. New York: Capricorn, 1964.

Taylor, J. M. *Eva Perón: The Myths of a Woman.* Chicago: University of Chicago Press, 1979.

Terrill, Ross. *The White-Boned Demon: A Biography of Madame Mao Zedong.* London: Heinemann, 1984.

Tolchin, Susan, and Martin Tolchin. *Clout: Woman Power and Politics.* New York: Coward, McCann & Geoghegan, 1974.

Toynbee, Polly. "Is Margaret Thatcher a Woman? No Woman if She Has to Make It in a Man's World." *Washington Monthly* 20 (May 1988): 34–38.

Thompson, Dorothy. "Women and Inflation." *Ladies Home Journal,* December 1941, 6.

Tickner, J. Ann. *Gender in International Relations: Feminist Perspectives on Achieving Global Security.* New York: Columbia University Press, 1992.

Van Devanter, ed. *Vision of War, Dream of Peace: Writings of Women of the Vietnam War.* New York: Warner, 1991.

Van Seters, Deborah. "'Hardly Hollywood's Ideal': Female Autobiographies of Secret Service Work, 1914–45." *Intelligence and National Security* 7 (October 1992): 403–424.

Veblen, Thorstein. *The Theory of the Leisure Class: An Economic Study of Institutions.* 1899. Reprint, London: George Allen & Unwin, 1922.

Vickers, Jeanne. *Women and War.* London: Zed, 1993.

Violette, Augusta Genevieve. *Economic Feminism in American Literature Prior to 1848.* 1925. Reprint, New York: Burt Franklin, 1971.

Volkogonov, Dimitri. *Stalin: Triumph and Tragedy,* edited and translated by Harold Shukman. London: Weidenfield & Nicolson, 1991.

Wales, Nym. *Inside Red China.* New York: Doubleday, Doran, 1939.

Walker, Cherryl. *Women and Resistance in South Africa.* London: Onyx, 1982.

Walker, J. Samuel. *Henry A. Wallace and American Foreign Policy.* Westport, Conn.: Greenwood, 1976.

Walzer, Michael. *Just and Unjust Wars: A Moral Argument with Historical Illustrations.* New York: Basic Books, 1977.

Wank, Solomon, ed. *Doves and Diplomats: Foreign Offices and Peace Movements in Europe and America in the Twentieth Century.* Westport, Conn.: Greenwood, 1978.

Ware, Susan. *Beyond Suffrage: Women in the New Deal.* Cambridge, Mass.: Harvard University Press, 1981.

———. *Partner and I: Molly Dewson, Feminism, and New Deal Politics.* New Haven: Yale University Press, 1987.

———. *Still Missing: Amelia Earhart and the Search for Modern Feminism.* New York: Norton, 1993.

Weibel, Kathryn. *Mirror Mirror: Images of Women Reflected in Popular Culture.* New York: Anchor/Doubleday, 1977.

Welch, Richard E. *Response to Imperialism: The United States and the Philippine-American War, 1899–1902.* Chapel Hill, University of North Carolina Press, 1979.

Welch, Susan. "Are Women More Liberal than Men in the U.S. Congress?" *Legislative Studies Quarterly* 10 (February 1985): 125–134.

Wilkie, James W., and Monica Menell-Kinberg. "*Evita*: From Elitelore to Folklore." *Journal of Latin American Lore* 7 (1981): 99–140.

Williamson, Edwin. *The Penguin History of Latin America.* Harmondsworth, England: Penguin, 1992.

Wilson, Joan Hoff. *See* Hoff, Joan

Wiltz, John E. *From Isolation to War, 1931–1941.* London: Routledge and Kegan Paul, 1967.

———. *In Search of Peace: The Senate Munitions Inquiry, 1934–36.* Baton Rouge: Louisiana State University Press, 1963.

Winner, David. *Eleanor Roosevelt: The Woman Who Pioneered the Universal Declaration of Human Rights.* Watford, England: Exley, 1992.

Winkler, Allan M. *Life Under a Cloud: American Anxiety about the Atom.* New York: Oxford University Press, 1993.

Witke, Roxane. *Comrade Chiang Ch'ing.* Boston: Little, Brown, 1977.

Witt, Linda, Karen M. Paget, and Glenna Matthews. *Running as a Woman: Gender and Power in American Politics.* New York: Free Press, 1993.

Woodruff, William. *America's Impact on the World: A Study of the Role of the United States in the World Economy, 1750–1970.* London: Macmillan, 1975.

Woodward, C. Vann. *Tom Watson: Agrarian Rebel.* New York: Rinehart, 1938.

Wynn, Neil A. *From Progressivism to Prosperity: World War I and American Society.* New York: Holmes and Meier, 1986.

Young, Hugo. *One of Us: A Biography of Margaret Thatcher.* London: Pan, 1990.

INDEX

Abdullah ibu-Hussein (king of Jordan), 164
ABM (anti-ballistic missile) system, 122–123
Abzug, Bella S., 83, 170, 180, 192, 196, 235n92; achievements, 9–10, 143, 145–146, 149, 154; background and views, 132–133; dismissed by President Carter, 151; feminist, 135, 148, 151; gender gap, 132, 136, 143, 149, 153, 154; image, 131, 189; Israel, 144–145; military assistance, 144, 233n62; opposes nuclear arms race, 147–149; opposes Vietnam War, 128, 132, 154; role in ending Vietnam War, 135–140; trade, 146–147; women's support for, 142–143, 148, 152
Abzug, Martin, 132
Adams, Brock, 3
Addams, Jane, 3, 6, 66–67, 96, 133; background, 12–13; beliefs and ideas, 13, 19, 205n24; disarmament campaign, 54; outlawry of war, 35–36; president WILPF, 18; smeared as Red, 26; World War I opposed by, 13–14
Agnew, Spiro, 123
Agricultural Adjustment Act (1933), 85
Agricultural Adjustment Administration (AAA), consumer representation in, 86, 88

Albring, Ursula Seiler, 236n5
Albright, Madelaine, 175
Alliance of Women for Peace, 14
Alonso, Harriet Hyman, 6–7
America First, 98
American Association of University Women, 30–31, 34–35
American Farm Bureau Association, 30
American League against War and Fascism, 82
American Legion, 73, 80
American Peace Society, 14
American School Peace League, 23
American Union Against Militarism, 15
Andrews, Fannie Fern, 25
Angola, 186
Another Mother for Peace, 142
Anti Price Rise Movement (Bombay), 180
Aptheker, Bettina, 141
Aptheker, Herbert, 141, 233n47
Aquino, Maria Corazon, 156–157, 167, 236n7
Argentina, 156, 161
arms embargoes, 70, 77, 81
Ashrawi, Hanan, 236n5
Aspin, Les, 143
Astor, Nancy, 16, 197; background, 91; World War II, 92
Attlee, Clement, 162, 237n19
Aung San Sun Kui, 156–157, 167

Baez, Joan, 3, 141
Bailey, Hannah, 15
Bailey, John, 187
Balch, Emily Greene, 6, 20, 67;
dismissed from Wellesley College,
26; on nurturant motherhood, 5,
18–19; secretary-treasurer WILPF,
18
Baldwin, Louise G., 56–57
Bandaranaike, Sirimavo, 121, 156, 158,
167, 175, 236nn3, 7; and nonalign-
ment, 155; world's first woman
premier, 156
Bang, Fru Nina, 155
Bangladesh, 155–156, 166–167
Barnes, Harry Elmer, 74
Barnes, Julian, 161
Barth, Ramona, 128
Baruch, Bernard, 85
Beard, Charles A., 74
Beard, Mary: on Carrie Catt, 100; on
women and war, 5
Berger, Jason, 96
Bhutto, Benazir, 4, 156–157, 185,
236n7; career and image of, 167
Bhutto, Zulfikar, 167–168
"Billion Dollar Navy Bill" (1933), 71–
73. See also Vinson-Trammel Act
(1934)
Blue Star Mother organization, 98
Boeckel, Florence: on paucity of
women in high office, 153; on
public opinion, 37; on women's
peace movement, 30
Boeckel model on women's foreign-
policy impact, 36, 48, 74–75
Bohlen, Avis T., 177
Bolivia, 77
Bolton, Frances P., 95–96, 108, 222n54
Borah, William E., 32–33, 68, 74, 78,
82; naval reductions, 31
Boulding, Elise, 134
Boxer, Barbara, 186, 240n4
breakthrough syndrome, 4, 105, 116,
132, 154, 198; corruption, 149;
defined, 1–2, 4, 157–158; flaws in
hypothesis concerning, 2, 192–193;
World War I, 1, 11–12
Briand, Aristide, 35

Britain, 198. See also United Kingdom
Brundtland, Gro Harlem, 156–157,
197; background and policies, 169–
170
Brundtland Commission, 170
Bryan, William Jennings, 74, 185
Buck, Pearl, 71, 197
Burdick, Eugene, 179
Burma, 156, 167
Bush, George, 94, 114, 154, 170, 185,
193–194
Bye, Raymond T., 44
Byron, Beverly, 187
Byron, Katherine E., 95, 185, 222n54

Calkin, Homer, 175
Cambodia, 126, 145
Camp, Katherine L., 128
Campbell, Kim, 156–158, 172–173,
238n40, 239n49
Campbell, Persia, 94, 180
Canada, 156, 158, 172, 178, 198;
women in politics, 239n49
Caner, Ann, 86
Caraway, Hattie W., 95, 185, 216n37,
222n54, 224n6
Carnegie, Andrew, 201n1, 205n24
Carroll, Susan, 193–194
Carson, Everett, 127
Carter, Jimmy, 103, 114, 181; seeks
and loses women's support, 150–
153
Carter, Rosalynn, 151
Castle, Barbara, 156
Cather, Willa, 19–20
Catt, Carrie Chapman, 6, 20–21, 43,
157; background and beliefs, 1, 11;
disowns socialists, 61, 110; League
of Nations, 27; peacetime pacifism,
1, 25, 28, 100; radio broadcast for
President Hoover, 61. See also
World War I: Catt-Wilson deal in
Ceylon. See Sri Lanka
Chaco War (1932–1935), 77
Chafe, William H., 36
Chamberlin, Hope, 154
Chambers, Marjorie Bill, 152
Chamorro, Pedro Joaquin, 238n36
Chamorro, Violetta de, 156, 168,

238n36

Charles, Eugenia, 156–157, 178

Chase, Margaret. *See* Smith, Margaret Chase

Chile, 145, 147

China, 68, 70, 104, 123, 153, 162, 166; women and education concerning, 176, 197, 215n20

Chisholm, Shirley, 140, 142, 145, 189; foreign policy concerns of, 137

Churchill, Winston L. S., 163, 239n47

CIA (Central Intelligence Agency), 117

Ciller, Tansu, 156–158, 163, 238n40

Civil Rights Act (1964), 177

Civil War (1861–1865), women in, 6

Clinton, Bill (William Jefferson Clinton), 3, 104, 174–175, 181; appoints women to cabinet, 199; supported by women in 1992 election, 194

Clinton, Hillary, 199

Cohen, Warren I., 74

Cohn, Carol, 8

Cold War: its demise an opportunity for women, 181; women and ending of, 10, 130, 154, 186, 194, 196

Cole, Wayne S., 217n59

Congress, women in, 189, 197, 242nn37, 38; dynastic factor, 183–188, 242n33; 1930s, 75, 216n37; 1941, 95, 98, 100, 222n54; 1960s, 175, 227n62; 1990s, 3, 175, 185–188, 196, 340n4; opposition to Vietnam War, 142; widows, 36, 75, 106, 183, 184. *See also under names of committees and individuals*

Congressional Union for Woman Suffrage, 21

consumerism: defined, 38–39; mystique, 86; tariff, 38, 55, 58, 180

Contras, 185–186

Cook, Blanche Weisen, 102

Coolidge, Calvin, 33, 72

Corbett, Raymond, 146

Costigan, Mabel C., 40

Cox, James, 27

Crapol, Edward P., 7

Crater, Robert, 138

Cresson, Edith, 156, 163

Crosland, Anthony, 158

Crosland, Susan, 158, 236n7

Cuba, 190

Cuban Missile Crisis (1962), 119

Damanaki, Maria, 156

Daniels, Joseph, 31

Darrow, Clarence, 86

Day, Dorothy, 133

DeBenedetti, Charles, 135–136, 138

Degler, Carl, 179

Dellums, Ronald V., 143

Denison, Ray, 146

Denmark, 155

Dennett, Mary, 15

Denny, Ludwell, 215n18

Detzer, Don, 66–67

Detzer, Dorothy, 96, 115, 137, 212n9, 215n23; background and views of, 65–67, 69, 218n60; critical of Mary Woolley, 54; early critic of Hitler, 69, 214n16; effectiveness as lobbyist, 66, 217nn57–59; evaluations of, 80–81, 217nn57–59; inspired by Jane Addams, 15; Manchurian Crisis, 69–71; marriage, 214n6, 215n18; neglected, 213n1; and President Hoover, 53; opposes Lend-Lease, 65; regrets Spanish arms embargo, 82; tactics of, 68, 77–79

Detzer, Karl, 66

Dewson, Mary Williams (Molly), 36, 75, 85, 87–88, 91, 97

Didion, Joan, 142

difference, 199; changes over time, 8–9, 84, 93–94, 104, 132, 144, 173, 188; defined, 10, 173; end of, 174; foreign policy and, 2, 66, 99; and Margaret Chase Smith, 107–108

discourse: of dress, 160, 164; male, on political women, 189; male, on war, 19–20, 27–28; of toys, 76

Disraeli, Benjamin, 163

Dole, Elizabeth, 192

Dominica (West Indies), 156

Douglas, Helen G., 116, 144, 180–181, 193; attacks military assistance,

Douglas, Helen G. (*continued*)
100; background and foreign-policy
stance of, 113–114
Douglas, Paul, 88
Douglass, Frederick, 154
Dryden, John, 168
Dukakis, Michael, 182
Dulles, Eleanor Lansing, 176

Earhart, Amelia, 3, 54, 100; endorses
Senate Munitions Inquiry, 77
Eastman, Crystal, 15
Eastwood, Clint, 189–190
Edgerly, Cora, 106
Edwards, Don, 138
Egypt, 145, 153
Eisenhower, Dwight D., 103, 115, 118;
military industrial complex, 83;
opposes human rights declaration,
9; women's support for, 133
Elizabeth of Toro, 178
Elliot, Harriet: appointed to NDAC,
89; background, 84–85; rebellions
and resignation, 90–92
Emergency Price Control Act (1942),
92
Engelbrecht, Helmuth C., 74, 77
environment, as international women's
issue, 154, 170
Equal Rights Amendment. *See* ERA
ERA (Equal Rights Amendment), 101,
103, 152; League of Nations split,
35; women's peace movement split,
97
Etheredge, Lloyd, 7–8
Ethiopia, 81

Fair Tariff League, 41–43
Falklands/Malvinas War (1982), 161–
162, 191, 237n17
Farley, James A., 75, 85
Federation of Business and Professional Women's Clubs, 31–32
Feinstein, Dianne, 189, 240n4
Felton, Rebecca L., 45–46, 224n6
feminism: in ending of Vietnam War,
135, 140; 1960s revival, 118, 175–
176; pacifism and, 12, 150; peace
and, 15, 69; in Scandinavia, 3, 171–

172, 239n47; tariff, 29–30, 85, 146
Fenwick, Millicent Hammond, 185
Ferraro, Geraldine A., 132, 195;
background and career, 192–193;
1984 election, 194; victim of
smears, 153
Ferrell, Robert, 31, 35
Finland, 172
Finnbogadóttir, Vigdís, 156, 236n7;
first woman elected head of state,
168–169
first ladies. *See* Carter, Rosalynn;
Clinton, Hillary; Hoover, Lou;
Johnson, Lady Bird; Reagan,
Nancy; Roosevelt, Eleanor; Wilson,
Edith Galt
Fish, Hamilton, Jr., 70
Fiske, Bradley Allen, 34
FitzGerald, Frances, 142
Fonda, Jane, 3, 142
Ford, Henry, 13
Fordney, Joseph W., 42
Fordney-McCumber Tariff (1922), 41–
43
foreign policy, impact of women on:
domestic comparative, 12, 49,
211n69; foreign women, 157; U.S.
women, 2, 8, 73, 83, 196–197. *See
also* Boeckel model; breakthrough
syndrome; environment; peace;
tariff; war; *names of conferences,
episodes, individuals, tariffs,
treaties, and wars*
Forrestal, James V., 108
Fowler, Robert Booth, 11
France, 156
Frankovic, 183–184
Fraser, Antonia: on Boadicean women,
6; on U.S. republicanism, 8
Frazier, Lynn J., 43, 110
Frazier amendment, 43, 68, 110
Freedman, Lawrence, 162
Fried, Ella, 32
Friedan, Betty, 131, 137, 152, 235n92;
opposes Vietnam War, 140
Frost, Jean, 71
Fulbright, J. William, 115, 125

Gadhafi, Muammar, 162

Gage-Colby, Ruth, 140
Gandhi, Indira, 4, 156–157, 167–168, 170, 180, 185, 236n7; background, 165; career and reputation, 165–166
Gannett, Guy P., 111, 122
Gardener, Helen H., 22
Gelb, Joyce, 171
gender gap, 10, 29, 104, 129, 182, 194–195, 198, 235n100; and Ferraro candidacy, 192; and insiders, 188; in 1980 election, 153; in Norway, 172; significance for foreign policy, 182; statistically confirmed, 84, 99; in U.K., 161
Geneva World Disarmament Conference (1932), 53–54, 65, 68
George, David Lloyd, 163
George, Walter F., 45–46, 94, 211n61
George amendment, 45
Germany, 81–82, 130, 145
Gladstone, William Ewart, 163
Glaspie, April C., 178
Gleason, S. Everett, 81
Goldwater, Barry M., 121
Good Neighbor Policy, 69, 196; coffee prices, 92
Gorbachev, Mikhail S., 154, 169, 182
Grasso, Ella, 142
Grattan, C. Hartley, 74
Graves, Anna, 82
Greece, 114
Grenada, 191, 193
Gromyko, Andrei, 184
Grover, James, 189
Guigon, Elisabeth, 236n5
Gulf War (1991), 178, 194; women in, 6
Gurney, Chan, 116
Guy Gannett press, 114–115, 120, 225n30

Haïti, 156, 241n17
Hamilton, Walton H., 88
Hanighan, Frank C., 74
Harbord, James G., 33
Hard, Anne, 46
Harding, Warren G., 27, 32; respects women's peace vote, 32
Harriman, Edward Henry, 86, 221n45
Harriman, Florence Jaffray (Maisy),

221n45
Harriman, Mary. See Rumsey, Mary Harriman
Harriman, W. Averell, 90–91
Harrington, Michael, 138
Hasford, Gustav, 8
Hasima, Sheikh, 155
Hathaway, William D., 126–128
Hawley, William C., 42, 48
Hawley-Smoot Tariff. See Smoot-Hawley Tariff
Hayes, John L., 38
Hebert, Felix, 59
Heckler, Margaret, 192
Henley, Helen, 112
Hepburn, Katherine, 100
Hildreth, Horace, 110
Higgins, Marguerite, 142
Hillman, Sidney, 89
Hills, Carla, 94, 180
Hiss, Alger, 112, 115
Hitler, Adolf, 82, 91, 95, 99, 201n1
Ho Chi Minh, 126
Hoff, Joan, 17, 52, 191
Holocaust, 97, 102, 221n44
Holtzman, Elizabeth, 181
Hong Kong, 162
Hoover, Herbert C., 9, 68, 72, 212n23; his appeals to women in 1932 election, 50–51, 58–60, 62–64; sympathetic to women, 51–52; Woolley nomination, 53
Hoover, J. Edgar, 103
Hoover, Lou, 51
House Armed Services Committee, 108, 143, 186–187; women on, 243n38
House Foreign Affairs Committee: dynastic women on, 185; women on, 95, 187, 243n37
House Military Affairs Committee, 107
Howe, Louis, 72, 215n23
Hoyt, Elizabeth E., 41
Hughes, Charles Evans, 32–33
Hull, Cordell, 78–79, 87; reciprocal trade agreements, 59
Hull, Hannah Hallowell Clothier, 15, 65
Hussein, Saddam, 178, 201n1

Iceland, 156, 168–169, 172
India, 144, 156, 165–167, 170–171, 180, 198, 237n30
Indian Mutiny (1857), 163, 171
Indo-Pakistan War: 1965, 165; 1971, 166
Industrial Workers of the World (IWW), 133–134
Inouye, Daniel, 3
International Bureau for Peace, 15
International Committee of Women for Permanent Peace, 18
International Council of Women, 25
International Women's Year (1975), 149, 150
Iran, 190
Iraq, 178, 194
Ireland, Republic of, 156
Irish Americans, and League of Nations, 49, 211n69
iron doves, 4, 158, 168–170, 192, 198
iron ladies, 1, 4, 158, 164, 168, 188, 198; Margaret Thatcher as archetype, 159, 161, 198; myth of, 158, 189, 192, 195; as products of breakthrough syndrome, 158, 193; redefined, 161, 195, 198
Israel, 144–146, 153, 156, 164, 198
Italy, 81, 176

Jacobs, Helen Hull, 60
James, William, 205n24
Japan, 68–70, 130; attacks Shanghai, 54; invades Manchuria, 51; Pearl Harbor, 92, 97
Jeffords, Susan, 7–8, 175
Johnson, Hiram, 74
Johnson, Hugh, 78, 88
Johnson, Lady Bird, 117, 123, 142
Johnson, Lyndon B., 117, 122, 137; special relationship with Margaret Chase Smith, 122–123, 125–126

Kahn, Florence Prag, 75, 209n29, 216n37
Kahn, Julius, 75, 216n37
Kassebaum, Nancy Landon, 187–188, 240n4
Kelley, Florence, 38

Kellogg-Briand Pact (1928), 36, 60, 68–69, 196
Kellogg, Frank B., 36
Kelly, Petra, 156
Kennedy, Caroline, 134
Kennedy, John F., 117–119; appoints Eleanor Roosevelt to U.N. delegation, 103; influenced by Women Strike for Peace, 134
Kennelly, Barbara, 187
Kessler-Harris, Alice, 39
Khan, Ishaq, 167
Khrushchev, Nikita, 105; denounces Margaret Chase Smith, 119
Kirchwey, Freda, 176
Kirkpatrick, Jeane, 104, 192, 194–195; career and outlook of, 190–191; impact at U.N., 190, 243n45; isolation of, 174–175
Kissinger, Henry, 104, 123, 139; male chauvinism of, 137, 142
Kitt, Eartha, 142
Koch, Edward I., 138, 145, 150, 189
Korean War (1950–1953), 9, 113, 115, 133, 162
Krock, Arthur, 48
Kumaratunga, Chandrika Bandaranaike, 156, 167
Kyrk, Hazel, 41, 55, 94
Kyros, Peter N., 126

La Follette, Robert M., Jr., 74, 78
LaGuardia, Fiorello H., 103
Landon, Alfred M., 187
Langer, William L., 81
Laos, 119, 127
Lazarsfeld, Paul, 37
League of Nations, 12, 68–69, 71, 99; undermined by U.S. women, 35; and women's franchise, 23, 25, 27
Lebanon, 191
Lederer, William, 179
Lend-Lease Act (1941), 65, 83, 95–96, 99, 109
Lewis, Ben, 91
Lewis, William C., Jr., 106, 110, 119, 128; background and significance of, 109; heart attack of, 127
Lewy, Guenter, 182

Liberia, 82
Libya: U.S. air strike on (1982), 161–162
Lippmann, Walter, 33, 208n20
Lithuania, 156
Livermore, Mrs. Arthur L., 58
Lockwood, Belva, 15, 121
Lodge, Henry Cabot, 24–26
London Naval Conference (1930), 53, 68
Long, Russell B., 94
Lothian, Lord, 92, 97–99
Lowell, Josephine Shaw, 38
Luce, Clare Boothe, 107, 176
Luce, Henry, 176
LWV. *See* National League of Women Voters

McAdoo, Eleanor (Wilson), 27
McAdoo, William Gibbs, 207n51
McCarthy, Joseph R., 106, 112–113, 115, 129, 144
McCarthy, Mary, 142
McCarthyism, 112–114, 176, 214n1
McCloskey, Paul N., Jr., 138
McCumber, Porter James, 42–43
MacDonald, Flora, 236n5, 240n49
MacDonald, Ramsay, 53
McGee, Willie, 132
McGovern, George, 129, 139, 142–143; and women's issues, 152
MacLaine, Shirley, 142, 152
McLaughlin, Audrey, 239–240n49
McMahon, Theresa S., 41
McNamara, Robert S., 119, 121–122, 124
Mahler, Josephine, 98
Mailer, Norman, 131
Malvinas War. *See* Falklands/Malvinas War
Mandel, Ruth B., 131, 149
Mandela, Winnie, 156, 178
Mao Tse-tung, 185
Marcantonio, Vito, 110, 112, 114, 181, 225n27, 226n46
Marshall Plan (1948), 109, 111, 114
Mason, Alfred B., 43
Mayo, Katherine, 171
Mead, Lucia, 14, 17

Mead, Margaret, 180, 241n22
Meir, Golda, 4, 144, 156–157, 165, 236nn5, 7; background and career of, 164
Mellon, Andrew, 70
men: as consumers, 93–95; influenced by women politically, 37, 196; Vietnam War, 8; warlike proclivities of, 7. *See also* discourse
"merchants of death," 18, 65, 74
Mexico, 178
Mikulski, Barbara A., 189, 240n4
Miles, Herbert E., 41
Miller, Arthur, 182
Miller, Emma Guffey, 71–72
Miller, Fishbait, 131, 137
Millis, Walter, 74
Mink, Patsy T., 142
Mitchell, Wesley C., 40
Moley, Raymond, 59
Mondale, Walter F., 153, 192, 194
Montevideo Pan-American Conference (1933), 69
Morgan, Robin, 140
Morgan, Sidney, 86–88
Moskowitz, Belle, 36, 209n30
Mosley, Oswald, 190
Mothers of Sons Forum, 98
Mott, James W., 48
Moynihan, Daniel Patrick, 150
Muir, Kate, 6
Muskie, Edmund, 127
Myanmar. *See* Burma
Myrdal, Alva, 236n5

Nader, Ralph, 39
National Advisory Committee for Women, 150, 152
National American Woman Suffrage Association (NAWSA), 1, 17; supports World War I, 22
National Committee on the Cause and Cure of War, 34; changing nomenclature of, 100
National Congress of Parents and Teachers, 31
National Consumers' League, 38, 46
National Council for Prevention of War, 30

National Defense Advisory Commission (NDAC), 84, 89

National Industrial Recovery Act (1933), 85

National League of Women Voters (LWV), 17, 31; elitist composition, 45, 47, 56–57; home economics legislation, 40; tariff education program of, 55–57; tariff question, 43–44

National Organization of Women. *See* NOW

National Recovery Administration (NRA), 77; consumer representation in, 86, 88

National Student Committee for the Limitation of Armaments, 31

National Woman's Party, 16, 31, 54, 103; endorses Al Smith, 52

National Women's Political Caucus, 137, 182

NATO (North Atlantic Treaty Organization), 169

Nehru, Jawaharlal, 165

Neuberger, Maurine Brown, 227n62

New Deal, 86, 92, 109; price maintenance in, 85

Newman, Sarah, 180

Nicaragua, 35, 156, 168, 193; Dorothy Detzer and U.S. withdrawal from, 68–69; Geraldine Ferraro on, 153, 193; Jeane Kirkpatrick on, 190; Nancy Reagan on Contras in, 185

Nixon, Richard M., 112, 114, 123, 126, 136, 139, 144, 147, 226n46

Norris, George W., 78, 79

North American Free Trade Agreement (1993), 94

North Atlantic Treaty Organization. *See* NATO

Norton, Mary T., 95, 216n37, 222n54

Norway, 156, 169–170, 172, 221n45

NOW (National Organization of Women), 128, 182

Nuclear Test Ban Treaty (1963), 119, 134, 197

Nye, Gerald P., 65, 74, 78, 80–81, 217n59; background and congressional tactics of, 79

Nye investigation. *See* Senate Munitions Inquiry

O'Day, Caroline Love Goodwin, 76, 96, 222n54; equates tariffs and war, 44

Office of Price Administration, 89, 92

Office of War Information: 1942 survey of women's attitudes to World War II, 37, 99–100, 222n52

Okin, Susan Moller, 172

Olmstead, Mary S., 177

OPEC (Organization of Petroleum-Exporting Countries), 146

opinion polls: on Abzug's dismissal, 152–153; advent of, 104; gender difference over Vietnam War, 94, 129, 141, 180; in Norway, 172; women in armed services, 108; women and "hot" wars, 116, 182–183; women and nuclear deterrence, 9

Orvis, Mrs. George, 40–41, 44–45

Owen, Ruth Bryan, 75, 175, 185

pacifist, defined, 201n1

Packwood, Robert, 3

Paine, Tom, 131

Pakistan, 144, 156, 166–167

Palmer, Alison, 177

Palmerston, Lord, 163

Panama, 153

Paraguay, 77

Paris Peace Conference (1919), representation of women at, 25–26

Park, Maud May Wood, 111

Pascal-Trouillot, Ertha, 155–156, 178; Jean-Bertrand Aristide on, 241n17

Paul, Alice, 16, 18; background and beliefs of, 15–16; death of, 205n16; expelled from NAWSA, 21; in prison, 27–28

Pax Britannica, nature of, 163, 237n20

PC. *See* political correctness

peace: cultural contexts of its female advocates, 17, 170–173; and tariff, 29, 94; women as champions of, 4–5, 14, 18–19, 63, 97–98, 180. *See also* pacifist

Peace Congress of Women, 14

Pearce, Allan, 85

Pearson, Drew, 80, 217n56

Peel, Robert, 163

Peixotto, Jessica B., 41

Perkins, Frances, 38, 75, 78, 86, 88, 109; on President Roosevelt's pacification of women, 89

Perón, Evita (María Eva Duarte de Perón), 178

Perón, Isabel (María Estela Martinez de Perón), 155–156, 178, 236n2

Perón, Juan Domingo, 185, 190

Perot, Ross, 194

Philippines, 147, 156, 167, 204n11

Pike, Otis G., 189

Pitt, William (the Elder), 163

Pitt, William (the Younger), 163

Piven, Frances F., 134

Poland, 156

political correctness (PC), 4, 199; defined, 174, 240n1

Poole, Grace Morrison, 59

Portugal, 144–145

Powell, Jody, 152

presidency, U.S., women candidates for: Dorothy Detzer, 83; failures of, 2, 174, 178; Jeane Kirkpatrick, 190; Belva Lockwood, 121; Margaret Chase Smith, 120, 228n76; Victoria Claflin Woodhull, 121

Prunskiene, Kazimiera, 156

public opinion, 3; Dorothy Detzer's faith in, 67, 75; and naval disarmament, 31–33; and U.S. hegemony, 69; Walter Lippmann on, 208n20; women's impact on, 48, 176. *See also* opinion polls

Putnam, George P., 77

Qiang Qing (widow of Mao Tse-tung), 156, 185

Ralph Nader Congress Project, 127

Rani Jhansi, 171

Rankin, Jeannette, 15–17, 72, 76, 133, 222n54; criticizes women's

passivity over Vietnam War, 140; death of, 205n18; in Georgia, 46; in Montana, 16, 98–99; protests Vietnam War, 141; votes against World War I, 16; votes against World War II, 16, 99

Reagan, Nancy, 184–185, 192–193

Reagan, Ronald, 141, 152–154, 161, 169, 174, 185, 190; and gender gap, 192–193; vulnerability to women's peace vote, 182; wins plurality of women's vote in 1984 election, 193

Reciprocal Trade Agreements Act (1934), 87, 196

Red-baiting: decline of, 195; in 1980s, 109, 114; in 1920s, 30, 33–34, 37; in Nixon-Douglas contest, 113–114, 226nn42, 46; and Margaret Chase Smith, 105, 109, 114; and WILPF, 141, 182. *See also* McCarthyism; smears

Reed, Donna, 142

Regan, Donald, 185

Rehn, Elisabeth, 172, 239n48

Reykjavík summit (1986), 169

Rhodesia, 147

Richards, Ann, 189

Richardson, Bertha June, 40

Richardson, Lewis Fry, 162

Ridgeway, Rozanne L., 177

Ritchie, Lawrence, 58

Roberts, Alfred, 159

Robinson, Mary, 156–157

Rogers, Edith Nourse, 95, 185, 209n29, 216n37, 222n54; background of, 45; Jewish Children's Refugee Bill sponsored by, 102; opposes neutrality legislation, 75; radio broadcast for President Hoover, 61; supports higher tariffs, 45

Rogers, James Grafton, 70, 212n9

Rogers, John Jacob, 45

Rogers, Will, 64

Roosevelt, Eleanor, 3, 38, 64–65, 77, 83, 114, 131, 175, 213n1, 221n41, 223nn58, 61; achievements, 104; and Lady Astor, 92; background and inspiring qualities of, 101–

Roosevelt, Eleanor (*continued*)
102; on difference, 4, 101; Human Rights Commission on Refugees, 102; mocked by President Eisenhower, 103; peacetime pacifist, 1, 96, 150; U.N. supported by, 100–101; United Nations Universal Declaration of Human Rights, 9, 84, 102–103, 196; views on war and peace, 75–76; and women's network, 134. *See also* smears

Roosevelt, Franklin Delano, 69, 71, 74, 108, 221n45; avoids Dorothy Detzer, 72, 215n23; courtship of women as consumers, 86, 89; pacifism of women feared by, 97, 99; peace standard deserted by, 96; political skills and tactics of, 78–80, 85, 89–90, 95; protectionist policies, 85; vacillates on tariff in 1932 election, 57, 59, 212n23; and woman voter in 1932 election, 50, 57, 64

Roosevelt, Theodore: and pacifist women, 14; and war and peace, 201n1

Root, Elihu, 201n1

Rosenberg, Emily S., 7

Rubin, Cora, 78

Rudd, Mark, 140

Rumsey, Mary Harriman, 86–87; death of, 88

Rushdie, Salman, 4, 167

Rwanda, 156

Ryan, William F., 138–139

Sahgal, Nayantara, 165–166

SALT (Strategic Arms Limitation Talks/Treaties/agreements) I (1972), 123, 148

SALT II (1975, 1979), 148, 151–153

Sandino, Augusto, 68, 214n13

SANE (National Committee for a Sane Nuclear Policy), 134

Savitski, Bella, 132. *See also* Abzug, Bella

Schechter v. United States (1935), 88

Schlesinger, Arthur M., Jr., 86

Schroeder, Patricia S., 143, 186, 189

Schwimmer, Rosika, 18

Scobie, Ingrid, 75

SDI (Strategic Defense Initiative/Star Wars), 161, 186; opposed by women, 183

Seldes, George H., 72–73, 215n24

Senate Armed Services Committee, 116–117, 122

Senate Foreign Relations Committee, 2, 68, 187

Senate Munitions Inquiry (Nye investigation), 65, 73, 75, 77, 79, 81–82, 196; evaluations of, 81, 218n61

Sewell, Sumner, 110

Shastri, Lal Bahadur, 165

Sherwood, Robert, 89

Shields, John K., 22–23

Shipstead, Henrik, 74

Shultz, George P., 184

Sinclair, Upton, 39

Six Day War (1967), 164

smears: ageist, 128; concerning graft, 153, 193; against Eleanor Roosevelt, 3, 105; sexual, 3, 105–107, 109, 127, 141, 181, 197; against Margaret Chase Smith, 3, 105–107, 109, 127–128. *See also* McCarthyism; Red-baiting

Smedley, Agnes, 176, 197, 215n20

Smith, Alfred Emanuel, 36, 52, 61

Smith, Clyde, 106–107, 109, 116, 224nn3, 5, 7, 8

Smith, Margaret Chase, 131, 143, 157, 181, 185, 191, 193, 196–197, 222n54, 224nn3, 8; ABM system opposed by, 122–123, 125; background and political character of, 105–107, 109, 111–112, 118, 227n63; Declaration of Conscience, 113–114, 125, 224n11; isolation of, 117; Khrushchev on, 4, 105; her lollipop diplomacy, 145; and Robert S. McNamara, 119, 121–122, 124, 126; not a feminist, 4, 107; on nuclear strike, 9, 115; and nuclear test ban treaty, 118–120; reservations concerning

Vietnam War, 123; significance and achievements of, 129; support for Vietnam War, 106, 124–126, 128; support for World War II, 95; views on foreign policy, 111–112; and women voters, 111–112. *See also* Red-baiting; smears

Smith-Connally Act (1943), 109

Smoot, Reed, 42, 48, 62

Smoot-Hawley Tariff (1930), 44–47, 58, 146, 219n9; criticisms of, 54–55; in 1932 election, 62

Snow, Helen Foster, 215n20

Snowe, Olympia J., 187

South Africa, 137

Southern Tenant Farmers Union, 68

Soviet Union (USSR), 147, 151, 166, 190, 194

Spain, 81, 144–145, 163

Spanish-American War (1898), 13, 14

Spanish Civil War (1936–1939), 96

Spencer, Anna Garlin, 18

Sri Lanka: first nation to elect a woman premier, 155–156; first nation to elect a second woman premier, 167

Star Wars, 183, 202n1. *See also* SDI

Steinem, Gloria, 4, 137, 140, 152

Steinson, Barbara, 6

Sternberger, Estelle, 77

Stimson, Henry L., 53–54

Stone, I. F., 115

Stratton, Samuel S., 189

Streisand, Barbra, 142

Strong, Anna Louise, 142, 215

Strother, French, 59

Suchoka, Hanna, 156, 163

suffrage amendment, in U.S. Senate, 22–27

Sugar Control Act (1937), 88, 91

Sumner, Jessie, 96, 222n54

Sweden, 171

Swerdlow, Amy, 133–140, 145, 231n9; peace mission to Hanoi, 141

Swisher, Idella G., 56

Sykes, Patricia Lee, 159

Taft, William Howard, 201n1

Takako Doi, 156

Tansill, Charles C., 74

tariff: as cause of war, 44; as feminist issue, 29; and U.S.–Latin American relations, 54–55; and prices, 19, 39; and women, 9, 94–95, 147; and women's peace movement, 29. *See also under names of individual tariffs*

Tasca, Henry J., 90–91

Taussig, Frank W., 53, 56–57

Temple, Shirley, 3, 175–176

Tet offensive (1968), 125–126

Thatcher, Margaret, 4, 6, 118, 156–157, 164–165, 168, 236n10; alleged male attributes of, 158; background and political character of, 159–160; as behavioral model, 163; as iron lady, 2

Thomas, Norman, 57, 61, 68

Thompson, Dorothy, 100

Tonkin Gulf resolution (1964), 124, 126

Toynbee, Polly, 4

Trammell, Park, 73, 79, 215n21

Truman, Harry S., 102, 108

Truman Doctrine (1947), 114

Tumulty, Joe, 21

Turkey, 114, 156, 158, 187

Underwood Tariff (1913), 42

United Kingdom, 156

United Nations, 84, 109, 114, 150; service by American women in, 175; women's support for, 99–101

United Nations Universal Declaration of Human Rights (1948). *See* Roosevelt, Eleanor

Universal Peace Union, 15

USSR. *See* Soviet Union

Uwilingiyimana, Agathe, 156, 178

Vandenberg, Arthur H., 116

Veblen, Thorstein, 40

Vernon, Mabel, 15, 76; on the Roosevelts, 64; Transcontinental Peace Caravan, 54

Vietnam War (1964–1973), 121, 123–126, 128–129; Benazir Bhutto protests, 167; its impact on

Vietnam War (*continued*)
women, 4, 8; Jeane Kirkpatrick
favors withdrawal from, 191;
normalization of opposition to,
135–136, 138, 143; opposed by
women writers, 142; sexism in
protest movement against, 140;
women's opposition to, 116, 197.
See also Abzug, Bella; feminism;
Friedan, Betty; Smith, Margaret
Chase; men; opinion polls;
Rankin, Jeannette
Villard, Helen Frances Garrison
(Fanny), 17–18, 210n51
Vinson, Carl, 72, 79, 108, 116, 215n21
Vinson-Trammel Act (1934), 215n21

Wagner, Robert F., 102, 154
Wald, Lillian D., 14
Wales, Julia Grace, 13
Wales, Nym. *See* Snow, Helen Foster
Walpole, Robert, 162
war: and prostitution, 77, 108; women
degraded by, 8, 20, 239n47; women
as warriors, 6. *See also under
names of wars*
Ware, Caroline, 91
Ware, Susan, 74, 100
Washington Conference (1921), 196;
and women's lobby, 31–33
Washington Conference (1931), 69
Watson, Thomas Edward, 45
Weeks, John D., 33–34
Wellington, Duke of, 158
We, the Mothers Organize for
America, 98
Wheeler, Burton K., 74
White, Anna, 14, 17
Wilkinson, David, 162
Wilson, Dagmar, 118, 134
Wilson, Edith Galt, 26
Wilson, Margaret, 27
Wilson, Woodrow, 74, 81, 201n1;
211n69; his promises on peace, 20;
his reluctance to endorse women's
suffrage, 21; his responses to
women, 26–27, 207n51; supports
suffrage, 22–23. *See also* World
War I: Catt-Wilson deal in

Winslow, Dorothy Sabin, 110
"Wise Men," 137
Wold, Emma, 31
Woman's Peace Party, 15, 18, 21–22,
29, 210n51; excluded from Paris
Peace Conference, 26
women: as ambassadors, 75, 97, 174–
175, 177–179, 190–191, 221n45;
American, as missing sisters of
world politics, 2–3, 64, 157, 174–
175, 178, 198; beneficiaries of
democracy, 198; champions of
moral and economic consumerism,
38–39; champions of national
security, 197; and China, 71;
conservative drift in 1990s,
238n40; as consumers, 9, 40–41,
51, 84, 93, 221n37; cultural factors
and rise to world leadership, 179–
180, 199; and decolonization,
239n47; distinctive voting behavior
of, 37; as distinct pressure group
on foreign policy, 2, 17; as dynastic
leaders, 158, 165, 167–168; as
foreign ministers, 236n5; as a
national lobby, 47, 50, 87; and
nuclear deterrence, 9; opposed to
"hot" wars, 9–10, 116, 123, 182–
183, 191, 197; and peace, 14, 63; as
peace voters in New Jersey,
204n10; political network of, in
1930s, 74, 87; as prime ministers
and presidents (table), 156; "stars"
in peace movements, 3, 54, 100–
101, 141; in State Department,
176–178; and tariff, 80; in U.S.
foreign service, 4, 175–177. *See
also* foreign policy
Women's Action Organization, 177
Women's Armed Services Act (1948),
108
Women's Campaign Fund, 182
Women's Christian Temperance
Union, 15, 31
Women's Committee for World
Disarmament, 31–32
Women's Foreign Policy Council, 154
Women's International League for
Peace and Freedom (WILPF), 65,

68, 70–72, 75–77, 79, 101, 115,
133–134, 141, 182, 210n51;
formed, 18; growth, 67; Mayflower
complex in, 74, 216n34; military
reduction campaigns, 34; naval
disarmament, 53; opposed to
Pacific nuclear tests, 118; rejects
merger with men, 98; supports
Kellogg-Briand Pact, 35–36
Women's Missionary Council, 31
Women's Non-Partisan League, 31
Women's Peace Parade Committee,
17–18
Women's Peace Union, 43, 65, 110;
provenance, 210n51
Women Strike for Peace (WSP), 133–
136, 141, 147; supports nuclear
test ban treaty, 118–119, 134–135
Woodhull, Victoria Claflin, 121
Woods, Amy, 68–69
Woolley, Mary Emma, 17, 212n9;
attacks militarism, 14; background

of, 53; radio broadcast for President Hoover, 61–62; U.S. delegate
at Geneva conference, 53–54
World Court: and LWV, 52; supported
by Dorothy Detzer, 68
World Court Committee, 35
World War I (1917–1918): Catt-
Wilson deal in, 1, 11, 14, 15, 17,
20, 23–25, 35, 100; impact on
peace feminism, 20; revisionists
and, 74, 81
World War II (1941–1945): women's
opposition to, 97–100; women's
support for, 95–97
Wydler, John W., 189

Yom Kippur War (1973), 164
Young, Andrew, 153

Zaccaro, John A., 192
Zelaya, José, 69
Zia, Begum Khaleda, 155–156, 167

ABOUT THE AUTHOR

Rhodri Jeffreys-Jones was born in Wales and received his Ph.D. from Cambridge University. Currently a Reader in History at Edinburgh University, he has held postdoctoral fellowships at Harvard, the Free University of Berlin, and the University of Toronto. His several books include *The CIA and American Democracy* (1989).